*Policing Protest*

GLOBAL AND INSURGENT LEGALITIES

*A series edited by Eve Darian-Smith and Jonathan Goldberg-Hiller*

*Paul A. Passavant*

# POLICING PROTEST

*The Post-Democratic State and
the Figure of Black Insurrection*

DUKE UNIVERSITY PRESS  DURHAM AND LONDON  2021

Production editor: Lisa Lawley
Designed by Aimee C. Harrison
Typeset in Portrait Text and ITC Franklin Gothic
by Westchester Publishing Services

Library of Congress Cataloging-in-Publication Data
Names: Passavant, Paul A. (Paul Andrew), author.
Title: Policing protest : the post-democratic state and the figure
of Black insurrection / Paul A. Passavant.
Other titles: Global and insurgent legalities.
Description: Durham : Duke University Press, 2021. | Series:
Global and insurgent legalities | Includes bibliographical
references and index.
Identifiers: LCCN 2020042807 (print)
LCCN 2020042808 (ebook)
ISBN 9781478010456 (hardcover)
ISBN 9781478011439 (paperback)
ISBN 9781478013013 (ebook)
Subjects: LCSH: Police—United States. | Militarization of police—
United States. | Police brutality—United States. | Protest
movements—United States—History—21st century. | Black lives
matter movement. | Occupy movement—New York (State)—
New York. | Neoliberalism—History—21st century. |
Authoritarianism—History—21st century.
Classification: LCC HV8141 .P28 2021 (print) | LCC HV8141
(ebook) | DDC 363.32/30973—dc23
LC recordavailableathttps:/ /lccn.loc.gov/2020042807
LC ebookrec ordavailableathttps:/ /lccn.loc.gov/2020042808

Cover art: Protesters in Washington, DC, demonstrate
against the death of George Floyd under the knee of
policeman Derek Chauvin on May 31, 2020, in Minneapolis.
Photo by Alex Wong/Getty Images.

Duke University Press gratefully acknowledges the support of
Hobart and William Smith Colleges, which provided funds
toward the publication of this book.

*For Jodi, with my love*

# Contents

*Acknowledgments*

This book took a long time to conclude. Consequently, the number of people to whom I am grateful for supporting its completion is likewise a long list. I am grateful to Courtney Berger, for agreeing to take on this project and for her patience as I completed it. I would also like to thank Sandra Korn, Lisa Lawley, and the Duke University Press staff for their assistance at its end. The two anonymous outside reviewers exemplified the highest standards of generosity, and their constructive comments improved the manuscript greatly.

Numerous colleagues offered me support while I was in the middle of this project. I never would have finished without the encouragement, friendship, shared meals, drinks, suggestions, and stories shared with Eve Darian-Smith, Jon Goldberg-Hiller, Renisa Mawani, Susan Coutin, Jonathan Simon, Marianne Constable, Renee Cramer, Keramet Reiter, Jinee Lokaneeta, Lennie Feldman, Andrew Dilts, Libby Anker, Chad Lavin, and Ashleigh Campi.

Jon Gould, Bert Kritzer, Cristina Beltrán, Georgia Decker, Anna Kornbluh, Helena Silverstein, Tom Keck, Lynn Mather, and Christine Harrington made suggestions, gave help, asked questions, or offered encouragement that furthered my thinking and the construction of the manuscript. Erin Pineda gave incisive and deeply engaged comments on a draft of a chapter. I value Susan Burgess's generosity and her feedback on work closely related to this book, as I do the feedback I received from Hannah Dickinson, Rob Maclean, and Joe Mink. Ricky Price has helped broaden my thinking around policing and security, as have interactions with Quinn Lester. I value learning about the effects of "Broken Windows" policing in Montreal, as well as low-level courts and the struggles of precarious peoples, from Véronique Fortin. When weather stranded us together in Charlottesville, Virginia, Maria Aristodemou, Costas Douzinas, and I were given a fortuitous opportunity to reconnect in a way that goes beyond a shared meal at a conference.

Lester Spence has been exceptionally generous, from making suggestions of scholarship to consult, inciting engagements between myself and those who disagree with me, and then reading part of the manuscript. Oh yeah, then there were the occasions of shared drinks. Paul Apostolidis's questions over the years helped improve this project. When I realized that the answer to one of his questions was the argument of another chapter, I knew I was nearing completion, and his good humor helped me get there. Not only have James Martel and Jackie Stevens been long-term intellectual interlocutors as this book developed, the shared meals and friendship sustained its writing. Corey Robin's empathy and kind words helped get me through the last stage of this project.

I learned greatly about technical aspects of legal practice, courts, and policing protests from upstate New York lawyers who have devoted their careers to supporting protesters seeking justice. These include Mark Mishler, Joe Heath, and Sujata Gibson, in addition to Ray Schlather. I've also learned from Mara Verheyden-Hilliard and Nahal Zamani. I am grateful for all I learned about policing protest from former Madison Police Chief Noble Wray, former Chief of State Capitol Police Charles Tubbs, Deputy Chief Dan Blackdeer, Dane County Sheriff Dave Mahoney, and former University of Wisconsin, Madison Police Chief Sue Riseling. I learned about what it was like to be a protester inside the capitol building during the Wisconsin uprising from union leaders.

This book could not have been written without the generosity of activists and lawyers who agreed to share with me their experiences, observations, and knowledge regarding Occupy Wall Street and how the New York Police Department policed this uprising. Thank you for everything. Other lawyers based in the New York City area helped in absolutely critical ways, but must remain unnamed to preserve the anonymity of those interviewed. Please accept my deepest gratitude. Several journalists provided insight or assisted me with sources. These include Matt Apuzzo, Nick Pinto, and Chris Faraone.

I received library and research support from Vince Boisselle, Dan Mulvey, Joseph Chmura, Jennifer Nace, and Emily Underwood. I received technological support from John Lord, Dusan Ducic, Michael Carroll, Jeff DeVuyst, and Roy Dewar. I thank Arianna Fishman and the New York Civil Liberties Union for supporting links to key New York Police Department documents regarding preparations for the 2004 Republican National Convention. Thanks also to Jean Salone for administrative support. I learned from Michael Ortiz and Ivan Guzman. My honors students Ellie Dieter (Afro-pessimism, policing, and punishment) and Isaac DuBois (melancholia, depression, and Mark Fisher) did amazing work that furthered my intellectual growth. Thank you to undergraduate student research assistants Emily Corcione, Steve Higgins, Matt Simpson, and Nikki Vairo, and I must acknowledge Hobart and William Smith Colleges Faculty Research Awards, which helped support some of this research. Thanks also to Anne Frantilla at the Seattle Municipal Archives.

An early version of part of chapter 1 was published as "The Governmentality of Consumption," *Interventions* 6, no. 3 (2004). An early version of another part of chapter 1 was published as "Policing Protest in the Post-Fordist City," *Amsterdam Law Forum* 2, no. 1 (2009). An early version of part of chapter 4 was published as "Neoliberalism and Violent Appearances," in *Capital at the Brink: Overcoming the Destructive Legacies of Neoliberalism*, edited by Jeffrey Di Leo and Uppinder Mehan (University of Michigan Press and Open Humanities Press, 2014). An early version of part of chapter 5 was published as "I Can't Breathe: Heeding the Call of Justice," *Law Culture, and Humanities* 11, no. 3 (2015). An early version of my research on the Wisconsin uprising appeared as "Uneven Developments and the End to the History of Modernity's Social Democratic Orientation: Madison's Pro-Union Demonstrations," in *The Ends of History: Questioning the Stakes of Historical Reason*, edited by Amy Swiffen and Joshua Nichols (Routledge, 2013).

The invitations to discuss my research have been invaluable. Thank you to Jeff Dudas and Meghan Bowden Peterson at the University of Connecticut. In addition to this visit, I have benefited not only from Jeff's questions at conferences, but from his friendship over the years. Thank you to Jeffrey Di Leo and Uppinder Mehan for inviting me to the University of Houston–Victoria, to Amy Swiffen for inviting me to Concordia University in Montreal, and to Megan Wachspress and the law students at Yale University for inviting me to speak at the annual Rebellious Lawyering (RebLaw) conference hosted by the Yale Law School. Thank you to Ruth Buchanan, an old friend, for inviting me to speak at Osgoode Hall Law School at York University in Toronto.

Regretably, Joel Grossman and Peter Fitzpatrick would not see the completion of this book, though I could not have written it without having learned much from each of them. Sadly, my uncle Charles and my cousin Roland passed away as I wrote this book. Nevertheless, I am grateful for the support, enthusiasm, and questions I've received from my Passavant, Hesselson-Passavant, Hea, and Laufer cousins and relatives as I concluded this project. I also acknowledge the gifts (from delicious cheese and sausage to paper towels and disinfectant) from my sister and brother, as well as my parents.

As I finish this project, Kian and Sadie KD are now very smart and very funny adults. No one, though, has supported this endeavor the way Jodi Dean has. Jodi commented on every chapter almost as soon as it was written. She is both my sharpest critic and my most enthusiastic reader. I dedicate this book with my love to her.

# Policing Protest and the Post-Democratic State

And protest begot reaction.
—SAMUEL WALKER, *Popular Justice* (1980)

THIS BOOK ADDRESSES NARROW QUESTIONS: Has the policing of protest become more aggressive and violent? If so, how did this happen? What does this mean? The answers to these narrow questions lead to disturbing conclusions with broad theoretical and normative importance. Yes, the policing of protest has become more hostile to protesters. Systematic abuse of those exercising their First Amendment rights points to the emergence of a distinctive state formation I call *neoliberal authoritarianism*. Neoliberal authoritarianism is a state formation that is post-democratic and postlegitimation. Those political subjects who are affectively attached to this state—who provide it political support—enjoy its expressive cruelties. The narrow question of policing protest provides an opening through which we can see that we have entered a new political era of government and political sensibility in the United States.

Protest policing has become more aggressive, violent, and cruel. On September 24, 2011, after a march to Union Square, a small group of women involved with Occupy Wall Street (OWS) protests were captured by the New York Police Department (NYPD) within orange police netting. They were then cruelly, and unnecessarily, pepper sprayed by now-retired NYPD Deputy Inspector Anthony Bologna. As they fell to the ground in pain, *New York Daily News* reporters were nearby, and video of the attack went viral. Less visible were the vindictive NYPD beatings of Occupy activists in Zuccotti Park under cover of the night on Occupy's six-month anniversary, March 17, 2012. As they threw peaceful Occupy protesters to the ground and battered them, NYPD officers repeated, by rote, "Stop resisting!" Officers of the NYPD say, "Stop resisting," when they are beating someone and others are witnessing or videotaping their abuse of force. Between September 17, 2011, and September 17, 2012, the message of Occupy's demonstrations seeking to draw attention to deepening economic inequalities, and the capture of the state by oligarchs and corporations, became derailed by the persistently hostile protest policing of the NYPD.

Seven years earlier, protesters arrested when New York City hosted the 2004 Republican National Convention (RNC) were subjected to excessive, degrading, and in some cases torturous custody for "processing" after their arrest. Arrestees endured detentions lasting over twenty-four, thirty, forty, and, in some instances, over fifty hours. In one case, a woman on her way to purchase a milkshake was swept up in an indiscriminate NYPD arrest and spent over fifty hours in custody. Other arrests were clearly targeted based on police intelligence gathering. Conditions at Pier 57—the hastily constructed detention facility for RNC arrestees located in a former bus depot—were filthy, with grime and hazardous chemicals on the floor. Makeshift cells were fashioned from chain link fencing topped with razor wire. With insufficient and overflowing porta-potties, many detainees had no choice but to relieve themselves on the floor. No sanitary items were available for women. Police officers also subjected protesters and arrestees to verbal abuse. Over 1,800 were arrested during the RNC, and more than 90 percent had their charges dismissed or were acquitted.[1] But their time in custody after their arrest meant that the NYPD had already punished the protesters extrajudicially.

On the evening of December 4, and into the early morning hours of December 5, 2014, protesters expressed outrage at a Staten Island grand jury's failure to indict NYPD Officer Daniel Pantaleo for Eric Garner's death. In response, the NYPD deployed a Long Range Acoustic Device (LRAD) in close range against protesters, chasing after them and repeatedly engaging the weapon against them from just ten feet or even a car's width away. An LRAD is also known as a sound cannon. It is a weapon developed initially for the military, and it uses sound as a method of obtaining compliance through pain.

Over the last twenty years, the NYPD, in conjunction with the City of New York's other governmental bodies, denies large antiwar marches access to public streets and public parks, and denies union demonstrators access to plazas. If protesters refuse to be penned and insist on their rights to assemble in public parks, they face abuse and arrest, if not brutality and violence. If they comply with the NYPD's restrictive conditions for protests, they still risk abuse and arrest, if not brutality and violence.[2]

Scholarship on policing often underscores that in the United States, policing is decentralized. Is abusive protest policing unique to the NYPD? In Oakland, Scott Olsen, who survived two tours of duty in the Iraq war, was nearly killed participating in an Occupy protest when he was shot in the head by a bean bag round (a nylon bag filled with lead pellets fired from a shotgun). Police then fired a flashbang at those who tried to help him. He suffered a fractured skull, broken neck vertebrae, brain swelling, and permanent brain damage.[3] One night at Standing Rock Reservation in the Dakotas, police injured more than three hundred—with twenty-six people requiring hospitalization—when they shot those protesting the Dakota Access Pipeline with water cannons in freezing weather, and with projectiles such as rubber bullets.[4] Police at Standing Rock partnered with TigerSwan in their response to the protests (despite TigerSwan not being licensed to provide security services in the state of North Dakota at that time). TigerSwan is a Pentagon and State Department contractor and considered the protesters to be an insurgency requiring tactics that included infiltration, surveillance, counterpropaganda disseminated through media outlets, and force to suppress them.[5] During the uprising demonstrating outrage over the killing of black teenager Michael Brown by white police officer Darren Wilson, Ferguson, Missouri, looked like a battlefield in a war zone. From Oakland, California, to New York City, from North Dakota to Ferguson, Missouri, police departments engage in abusive protest policing. In other words, there appears to be a broad pattern of aggressive and violent protest policing in the United States that goes beyond any one police department.

Those who study the policing of protest describe how, during the 1960s, protest policing was undisciplined and used force abusively. When police would encounter protesters, according to this model of policing protest known as escalated force, police would mobilize a show of force and expect protesters to back down and disperse. If protesters failed to disperse, then police would confront them and escalate their level of force until they did. Under the model of escalated force, protesters were not exercising First Amendment rights. They were a mob. According to studies of protest policing during this era, escalated force tended to produce violent, disorderly outcomes as police aggression incited an aggressive response from protesters. One well-known example of the escalated force model is the 1968 Democratic National Convention (DNC) held in Chicago.[6] Old videos (now uploaded to YouTube) show police chasing protesters, trying to catch someone to beat. A high-level commander described the police during the event as "out of control."[7]

A number of vectors converged to transform the policing of protest away from the escalated force model. Supreme Court rulings on speech and assembly in a "public forum"—such as public sidewalks, parks, and streets—required police to respect the First Amendment rights of demonstrators, even if speech disturbed onlookers. Other Supreme Court rulings led to controls on police use of force. In 1967, President Lyndon Johnson established the National Advisory Commission on Civil Disorders, more popularly known as the Kerner Commission, after its chair, Illinois Governor Otto Kerner, to study why the urban riots occurred and how to prevent them. The commission issued a report on civil disorders in urban areas during the 1960s that included trenchant critiques of ordinary police conduct. Other presidential commissions also established to study policing and violence during this period echoed many of these findings and criticized inflammatory overreactions by police to demonstrations. A startling percentage of police officers freely expressed themselves using racist language. Often, police were not merely verbally abusive, but physically abusive to city residents. They were poorly trained and few had been to college. Images in the media of civil rights marchers in Birmingham or Selma, Alabama, or protesters at the 1968 DNC being attacked by police, or antiwar demonstrators being killed by the National Guard at Kent State University, shocked the national conscience. The public reception of commission reports, and gradual support for reform by the International Association of Chiefs of Police, set in motion changes in policing to make police more accountable legally.[8] Police should function as a law enforcement agency, not a group of vigilantes who inflict arbitrary, on-the-spot, back-alley "justice" in lieu of an arrest. Training for policing demonstrations also changed by the early 1970s. These vectors converged to institutionalize a transformation of protest policing in a more tolerant direction.

Beginning in some cities in the 1970s, and through the 1980s and into the 1990s, the negotiated management model of protest policing became established as the dominant model for policing protest. Police should understand their role as helping to protect First Amendment rights. They should encourage demonstrators to apply for permits, and they should reach out to political groups and establish lines of communication. They should even work with groups planning acts of civil disobedience as part of a demonstration, negotiating how arrests should be conducted. Police should expect and tolerate a certain amount of disruption to everyday routines when citizens exercise their First Amendment rights. Not only should police maintain lines of communication prior to events, they should engage in dialogue with protesters throughout a demonstration. During protests, police should avoid using force, and avoid making arrests except where absolutely necessary. When arrests occur, they should be conducted only after numerous warnings, and they should be conducted in as orderly a manner as possible to avoid unnecessary injury, or agitating protesters and onlookers, in order not to threaten public safety. After arrests, booking processes should be as efficient as possible.[9]

Negotiated management presents a stark contrast with contemporary protest policing. In the 1960s, Madison, Wisconsin, police looked like the military when they confronted student protesters. That changed when David Couper took over as police chief in 1973. Police should appear like human beings or fellow citizens at a protest; they should not appear like an occupying army. At a massive antinuclear protest in New York City during the early 1980s, there were more arrests than on any given day at the 2004 RNC, but arrestees were processed in a matter of a few hours, not days.[10] When Chicago hosted the 1996 DNC, protesters found it difficult to get arrested. One study of groups that used disruptive forms of civil disobedience in the mid-1990s reported that the use of force by police when encountering disruptive protest tactics was strikingly rare.[11]

Protest policing, as the contrast between the examples of contemporary abusive protest policing above and the description of negotiated management indicates, has changed again. The policing of protest no longer functions according to the tolerant norms of negotiated management. As I describe in this book, today police enjoy dressing aggressively to intimidate protesters while policing protests (they enjoy dressing in an intimidating manner for ordinary patrols as well). Police now arrest protesters for the most minor violations. They make preventative or proactive arrests—arrests that may lack a legal basis because they occur prior to a legal infraction and are based on police prejudging certain protesters to be lawless. Often, protesters may be just snatched from a group and arrested. Instead of a warning, a commander will point and an officer will snatch and arrest the demonstrator. There is no dialogue. There may, though, be verbal abuse from police directed toward protesters. Force may be used gratuitously, and some officers look forward to an opportunity to beat protesters.[12] Custody incident to an arrest for processing is lengthy, if not punitive. Instead of order, police may actively create disorder to scare protesters by kettling them—by trapping a group so they cannot escape, and then arresting all those trapped in a mass arrest. Contemporary protest policing provides a dramatic contrast with the negotiated management model.

When did the shift from negotiated management to more aggressive and violent protest policing practices occur? This question is significant because its answer highlights or diminishes different forces. Almost by convention, many scholars point to the attacks of September 11, 2001, as causing more repressive practices in law and policing. Whether motivated by an unreflective 9/11 narrative device, or forcing a theory of unitary sovereign decisionism upon an institutionally plural and decentralized state structure, the attacks of September 11, 2001, did not cause the policing of protest to become more hostile.[13] The policing of protest in the United States was already becoming less tolerant of democratic practices, and more aggressive and violent, prior to the attacks of September 11, 2001. Reaction to those attacks amplified a transformation already in process, but it did not cause the change.

As is well known, the Seattle Police Department reacted forcefully to those protesting neoliberal globalization when Seattle hosted the World Trade Organization meetings in 1999. Perhaps less well known to those outside of New York City, the NYPD responded to the 1998 Million Youth March by riotously rushing the stage, with helicopters hovering from above, the instant time ran out on their permit. The NYPD also refused to negotiate with demonstrators, trampling them with horses instead, at the Matthew Shepard Emergency Demonstration, also in 1998.[14] So negotiated management was already unraveling before September 11, 2001. The security institutions, personnel, weaponry, and culture that have been built, hired, funded, and communicated in the aftermath of those attacks were not the beginning but the intensification of changes already proceeding in the United States. To grasp how protest policing in the United States has become increasingly inimical to democratic practices, we must not think reactively to an event or a decision, but explore more complex institutional and cultural transformations.[15] We need to understand the emergence of a distinctive state formation.

A range of forces converged to lead the policing of protest to become more legally accountable and accommodating to marches and demonstrations in the 1970s–1990s, and a range of reactionary vectors converged to lead protest policing to become less hospitable to mobilizations and assemblies of the people by the late 1990s. These reactionary forces began to constellate in the 1960s and 1970s, and they were set in motion by three interrelated crises: a crisis of democracy, an urban fiscal crisis, and a crime crisis. The reactions to these crises set in motion transformations in political culture and law, urban political economy, and policing and punishment. These vectors of reaction became sufficiently institutionalized by the 1990s that a noticeably distinctive model of policing protest emerged—one that I am calling the security model of policing protest.

### Crisis of Democracy

The crisis of democracy represents the reaction against democracy. Harvard University's Samuel Huntington argued, "Marginal social groups, as in the case of blacks, are now becoming full participants in the political system," creating a "danger of overloading the political system" with their demands.[16] Huntington added his voice to those who perceived in the protests of the 1960s a "crisis of democracy"—a crisis produced by too much democratic mobilization. American political culture was developing an exhaustion, if not an antipathy, toward democracy.

For those with more democratic sensibilities, the demonstrations of the Civil Rights movement and the urban riots of the 1960s engendered a sense that the United States faced a legitimation crisis.[17] The Kerner Commission's report expressed this orientation when it criticized policing in urban areas as inconsistent with the role of police in a democratic society. It urged that the gap between democratic norms of equality and the reality in major cities of material deprivation and symbolic degradation of black people be reduced. The Kerner Commission exemplified the orientation to social democracy that was hegemonic in the 1960s, and its report not only became the focus of serious discussion, it also became a best seller.[18] From this social democratic orientation, urban civil disorder represented a legitimation crisis.[19]

Richard Nixon splintered the hegemony of the Kerner Commission's more social democratic orientation with his successful campaign for the presidency in 1968. When the Kerner Commission's report was released, he complained that the report blamed everyone for the riots except those who rioted.[20] He accepted the Republican Party's nomination at the RNC on behalf of the "great majority of Americans, the forgotten Americans—the non-shouters; the non-demonstrators," who were "not guilty of the crime that plagues the land."[21]

Nixon projected the voice of conservatives who had railed against civil rights demonstrations like the 1964 March on Washington.[22] He also made them matter legally with his four appointments to the Supreme Court, including its new chief justice, Warren Burger. The Burger Court buried important legal doctrines holding that when there was a conflict between constitutional values like free speech and property rights or commerce, the First Amendment held a preferred position due to the constitutional commitment to democracy. The preferred position doctrine had guided the Court for decades in the middle of the twentieth century. Under the Burger Court, this hierarchy of constitutional values was upended and commerce was privileged over speech rights.

The Burger Court's post-democratic jurisprudence overturned earlier legal precedent that demonstrators should be able to express themselves in public spaces even if those public spaces were under private ownership. More compelling to the Burger Court than the value of public space for a democracy was extending the image of a homeowner's power to control what they chose to listen to in their own home by analogy to the owner of a shopping mall. By permitting the power of authoritarian government over privately owned public spaces like shopping malls, it enabled authoritarian government over a space that was becoming socially, geographically, and economically significant to American life in the 1970s and 1980s. Malls exercised their control over space for purposes of aesthetic governance to create environments that incited consumerism, subsuming and simulating the appearance of community by foreclosing the appearance of political antagonism.

In the late 1970s and through the 1980s, developers were introducing malls to cities as a component of urban regeneration. By the 1990s, the logic of the mall was guiding urban design. With most of their manufacturing jobs of the Fordist era gone (named after manufacturing pioneer Henry Ford), cities were being redeveloped according to post-Fordist forms of symbolic or cultural production and branded aesthetic experiences.

I argue in the first chapter that as significant as the privatization of space is, of perhaps greater importance is how public urban spaces have been governed since the 1990s. I look at how New Jersey, one of the few states to require malls to respect state constitutional speech rights, understands what those rights of expression mean in that state's shopping malls. The New Jersey State Supreme Court requires that the exercise of speech rights not be disruptive to commerce and speaks supportively about zoning speech to a "community booth." As cities redirect urban political economies to post-Fordist aesthetic experiences, New Jersey's cramped model of speech rights like-wise migrates from privately owned suburban malls to guide First Amendment jurisprudence in urban public spaces. Some political theorists rightly criticize the authoritarian governance of privately owned public spaces like malls because of the detrimental normative consequences for democracy.[23] As important as those insights are, I go further to argue that the limited understanding of speech rights available to speakers in New Jersey shopping malls supplies the juridical key for comprehending how the right to expression has been reformatted within cities engaged in neoliberal, post-Fordist symbolic production. That is, authoritarian government introduced as a model for control over privately owned public space is now the model for government of urban public space under neoliberal, post-Fordist conditions of political economy.

### Urban Fiscal Crisis

The second crisis of the 1960s and 1970s that set in motion forces of reaction that shape the security model of protest policing was the urban fiscal crisis of the 1970s. In 1975, New York City was unable to find purchasers for its debt. The Ford administration made a national example of New York, and only provided the city help on the condition that New York dismantle its support for social reproduction and govern residents instead through social austerity.[24] In the 1980s and 1990s, the administrations of Ronald Reagan and George Herbert Walker Bush severely slashed federal funding for urban programs, exposing cities directly to markets, forcing them to govern for markets, and compelling cities to become market actors themselves. In other words, urban governments were compelled—as New York was—to become neoliberal: a practice of governing for markets and embedding market logics within practices of government.[25]

In addition to creating favorable environments for the finance, insurance, and real estate industries, cities began to reorient their infrastructures away from residents and toward nonresidents who might visit the city.[26] Having lost not only substantial numbers of manufacturing jobs but also residents, cities like New York sought to bring those who lived in the suburbs—or other tourists and conventions—back to the city as a source of revenue. The city was now a place for visitors to shop, dine, patronize museums or the theater, enjoy art galleries, visit an aquarium, and attend sports events. Urban political economy was becoming post-Fordist, and cities focused on producing aesthetic environments conducive to cultural experiences and symbolic production. They branded themselves (I ♥ NY) and marketed themselves in competition with other cities seeking to do the same thing.[27]

Cities also compete to host mega-events to brand and market themselves. The most significant mega-events are classified as national special security events (NSSEs), the highest security classification in the United States. Examples of NSSEs are presidential inaugurations, presidential funerals, major international summits, major party conventions, the Olympics, and the Super Bowl. When a city wins a bid to host a mega-event classified as an NSSE, police executives will often visit a city that is presently hosting an NSSE to prepare for managing NSSE security in their own city. From the perspective of the host city's branding and marketing goals, success in producing the spectacle of a mega-event means that there can be no disruption to the event, whether the disruption is a terrorist attack, some other emergency or disaster, crime, or a protest. Protest is represented not as a democratic practice but as a threat equivalent to crime, or any other risk to the event that must be prevented. Mega-event and NSSE security planning materials reinforce the market-based calculations of entrepreneurial cities.[28]

In chapter 2, I examine how the NYPD policed the 2004 RNC, and how it prepared for the 2004 RNC by hosting the 2002 World Economic Forum (WEF). I argue that when cities host mega-events, they are left with a security legacy that persists in the city after the event is over. This legacy can be armored vehicles, weapons, or security cameras that become embedded within the fabric of the urban environment. In the case of New York, hosting the 2002 WEF and the 2004 RNC would lead to a security legacy of institutional development in two areas: expanding the capacity of the NYPD's Intelligence Division and changing arrest policies linked to its mass arrest processing. Although the NYPD's 2004 RNC practices would be judicially legitimized at the time as necessary for the exceptional event of the 2004 RNC, politically motivated intelligence gathering and needlessly punitive arrest processing practices have become institutionalized as normal policing practices and have been redeployed, as I argue in later chapters, against Occupy Wall Street and #BlackLivesMatter protesters in New York.

Scholarly characterizations of protest policing at major events frame its practices as extensions of actuarial calculations for efficient risk management. This kind of efficient risk management calculation is central to portrayals of neoliberalism as coldly utilitarian in its minimization of costs. Because after-action assessments of the NYPD's WEF protest policing show how the NYPD enjoyed intimidating demonstrators, and because the NYPD's harsh policing of the 2004 RNC led to the largest civil settlement arising out of abusive protest policing in U.S. history, representations of neoliberal protest policing as calculatingly, economically efficient are misplaced and may overlook sources of political support for the neoliberal state that enjoy its cruelties. Perhaps the neoliberal state's practices of protest policing—or police practices more generally—derive political support because of, and not despite, their abuses.

## The Crime Crisis

In the 1960s, conservatives fueled perceptions of a crime crisis by conflating, in their resistance to the Civil Rights movement, civil rights, crime, protest, and violence. Where supporters of the Civil Rights movement may have seen core First Amendment activities such as marches and demonstrations, or where supporters and participants may have seen citizens rightfully seeking access to public places and services guaranteed to them by the Constitution, conservatives saw violations of state segregation laws. In a word, they saw crime.[29] Nixon's Southern strategy to split the Democrats and win the White House echoed these ostensible law-and-order themes that likewise elided protest and political equality with crime and violence. His 1968 RNC speech discussed above valorized the "non-demonstrators" who were "not guilty of the crime that plagues the land."[30] The "crime" of the crime crisis was always more than ordinary crime. The forces mobilized by the crime crisis reacted against the crime of political equality, and the crime crisis supplied affective attachment to authoritarian policies of policing and punishment.

Though Nixon would announce a "war against criminal elements," the presidencies of Reagan, Bush, and Bill Clinton were the ones that fought this war with institution building, resources for state and municipal police, and political commitment. Crime was not merely racialized during the 1980s and 1990s, but politicized and militarized. Crime legislation passed in even-numbered—that is to say, election—years. The 1984 Crime Bill expanded "asset forfeiture," making it easier to seize assets thought to be associated with a crime, providing a source of revenue to police that could be used to purchase military-grade weaponry, vehicles, and uniforms.[31] Clinton expanded state and local police access to military surplus through the 1033 Program. Police became better armed and enacted a spectacle of shock and awe in the course of their normal duties.[32]

Police also began to target minor forms of disorder with zero tolerance in the 1990s. In 1982, George Kelling and James Q. Wilson's essay "Broken

Windows" provided the ideational template for this transformation of local police forces. Pushing back against the Kerner Commission's orientation to policing as law enforcement, the "Broken Windows" concept of policing urged police to go beyond law enforcement to target the disorder of the visibly poor. The authors quoted an officer who described how he policed public housing: "We kick ass."[33] When Rudy Giuliani won election to become New York City's mayor in 1993, he appointed "Broken Windows" adherent Bill Bratton to become the NYPD commissioner. Under Bratton, the "Broken Windows" concept of policing ruthlessly transformed the NYPD and became institutionalized.[34] Bratton and Giuliani spoke all over the United States and the world promoting the "Broken Windows" concept of policing.[35] Between these promotional efforts, and with high-level executives from the NYPD accepting positions with other major city police departments or work with private security firms, the "Broken Windows" concept of policing transformed policing all over the United States.

The transformation of policing in the direction of zero tolerance, quality of life, order maintenance policing—and enjoyment of "kicking ass"—was at odds with the principles of tolerance and restraint informing the negotiated management model of protest policing. It also injected an affective charge into policing much like patrolling in "battle dress uniforms" did. Within only a few years, negotiated management would erode under the pressure of order maintenance policing inspired by "Broken Windows." Mobilization motivated by the crime crisis set in motion transformations in policing that would lead to a more aggressive and violent model of protest policing.

In chapter 3, I describe how the NYPD's policing of OWS protests reacted excessively and dramatically to the most minor disorder. In this regard, I agree with other protest policing scholarship finding that NYPD protest policing is an extension of their commitment to the "Broken Windows" concept of policing.[36] I diverge from this scholarship insofar as its portrait of NYPD policing of protest presents a picture of a hyper-Weberian force that ruthlessly and dispassionately polices law to its letter. In contrast, I attend to the excesses in the NYPD's protest policing. Characterizing the NYPD as strictly enforcing the minutiae of legal regulations does not address the use of disproportionate force to conduct an arrest for something so minor as a protester briefly stepping into the street when police wanted the march to stay on the sidewalk. It cannot account for the NYPD's extralegal practices such as baseless arrests or kettling protesters to scare them. Nor can it account for the officer who screamed at an Occupier in custody, "You motherfucking protesters, every time you come back to that park, we're going to kick your ass!" In other words, I underline affective attachment expressed by members of the NYPD to defeating and degrading OWS.

We see this NYPD institutional dedication to defeating OWS in the excessive lengths of custody Occupy arrestees suffered. We also see this dedication to defeating OWS with the NYPD's deployment of the Intelligence Division's resources against OWS. Both the mass arrest processing and the use of the Intelligence Division against nonviolent protesters built upon the NYPD's policing of 2004 RNC protesters. The NYPD not only criminalizes protesters like OWS, it seeks to defeat them. I refer to this institutional ambiguity in NYPD protest policing that goes beyond criminalizing protest, but stops short of war, as the security model of protest policing. This security model of protest policing is underwritten politically by subjects affectively attached to the defeat of protesters critical of neoliberal authoritarianism.

By looking at how the NYPD policed the 2004 RNC in conjunction with how it policed OWS, we can understand how protest policing has become more hostile to public assemblies and demonstrations. The increasingly authoritarian policing of protest that has taken shape in the United States since the 1990s is the product of two institutional influences. On the one hand, it results from the vertical influence of protest policing knowledge, strategies, institutional supports, resources, and weaponry that are disseminated from federal sources when cities host NSSEs like the RNC. On the other hand, it results from the horizontal influence of the "Broken Windows" concept of policing that is disseminated by the circulation of police managers through different police forces and private security firms, and by its promotion from boosters in the 1990s and 2000s. Therefore, the aggressive policing of protest is overdetermined. New York is a city that is well known both for the mega-events that it hosts and for its commitment to the "Broken Windows" concept of policing, and the NYPD is exemplary for its aggressive protest policing.

### Communicative Production

Protest policing has become expressively aggressive and violent. Moreover, images of protesters being pepper sprayed or subjected to flashbangs, tear gas, LRADs, and water cannons, or being confronted by riot police dressed for battle, or by armored vehicles designed to withstand land mines while on patrol in Iraq, circulate widely in the news media, on social media, and on YouTube. If these images are so widely disseminated, then why do we not see the nation's conscience shocked and a reform movement mobilized to rein in protest policing today like the reform of protest policing that took shape in the 1970s?

Capitalism in the United States—and globally—has become more communicatively productive. "Communicative capitalism" depicts how communication has become subsumed within capitalism.[37] Capitalism has become communicative and incorporates, mediates, arranges, and fragments virtually all spheres of life. By engendering a reflexive experience of communicative potential inciting new market niches to express subjective preferences, and by creating nonunified experiences for diverse users, communicative capitalism incites a disintegration of the disciplined, social democratic subject symbolically undergirding social welfare democracies in the 1960s.

The centrality of the political subject oriented to a social democratic horizon has been displaced and takes up a position of communicative equivalence alongside other subjective orientations. On the one hand, the reflexive experience of communicative multiplicity enables a subjectivity that enjoys interpretive pluralism and communicative multiplicity for its own sake. We can call this manner of subjectivity "whatever being."[38] Whatever being enjoys, and is flexibly open to, the communication of . . . whatever. On the other hand, whatever being has a doppelganger. Under conditions of reflexive, communicative multiplicity, the doppelganger's preferences are as good as anyone else's (since "everyone is biased"), but the doppelganger is not open to whatever. The doppelganger remains stuck within—or affectively attached to—the political coordinates of 1968. The doppelganger's enjoyment of its citizenship has been stolen by rioting black people and the liberal elites who coddle them at the doppelganger's expense (a psychic tax expressed in overt political discourse as "taxes"). In the election of 1968, Nixon (and George Wallace) provided a communicative space for these "forgotten Americans," and communicative capitalism provides a habitat enabling these forgotten Americans to enjoy communicating their resentment for having lost the enjoyment of their citizenship.

Under the conditions of communicative capitalism, these disintegrated subjectivities proliferate. Moreover, with the viral circulation of memes, the image of police violence is disintegrated. Indeed, the social itself is disintegrated by the circuits of communicative capitalism and the technologies of control they enable. Under these conditions of communicative capitalism, I argue in chapter 4, images of police abuse of protesters—like the viral circulation of protesters being pepper sprayed—fail to shock a social conscience. They become the opportunity for a meme. And maybe the meme is funny, sort of. These images can be interpreted in a multitude of ways. Or, more disturbingly, they are enjoyed. They are not, however, understood as images of a wrong. Therefore, despite protest policing becoming more aggressive and violent, the circulation of these images of protesters being abusively policed fails to shock a hegemonic subject's conscience under conditions of communicative capitalism.

### The Haunting Figure of Black Insurrection

The erosion of negotiated management, a more tolerant and dialogic relation between protester and police, and the emergence of a more hostile form of protest policing I am calling the security model occurred due to a series of reactions to three crises of the 1960s and 1970s: a crime crisis, an urban fiscal crisis, and a crisis of democracy. The reaction to the crime crisis led to zero tolerance policing that targeted perceptions of disorder. This style of policing focused on aesthetic perceptions and affective encounters, such as fear of crime in the presence of the visibly poor. This aesthetic dimension to the "Broken Windows" concept of policing complemented transformations in urban political economy in response to the urban fiscal crisis of the 1970s that prioritized symbolic or cultural production. Not only did aesthetic government become an integral aspect of everyday urban post-Fordist production, it became vital for the controlled production of spectacle when cities hosted mega-events. The sense of antipathy toward political mobilization spurred by the crisis of democracy accommodated the institutional developments produced by the reactions to the crime crisis and the urban fiscal crisis.

The spectral figure of black insurrection haunts all three crises. The "crime" of the crime crisis is the crime of the Civil Rights movement—demonstrations claiming rights to political and civic equality. The response to the crime crisis also seeks to replace welfare, which reactionaries view as being for black people, with authoritarian policing and punishment. The attack on institutions providing for social reproduction is therefore also haunted by the spectral figure of black insurrection. The crisis of democracy, in turn, is a reaction against black political mobilization overloading the governmental system. In sum, the state of neoliberal authoritarianism is haunted by the spectral figure of black insurrection, and it is built upon the premise of repressing this haunting figure's appearance.

Perhaps we should not be surprised, then, that we can see all three crises intersecting with particular intensity in the policing of #BlackLivesMatter

(BLM). Simmering and long-standing anger at the institutionalized degradation ritual of stop and frisk garnered national attention and nationwide protests with the police killings of Eric Garner and Michael Brown. Reflecting the institutional developments reacting to the crime crisis, police in Ferguson, Missouri, responded with an excessively militarized mobilization. Police in New York engaged in pervasive surveillance and infiltration of BLM protests. As part of the reaction to the urban fiscal crisis, New York acquired two LRADs in its preparations to host the 2004 RNC. As part of the security legacy of having hosted that event, it still possessed LRADs in December 2014, when BLM protested a Staten Island grand jury decision not to indict NYPD Officer Pantaleo, whose chokehold on Eric Garner was responsible for Garner's death. Though justified in 2004 as a glorified public address system, the NYPD has only used LRADs at protests and routinized its LRAD use against BLM protests. Finally, the reaction to the crisis of democracy creates an accommodating political culture for the postlegitimation, post-democratic response of the Memphis Police Department (MPD) to BLM of politically targeted surveillance and blacklists in violation of a forty-year-old judicial consent decree forbidding such practices.

The policing of BLM protests exhibits the forward edge of contemporary protest policing. Today, protest policing is developing two postlegitimation, post-democratic tendencies. The first is an increasingly militarized response to protest, and the second is the increased deployment of postdisciplinary control technologies to monitor and manage protests.

The militaristic response to BLM in Ferguson and New York indicates how the spectral figure of black insurrection continues to haunt contemporary policing and American political culture. This militaristic response acknowledges the appearance of a political antagonism and a political subject. This political subject—BLM and its spectral evocation of the haunting figure of black insurrection—represents a relation of enmity to the state formation of neoliberal authoritarianism. The mobilization of forces by neoliberal authoritarianism to defeat this political subject acknowledges and responds to this political subject. This communication of mutual enmity has important theoretical significance.

For scholars like Frank Wilderson who work in the field of Afro-pessimism, the state, civil society, indeed, the Human, is constituted in a relation of ontological antagonism to Blackness. The practice of enslaving the Black established by negation a world; it constituted being through the nonbeing of the Black. From the perspective of Afro-pessimism, then, Blackness is not a social position but is outside social relationality as a "structural position of non-communicability in the face of all other positions."[39] Ontologically structured as a position of social death or a human void, Blackness is "perpetually open to gratuitous violence."[40] The militarized response in Ferguson and New York would seem to confirm this ontological analysis.

In chapter 5, I argue that we understand the antagonistic relation between police departments and BLM better as a political antagonism, rather than as an ontological condition. The militarized response to BLM in Ferguson and New York exceeds normal responses to crime in civil society. As Carl Schmitt famously urges, the friend-enemy relation expresses the essence of politics, and it is the "most intense and extreme antagonism."[41] Participants in political relation must judge "whether the adversary intends to negate his opponent's way of life."[42] Rather than conceptualizing the relation of police and BLM as an ontological void of nonrelation, I contend that we do better to understand the antagonism between neoliberal authoritarianism and BLM as a political relation. The spectacular excesses of the police reactions in Ferguson and New York communicate—they communicate enmity. The intense political antagonism BLM forces to appear with its mobilization should not be displaced and depoliticized as an ontological condition of being.

Why address such deeply philosophical questions—the ontological claims made by Afro-pessimists—here? Understandably, concern with policing, police violence, and incarceration runs throughout the works of Afro-pessimists.[43] Afro-pessimism's ontological focus on being and its essential qualities, though, cannot explain periods when socioeconomic conditions have improved for black people, among others in American society, or why the violence of state practices may have become more constrained.[44] Such distinctive periods make apparent how political mobilization can result in improvements in social well-being or reductions in state violence, and how reactionary movements can cause social well-being to deteriorate and state violence to become more widespread or more intensely brutal. Therefore, political analyses do well to identify these differing historical periods and to make the best effort possible to comprehend why and how such changes occur—particularly if we seek to remedy our deepening exploitation, expropriation, and collective political disempowerment. In other words, the depoliticizing logic of ontological thinking, though currently prominent, hinders political understanding.[45]

The second tendency we see in contemporary protest policing is an increasing use of postdisciplinary control technologies. As theorized by philosopher Gilles Deleuze, control technologies "dividuate," fragment, divert, control points of access, manage or minimize risk to a system, create graduated stages of access or denial, or use aggregations of data produced by our participation in communicative capitalism to calculate risk levels to systems. They create lines of association and reflexively construct possibilities and probabilities of threats.[46] Control technologies are postdisciplinary in the sense that they do not train subjects, normalize or socialize subjects, or correct subjects and seek their reintegration as productive members of society. By their dividuating or fragmenting tendencies, they function according to a logic of subjective and social disintegration—they prevent the formation of a political subject from appearing or assembling power. Or, by deploying technologies of control, police can monitor and manage protesters, and displace or disassemble the appearance of a political subject, which is what the MPD sought to do by deploying control technologies in its policing of BLM and those possibly associated with BLM.

Although a federal court ruling found the MPD to be in violation of a judicial decree limiting its political surveillance, Memphis argued, and not without reason, that their policing of social media represents a best practice in the field of policing. The plausibility of their claim is indicative of how protest policing has been transformed since the negotiated management era. This transformation, however, has deeply disturbing consequences for democratic practices and the power of the people.

Today, courts permit police and city governments to zone protesters to marginal locations, justifying their displacement from more publicly central locations—or their ability to stage an antagonism by confronting those with whom they have political grievance—on the grounds that modern communications, such as the internet, enable protesters to communicate even if no one is physically present to see or hear them. These judicial rulings force protesters to participate in the domains of communicative capitalism and to become present to technologies of control. Taken to its logical extreme, access to public space could be totally denied to protesters as long as Twitter or Facebook exist. More problematically, police have shut down internet and cellular communications to prevent protests from occurring within the Bay Area Rapid Transit system. The combinatory effects of law and policing compel protest to become subsumed within the circuits of communicative capitalism, where protest's communicative possibility is then conditioned upon the decisions of those who control access to communicative capitalism, and how police use control technologies. By considering how law works in relation to policing's use of control technologies, we can apprehend how a postlegitimation and post-democratic state formation is taking shape—the state of neoliberal authoritarianism.

Contemporary protest policing may be self-evidently post-democratic for its militarized efforts to defeat those seeking to raise grievances to government, or to prevent the assembly of a political subject that would make an apparent political grievance.[47] But how is it postlegitimation? The preemptory, politically targeted, and excessive dimensions of the security model of protest policing violate the most basic conditions of legitimation through discourse ethics, as theorized by Jürgen Habermas. By repressing the political participation of neoliberal authoritarianism's critics, contemporary protest policing violates the premise that only the force of better arguments rather than brute force is normatively acceptable for political discourse.[48] If legitimation is posited in terms of consent, then these methods of policing protest are determined efforts to prevent the appearance of a withholding of consent. Finally, in the most narrowly understood sense of liberal legalism, the security model of protest policing is postlegitimation because it polices in a non–legally discriminate manner. For example, the appearance of disorder is a legally arbitrary determination. The LRAD's logic of pain compliance is a non–legally authorized punishment for protesting. Additionally, anyone in an area is subjected to the pain of sound, not merely those allegedly in violation of a law. Similarly, control technologies function according to a logic of association, in violation of liberal legal principles of individualized guilt. Therefore, the security model fails not only rigorous standards of legitimation but the most minimal standards of normative legitimation.

The excesses of contemporary protest policing presented here shed new light on the neoliberal state. Conventionally, theorists like Wendy Brown conceptualize neoliberalism in terms of "economizing" approaches to public policy neglectful of nonmarket values in its cost-benefit analyses—a governmental rationality that is a "steroidally charged form of Weberian instrumental rationality."[49] The neoliberal state, therefore, is one that "will eschew *excessive* uses of violence or extraconstitutional conduct."[50] The chapters that follow are filled with examples of excessive violence and extraconstitutional conduct that are increasingly integral to contemporary protest policing. Moreover, the numerous and repeated settlements resulting from civil rights litigation do not indicate an economizing disposition on the part of the neoliberal state either. In contrast, I argue that the excesses increasingly apparent in contemporary protest policing are indicative of affective attachment to the neoliberal state's practices.[51] That is, the neoliberal state's cruelties are practices of affective enjoyment by and for the neoliberal state's political subjects. I contend we fail to grasp political support for the neoliberal state if we neglect how its political subjects are attached to seeing these cruelties expressed and enacted. In sum, narrow questions regarding the policing of protest provide an opening through which the contours of a distinctive state formation, the postlegitimation, post-democratic state of neoliberal authoritarianism, become apparent.

On May 25, 2020, Minneapolis police officer Derek Chauvin, aided by three other officers, Thomas Lane, Tou Thao, and J. Alexander Kueng, arrested George Floyd, a black male, and forced him face down onto the pavement. Chauvin placed his knee on the back of Floyd's neck for almost nine minutes, killing Floyd. Like Eric Garner, Floyd repeatedly called out in his last moments of life, "I can't breathe. . . ."[52]

As video recordings of the Minneapolis police officers killing Floyd circulated, massive protests erupted in Minneapolis and around the country. Protests linked recent police and vigilante killings of black people including Ahmaud Arbery, Breonna Taylor, Elijah McClain, and Daniel Prude to the killing of Floyd. The protests continued through the summer and into the fall of 2020, fueled by needless police shootings of black people. Jacob Blake was shot in the back by police in Kenosha, Wisconsin, on August 23 as he walked away from police and was opening the door to his car. Walter Wallace Jr. was suffering a mental health crisis when he was shot by Philadelphia police on October 26. By the summer of 2020, the *New York Times* considered the uprising protesting police and vigilante killings of black people to be the largest movement in U.S. history. On June 6, over half a million people demonstrated in 550 places around the country. By July, polling found that between 15 million and 26 million people had participated in these protests.[53] More than 93 percent of the protests were peaceful.[54]

Some protests, though, were marred by violence. Members of the right-wing group seeking to ignite a second civil war, the Boogaloo Bois, were charged with inciting violence in Minneapolis. The charges included firing into a police station and setting the building ablaze.[55] Kyle Rittenhouse, a seventeen-year-old Blue Lives Matter enthusiast, traveled to Kenosha from Illinois and associated himself with militia members. Shortly after the group received bottles of water and words of appreciation from police operating an armored vehicle, he shot three BLM protesters, killing two.[56]

Most of the violence during the uprising of 2020, however, was perpetrated by police themselves. On the evening of June 3, NYPD riot police kettled protesters in Brooklyn's Cadman Plaza. According to reports, for the next twenty minutes, "officers swinging batons turned a demonstration that had been largely peaceful into a scene of chaos."[57] During the late spring and early summer of 2020, the *New York Times* collected and published video that captured NYPD officers picking up and body slamming a protester into the street; an officer who pushed a woman so hard that she fell backward onto the pavement; multiple officers who caught a man running from the police to swarm him and beat him with batons (and when a high-level "white shirt" joined the melee, he "stepped on the man's neck"); officers who hit people "walking away from them"; officers who "grabbed people from behind"; officers who "attacked people who had their hands up"; officers who "repeatedly pummeled people who were already on the ground"; and officers who "responded to words with punches and pepper spray." Many of the police attacks "were led by high-ranking officers" and were "not warranted."[58] The NYPD's excessive response to protests was the cause of violence and disorder on New York City streets, sidewalks, and plazas.[59] In addition to high-ranking officers' concerning role in the abuse of force was the disturbing fact that gratuitous police violence against protesters occurred while police had to have known they were being watched and video recorded as they reacted against protests of police abuse of force. This suggests that the police violence against protesters had an expressive element—the police response expressed opposition to BLM, to democratic assemblies, and to the claim that police should be legally accountable. They were responding to political antagonism.

The NYPD and its policing of the 2020 uprising represented a more general institutionalization of a post-democratic, postlegitimation state as police in numerous cities responded with excessive force to the protests. In Washington, D.C., on June 1, 2020, during the early evening, police from multiple agencies, supported militarily by the National Guard, physically brutalized peaceful demonstrators in Lafayette Square. If there was a warning to disperse, it went unheard by protesters and reporters. Police in riot gear used shields and batons and fired flash and smoke grenades, as well as chemical irritants, to attack the protesters and drive them out of the square. Reporters for the *New York Times* described the "scene of mayhem" as one "more commonly associated with authoritarian countries." The attack on the peaceful protesters was purposeless from a public-safety perspective; its purpose was to remove the protesters from Lafayette Square so President Trump could be photographed holding a bible in front of a church located by the square, "demonstrating toughness."[60] Later that evening, military helicopters flown by the National Guard conducted shows of force against protesters by flying low and shining searchlights directly on demonstrators. The tactic is one used by the military "in combat zones to scatter insurgents."[61] The force of the wind generated by the helicopter propellers snapped tree limbs and tore signs from buildings, while the noise caused by the force of air generated by the propellers was characterized as "deafening."[62] One of the helicopters engaged in the maneuvers bore a Red Cross emblem, the misuse of which violates the Geneva Conventions.[63] The attack on peaceful protesters by multiple police, security, and military forces on June 1, 2020, exemplifies how protest policing in the United States is a hybrid of policing and military actions, which I describe as the security model of protest policing.

This security model of protest policing was evident in Oregon, where Portland police and federal agents used batons and fired projectiles—often containing chemical irritants—against passive protesters. Evidence suggests they targeted medics providing medical aid to the injured, in violation of international human rights principles.[64] Protesters in Portland were abducted by unidentified federal agents and taken away in unmarked vans.[65] Patrolling Portland streets wearing camouflage and tactical gear blocks away from any federal building they might have been justified legally in guarding, federal agents arrested dozens of protesters on federal charges.[66] Among the federal agents deployed to Portland was a group known as BORTAC, a Border Control unit that some compare to a SWAT team and others compare to a special forces unit within one of the armed services.[67] According to Mary McCord, a professor at Georgetown Law and a former national security official at the Department of Justice, "This is the kind of thing we see in authoritarian regimes."[68]

As the response to the uprising of 2020 indicated, the security model of protest policing is one dimension of post-democratic state formation. Expressing a post-democratic political culture, on a conference call about BLM protests, U.S. Attorney General William Barr told governors to "dominate the streets."[69] Secretary of Defense Mark Esper represented policing protest as a "battlespace" to be controlled.[70] Trump asserted, "You have to dominate," and, expressing a postlegitimation orientation to state power, "You have to do retribution." Summing up the post-democratic orientation to political culture, as well as an attachment to repressing the spectral figure of black insurrection, Trump referred repeatedly to protesters as "terrorists."[71]

Marching under BLM banners, protester chants and speeches were not limited to the memories of those whom police had killed. Protesters condemned police abuse of force and called for police accountability. They also called for defunding the police so governments could fund programs responsive to a plethora of human needs and social well-being. Protesters called most obviously for improvements in mental health services: when police are those who respond first to persons suffering mental health crises, the results can be deadly for the person suffering the crisis, as Daniel Prude's death—caused by Rochester, New York, police—illustrates. Free the People Roc, which has organized the main demonstrations against the conduct of Rochester Police and Rochester's Mayor Lovely Warren since the disclosure of Prude's death, has called for healthcare and improving mental healthcare capacity, improving education, enriching the lives of young people, valuing the lives of LGBTQ+ people, redressing the injustices of the carceral state, abolishing the death penalty, providing access to housing, providing local jobs and fair wages, enacting programs to prevent evictions, ameliorating poverty, evaluating government budgets in terms of principles of justice, and putting people before profit.

Free the People Roc represents a fundamental challenge to neoliberal authoritarianism by calling for a response to the crisis of social reproduction. Their political program does not receive adequate political representation through either of the two main political parties in the U.S.—certainly not in comparison to the competition by major party candidates for endorsements of police, police associations, and police unions. This highlights the political significance of protest and the uprising of 2020, and it highlights the significance of the abusive response to this uprising expressed by the increasingly militarized security model of protest policing. This confrontation on streets across the country represented key dimensions of political antagonism that cannot be redressed without taking on the institutional structures of the post-democratic, postlegitimation state shaped by neoliberal authoritarianism and haunted by the figure of black insurrection.

Fifty years ago, social scientists documented that when police initiate a confrontation with protesters by aggressively escalating their level of force toward a demonstration, this manner of policing protest produces disorderly, if not violent, outcomes, is contrary to public safety, and contradicts First Amendment values. Police responses during the uprising of 2020 seeking to "dominate" protesters with excessive exercises of force produced similar and predictable outcomes. Such protest policing escalates violence and is counterproductive in terms of building either consent or legitimacy for state institutions or policies. The policing of protest during the uprising of 2020 indicates the institutionalization of the security model of protest policing, and it points to an affective attachment to dominating protesters expressed by state actors and political subjects. *Policing Protest* analyzes the institutional developments in law and political culture, urban political economy, and policing and punishment that have brought state practices and politics in the U.S. to this point.

# Chapter One

# Aesthetic Government
# Neoliberal Authoritarianism
# and the Post-Democratic
# Right of Expression

Wherever the title of the streets and parks may rest, they have immemorially been held in trust for the use of the public and, time out of mind, have been used for the purposes of assembly, communicating thoughts between citizens, and discussing public questions. Such use of the streets and public places has, from ancient times, been a part of the privileges, immunities, rights, and liberties of citizens.
—JUSTICE OWEN ROBERTS, *Hague v. C.I.O.* (1939)

If speech is to reach these people, it must reach them in Lloyd Center.
—JUSTICE THURGOOD MARSHALL, U.S. Supreme Court, dissenting,
*Lloyd Corp. v. Tanner* (1972)

Shopping can be accomplished even with mouths shut and minds closed.
—JUSTICE MARIE GARIBALDI, New Jersey State Supreme Court, dissenting,
*New Jersey Coalition against War in the Middle East v. J.M.B. Realty Corporation*
(1994)

POLITICAL THEORISTS CRITICIZE privatization leading to the disappearance of public space for undermining democracy and removing conditions necessary for freedom of speech.[1] Public space facilitates exposure to new or unconventional ideas and speakers. An unforeseen encounter with a homeless person can remind one that a seeming consensus either overlooks or actively occludes pressing concerns pertinent to human dignity and the welfare of all. Because private ownership implies control over space and the right to exclude unwanted persons—including unwanted speakers—political theorists argue we must defend a right to both free speech and public spaces in which to exercise this right. Otherwise, we won't know what we are missing. Or we can too easily avoid the dissonance or epiphany that can accompany an unplanned, or perhaps disturbing, encounter.

But: Is a shopping mall, despite its private ownership, not a public place—a place where friends gather, consumers shop, and civic organizations reach out to passersby? Can a shopping mall exercise the same control over visitors that individuals can exercise over what someone says, watches, or wears in their living room? While a living room or bedroom is private, isn't a mall meaningfully public, particularly as malls update themselves to subsume more and more aspects of human life? Consider the Streets at SouthGlenn in Centennial, Colorado.[2] The redevelopment of this shopping mall in the mid-to-late 2000s removed the walls and introduced an "open air footprint." Instead of corridors, now there are paved streets, sidewalks, and new businesses like Whole Foods alongside retail outlets one more conventionally finds in shopping malls, like Victoria's Secret, Old Navy, or H&M. The developers promote their residential apartments and have hosted summer concert series. The Streets at SouthGlenn advertises itself as a place to "shop, work & live."[3] In other words, it advertises how it has subsumed human life and capitalizes social reproduction. It owns spaces we imagine or experience as both public and private.

The Streets at SouthGlenn is a space for differentiated consumerism, and the enjoyment of experiences, memories, and photo or video opportunities reliant upon social media. It also is a site of nonfactory work for selling commodities; providing cognitive labor to the finance, insurance, and real estate (FIRE) industries; and immaterial or affective labor providing affective experiences, cultural production, and forms of symbolic production, such as marketing and branding. Some social scientists and theorists refer to the niche-based, expressive contemporary political economy as post-Fordist, in contrast with the mass production of uniform products for mass markets Henry Ford helped build. Others express how different political economy is today from the Fordist era using a variety of terms in addition to post-Fordism, such as semio-capitalism, cognitive capitalism, or communicative capitalism.[4] The Streets at SouthGlenn illustrates the privatization of public space that facilitates the distinctive image and affect-oriented contemporary political economy social scientists and theorists depict because privatization enables greater control of aesthetic production and experience.

According to U.S. constitutional law today, shopping malls are considered to be private property that a mall developer can govern much like individuals can control their living room or backyard. Constitutional law has not always treated shopping malls or privately owned towns as spaces where owners can treat those living, working, or visiting arbitrarily. Such spaces were previously treated as fulfilling public functions, and the Supreme Court protected the First Amendment rights of those within these privately owned public spaces offering public functions. The Supreme Court, however, shifted its conceptualization of the mall in the 1970s, neglecting its earlier public function doctrine, which had played a crucial role in democratizing the United States. This shift by the Supreme Court is part of a deeper crisis of democracy, the effects of which continue to afflict U.S. political and legal culture today.

I argue that the changed treatment of malls by the Supreme Court reflects a shift from prioritizing democracy over economics to privileging commercial life over democracy. This shift is one part of the deeper movement away from a horizon of government we can call social democracy toward a state formation we can call neoliberal, where the state governs for markets and encourages market sensibilities.[5] As troubling as political theorists find the privatization of public space, I contend that the shopping mall, and the jurisprudence governing the space of the mall, have become models for the government of public space. This means, on the one hand, that urban governments have increasingly privileged, in addition to the FIRE industries, the aesthetic experiences of visitors or residents, and cultural or symbolic production. It also means, on the other hand, that First Amendment rights to free speech and assembly are increasingly displaced or are tightly controlled—much like they are within shopping malls—in favor of the image a city seeks to project for itself or the forms of aesthetic or cultural experiences it offers. That is, we see the emergence and growth of a legality that accommodates this downgrading of democratic rights and practices—like rights to assembly and protest—in favor of the state's promotion of markets, post-Fordist symbolic production, and communication of images. Authoritarian control is not limited to the home or mall, but has migrated to the government of public space. Therefore, the crisis of democracy these changes express is part of a broader state structure, one we can call neoliberal authoritarianism. As I shall argue here and throughout this book, neoliberal authoritarianism is a state formation that is post-democratic.[6]

Between the 1930s and 1960s, policy making in the United States at the national level occurred within broad parameters of social democracy. The New Deal of the 1930s included work programs from the arts to infrastructure, enacted Social Security, regulated the banking and financial markets, established a minimum wage, and protected the right to join a union. In the 1960s, this commitment to social democracy continued, from civil rights legislation to support for public education, job training, welfare, and housing. In the era preceding the New Deal, the Supreme Court regularly struck down such legislation for violating its beliefs in social Darwinism.[7] Beginning in 1937, though, the Supreme Court shifted course, and in 1938 the Court developed a theory of judicial review for a constitutional democracy. In the famous footnote number four of *United States v. Carolene Products*, Chief Justice Stone laid out the relation between the Court and the other branches of government.[8] In the future, according to Stone, the Court would normally defer to the policy making of those more politically accountable branches, asking only that legislation demonstrate a rational or reasonable relationship of means to constitutionally permissible ends. Such deference—a contrast with the pre–New Deal Court—was based upon a presupposition of a functioning constitutional democracy. If, however, legislation passed putting such a presupposition into question—policies abridging fundamental rights, rights integral to the democratic political process, or burdening "discrete and insular minorities" vulnerable within a majoritarian process—then the Court would engage in "strict scrutiny" of such legislation, and it would inevitably result in the law being struck down as unconstitutional.

This broad theory of the relation of the judiciary to the legislative and executive branches of government included special importance for the First Amendment. The First Amendment should have a "preferred position" among constitutional rights.[9] If policies burdened First Amendment rights or if constitutional rights were in conflict, the Court granted the First Amendment priority. Why this order of priority? While the First Amendment is a constitutional right, no particular economic policy has constitutional status. Moreover, if a particular economic policy produces immiseration but institutions of collective deliberation and decision making still function, then people can change economic policy. If collective deliberation and decision-making processes have been suppressed and do not function, then the people cannot govern the economic conditions determining their lives or collective well-being—they are no longer self-governing. Therefore, the First

Amendment's relation to democracy represents a fundamental value for the Supreme Court's footnote number four jurisprudence.

By the 1960s, the Supreme Court had become an active guardian of democratic practices. It protected the right to vote from being denied or abridged by upholding the Voting Rights Act of 1965 and by striking down forms of gerrymandering and malapportionment giving unequal weight to votes.[10] It also struck down the use of a poll tax in state elections and upheld legislation extending the right to vote to those age eighteen or older in federal elections.[11] The Court protected the right to participate in the political process by striking down primary elections limited to white people.[12] It ruled racial segregation in public education was unconstitutional in language highlighting the importance of education for equal civic participation of citizens, and struck down racial segregation in other public places as well.[13] It prevented police from using vague laws to remove the poor from public spaces.[14] The Court also protected rights of free speech and assembly in public places even if such speech caused anger or upset.[15] These decisions reinforcing democratic principles complemented national policy making, such as the Civil Rights Act of 1964 and the Voting Rights Act of 1965, as well as constitutional amendments prohibiting poll taxes in federal elections and extending the right to vote to those eighteen or older in all elections. A movement was also afoot to pass a constitutional amendment guaranteeing equal rights to women. The hegemonic political culture was oriented to the horizon of social democracy, and the Court's jurisprudence reflected this political culture.

When shopping malls became prominent in the 1960s, the Supreme Court looked to its earlier precedent, *Marsh v. Alabama* (1946), to adjudicate the relative importance of First Amendment rights of picketers and the property rights of a mall owner. *Marsh v. Alabama* involves a woman who, as a Jehovah's Witness, sought to distribute religious literature in Chickasaw, Alabama, a company-owned town. She was told to stop leafletting and was asked to leave both the sidewalk and the town. Marsh was arrested for trespass when she refused to leave, and was convicted of trespass in the Alabama courts despite her argument that the arrest and conviction violated her First Amendment rights. Justice Black, speaking for the Supreme Court, observed that ordinarily, such an arrest for trespassing would easily be reversed but for the fact that the Gulf Shipbuilding Corporation owned Chickasaw. Therefore, the legal question the case presented was whether people "who live in or come to Chickasaw [can] be denied freedom of press and religion simply because a single company has legal title to all the town."[16]

According to Alabama, "the corporation's right to control the inhabitants of Chickasaw is coextensive with the right of a homeowner to regulate the conduct of his guests." In other words, Alabama is arguing that the corporation, because it owns the property of Chickasaw, should enjoy authoritarian power of government over those who work in, live in, or visit the town. According to Black, however, "We cannot accept that contention." The Court cannot "agree that the corporation's property interests settle the question."[17]

Black argues, the more an owner opens property "for use by the public in general, the more do his rights become circumscribed by the statutory and constitutional rights of those who use it." As examples of property fulfilling a "public function," Black refers to "privately held bridges, ferries, turnpikes and railroads" as performing "essentially a public function."[18] Because the town and its shopping center were indistinguishable from any other town and shopping center, on the one hand, and because of the "preferred position" of First Amendment rights when they are balanced against the rights of "owners of property," on the other, it does not matter "whether a corporation or a municipality owns or possesses the town," because "the public in either case has an identical interest . . . that the channels of communication remain free."[19] In the mid-twentieth-century constitutional framework, free speech and public space are superior values to merely economic interests in property rights, and these values are embedded within the Court's "preferred position" and "public function" doctrines informing its constitutional jurisprudence.

The decision in *Marsh v. Alabama* is consistent with Justice Roberts's earlier opinion in the Supreme Court's landmark public forum case, *Hague v. C.I.O.* (1939). A "public forum" is a space where one's First Amendment rights are on their strongest grounds. According to Roberts, who ruled that Jersey City could not forbid public assembly, dissemination of information, and discussion of the National Labor Relations Act, "*Wherever the title of the streets and parks may rest*, they have immemorially been held in trust for the use of the public and, time out of mind, have been used for the purposes of assembly, communicating thoughts between citizens, and discussing public questions."[20] The Roberts opinion anticipates Black's seven years later: wherever legal title to public space rests, whether it is privately owned or is publicly held, it must be open to the public and is where First Amendments rights should be most fully protected.

Shopping malls emerged at a time when the preferred position doctrine and the public function doctrine continued to be operative. In *Amalgamated Food Employees Union v. Logan Valley Plaza* (1968), a Pennsylvania court had enjoined the union from picketing a supermarket on the premises of a mall for using nonunion labor.[21] The question this presented to the Supreme Court was whether the mall should be considered to be performing a public function as described by *Marsh v. Alabama*. If so, then despite the shopping center's private ownership, the union would still have a First Amendment right to picket one of the stores located at the shopping mall. The Court's decision, by Thurgood Marshall, found the "similarities between the business block in *Marsh* and the shopping center in the present case," Logan Valley Mall, to be "striking."[22] The "shopping center premises," it found, were "open to the public to the same extent as the commercial center of a normal town."[23] Economic change also underscored the importance of shopping malls as locations for communication and criticism of business practices. Malls would thwart the purpose of the First Amendment if they could create a "cordon sanitaire" of parking lots around their stores to "immunize themselves" from the kinds of "on-the-spot public criticism" downtown businesses were subject to from workers, consumers, or those who faced discrimination. The rise of the "suburban shopping center" had accompanied the "large-scale movement" from "cities to the suburbs," and the percentage of all retail sales for which malls were responsible by 1968 was "significant." Marshall therefore concluded, based on the First Amendment's values, as well as the geographic and economic importance of the shopping mall to American life in 1968, that malls had become the "functional equivalent of a business block" in a normal town and "must be treated in substantially the same manner."[24] Unlike a "person's home," Marshall contended, "no meaningful claim to protection of a right to privacy" could be put forward by the shopping center because it had opened itself to the public. All the shopping mall could assert was "naked title" devoid of constitutional values.

In the Supreme Court's mid-twentieth-century jurisprudence, the public function doctrine played an important role in combating antidemocratic values. In the context of company-owned towns and shopping malls, as we have just seen, the public function doctrine guarded against public space becoming subordinated to the authoritarian control of its owner to preserve First Amendment values critical to the Supreme Court's broader jurisprudence. The public function doctrine also played a significant role in the Court's ruling that the Texas Democratic Party could not exclude black voters from participating in the selection of its candidates through primary elections.[25] Additionally, the public function doctrine supplied the legal grounds for the Supreme Court to rule that the public character of parks meant that access to and use of a park—"regardless of who now has title [to the park] under state law"—could not be limited to white persons.[26] Therefore, the Supreme Court's mid-twentieth-century jurisprudence opened centers of commerce to which the public is invited, elections, and parks to the public and pre-served these spaces and institutions from authoritarian control, whether such authoritarianism was exercised for reasons of economic control or for the maintenance of racial apartheid.

### The Demise of Democracy and the Priority of Commerce

The Supreme Court decided *Logan Valley Plaza* in 1968, a presidential elec-tion year. Richard Nixon waged his campaign that year on behalf of the "forgotten Americans," the "real voice of America," those who are the "great majority of Americans" who are the "non-demonstrators," and who are "not guilty of the crime that plagues the land."[27] Even before Election Day 1968, *Time* magazine observed that "law and order" had become a "loaded catchall, with room for every suspicion, grudge, fear, resentment and jealousy that divides the American electorate." Nixon was the candidate who would "'do something' about rising crime rates, unsafe streets, noisy demonstrators and restless blacks." It predicted that 1968 "could be the most corrosive campaign in memory—one that could cause the U.S. to avert its eyes from the goals of justice and equal opportunity for years to come."[28] Once elected, Nixon was able to redirect the Supreme Court's jurisprudence with four appoint-ments, including a new chief justice, Warren Burger. The presidency, and certain strands of U.S. political culture, expressed exhaustion, if not antipa-thy, toward social democracy and placed new priority upon commerce and consumerism. The Supreme Court's jurisprudence reflected this turn.

The Supreme Court began backtracking from *Logan Valley Plaza* merely four years after its ruling. The Court's changed membership and correspond-ingly changed prioritization of democracy and commerce was evident in a 1972 case involving anti–Vietnam War demonstrators distributing leaflets in the Lloyd Center, a mall owned by the Lloyd Corporation in Portland, Oregon. Justice Lewis Powell's opinion reversed district and appeals court decisions recognizing the First Amendment rights of those distributing the antiwar leaflets, and Powell ruled, in this 5–4 decision, that the anti–Vietnam War demonstrators were not entitled to exercise their First Amendment rights on mall premises.[29]

Powell's appreciation for the controlled aesthetics of a mall, and the way that can facilitate consumerism, was apparent in the opening of his opinion. There, he described the Lloyd Center's functions as "both utilitarian and esthetic" and underscored how the mall provided a "controlled, carefree environment" to "make shopping easy and pleasant."[30] In conjunction with its aesthetic design, the mall sought to stimulate "customer motivation" and "goodwill in the community" by inviting groups to use its auditorium (civic and charitable organizations like the Cancer Society and Boy and Girl Scouts were allowed to use it without a fee), allowing presidential candidates to speak at its auditorium, allowing the American Legion to sell poppies and the Salvation Army to solicit Christmas contributions at the mall. The mall's close attention to creating and securing a particular aesthetic environment, however, meant that it prohibited leafletting, which it believed to be "incompatible with the purpose of the Center and the atmosphere sought to be preserved."[31]

The Lloyd Center has selected elements from society to aggregate and subsume within the mall. This subsumption enables the mall to project an image of community within its space, to associate the mall with community. By associating itself with community and by integrating certain community activities within the mall, Lloyd Corporation draws potential customers to the mall as shoppers, though within a particular aesthetic or imaginary plane. Expression and communication are integrated within the Lloyd Center, which permits meetings, presidential candidate speeches, football rallies, parades with "flags, drummers, and color guard units," and a speaker who delivered an address on the "meaning of Veterans Day and the valor of American soldiers."[32] The Lloyd Center therefore highlights the image production of post-Fordism. This aesthetic production, this image of community, is the Lloyd Corporation's expression, and it incites and manages participation in this expression. The condition of the mall's successful image production, of course, is its capacity to prevent disruption to the creation of this aesthetic environment. Thus, those who come to the mall participate in the mall's image production, and do so under conditions of authoritarian control, as the exclusion of those seeking to distribute antiwar leaflets shows. Lloyd Center's post-Fordist success produces a relation of antagonism, but that antagonism must not appear within the space of the mall.

Powell's disagreement with the Court's ruling in *Logan Valley Plaza* is unmistakable, though his opinion in *Lloyd Corp.* stops short of overruling it. Powell asserts that *Logan Valley Plaza* misinterpreted *Marsh*. *Marsh* represented a special situation where a company-owned town encompassed all the characteristics of an American town, and incorporated everything an American town might have. *Logan Valley Plaza* erroneously focused just on the similarities between the Chickasaw business district and the shopping plaza at issue in *Logan Valley Plaza*.[33]

Must a privately owned corporation encompass key public attributes for the public function doctrine to apply, or must it encompass all the attributes of a municipality before the public function doctrine applies? For the majority in *Lloyd Corp.*, the answer was that a privately owned entity must encompass all attributes of a municipality before the public function doctrine applies. To this end, Powell's opinion emphasizes the "limited scope of the shopping center's invitation to the public," which is to "do business with the tenants," and that the purpose of allowing the groups to express themselves that the mall has permitted is to "create a favorable impression and to generate goodwill."[34] Commerce, commercial post-Fordist communication, and private rights are given precedence over the First Amendment, the value of democracy, and the sovereignty of the people.

Speaking for the four dissenters, Justice Thurgood Marshall argues that Powell's reasoning not only is at odds with *Logan Valley Plaza*, but constitutes an "attack" on the Court's long-standing principles guiding its ruling in *Marsh*.[35] Marshall spotlights how *Marsh* is based on the preferred position of freedom of speech in the constitutional hierarchy of value, and how the Court in *Marsh* refused to allow a corporation to govern citizens by limiting their fundamental rights. The Court's decision in *Lloyd Corp.*, however, contradicts this value scheme when it gives priority to commerce over speech integral to democracy.[36]

For Marshall, a mall cannot be analogized to a private residence. Criticizing Powell's neglect of the public function doctrine in *Lloyd Corp.*, Marshall points out that the Lloyd Center is even more like the company town Chickasaw than was the shopping center at issue in *Logan Valley Plaza*. Portland vacated land for the Lloyd Corporation's use in building the mall so that it could function as a "general retail business district" for the city. Portland hoped employment within the mall would benefit the city economically; the Lloyd Center is integrated into the pattern of city streets; Portland planned future street patterns around the center; it granted the private security employed by Lloyd Corporation full police powers; and the range of businesses and services available at the mall is so extensive, according to Marshall, that residents of Portland could easily satisfy their needs and wants there without ever going anywhere else. Like any municipality, the Lloyd Center has invited the public into its space, and it permits a broad range of noncommercial, speech-related activities within it. Portland has made the Lloyd Center functionally integral to the city. The distribution of leaflets inviting patrons to an antiwar meeting, therefore, is in keeping with the normal patterns of activities in the space because it is meaningfully the equivalent of public space even if it is privately owned.[37]

Marshall continues to demonstrate the sensitivity to the way that jurisprudence must respond to changing economic conditions that he showed in *Logan Valley Plaza*. For the preferred position doctrine to retain vitality in the face of growing corporate concentration of media ownership, people of ordinary means must be able to use "relatively inexpensive means of communication," such as handbills or pickets, in areas where "most of their fellow citizens can be found." This, according to Marshall, "is why respondents have a tremendous need to express themselves within the Lloyd Center." Marshall discerns how privatization is diminishing public space. If the Court fails to respect the public function doctrine, then, Marshall anticipates, it will become "harder and harder for citizens to find means to communicate with other citizens," and only the "wealthy may find effective communication possible."[38] In short, Marshall foresees the emergence of neoliberalism (government relieving itself of public responsibilities through privatization and reliance on markets), the way this will disconnect freedom of speech from democracy, and how this will greatly advantage the political power of the wealthy, if the jurisprudence of the majority in *Lloyd Corp.* should become the jurisprudence of the future. Effective communication means speech is connected with power, and *Lloyd Corp.* disempowers people of ordinary means from reaching their fellow citizens.

As Marshall observed, the grounds of the Court's decision in *Lloyd Corp.* was at odds with its prior rulings in *Logan Valley Plaza* and *Marsh*. A mere four years after the Court decided *Lloyd Corp.*, it made this clear by overruling *Logan Valley Plaza*.[39] Since then, *Marsh* and the public function doctrine have remained neglected. The Burger Court's First Amendment jurisprudence would continue to give priority to commerce over speech, further unsettling the preferred position doctrine and the deeper juridical framework of which it was a part.[40] The Supreme Court, though, has permitted state courts to take a broader view of free speech in their state constitutions—one that would extend a state constitutional right of free speech to mass private property controlled by malls.[41] Most states, however, have declined that invitation. For example, the high court in New York has followed the Supreme Court's lead in its SHAD *Alliance* decision finding the character or use of privately owned property is "immaterial" to a finding of state action implicating a constitutional right, and that the "nature of the property" does not "transform a private actor into a public one."[42] In New York, only a state actor can violate its state constitutional right of freedom of speech. Because most states have not chosen to protect freedom of speech more broadly than the U.S. Supreme Court, this indicates the Supreme Court's post-1968 jurisprudence is in keeping with broader patterns of post-1968 political culture expressing a postdemocratic acceptance of authoritarian control over public spaces.

### The Demise of the Public Function Doctrine
### and the Mall's Subsumption of Human Activity

In *Lloyd Corp.* the Supreme Court significantly narrowed the public function doctrine presented in *Marsh* when Powell asserted that mass private property had to take on all the attributes of a municipality before incurring the obligations of the public function doctrine.[43] In *Marsh*, Black explained the public function doctrine as follows:

> Ownership does not always mean absolute dominion. The more an owner, for his advantage, opens up his property for use by the public in general, the more do his rights become circumscribed by the statutory and constitutional rights of those who use it. . . . Thus the owners of privately held *bridges, ferries, turnpikes and railroads* may not operate them as freely as a farmer does his farm. *Since these facilities are built and operated primarily to benefit the public and since their operation is essentially a public function it is subject to state regulation.*[44]

In contrast with the Court's interpretation of the public function doctrine in *Lloyd Corp.*, Black uses "bridges, ferries, turnpikes and railroads" as examples of privately held property that fulfill public functions. These forms of property do not exhaust what a municipality or a state might do, though they are certain functions that are used by the public and should be governed accordingly.

Likewise, as important as elections are to formal processes of representative government, and as important as parks are to constituent assemblies making present the will or grievances of the people, they do not exhaust the attributes of a state or municipality. Nevertheless, as previously discussed, the Court has found these to fulfill essentially public functions. The suppression of the public function doctrine in contemporary constitutional law, then, is forceful evidence of the emergence of a distinctive post-democratic state formation. This state formation is antagonistic to the principles of equal protection and the sovereignty of the people that the public function doctrine defended against race-based and corporate-based machinations at odds with those commitments. The regime of visibility communicated within the mall and enforced by police, private security, and the law renders the people claiming they should count invisible; or it renders them visible only as signs of disorder to be policed.

At the same time as the public function doctrine has been subordinated to the interests of property owners and their control over privately owned public spaces, malls and "mass private property" have subsumed more and more areas of human activity.[45] This expanded integration of human activities within shopping malls increasingly realizes the aspirations of the father of the shopping mall, architect Victor Gruen. As Gruen envisioned the shopping center, it should do more than merely provide the necessities of life to those who live in the suburbs. Malls should fulfill civic, cultural, and other community needs that enrich the lives of suburban residents.[46]

The mall, for Gruen, was not an alternative to the city; it was a better city: "a shopping center must be a carefully planned urban organism."[47] To this end, he urged that malls be designed so they could host public events like "band concerts, fashion shows, and special merchandising promotions." These, and "holiday celebrations, exhibitions, social events, are all part of life in these open spaces."[48] By including auditoriums that can host civic meetings, performances, educational courses, and church services, and by including nursery schools, play areas for children, and theaters, malls would incorporate social life. This, in conjunction with hosting special events, would foster a strong identification between residents and the mall, making the mall a "real community center."[49] Writing of his design for Northland Center outside Detroit, Michigan, Gruen boasted it would include "a community center—auditorium, club rooms and other facilities—for the use and enjoyment of the entire community."[50] A decade later, Gruen applauded how the regional shopping center was not merely a commercial center, but a "social, cultural, and recreational crystallization point" for the suburban region. They had only fallen short in one respect—one which contemporary mall redesigns are seeking to remedy—a failure to include residences.[51]

Several major shopping malls in the United States approach Gruen's aspirations that the mall incorporate as much of life as possible, and become a "social, cultural, and recreational crystallization point."[52] For example, Frances Viglielmo was arrested for trespass at Hawai'i's Ala Moana shopping center while she was leafleting and picketing a Kay-Bee Toys store for its sale of militaristic toys to children. The Ala Moana mall "is situated on fifty acres, hosts over two million people each month, houses more than two hundred retail stores, holds nearly 550 performances each year, includes a central bus transfer station . . . a United States Post Office, and a Honolulu satellite city hall."[53] The Mall of America is even larger. It encompasses 4.2 million square feet, has 37.5 million visitors a year, and has more than four hundred retail establishments. Its tenants include "movie theatres and entertainment venues, the nation's largest indoor amusement park, a wedding chapel, a post office, a police substation, and an alternative school."[54] It even functions as a vacation destination. With not only private entities but governmental offices and schools situated within the mall, now municipal government, and even the federal government, can enjoy the cordon sanitaire insulating them from protest by locating their offices within the mall. Nevertheless, state supreme courts in Hawai'i and Minnesota cite *Marsh* in order to dismiss it.

*Marsh* is regularly evoked in state court decisions regarding malls, if only to be ritualistically rejected. This active suppression and symbolic degradation of *Marsh* and the public function doctrine occurs as privately owned public spaces subsume increasing spheres of human activity—as *Marsh* becomes increasingly germane to the spatial government of human interaction in the United States. Indeed, the standards for the public function doctrine are so impossible to meet that, as municipalities increasingly slash services or contract out their delivery to private entities—as municipal governments privatize public services and social reproduction—the public function doctrine as presently construed would be difficult to apply to municipal creatures of the state if judged by the same standards as the owners of privately owned public spaces.

As significant as the demise of the public function doctrine is, we should not lose sight of the ways that states more directly and proactively encourage large-scale privately owned developments. Municipal governments accommodate, embed, and connect such significant, privately owned public spaces to their urban fabric, and their urban planning invests in the continued existence of these privately owned public spaces, as Marshall observed with respect to the Lloyd Center in Portland. Malls require numerous approvals (and often, code exemptions) from municipal and state bodies, and state taxpayers fund improvements to roadways connecting malls to cities and regions. Police and mall security become mutually entangled with police substations located in malls. These state actions arising from cooperative ventures, symbiotic relations, and mutual entanglements raise the question: should states bear responsibility for the regulation of speech that occurs in malls because the mall wouldn't exist but for the state, and the mall's success is the state's purpose?[55] If so, then such speech regulations malls consider vital to their success should be considered by courts as direct violations of constitutional rights because they are extensions of the state's purposeful actions.

## Stephen and Roger Downs Wear Peace T-Shirts at the Mall

Malls incite some communication and actively repress other communication they consider to be disruptive to the aesthetic experience they seek to create. These acts of repression are enabled by cooperation between private security and the state. As we shall see, even the state's cooperative entanglement with corporate management of communicative experiences and symbolic production fails to register as state action violating free speech rights. This legal framework, in turn, can shield state practices from critique by preventing the appearance of antagonism. In other words, at the level of the image and affect, symbolic production in conjunction with prevention-oriented policing in malls helps produce an *aesthetics of consent* by the foreclosure of antagonism's appearance.[56] Therefore, the policing that emerges from the cooperation of private security and municipal police can insulate the state from democratic practices integral to normative legitimation or delegitimation.

On March 3, 2003, as the Bush administration was moving toward invading Iraq, Stephen Downs was arrested at the Guilderland Crossgates Mall, a shopping mall just outside Albany, New York, for wearing a T-shirt he had purchased at a store in the mall. The shirt read "Peace on Earth" on the front and "Give Peace a Chance" on the back.[57] A private security officer employed by the mall told Downs, who was also the chief attorney with the New York State Commission on Judicial Conduct, and his adult son Roger, that they had to either remove their shirts or leave the mall. Though Roger Downs complied, and therefore was not arrested, Stephen Downs refused, was arrested by a Town of Guilderland police officer, and charged with a trespassing violation.[58]

Two days later, over 150 protesters showed up at the mall wearing T-shirts similar to the one Downs wore when he was arrested. They marched through the mall and sat at tables in the food court (where security had confronted Downs).[59] Editorials and letters to the editor opposed to the arrest of Downs appeared throughout the country.[60] In reaction to the firestorm of protest, the mall dropped the charges, and they were dismissed.[61]

Downs then began legal action arguing that his removal from the mall and arrest violated his freedom of speech. The case Downs presented at the appellate level differed from the frequently made claim that malls fulfill a public function. Instead, Downs questioned how private a mall really is.

Contending that his speech rights were violated, Downs makes two arguments in his appeal of the lower court's ruling against him when he contended that the mall and the town had violated his speech rights.[62] First, Downs argues that the mall and Guilderland police constitute a "joint enterprise" because the town and mall are closely intermeshed. Given this joint enterprise, Downs's arrest for trespassing when he refused to remove his shirt meant that there was state action, which, in turn, triggers constitutional obligations like the right to free speech. Second, Downs argues that he suffered a "false arrest" (an arrest without legal basis) because a mall is a public accommodation to which the public is openly invited, and public accommodations in the state of New York may not violate a panoply of rights, including discrimination based upon one's creed.

Downs turns to a Civil Rights–era decision to elucidate the concept of a joint enterprise. In 1964, a white teacher named Sandra Adickes went with her black students to the public library in Hattiesburg, Mississippi. The librarian refused to serve the black students, informed Adickes that the library was closed, and asked them to leave. The group then went to the Kress store for lunch. While there, a police officer came into the restaurant and observed Adickes in the company of black people. The waitress who then came to the booth took the orders of the black students but refused service to Adickes because she was sitting with her black students. After the refusal of service, they left the restaurant and once outside, the officer who had been inside the store came out and arrested Adickes for vagrancy. According to the U.S. Supreme Court, Adickes was entitled to damages if she could show that the store and the officer had come to some mutual understanding or "meeting of the minds" about denying Adickes's civil rights. In other words, if the privately owned store and the police officer were cooperating as a "joint-enterprise" to violate Adickes's civil rights, such state involvement would amount to "state action" contravening federal law protecting civil rights from violation under "color of law."[63]

How are the mall and Guilderland intermeshed such that Downs can argue they constitute a joint enterprise? The mall provides the Guilderland Police Department rent-free space for its police substation located in the mall. Guilderland requires the rent-free police substation as a condition placed upon the special use permit it issued authorizing construction of the mall. In addition to its ordinary taxes, to help defray the cost of extra police services Guilderland provides the mall, the latter pays an annual fee of $25,000 to the town. According to the Appellants' Brief, "the degree of police presence in the Mall in this case is precisely what enabled the Mall to rely upon the power of the state, in the form of Town law enforcement, to exclude and eject (by means of arrest) Mr. Downs based on the ideological content of his T-shirt."[64] Moreover, we can see the entanglement between Guilderland and the mall in the way that the arrest occurred. With respect to the two private security officers who told Downs to remove his shirt and the Guilderland police officer who arrested Downs, there was an "extended process involving much discussion among themselves, multiple efforts to negotiate with Mr. Downs, and repeated checking with superiors both in the Mall management and the Town Police Department and Town's attorney's office for instruction and direction." Therefore, the decision to arrest Downs was the product of "an evolving process involving all three of them (plus input from their respective supervisors by phone) in which [the three officers representing the Town and the Mall] each contributed information, encouragement, support and guidance leading to the eventual determination to place Mr. Downs under arrest." As Downs's Reply Brief states, "Neither the Town nor the Mall would have proceeded to an arrest without the prior knowledge, consent and support of the other."[65] Because both sides agreed to arrest Downs only with each assuring the other that it would validate the arrest, the arrest is a product of the joint enterprise composed of the Town of Guilderland and the Pyramid Crossgates corporation resulting in state action suppressing Downs's antiwar message.

By establishing state action, Guilderland and the mall violated Downs's speech rights in three very straightforward ways. First, the mall permits other groups to express messages in common areas of the mall, and activities include "fund-raising events, military recruiting, and dissemination of religious material and information." Some of the groups that have used the mall to communicate their message include the Chabad Center (a Jewish religious organization), the Salvation Army (a Christian organization), and the U.S. National Guard.[66] By allowing groups to communicate their messages, there is state action creating a public forum. If a public forum has been created, then allowing these groups to communicate their respective views to others but refusing Downs the opportunity to communicate his opposition to the Iraq War with others violates his constitutional rights in a straightforward way.

Second, the mall justifies its decision to tell Downs to remove his shirt or be arrested on the grounds that he was causing disorder. Events described in legal briefs, however, indicate that the disorder flows from disagreement with his message opposing an invasion of Iraq, not that Downs was engaged in disorderly conduct himself. In fact, they show that other mall patrons verbally harassed and threatened Stephen and Roger Downs. Even when the Guilderland police officer was telling Downs and his son to remove their shirts or else they would be arrested, a mall patron walked up to them and told Stephen and Roger Downs, "I ought to kick the shit out of you mother-fuckers!"[67] The person who accosted Stephen and Roger Downs and threatened them with violence was not warned or arrested by the police officer. Rather, it was Stephen Downs who was arrested. Arresting a speaker when someone threatens him with violence due to disagreement with the speaker's message is a straightforward example of a "heckler's veto" that violates the First Amendment.[68]

Third, Roger Downs took off his antiwar shirt and was not arrested. Stephen Downs did not take off his antiwar shirt, and he was arrested. Because both of them were walking together and engaged in the same course of conduct, the only difference between them that could distinguish why Stephen was arrested but not Roger was Stephen's refusal to remove his shirt. The decision to arrest Stephen Downs for wearing an antiwar shirt, and not to arrest Roger once he removed his antiwar shirt, was a decision based on the content of the speech Stephen Downs insisted on continuing to express. Such content-based (and viewpoint-based) discrimination is a straightforward violation of speech rights.

The second legal argument Downs makes is that he suffered a "false arrest" at the hands of the Guilderland police when they arrested him for trespass. The order requiring Stephen Downs to leave the premises was not a lawful order. Therefore, Downs was falsely arrested for trespass.

Why is the claim that Downs was trespassing groundless? A mall like the Pyramid Crossgates is a public accommodation under New York law. Public accommodations are places typically (but, according to New York law, not necessarily) privately owned, but open to the general public. Examples include hotels, motels, restaurants, pubs or bars, and parks. A public accommodation in New York, like other states, is forbidden from discriminating against people on a variety of grounds. In New York, they may not discriminate based on "race, creed, color, national origin, sexual orientation, military status, sex, disability or marital status of any person."[69] Creed refers to religious belief, faith, or a "set of beliefs or aims which guide someone's actions."[70] Because the mall, unlike someone's home, is open to the general public, Downs had a right to be in the mall. He was arrested for trespass because he refused to remove his shirt that expressed his belief in peace, hence his opposition to the impending invasion of Iraq. His shirt was an expression of Downs's beliefs, his creed. By arresting Downs on the grounds of his creed, the mall and the Guilderland police violated New York law and falsely arrested him.[71]

Downs relies on the New York state court decision in *People v. Leonard* (1984), finding that when "property is 'open to the public' at the time of the alleged trespass . . . the accused is presumed to have a license and privilege to be present," and the state has the burden of proving that the order excluding the defendant from the premises is valid.[72] A decision to exclude that "impermissibly inhibits a constitutionally or statutorily protected activity will not be lawful."[73] Therefore, since the mall and the town sought to exclude Downs on legally prohibited grounds (for his creed), the trespass charge was not valid and he was falsely arrested. This argument is situated not on the premise that a mall fulfills a public function, but that it is a public accommodation, and as such, it may only be operated in accordance with New York law. Operating a mall is not the same thing as a homeowner excluding an unwanted person from entering the house.

The town and Pyramid Crossgates insist that Pyramid Crossgates is not a state actor, and that the mall's behavior code was not written with any state actor.[74] They refer to the onsite police substation as "strictly for convenience" because the police station is across town, and that the annual payments Pyramid Crossgates makes to Guilderland for additional police services are insufficient to create state action.[75] The town and Pyramid Crossgates invoke the imagery of a person "call[ing] the police to remove a trespasser from his or her property," arguing that the use of police to enforce such private rights cannot be considered state action without stretching the concept beyond recognition.[76] By creating an imaginary association between a mall with 246 tenants and a person's private property, the town and Pyramid Crossgates occlude how the mall is a different species of property than, for instance, someone's home or yard. A mall is a public accommodation under New York law, and the public has a different relation, hence different rights of access and against removal, to a public accommodation, as opposed to a person's home or yard. Arguing that none of the different forms of collaboration between the town and the mall were sufficiently significant to create state action, the town and Pyramid Crossgates urge that the ruling in *SHAD Alliance* means that they were within their rights to remove Downs for causing a disturbance.

In a short opinion, an intermediate appeals court upheld the lower court's judgment in favor of the town and Pyramid Crossgates Mall. The court largely ignored the concept of a joint enterprise Downs put forward, and did not find other examples of town-mall cooperation sufficient indicators of state action. More compelling than the mall's status as a public accommodation was the imaginary association the town and Pyramid Crossgates put forward that the mall was like a person who owned property. As Judge John Lahtinen wrote, "involvement of the Town police officer at the request of the mall to enforce the rights of the private property owner under these circumstances did not constitute state action."[77] Under New York law, malls, with support from the state, enjoy the same kind of authoritarian control over those within the mall—extending to control over what they wear—as a person might enjoy in the privacy of their own home.

If we consider the neglect of the concept of a joint enterprise between a private and state actor implicating the state in the denial of rights in conjunction with the active neglect of the public function and preferred position doctrines, a post-1968 legal arrangement emerges that is distinctive from the Supreme Court's mid-twentieth-century constitutional jurisprudence. Now, commerce supersedes democratic practices as a state purpose, and the image of homeowners with authoritarian power to control their home supersedes a concept of publicness or public space as the imaginary of government. In this regard, the question of empirical state involvement in the violation of rights is displaced by the lack of normative significance attributed to state participation in the exercise of authoritarian power furthering commerce or markets. That is, we are seeing the emergence of a legal formation corresponding to a post-democratic state formation.

### From Privatization to State Formation: Malls as Models for Urban Design

What does such authoritarian control exercised through the joint enterprise of the state and capital over the spaces of our lives mean for our daily aesthetic experiences? After the attacks of September 11, 2001, President Bush incited consumers with a statement asserting the terrorists will have succeeded if Americans no longer go shopping as part of a return to normalcy.[78] Capitalism also responded to those attacks by communicating nationalism throughout the landscapes of our everyday lives in the United States. Stores within malls across the United States posted American flags in their windows, doors, and on their cash registers, creating a visual association between consumerism and support for the global war on terrorism.[79] In conjunction with the anniversary of the attacks, and coinciding with both congressional discussion about giving the Bush administration authority to decide whether or not to attack Iraq, and the holiday shopping season, signs went up at retail outlets remembering and commemorating the attacks of September 11 during the fall of 2002. Many of these remained up for months after the anniversary of those attacks due to managerial inertia.[80]

The images commodities help produce become a particularly significant attribute of post-Fordist capitalism, and the imagery produced in the aftermath of September 11, 2001, was notable.[81] With the Bush administration's nationalistic and militarized response to the attacks of September 11, commodities gained a new consumer niche to fill. Crossing private and public space, consumer items flourished bearing the signs of 9/11. The sale of American flags increased substantially.[82] Consumers could purchase T-shirts with the message "Osama—yo mama," a cap with the slogan "Operation Enduring Freedom," or "Let's Roll."[83] Computer and video games were released in October 2002—timed to coincide with the anniversary of September 11 and the holiday retail season—by Gotham Games for PlayStation2 based on post–September 11 Iraq War themes that consequently coincided with Bush's push for war against Iraq.[84] Trading cards for 9/11 and Iraqi "most wanted" playing cards were marketed.[85] In the aftermath of September 11, NBC redecorated its trademark peacock in stars and stripes, much the way politicians associating themselves with the global war on terror wore American flag lapel pins.[86] Bumper stickers commemorating 9/11 remained on automobiles and created an aesthetics of consent for the looming invasion of Iraq.[87] Articulating and amplifying these elements into an affectively associative composition, George Bush gave speeches in fall and winter of 2002–2003 on the threat posed by Iraq, mentioning the attacks of September 11 or terrorism numerous times.[88] If not a logical or an evidentiary argument for the invasion, his speeches nevertheless created a brand-like association between the attacks of September 11 and Iraq, supporting the U.S. invasion of 2003.[89]

Within this sensible environment, Stephen and Roger Downs created aesthetic discord by wearing their peace T-shirts. They disrupted the visuality produced by the state and corporations working in conjunction with each other, and they were threatened with violence by those affectively attached to this state formation's images—and not only Stephen and Roger. When 150 protesters returned to the Guilderland Crossgates Mall wearing antiwar T-shirts in support of Stephen Downs, "one man was punched by a bystander who shouted, 'Remember 9/11.'" According to the New York Times, no one was arrested.[90] Cooperation between private security and police helped create and enforce communicative participation in an expansive aesthetic environment crossing privately owned and state-controlled spaces.

The joint enterprise of the state and mall composing post-Fordism suggests we should expect this aesthetic crossing between spaces under state control and those under private ownership. Victor Gruen expresses this mutual transference in his aspirations for the mall. Not only did Gruen view the mall as bringing urban values to the suburbs, he touted the mall as a model for urban design. In a 1955 interview with *Business Week*, he stated that the regional shopping mall has "taught us a lot about planning commercial centers. And these lessons—learned in the suburbs—can be the salvation of downtown." For Gruen, the "best model available for rebuilding [downtowns] is the regional shopping center."[91]

Gruen reiterated these claims in his 1964 book *The Heart of Our Cities: The Urban Crisis*. There, he found that regional shopping malls were as "busy as the long lost town square of our urban past" and, as such, were a "great step forward."[92] They created "trouble-free, safe and well designed public spaces."[93] By the 1990s, architect John McMorrough found the mall to be the "de facto model for city planning."[94] For McMorrough, the decline of its rate of growth by the 1990s did not "mean that its influence [was] waning." Rather, the logic of the mall had become embedded "into the very idea of urbanity."[95] This logic prioritized the aesthetic government of space for the purpose of shopping and commerce, on the one hand, and security, on the other.[96] The emphasis on security rendered crime and protest equivalent forms of disorder to the mall's aesthetic order. As urban planners Bernard Frieden and Lynn Sagalyn wrote at the end of the 1980s regarding antiwar protests at malls, "Strident protests against a grim war would be about as helpful to this atmosphere as a child molester in Disneyland."[97]

Given the significance of the mall for the design of urban space, we can look at how the right of speech has been reconfigured in one of the few states that has required malls to permit expression as indicative of how speech has been reshaped in public spaces under the neoliberal state. In *New Jersey Coalition against the War in the Middle East v. J.M.B. Realty* (1994), an antiwar coalition wanted to leaflet in malls where businesses displayed posters demonstrating support for President George H. W. Bush's 1991 Gulf War. New Jersey's state supreme court maintained that malls must allow leafleting, finding that the normal use of malls is "all-embracing," projecting a "community image" and "encompassing practically all aspects of a downtown business district."[98] The court held that "no private property . . . more closely resembles public property" and found that the "public's invitation to use the property . . . is correspondingly broad," and leafleting was "wholly consonant with the use of these properties."[99] The New Jersey state constitution created a "constitutional obligation" that malls must recognize speech rights.[100] Instructive, though, is how the court's opinion imagined this right in practice.

The New Jersey court expects that free speech will be "carefully controlled by these centers." By limiting its holding to leafleting, the court limits expression in malls to that which is "least obtrusive and the easiest to regulate" so that it will be "consonant with the commercial purposes of the centers."[101] The court uses the policy of the Woodbridge Center mall to illustrate how speech can be regulated so it will not disrupt the aesthetic environment of the mall. The Woodbridge Center permits speech at its "Community Booth," but warns potential speakers they may use the booth "provided that you recognize and respect our right to maintain our center as [a] clean, neat, orderly, pleasant and harassment free environment for everyone."[102] The court continues, arguing malls have "full power to minimize whatever slight discordance might otherwise exist," so expression "does not interfere with the shopping center's business."[103] The right being recognized does not include "bullhorns, megaphones, or even a soapbox; it does not include placards, pickets, parades, and demonstrations; it does not include anything other than normal speech and then only such as is necessary to the effectiveness of the leafleting."[104] Here, the court is crafting a right of expression severed from the practices of democracy, the assembly of the people, and their assertion of power. That is, the court is making every effort to sever speech from something more that could function as a disruptive force by configuring speech to be as compatible as possible with a controlled, consumer-friendly commercial environment. The court is crafting a post-democratic neoliberal right of expression enabling freedom to appear associated with the mall.

For the dissenters, even this appearance of free speech is too much. They acknowledge community groups have been allowed in the mall, from the sale of Girl Scout cookies to free concerts. The point these examples make is that their purpose is to "draw people to the mall and thereby maximize sales and increase profits."[105] The dissenters highlight distinctions between malls and cities: "The inescapable mission of shopping malls is not to be the successor to downtown business districts; rather, it is to provide a comfortable and conducive atmosphere for shopping."[106] And "shopping," dissenters argue, "can be accomplished even with mouths shut and minds closed."[107] Besides, political speech may be connected to the appearance of antagonism. Recognizing this, and anticipating how Stephen and Roger Downs's seemingly innocuous peace T-shirts produced anger and threats of violence from other shoppers as another invasion of Iraq loomed, dissenters observe, "confrontation is an easily-foreseen outcome" when any political speech is allowed.[108]

Although Gruen considered malls as urban developments, by being racially and economically segregated from mid-twentieth-century cities, and by having been allowed to develop an authoritarian mode of government attentive to the aesthetics of space, malls were distinguishable from urban centers until cities modeled their design upon malls. Dissenters emphasize that the value of the suburban mall is its difference from mid-twentieth-century cities. The dissenting opinion may be more perceptive than the court's ruling in its recognition of the potentially disruptive force of political speech. Their reaction to suppress even the appearance of speech for fear it might lead to something more manifests the authoritarian orientation of contemporary jurisprudence that so many courts have adopted and enforce as part of a broader post-democratic state formation congruent with neoliberalism. The court's ruling holding out as exemplary a right of expression zoned to the Community Booth likewise manifests an authoritarianism in its broader disposition to depoliticize speech and disempower the people. The court's authoritarianism, though, projects an image of neoliberal freedom since individuals are still permitted to express themselves if they communicate within the mall's Community Booth. By permitting speech but prohibiting demonstrations of the people's strength out of concern it could disrupt commerce, the court's ruling provides a model for how speech is policed in contemporary urban space.

### The Neoliberal, Post-Fordist City

In his 1970 State of the Union Address, President Nixon identified the threat to "quality of life" posed by "violent and decayed central cities" as a major concern.[109] He argued, "if there is one area where the word war is appropriate it is in the fight against crime. We must declare and win the war against criminal elements which increasingly threaten our cities, our homes and our lives." The "Federal Government" had a "special responsibility," Nixon believed, in the areas of "crime, narcotics and pornography."[110] Important films of the early 1970s, such as *Taxi Driver* and *Dirty Harry*, amplified the associational constellation of crime, pornography, and urban decay in popular culture.

The Burger Court responded to this quality of life agenda, in part, by providing cities with legal tools for their aesthetic government of space directed to "quality of life" with decisions regarding the regulation of nonobscene "indecent" expression.[111] These tools did not allow local governments to censor indecent speech totally (cities could not forbid sexually oriented businesses from locating themselves in the city outright), but indecent speech could be significantly burdened in practice by being zoned. These burdens might even leave no viable spaces for such establishments in a given municipality without violating the Supreme Court's view of the First Amendment.[112] These judicial decisions helping cities manage sexual expression in order to spur urban redevelopment are similar to the logic of zoning expression to the Community Booth in malls that the New Jersey high court found to be exemplary. They also anticipate, as we shall see, how protests would likewise be managed by the neoliberal, post-Fordist city.

One dimension of this jurisprudence is the Supreme Court's legal reasoning pertaining to secondary effects. These rulings allowed cities to zone sexually oriented businesses to contain their effects. Cities might disperse such businesses throughout a city, cluster them within a particular zone, or regulate their proximity to homes, schools, or churches. Dancers at strip clubs could be required to wear minimal clothing, such as pasties or a G-string.[113] In this regulatory regime, the Court considered various secondary effects of urban disorder or crime to be mysteriously associated or correlated with the sex industry. If secondary effects were caused by sexual expression, then the regulations would violate the First Amendment for targeting speakers. As Justice Souter explained, men were not led directly by expression with sexual content to commit crime. It was simply the case that a "concentration of crowds of men predisposed to such activities" tended to congregate in the vicinity of such establishments.[114] We can analogize this reasoning to the regulation of speech in malls. The Town of Guilderland and Crossgates Mall argued that requiring Stephen and Roger Downs to remove their shirts or leave the mall because of the disruption caused by a man threatening to assault them was a content-neutral regulation. Likewise, city regulations of sexually indecent expression are targeted not at the expression but at the crime asserted to be associated with such indecent establishments, for whatever reason. Court-permitted regulations of "time, place, and manner," and of "symbolic conduct," to contain "secondary effects" associated with indecent speech provided local governments important legal tools. These tools could help prevent, in Justice Powell's words, a "modern city" from "deteriorating to an urban jungle," to the detriment of "social, environmental, and economic values" constituting a city's "quality of life."[115]

The Supreme Court's First Amendment jurisprudence had become a lever to promote quality of life and to manage secondary effects. As such, it helped remake urban space to further the neoliberal, post-Fordist city's orientation to distinctive districts, quarters, or zones as part of its attention to the FIRE industries (finance, insurance, and real estate). It would also assist cities to promote their branding and marketing efforts in the interurban competition for tourism. In other words, the Court's "secondary-effects" jurisprudence contributed to remaking urban political economies directed to "communicative," "semiotic," "symbolic," "immaterial," or entertainment-driven production.[116]

The Supreme Court's secondary-effects jurisprudence would be key, for example, in New York City's efforts to clean up Times Square so it would be aesthetically compatible with Disney's brand, while allowing New York City to associate itself with the family-friendly symbolic cachet of Disney's brand, creating state-capital brand synergy. As Frank Roost notes, Times Square is perhaps the "best-known example of entertainment-driven urban redevelopment."[117] According to Roost, before renovating the New Amsterdam Theatre, Disney negotiated not only financial incentives from the state but the "social transformation of Times Square," well known for its theaters that showed pornography, so that Disney's brand image would not be compromised.[118] In effect, Disney required as a condition for its investment that the city be changed to fit Disney's brand. Mayor Rudolph Giuliani assured Disney executive Michael Eisner that the porn would be removed. Fulfilling its end of the deal, the New York City Council passed zoning restrictions on the adult industry in 1995, requiring adult establishments to relocate to more peripheral commercial and industrial zones in the city. It also required that such establishments not be located within 500 feet of any "school, daycare center, or house of worship, nor within 500 feet of the edge of most residential areas . . . nor within 500 feet of any other adult establishment."[119] After court rulings sustaining the constitutionality of these zoning regulations, Times Square became a Disney-friendly zone.

Zoning based on secondary effects of sexual expression meshes with the zero tolerance, quality of life, "Broken Windows" theory of policing for which Giuliani and his first police commissioner, William Bratton, are well known. Quality of life policing addresses not only actual crime but signs, or the appearance, of economic distress and disorder, such as panhandlers, homeless, and "squee-gee men."[120] Similarly, the negative secondary effects cited to justify the removal of sexually oriented businesses from Times Square are aesthetically based perceptions. They include diminished property values (based significantly on perception and association) and a "perceived decline in community character." Like quality of life policing, secondary-effects rules are oriented toward creating and governing the aesthetic environment for a given zone—a project and projection that goes far beyond actual crime, since nonobscene sexual expression is protected by the First Amendment. They are part of an overall strategy of government producing post-Fordist urban space to promote the city to financial markets, global media conglomerates, the "creative class," visitors, tourists, and shoppers.[121] They are practices of communicative and affective production premised on the capacity to control space aesthetically. If there should be the appearance of expression or people who disturb this aesthetic regime, then these disruptions will be policed, displaced, or repressed.

The Supreme Court's jurisprudence permitting sexual expression to be zoned, dispersed, and marginalized is homologous to the way that the contemporary legal regime governs protests. In 1939, Justice Roberts could write for the Supreme Court, "one is not to have the exercise of his liberty of expression in appropriate places abridged on the plea that it may be exercised in some other place."[122] More recently, when protesters seek to use traditional public forums such as parks, streets, and sidewalks, they have found such forums closed to them. Demonstrators are penned into free speech zones or are zoned to peripheral areas of the city far from the event or government officials they wish to protest or petition for redress of their grievances. The management of protests displaces their force, similar to the way perceived secondary effects of sexual expression justified judicially sanctioned zoning regulations to displace such expression from spaces targeted for urban investment. Much like New Jersey malls can contain a speaker within the Community Booth to preserve their aesthetic environment from disruption, protesters in the city can express themselves, though such expression is contained for the purpose of maintaining a particular aesthetic environment free from disruption, or in the interests of mega-event management. Traditional public forums in the city are coming to be governed much like a shopping mall or Disney World. Otherwise put, urban life is becoming subsumed within spaces of neoliberal, post-Fordist capital.[123]

### Producing and Policing Aesthetic Experiences

The way that a post-Fordist urban aesthetic suffocates the right to protest is illustrated by an appeals court decision in a case involving a labor union representing hotel and restaurant workers, and the City of New York and Lincoln Center for the Performing Arts.[124] In the spring of 1999—significantly, this is prior to the attacks of September 11, 2001, and thus underscores the importance of the relationship between political economy and legal development—the union made several efforts to picket and distribute leaflets in the plaza outside Lincoln Center to show support for food service workers operating within the Metropolitan Opera. Lincoln Center governed the plaza for the city and scheduled events in the public areas of the plaza subject to the approval of the Parks Department. In other words, Lincoln Center was the agent for the City Parks Department. The policy of Lincoln Center was to limit approval for the use of the plaza to those events having a "performance, entertainment, or artistic component."[125] The dispute centered on whether Lincoln Center could prevent the union from picketing and leafleting. According to the appeals court, Lincoln Center's denial of permission for the union's planned rally did not violate the First Amendment. Even though the court assumed that Lincoln Center was a state actor since it managed the plaza on the city's behalf, it did not find this government of expression to violate the First Amendment. Instead, the court of appeals noted that Lincoln Center had governed this space in a generally exclusionary way (such exclusions, however, did not extend to those who passed through the plaza or sought to eat lunch in the plaza, nor to those who wanted to sun themselves there). Through its exclusion of political protesters and union picketers, while allowing musicians, Lincoln Center sought to create a "pleasing forecourt at the center of a prominent performance arts complex, to facilitate patrons' passage into the events taking place in the arts buildings, and symbolically to promote the cultural arts for the benefit of the community."[126]

In this case, despite the fact that authority for this plaza ultimately fell upon the city, the court upheld the tautological reasoning of Lincoln Center—because others have been excluded, it could exclude others in order to produce an aesthetic environment conducive to the consumption of the center's cultural offerings. The city's plaza, thus, is understood to be fulfilling an important and complementary function in relation to Lincoln Center—the production of a controlled environment in order to enhance artistic consumption—that a labor protest on behalf of the service workers employed by Lincoln Center would only disrupt. For present purposes, however, what is telling about this case is that a traditional or quintessential public forum has been closed (a plaza under the ultimate authority of the Parks Department) to those who wish to protest. In this particular case, the right to protest is displaced by an interest in maintaining a particular aesthetic order that will be conducive to the cultural experience for the consumer or the tourist in the center. To preserve the plaza as an entertainment zone or enclave that promotes the post-Fordist urban production of culture and affective experiences, the labor union protest was rightly regulated, according to the three-judge panel. The city's promotion of post-Fordist cultural production and its consumption means that the exercise of First Amendment rights in a manner that might disrupt this aesthetic order may be regulated.

Organizing the workplace was facilitated when businesses were located in cities. Workers could make use of well-traveled sidewalks and streets—quintessential public forums—in order to picket and leaflet. When such businesses moved out to suburban shopping malls, however, they became enclosed within privatized spaces, which presented an additional hurdle to those seeking to unionize these service sector jobs, as we have seen. Today, with such service sector jobs being central to the post-Fordist urban political economy, however, the city itself, as we can see from the example of the attempt to picket Lincoln Center in the city plaza in front of it, is coming to be governed by the authoritarian logic of the suburban shopping mall and its judicially validated control over the aesthetic environment. Thus, the neoliberal, post-Fordist "partition of the perceptible" has detrimental consequences for efforts to unionize the service sector, which is a particularly significant aspect of the post-Fordist economy.[127]

## Criminalizing Democratic Strength, Celebrating Diversity

On February 14, 2003, French Foreign Minister Dominique de Villepin made his historic statement against warmongering by the United States and in favor of peace through disarmament at a meeting of the United Nations (UN) Security Council, which was discussing the possibility of authorizing the use of force by the United States against Iraq. To coincide with this event, United for Peace and Justice (UFPJ) sought a permit from New York City to parade in front of the UN building. New York denied this permit request and refused to allow the group to parade anywhere in the city. The New York Police Department (NYPD) required the group to hold a stationary rally a few blocks from the UN building. At the stationary rally, the NYPD forced protesters into barricades forming pens, and used batons, horses, and pepper spray to keep the crowd within the pens or to disperse them.[128]

Arguing that to march past the UN building in its direct view was a "necessary part of the event," UFPJ challenged the denial of a parade permit. According to the NYPD, however, the march was too large—100,000 were expected—for the NYPD to secure the safety of UN headquarters, particularly after the attacks of September 11, 2001. Moreover, the NYPD denied UFPJ the right to march anywhere in the city. In response, UFPJ pointed out that numerous other cultural groups of similar size had been allowed to march in New York. The Dominican Day parade had 100,000 participants; the Puerto Rican Day parade had 100,000 participants; and the Saint Patrick's Day parade had 120,000 participants.[129]

District Court Judge Barbara Jones disagreed with UFPJ's arguments that the denial of a permit was content based, hence a violation of the First Amendment. She contended that the UFPJ protest was "markedly different" from the annual ethnic pride parades, which could be planned long in advance. Moreover, she viewed the requirement that the protest be a stationary one, confined within the pens, to be merely a regulation on the manner of the speech, and a regulation that was narrowly tailored to security concerns. Thus, it was not considered to be a restriction of the group's ability to communicate that would violate the First Amendment.[130]

Within the neoliberal, post-Fordist city, a political protest that makes manifest the broad strength of popular opposition to state policies now counts against the group's First Amendment rights. During the middle of the twentieth century, the Supreme Court recognized that political speech, and speech addressing broad, national questions or public issues, was the speech that should receive the greatest protection under the First Amendment. Now, it receives reduced First Amendment protection when compared to "large scale cultural and celebratory marches" that would be equally at home in a theme park as in a post-Fordist city like New York where the latter advertises itself as diverse.[131]

Additionally, we can draw a connection between the requirements that dancers wear pasties or a G-string as merely a regulation upon the manner of communication, and forcing UFPJ to hold a stationary rally confined within protest pens. Much like the forced, minimal clothing upon the body of the dancers is a sumptuary marker of state power, being forced into pens not only prevents UFPJ from showing the strength of the people to the rest of the city, it symbolically frames their message within state parameters. Onlookers could be forgiven if they perceived the NYPD's framing of the exercise of popular political strength and democratic aspirations as criminalized within the neoliberal, post-Fordist city. By containing demonstrators within barricades, the neoliberal, post-Fordist state preemptively disqualifies the political voice of the people.

New York is not alone in these practices. At the 2004 Democratic National Convention (DNC) in Boston, the Boston Police Department erected an eight-foot wire mesh fence lined with an opaque fabric so protesters could not breach the fence, and so protesters on the outside and dignitaries on the inside could not see each other. A demonstration zone (DZ) was created for protesters underneath elevated railroad tracks close to the convention site. The DZ was fenced in, covered with a "tightly woven mesh fabric," as well as "looser mesh netting," and covered with looped razor wire. District Court Judge Douglas Woodlock noted that a person of normal height could not stand and carry a sign because of the low height of the girders. The DZ's capacity was approximately one thousand, but even that number was potentially unsafe and a violation of the city's fire code. Because of these spatial controls, protesters would not be able to reach their intended audience, and Judge Woodlock conceded that the DZ reminded him of "Piranesi's etchings published as *Fanciful Images of Prisons*," and that the "overall impression created by the DZ is that of an internment camp." Nevertheless, he sustained the Boston police's decision to "coop them all inside a bleak enclosed pen" as the only practical way to maintain a "secured environment." Even with the judge's concession that the DZ was akin to an "internment camp," this time, place, and manner regulation was found to be constitutional in its penning of protesters. Again, democratic actions are displaced, contained, and visually criminalized in the neoliberal, post-Fordist city.[132]

In fact, the appeals court uses conditions of communicative capitalism to justify penning protesters within the DZ. Even though protesters and political dignitaries would not be visible to each other, considering this as suppressing protesters' rights of expression "greatly underestimates the nature of modern communications," such as "television, radio, the press, the internet, and other outlets."[133] A subsequent ruling upholding regulations at the 2008 Republican National Convention (RNC) preventing the likelihood of confrontation between protesters and delegates cites this portion of the appeals decision regarding the 2004 DNC in Boston with approval, arguing that the RNC protesters would still be able to "communicate."[134] In light of how prison-like conditions for protesters exercising First Amendment rights are justified by the existence of communicative capitalism, would such jurisprudence, taken to its logical conclusion, permit foreclosing all of the city to protesters during a mega-event as long as Facebook or Twitter exists?

*Maintaining the Environment for*
*Symbolic Production by Displacing Speech*

Hosting mega-events, such as sporting events like the Super Bowl or the Olympics, a major convention like the Democratic or Republican national conventions, or even New York's hosting of the Disney movie premiere of *Pocahontas* in Central Park, is a significant component of post-Fordist communicative production. When New York City hosted the premiere of *Pocahontas* in Central Park, the first time a public event on the Great Lawn had been ticketed, the crowd was estimated to be between 70,000 (police) and 100,000 (Disney).[135] According to Giuliani, the *Pocahontas* event would help promote New York City since the city would have shown "the largest movie premiere in history in the world's greatest park in the world capital city." Although the city would incur costs in staging the movie premiere, the event was expected to bring "tens of millions of dollars to the city in direct and indirect revenues," in Giuliani's view.[136] By hosting such mega-events, cities draw tourists, market themselves through the spectacle to potential visitors, market their capacity to produce a mega-event without disruption, and brand the city in accordance with a particular image.

To demonstrate New York City's recovery after the attacks of September 11, 2001, and to "galvanize the city's tourism industry," Mayor Michael Bloomberg made bids to host the 2012 Olympics and the Democratic and Republican national conventions. The bid for the RNC was successful. City officials, in collaboration with the White House, worked to showcase New York City by integrating the city's icons as a stage for the renomination of George W. Bush for a second administration. As we shall see in chapter 2, like New Orleans's hosting of the Super Bowl after Hurricane Katrina, New York approached the RNC as a "coming-out party" after a major disaster, as a generator of economic benefits from the convention, and as an "indicator" of the city's "ability to carry on events."[137]

With two wars, the passage of legislation restrictive of civil liberties, and a camp at a U.S. military base in Guantanamo Bay, Cuba, dedicated to keeping prisoners away from normal legal processes in the United States, numerous political groups planned to protest at the RNC. Of course, such protests could risk disrupting the mega-event of the first RNC after September 11, 2001. Such protests could also disrupt New York's efforts to market the city as reintegrated within the neoliberal and post-Fordist visitor economy, as it might raise questions about its readiness to host and produce mega-events.

In *National Council of Arab Americans and Act Now to Stop War & End Racism Coalition v. City of New York*, a federal district court addressed the council's attempt to get a permit to hold a demonstration of up to 75,000 people on the Great Lawn of Central Park in New York on August 28, 2004, during the RNC. The Great Lawn had symbolic significance for the council, as did the date of the planned demonstration. The date of the protest was important not only for the fact that it coincided with the RNC and thus presented an opportunity to protest against George W. Bush's policies in the Middle East.

The date also fell on the forty-first anniversary of the 1963 March on Washington led by Martin Luther King Jr., and therefore commemorated the struggle for civil rights. The Great Lawn, according to the council, is important not only because it could accommodate a demonstration of the size that the council expected, and because it was a large, unconfined, family-friendly mass rally venue. The Great Lawn is important because it is a place where mass assembly has taken place in the past; it represents the heart and soul of New York as the flagship for where people gather, and as such, it symbolizes a link of centrality, hence acceptance and equality for Arab American people. Since many major rallies had been held on the Great Lawn, such as a 1982 antinuclear rally, an antiapartheid rally in 1986, a Gay Pride rally in 1989, and Earth Day in 1990, assembly on the Great Lawn is part of the political message.[138]

The City of New York, however, sought to prevent the rally in order to protect the Great Lawn from possible damage. After years of what was now considered to be overuse, the lawn was restored in 1997 at a cost of over $18 million. Consisting of over twelve acres of hearty Kentucky blue grass, soil engineered to resist compaction, subsurface drainage lines, irrigation lines, pop-up sprinklers, and eight baseball diamonds, the Great Lawn is under a comprehensive management program by the City Parks Department, devised in consultation with turf specialists, engineers, and architects. This plan limits large events on the lawn to six a year (to allow for turf recovery, aeration, and overseeding), including two Metropolitan Opera productions and two New York Philharmonic productions. These performances are considered permissible, in significant part, because audiences do not exceed eighty thousand, and events are rescheduled if the weather is bad and the turf is wet. If the Great Lawn were damaged, according to the city, New Yorkers would lose something "sublime."[139]

In light of the importance of the governmental interest (the sublime Great Lawn), the fact that the permitting scheme is content neutral (i.e., not based on the content of the speech of the council), and the fact that the city had offered alternative venues that could accommodate the expected size of the rally, District Court Judge William Pauley refused to enjoin the city to give a permit to the council to rally on the Great Lawn. The alternative avenues for communication offered to the council included holding a smaller demonstration on the East Meadow of Central Park, or holding the demonstration in Flushing Meadows in the borough of Queens or Van Cortland Park in the borough of the Bronx, neither of which are on the island constituting the borough of Manhattan where the RNC was to take place.

Regarding the question of a public forum, we have a refusal to grant a permit for a political rally to occur during the RNC in a public park, which is a "traditional public forum."[140] The Supreme Court has frozen the development of its public forum doctrine historically in a manner that does not adequately account for more contemporary spatial developments, such as shopping malls or airports.[141] Even by limiting legal recognition of public forums to those spaces prominent when this juridical doctrine initially emerged in the 1930s, a park is a public forum.[142] First Amendment rights should be on their strongest grounds when their exercise occurs in a public forum.

As for the governmental interest in preserving the grass, a damaged lawn can be considered a secondary effect of the exercise of First Amendment rights in a public forum. In 1939, however, when New Jersey sought to prevent people leafleting in the public streets in order to prevent litter—also a secondary effect deriving from the exercise of First Amendment rights in a public forum—the Supreme Court invalidated the leaflet ban as a violation of the right of free expression, arguing that "streets are natural and proper places for the dissemination of information and opinion."[143] Although cleaning the streets might impose greater economic responsibilities on the state, they were understood to be a cost that a democratic society bears.

Today, the post-Fordist raison d'être for the Great Lawn as a main attraction in Central Park is as an environment for cultural productions for ticketed patrons of the arts, and as an attraction for visitors to the city. The value of this space has changed. In light of the lawn's post-Fordist purposes, its aesthetics have become particularly significant, as Judge Pauley's extended discussion of hearty Kentucky bluegrass and sophisticated turf maintenance regimes shows. The aesthetic project of creating an environment suitable for the consumption of culture, a primary goal for the post-Fordist city, means that unfortunate secondary effects of speech and its potentially disruptive possibilities—the role of litter in *Schneider v. State*—are now sufficient to justify the regulation of expression or its removal to other spaces.

Democratic politics actually might even count against the constitutional right to protest within neoliberal, post-Fordist aesthetic sensibilities. A protest of the sitting president's policies certainly counts as political speech. In the mid-twentieth century, political speech was considered to be the most important speech to protect.[144] Nevertheless, the political nature of the protest does not seem to cause Judge Pauley to hesitate in sustaining the denial of a protest permit to the group. In fact, if we consider his reference to the past of massive antinuclear rallies as the "dust bowl era" of Central Park, there may even be an affective aversion to democratic politics in his opinion. While

New York City's fiscal crisis in the mid-1970s caused upkeep of its parks, including Central Park, to be underfunded, Pauley's opinion creates a negative aesthetic association between the exercise of democratic rights and dirt that conflicts with neoliberal, post-Fordist mentalities of government that emphasize cleaning up the city.[145] The neoliberal, post-Fordist purpose of the Great Lawn is to produce cultural events like a Dave Matthews concert (which had over 85,000 patrons), a Met Opera concert, or a Disney movie premiere, and these purposes have displaced demonstrations of democratic strength.[146]

This examination of the contemporary juridical formation pointing to the emergence of a post-democratic state formation I am referring to as neoliberal authoritarianism bears significance for understanding the relationship between neoliberalism and the state. The relationship between neoliberalism and the state is more complex than privatization and the corresponding suggestion that the neoliberal state is small or weak. The neoliberal state is a distinct formation compared to the mid-twentieth-century Keynesian state oriented to social democracy.[147]

The state is deeply embedded in the construction of the neoliberal, post-Fordist landscape, whether we are referring to malls for consumer capitalism, the Superdome in New Orleans for the generation of spectacle, the remaking of Times Square for a global media conglomerate, or preventing the people from assembling to protest political illegitimacy, endless war, surveillance, torture, and internment camps. This is not a weak state—it is a distinctive state, and part of its power lies in the creation and enforcement of the aesthetic environment, including visual culture. This aesthetic regime is protected by neoliberal preventative policing and is accommodated by the emergence of a post-democratic juridical formation. Some political theorists explain hostility to protests in public places as a product of judicial preferences for statist conceptions of public property intellectually indebted to Thomas Hobbes.[148] I have shown here that we gain a better understanding of this hostility by connecting individual judicial decisions to a deeper post-democratic shift in post-1968 U.S. political culture and a corresponding neoliberal, post-Fordist transformation in U.S. political economy that we will explore further in chapter 2.

## Conclusion

This chapter describes how the Burger Court turned away from the Warren Court's requirement that malls respect First Amendment rights because they fulfill a public function despite the fact that they might be privately owned. In contrast, the Burger Court created a legal framework whereby malls could be insulated from labor pickets and political protests due to their private ownership, turning its back on the mid-twentieth-century juridical presupposition that the First Amendment ought to enjoy a preferred position within U.S. constitutional law. This is noteworthy in light of the aspirations that the father of the mall, architect Victor Gruen, held for the mall. Gruen did not think of the mall as an alternative to urbanity; he considered it as bringing a better urbanity to the suburbs, seeking to incorporate civic and social life within it. Despite privately owned public spaces actualizing Gruen's aspirations for the mall by subsuming human life, courts have turned away from the public function doctrine or from recognizing how state and capital cooperate as a joint enterprise. This turn highlights the post-democratic transformation of constitutional jurisprudence.

Although most states have followed the Supreme Court's lead and have refused to make free speech rights obligatory upon malls under state law, a few states do recognize limited expression rights within the mall. As one of those states requiring malls to protect some measure of speech rights, New Jersey has reformatted the right so that it will not disrupt either commerce or the aesthetic environment the mall endeavors to construct. By rendering speech rights as little more than a right of expression by severing them from democratic practices, the New Jersey court represents how speech rights are being reconfigured within a neoliberal jurisprudence.

Much as Gruen thought the mall could be used as a remedy by the city to solve its urban crisis, I suggest that the New Jersey courts have modeled speech rights for the neoliberal, post-Fordist city. By privileging ethnic pride parades, cultural production, and mega-events, while preventing or displacing assemblies of the people manifesting democratic strength, urban government extends this logic by managing the right of expression so it will be as compatible as possible with the city's branding and marketing strategies, and post-Fordist communicative production. By using communicative capitalism to justify the legal tools they provide local governments to police its aesthetic environment and to prevent its disruption, courts coerce communicative participation within the channels of communicative capitalism. In the mid-twentieth century, Supreme Court justices like Thurgood Marshall raised concerns about the effects on those of ordinary means and for democracy entailed by funneling expressive participation through oligopolistic media outlets. Today, the appearance of participation that is formally equal—opening a Twitter account is free—occludes the deeply unequal practical effects of the contemporary media formation.[149]

Some scholars describe the constriction of democratic possibilities in terms of growing privatization. To be sure, many services and spaces have been privatized in the last forty years. Referring to these changes solely in terms of privatization, however, misses deeper legal transformations that have facilitated these changes or have made them more damaging to egalitarian and democratic values. Additionally, it misses how the state is embedded in producing the contemporary landscape and can contribute to the misperception of the neoliberal state as either small or weak. It also neglects how public space is governed aesthetically in a manner quite similar to the government of mass private property, and the role law plays in this aesthetic government of public space. Therefore, we gain a more adequate understanding of these changes by attending to the emergence of this post-democratic jurisprudence as one aspect of the broader state formation of neoliberal authoritarianism. This is the postliberal, post-democratic state formation shaped by the reaction to a crisis of democracy in the late 1960s and 1970s.

# Chapter Two

# New York's Mega-Event Security Legacy and the Postlegitimation State

In a race between the executive and the judiciary,
the judiciary will mostly arrive too late.
—CARL SCHMITT, *Legality and Legitimacy* (2004)

IN THE 1970S, cities throughout the United States experienced an urban fiscal crisis, though factors contributing to the crisis had been set in motion earlier. At the close of World War II, most white-collar and manufacturing jobs were located in cities. Due to the federal policy of building an interstate highway system, manufacturing was able to relocate out of northern and midwestern cities, and white-collar workers were able to keep jobs in cities, but live in the suburbs, depriving cities of tax revenue for their dwindling population that was becoming poorer and, due to racial restrictions on obtaining housing in the suburbs, blacker and browner. Developers built shopping malls in the suburbs to capture this growing market of consumers. As a result, service sector jobs grew in the suburbs, and the incentive for suburban consumers to return to the city to shop in its department stores disappeared. For those who remained in cities, manufacturing jobs were not replaced by service sector jobs (which were being located in the suburbs), resulting in unemployment and diminished retail opportunities, from supermarkets to department stores.[1]

In the middle of the 1970s, New York City suffered a fiscal crisis when Wall Street refused to purchase its debt, Standard and Poor's suspended the city's A credit rating, and on October 29, 1975, in a famous speech to the National Press Club, President Ford threatened to veto any bill intended to bail out New York City.[2] The city and the state scrambled to avoid default. In June 1975, the state created an agency to issue bonds to retire the city's short-term debt, called the Municipal Assistance Corporation. In September, an Emergency Financial Control Board was created with powers over the city's budget and certain contracts, agencies, and institutions.[3] Representative government in New York City was suspended to address the fiscal crisis. With promises from unions and banks to purchase the city's debt, with city and state promises to raise taxes, and with city promises of wage and workforce austerity, as well as promises to cut social services and welfare, Ford signed legislation for loans to New York City on December 9.[4] New York City was forced by the Ford administration, in conjunction with the state, the financial sector, and major corporations, to dismantle its social democratic form of government and assistance for social reproduction, and to serve as an example for other major cities in the United States. The legacy of this fiscal crisis includes the continuing existence of a State Financial Control Board that reviews New York City finances, tax breaks for the city's biggest corporations and real estate, the dismantling and underfunding of services supporting social reproduction, a decline in middle-class jobs, and a poverty rate that remains significantly higher than it was in 1975, a year of global recession.[5] In a word, the legacy of the fiscal crisis for New York City has been neoliberalism.

New York was not alone in having been forced to restructure its government and political economy in response to the urban fiscal crisis. In addition to national trends regarding the loss of manufacturing and the growth of the suburbs, federal funding of urban programs was cut by 68 percent during the Reagan and Bush years.[6] As illustrated by California's Proposition 13 and Massachusetts's Proposition 2½, states restricted the ability of cities to raise revenue. Cities were becoming disintermediated from markets, becoming more dependent on debt markets to fund improvements, and were being forced to become more "entrepreneurial."[7] In response, cities reoriented their infrastructure away from residents and toward potential visitors as a source of revenue, in addition to becoming a hospitable environment for finance, insurance, and real estate industries.[8] Cities invested in shopping, sports stadiums, museums, performance arts, aquariums, historical or other themed districts, and fine dining. They advertised experiences and amenities to host conventions, lure those living in the suburbs to return on weekends, and compete in global interurban tourism markets.[9] Cities place branded themselves, and marketed themselves by hosting mega-events, or by demonstrating that they were "mega-event capable." How does this neoliberal, post-Fordist transformation of urban political economy privileging symbolic production affect the policing of protest?

Scholarship on policing protest finds that the policing of global mega-events, such as major economic summits, has become increasingly intolerant of protesters—and became so prior to the attacks of September 11, 2001, as illustrated by the policing of protests at the World Trade Organization (WTO) meetings in Seattle of 1999 and the G-8 meetings in Genoa, Italy, during the summer of 2001.[10] Explanations for this heightened police aggressiveness against protesters range from police knowledge (their operative rationalities, perceptions, or cultural expectations of protesters, though such knowledge may be inaccurate), a new type of transnational protester who may be more disorderly, or an interest in showcasing security to compete with other global cities as a potential mega-event host.[11] Irrespective of the explanation, these scholars find that police no longer adhere to the negotiated management style of tolerance for demonstrator rights of free expression by minimizing arrests and use of force.

Instead of negotiated management, important scholarship on policing protest finds that police engage in "strategic incapacitation" of protesters to minimize the risk of disruption.[12] Strategic incapacitation, developed initially from studies of protest policing at transnational summits, finds that police no longer follow the negotiated management style of policing protest. It attributes this break to a postliberal "new penology" informing policing and penology in the United States more broadly.[13]

According to Malcolm Feeley and Jonathan Simon, the new penology has superseded the normalizing institutions of disciplinary punishment and social control described by Michel Foucault in *Discipline and Punish*. While the latter seek to rehabilitate or to reintegrate offenders within society, the new penology does not concern itself with socialization of subjects with respect to legal or social norms. Instead, it is concerned with "identifying and managing unruly groups."[14] It assesses and manages risk with varying degrees of surveillance or control, utilizing selective incapacitation for those whom it identifies as high risk.[15] Strategic incapacitation of protesters, then, is part of a broader risk management determination to incapacitate the unruly.

This chapter elaborates how policing protest has become more aggressive, as illustrated by the quick resort to arrests and the use of force, than the negotiated management model of protester-police interaction describes. It does so by analyzing how the New York Police Department (NYPD) prepared for and policed the 2004 Republican National Convention (RNC), which was designated a national special security event (NSSE). The NYPD prepared for the 2004 RNC by hosting the 2002 World Economic Forum (WEF). Hosting the 2002 WEF and the 2004 RNC affected the NYPD by leaving a security legacy institutionalized within the NYPD regarding protest policing. This security legacy has had consequences for how protesters, like those involved with Occupy Wall Street, have been policed subsequently by the NYPD.

The RNC security legacy includes expanded use of surveillance for protest policing, preventative arrests, changes to mass arrest processing, extended detentions for arrested protesters that in many instances exceeded state constitutional norms, and degrading conditions of detention and arrest processing. These aspects of the RNC's security legacy, due to their extralegal and extrajudicial nature, represent a postlegitimation state formation—they are executive actions unbound from legal or judicial authorizations. The selectivity of arrests, the selective production of disorder by police, and the long detentions of arrestees can be linked to neoliberal, post-Fordist urban government because they contribute to the government of the city's market-oriented symbolic production. In this aesthetic regime, the city's brand image produced by hosting a mega-event is promoted and policed, while the visibility of the people exercising power is actively disrupted.

Finally, evidence of intentional efforts by the NYPD to intimidate protesters and of the degrading conditions of detention and arrest processing allows me to bring forward the disorderly and expressive dimensions of NYPD protest policing here. This is significant because the new penology—the premise of the strategic incapacitation understanding of protest policing—highlights efficient technocratic management and is associated with the emergence of an actuarial criminology.[16] The NYPD's excesses described here, however, indicate something more than coldly rational calculations of efficient managerialism. They manifest subjective attachment to, and affective enjoyment of, the neoliberal state's practices.

Although the WEF and RNC are mega-events that New York City hosted after the attacks of September 11, 2001, I do not mean to imply that reaction to those attacks was the primary factor leading to more aggressive policing of protests in the United States or in New York City. On the one hand, due to the post–fiscal crisis transformation of urban political economy, incentives for hosting mega-events—and securing them—preexisted those attacks. On the other hand, zero tolerance, order maintenance policing deriving from the "Broken Windows" concept of policing was adopted by New York City in the early 1990s and has also influenced its policing of protest, as chapter 3 will show.[17] Institutionally speaking, we should understand the aggressive policing of protest that has emerged since the late 1990s in the United States as the result, on the one hand, of the vertical dissemination of protest policing tactics that occurs when cities host mega-events. For instance, if the mega-event is classified as an NSSE by the secretary of Homeland Security, then the Secret Service becomes the lead federal agency for developing and implementing security for the event, coordinating federal agencies and state and local police.[18] Training materials prepared under the authority of the Department of Justice also help municipal and state police departments prepare for these events considered to have national or international significance. On the other hand, it is the result of the horizontal dissemination of the "Broken Windows" theory of policing through the movement of police executives among different policing agencies, the revolving door between municipal police and private security consultant services (who provide security services to governments not only within the United States but around the world), and through the promotional efforts of celebrity police chiefs and security consultants, often sponsored by think tanks.[19] While the present chapter focuses on institution building that occurs by hosting mega-events, we should bear in mind that the aggressive policing of protest is overdetermined, and the following chapter addresses continuities between the NYPD's general order maintenance policing, influenced by "Broken Windows," and its protest policing.

### Seattle's Legacy for Hosting Mega-Events

Training materials for cities hosting mega-events, produced under the auspices of the Department of Justice and summarized in the official publication of the International Association of Chiefs of Police, encourage police executives to respond to protests as a threat equivalent to a natural disaster, terrorism, or criminal act that must be prevented by police.[20] Unsurprisingly, such policing of protests at mega-events in the United States dating back to the WTO of 1999 has resulted in violations of First Amendment rights, surveillance of activists, excessive use of force, the use of preventative detention during the event, and a security legacy institutionalized within the host city and its police forces after the event has concluded.[21] The consequences of New York City hosting the 2004 RNC bore similar results. Police departments preparing to host mega-events seek to ensure that theirs will not become another Seattle, when police-protester interactions disrupted Seattle's hopes for promoting itself and the state of Washington by hosting the 1999 WTO.[22] New York likewise approached the 2004 RNC with similar aspirations for image-based promotion, and therefore was committed to avoiding the disorder of Seattle.[23]

By hosting the 1999 WTO, Seattle and Washington State looked forward to an "infusion of visitor dollars into the local economy," hoped to "solidify Seattle's reputation as a 'world class city,'" and sought to position themselves to influence future international trade decisions—as the protesters did, too, albeit for antagonistic political purposes.[24] The divergent perspectives in the various reports written on the event subsequently, however, make apparent that the policing of protest was in transition. The principles of negotiated management did not uniformly guide either the policing of the WTO or the evaluation of Seattle's policing.

The American Civil Liberties Union (ACLU) of Washington did use the principles of negotiated management in its evaluation of the WTO. It argued that police in Seattle were underprepared, then overreacted, and that the mayor, by declaring a "civil emergency," and by ordering a twenty-five-block area of downtown Seattle a "no protest zone," violated the First Amendment rights of protesters.[25] Its report counseled that democracy is "not always neat and orderly," and while the WTO protests were "disruptive," they were "overwhelmingly peaceful." It reminded readers of the "'continuum of force' principle requir[ing] that force be proportionate to the threat to which it responds," and that less-lethal chemical weapons or rubber bullets "should not be used simply to move a crowd." In particular, this weaponry "should not be used against nonviolent crowds," such as those engaged in nonviolent civil disobedience, and the indiscriminate use of such weaponry injured nonviolent demonstrators, shoppers, workers, residents, and fifty-six police officers.[26] The report by the Citizens' Panel on WTO Operations was also guided by the principles of negotiated management when it argued that protesters engaged in civil disobedience cannot complain if they are arrested, but their arrest should not be an occasion for "summary physical punishment."[27]

The *After Action Report* of the Seattle Police Department (SPD) represents the transition away from the principles of negotiated management. Its point of reference is the first WTO meeting, held in 1996 and hosted by Singapore, where Singapore "employed its military to ensure that security for the event was tightly controlled."[28] In its self-critique, the SPD concludes in a militaristic mode that it had approached the 1999 WTO by falling into the trap of "fighting the last war" rather than "the 'new war,'" and refers to protesters as a "well-trained and equipped adversary."[29] Continuing to situate its analysis within a militaristic framework in which protesters are an "adversary" rather than fellow citizens or members of civil society, the SPD faults the constraints of Seattle's city ordinance restricting surveillance, though the report does not indicate inaccurate "intelligence" that would have been remedied by amending this legal regulation.[30] In contrast to the ACLU of Washington, the SPD praises its use of chemical weaponry for limiting injuries to protesters.[31]

The report by consultants R. M. McCarthy and Associates (in conjunction with Robert Louden), like the SPD, took a different tack from negotiated management, one representing and contributing to changes in protest policing in a more forceful, aggressive, and security-minded direction regardless of effects on either democracy or normative legitimacy. It found, pointedly, that Seattle "over accommodate[d] protesters."[32] This report criticized the SPD for "disregard[ing] the abundance of information" from "open source documents" of the "real threat of massive disruptions" in its planning.[33] Despite the availability of such information, this report also criticized Police Chief Norman Stamper for not seeking to overturn the city's intelligence ordinance limiting surveillance "long before" the WTO and, contradicting its analysis elsewhere in the report, found the intelligence ordinance to have "hampered . . . planning efforts from the outset."[34] This report also advocated for a "visible deployment" of "demonstration management personnel in a pre-emptive role" that would "swiftly" arrest for legal violations—rather than negotiated management's tolerance for minor legal violations. It urged the establishment of a "restricted safety zone" to deter demonstrators and that police would defend against any demonstrators seeking to "breach."[35] Similar to the SPD's post-democratic orientation, the consultants subtracted protesters from the discursive domain of citizens, finding that the "rights of protesters were exercised to the detriment of local citizens."[36]

As we learned in chapter 1, no-protest zones or limiting the exercise of First Amendment rights to contained and marginalized zones would become accepted by the juridical regime emerging in the late 1990s and early 2000s. As we shall see in this chapter, swift, if not preemptive, arrests, the use of visible acts of intimidation by police of protesters, and the removal of constraints upon surveillance would all become institutionalized in the new protest policing regime that also took form in the late 1990s and 2000s. Planners in Seattle had considered and rejected some of these ideas prior to the WTO out of concern that the people of Seattle would perceive their implementation as "repressive."[37] The consultancy report to Seattle conceded this possibility, but defended its proposals as the "most effective of available alternatives," indicating the emergence of a post-democratic, postlegitimation protest policing regime.[38]

Under neoliberal, post-Fordist conditions of political economy that have emerged since the 1970s, cities host mega-events to demonstrate recovery as one dimension of image production. Much the way that New Orleans sought to host the Super Bowl to demonstrate its recovery from Hurricane Katrina, New York submitted bids for several mega-events after the attacks of September 11 and was successful in its bid for the 2004 RNC. And much the way New Orleans would prepare to host the 2013 Super Bowl by hosting both the Fiesta Bowl and the Sugar Bowl during the 2007–2008 college football season to prove it was mega-event capable, New York hosted the 2002 WEF prior to hosting the RNC in 2004.[39]

## Policing the 2002 World Economic Forum

The WEF moved its annual meeting from Davos, Switzerland, to New York in the winter of 2002 to show solidarity with New York after the attacks of September 11.[40] NYC and Company, a quasi-governmental agency, celebrated the decision's potential for increasing foreign tourism in the aftermath of the attacks: "Broadcasting overseas that New York City is open for business is priceless." A spokesperson for the city's Independent Budget Office also rejoiced at the opportunity to market and brand New York in the global interurban competition for visitors by proclaiming that the WEF "helps market and expand New York's image as a host of world and national and international forums." The chief economist with the city's Comptroller's Office likewise described the WEF as a "coming out party for the City of New York, and it's worth a lot of money."[41]

The WEF's decision to move its meetings to New York was also part of an effort to hinder the momentum that transnational alter-globalization protesters had achieved in the late 1990s and early 2000s. Although the WEF's executive director averred that the forum was not "turning our back on Davos," the Swiss economy minister stated that the condition of the WEF's return to Davos was "sufficient security." Those opposed to siting the forum in Davos referred to the G-8 protests in Genoa as a reason to move it out of Davos for 2002.[42] The move from Europe to the United States would be a hurdle for Europe-based protesters, hampering their presence at the summit.

The security concerns of the WEF's leadership converged with the interests of New York in proving it was ready to host mega-events without disruption and reposition itself within the global neoliberal, post-Fordist urban economy. Given the prominence of security concerns and the appeal to neoliberalism's advocates and beneficiaries of dampening the global anti-neoliberal social movement, some saw the decision to shift the venue from Europe to New York at a time of unquestioned support for police in New York as a "trap" for the "alter-globalization movement."[43] Other city boosters, like *New York Times* journalist Clyde Haberman, asked demonstrators to "be there" for the city during the WEF "by behaving."[44] Giving voice to New York's interest in proving itself mega-event capable, Mayor Michael Bloomberg stated that by hosting the WEF, the city "proved it can handle large events, which the city would like to attract." At the conclusion of the WEF, Bloomberg reported he had "plans to lobby Republican and Democratic Party leaders to hold their national conventions here in 2004."[45]

By mid-June 2002, Bloomberg had submitted a bid to host the 2004 RNC, citing the fact that New York had successfully hosted the WEF "without any major incident," along with declining crime rates in the city, as evidence in support of its bid (the proposal to host the 2004 DNC had been submitted in April).[46] By late January 2003, the Republican National Committee announced its selection of New York for the 2004 RNC, which was welcomed by New York's Governor Pataki and Bloomberg as a way to show New York as "doing well and . . . coming back."[47] New York's perceived interests in marketing and branding itself within the global neoliberal, post-Fordist political economy converged with those of the WEF in being insulated from potentially disruptive protesters, and it would converge with the RNC's political interests as well.

Immediately after the WEF concluded, key members of the NYPD circulated critiques of their management of the event in February to the commanding officer of the Disorder Control Unit (DCU), Inspector Thomas Graham. Graham then circulated an "After Action Report" on March 4, 2002. Collectively, these reports, though heavily redacted, provide evidence that the NYPD's approach to the WEF was not consistent with negotiated management. In them, we also find discussion and anticipation of tactics the NYPD would utilize during the RNC, and against Occupy Wall Street.

The critiques and Graham's "After Action Report" focused especially on the perceived psychological effects of major shows of force, the role of intelligence or surveillance like the use of "undercovers" to infiltrate groups of protesters, and the NYPD's "proactive arrest policy." For example, a critique submitted by Captain Timothy Hardiman praised the DCU for providing links via email to "protestors' homepages," and found that "undercovers from narcotics provided useful information" and that staging "buses with corrections officers" was "useful." The buses, which have windows that are reinforced and covered with metal grids, also had "a powerful psychological effect."[48]

Deputy Inspector Michael Shortell, the commanding officer of narcotics in Manhattan South, lists as a positive aspect of the NYPD's plan for the WEF the "staging of massive amounts of equipment in key areas." The memo is clear that the positive effect of this staging was not the utility of having equipment on hand, but the likely intimidation of protesters upon seeing certain kinds of equipment being staged in the NYPD's preparation for them. He identifies the type of equipment he thought had positive effects in being seen by protesters: "armored vehicles, command posts, prisoner wagons, Department of Corrections buses, city buses." He expects that the likely effects of making massive amounts of this equipment visible upon protesters would "cause them to be alarmed at the level of police readiness." He also singles out for mention the use of "undercover personnel in the ranks of the protesters" and the use of "Anti-Crime personnel to follow smaller groups leaving the area."[49] Considering that Shortell contextualizes this discussion by stating that the NYPD's plans and their implementation were "highly effective and deserving of the accolades it has received," we can observe that Shortell enjoys the intimidation of protesters by police.

Captain Bonifaci highlights the "proactive arrest policy" as part of the NYPD's WEF "success." He writes, "it should be noted that a large part of the success in policing the major demonstration on Saturday February 02, 2002 was due in part to the proactive arrest policy that was instituted at the start of the march at 59th St. and 5th Ave., and directed toward demonstrators who were obviously potential rioters."[50] Striking about this statement is the lack of evidence for a lawful basis for the arrests he is celebrating. Bonifaci points to no legal violation as the basis for the arrests—that, of course, is why he is referring to a proactive arrest policy.

This prevention-oriented policing of a mega-event fits with expectations derived from the scholarship on strategic incapacitation. It also converges, as we shall see in chapter 3, with the "Broken Windows" theory of zero tolerance, order maintenance policing. Policing a mega-event means policing the perception of disorder for the purposes of city marketing and branding—for urban participation in the neoliberal, post-Fordist communicative capitalist order. Bonifaci praises the proactive arrest of demonstrators who appeared, to police, to be obvious potential rioters—an assessment that must be based on appearances and conjecture since no legal violations are referenced. We should also note that Bonifaci's memo states it is a policy of the NYPD to arrest demonstrators based on their appearance and without a legal violation, indicating a post-legal-legitimation institutional orientation within the NYPD.

Based on this and other input, Graham echoes the memoranda in his "After Action Report" regarding the benefits of the NYPD expressing intimidation. Graham finds that the "staging of large amounts of personnel and equipment that was observed by protesters was a deterrent." He goes on to describe how "the wearing of disorder helmets" is a "deterrent to confrontation." Graham also refers to the expressive and chillingly intimidating effects of preventative arrests described by Bonifaci as setting "a 'tone' with the demonstrators and their possible plans at other demonstrations." Among Graham's recommendations for future NYPD demonstration planning is the proposal to use "undercover officers to distribute misinformation within the crowds."[51] The approval of policy actions in protest policing that are expressively intimidating and embraced for their chilling effects, like setting a tone that deters demonstrators, indicates a model of policing protest at odds with the concerns of negotiated management or political democracy more broadly. Instead of negotiated management's respect for First Amendment rights of speech and assembly, and maintaining lines of dialogic communication between protesters and police, the NYPD's form of policing shares purposes and tactics with what we can call a security model of policing more interested in suppressing or disorganizing the people. The latter is closer to a policing model that might be shared with more paramilitary or counterinsurgency-styled forces.[52]

Policing based on intimidation—affecting the psychological or subjective will of people to assert their rights—requires expressive acts, messages, and communication. Projecting such an image of the NYPD, its spokesman, Paul Browne, publicly acknowledged the use of "plainclothes officers" and "surveillance techniques to track and hopefully disrupt violent elements" during the WEF. A lawyer for demonstrators, Daniel Perez, noted the expressive, communicative elements of this manner of policing, saying it seemed like "something out of a battle zone."[53]

We can identify NYPD policing practices, as described by these NYPD memos and the WEF "After Action Report," as being directed to control and security.[54] The NYPD's institutional practices are motivated by something more than efficient technocratic management. The NYPD emerges in these reports as a police force, rather than a law enforcement agency, and its protest policing is a policy of excess beyond legal violation. Because the NYPD's policing is dedicated to control and security in excess of legal violations, it represents a postlegitimation state formation. Because, moreover, police managers single out extralegal intimidation of protesters as a benefit to their police practices, NYPD protest policing, as it appears in these after-action reports, is directed less by actuarial calculation than affective attachment to, and expression of, post-democratic policing.

Two of Graham's criticisms of how the NYPD handled the WEF would be addressed in the near future. First, Graham identifies a number of weaknesses within the Intelligence Division. He finds that "early intelligence was poor" with regard to potential WEF protesters, and that the Intelligence Division "gave out very little information." "No information developed from monitoring the demonstrators' radios" (by the Intelligence Division) was relayed to task forces, he added, though he acknowledged information "from sources within the crowd proved to be good information." The second weakness was arrest processing. The "urgency, in some cases, to 'scoop up' arrests and remove them from the scene . . . hastened the process adding to the confusion and increasing the potential for mistakes to be made." At the processing facility, in two instances when "inquiries were made" regarding "the number of prisoners being processed," the "answer both times was 'I have no idea.'"[55] As a lawyer who defends protesters described, at the WEF, "it was just obvious even to prosecutors [that] some [NYPD] supervisors said arrest these people, they did, and nobody could say what you did as opposed to what I did."[56] Between the WEF and the 2004 RNC, the NYPD would make institutional changes with respect to the Intelligence Division and with respect to its capacity for mass arrests.

### Preparing for the 2004 RNC and NYPD Institutional Development

*The Intelligence Division*

With regard to the Intelligence Division, Ray Kelly rejoined the NYPD as commissioner with billionaire global media mogul Michael Bloomberg's election as mayor after the attacks of September 11, 2001. Kelly kept the New York City Joint Terrorism Task Force office, created to encourage cooperation among different agencies and the Federal Bureau of Investigation (FBI), at arm's length, continuing the NYPD tradition of distrust where "outsiders"—or the actual city—were concerned. Instead, Kelly began building an equivalent to Central Intelligence Agency (CIA) operations within the NYPD's Intelligence Division.

Kelly offered the CIA's New York station chief, David Cohen, the job of deputy commissioner of the NYPD's Intelligence Division.[57] Cohen, in turn, hired CIA operative Larry Sanchez to assist him in remaking the Intelligence Division.[58] In his first year, Cohen began the legal process to have the "Handschu Guidelines" modified.

"Handschu" refers to a civil rights suit initiated against the NYPD in 1971 for widespread spying and infiltration of political organizations, and blacklisting of individuals, in New York City.[59] After lengthy negotiations, New York agreed to settle the class action lawsuit, putting the NYPD under a judicial decree governing how it conducts investigations of individuals and groups engaged in First Amendment activities.[60] The Handschu Guidelines are the regulations covering NYPD investigations of groups involved with political activities to make sure that investigations are not based on First Amendment activities.

The Handschu Guidelines required that the Intelligence Division be the only NYPD division to investigate groups involved with political activities, and created a Handschu Authority to oversee the Intelligence Division, which included one civilian member from outside the NYPD who would be appointed by the mayor.[61] The Handschu Guidelines placed a check on the conduct of investigations, monitored the NYPD's investigatory practices in an ongoing fashion, and gave individuals and groups a process of inquiry if they believed they were being improperly investigated by the NYPD. By placing a check on how investigations were conducted and by establishing a system for monitoring investigations in an entity that was not within the Intelligence Division, the Handschu Guidelines sought to prevent abuse from occurring and created mechanisms for discovering abuse should it occur.[62]

Cohen argued that the Handschu Guidelines were too restrictive for preventing terrorism and sought to do away with them because "to wait for an indication of crime before investigation is to wait far too long."[63] Though Cohen did not present concrete evidence showing that the Handschu Guidelines had prevented a needed investigation from occurring, Judge Haight, the judge assigned to the Handschu class action, ruled in favor of the NYPD's proposed changes to the Handschu Guidelines on February 11, 2003. In his ruling, Judge Haight accepted Cohen's promise that the "substance of the FBI Guidelines" for investigations, as amended in 2002, would be included in the NYPD Patrol Guide (but not in the consent decree). Cohen's assurances were important to Judge Haight because the FBI guidelines maintained at least some connection—if loose, because of the permissibility of an investigation where there is mere advocacy of unlawful conduct—between investigation and criminal activity.[64]

The 2003 Modified Handschu Guidelines deleted almost all of the original Handschu Guidelines. Removed were such items as the regulation limiting the kind of information that may be required of a group for event planning purposes, and requiring that the Intelligence Division request permission for the investigations of groups involved with political activities from the Handschu Authority, that the use of undercover personnel also be regulated according to the approval of the Handschu Authority, and that investigations be monitored and the results be reported annually. The Handschu Authority was reduced to a sole function of responding to those members of the public who believed they had been investigated by the NYPD in a manner that was not in conformity with the Constitution, and to conduct an inquiry into such an investigation. In other words, regulations to prevent police misconduct had been stripped from the guidelines, leaving only a process of inquiry into investigations after a potential harm to constitutional rights had already occurred.[65]

Almost immediately after the February 11 ruling, and before the revised consent decree had been finalized, the NYPD abused its powers. On February 15, as the United Nations Security Council met to hear the United States' argument for invading Iraq, and then on March 22 and March 27, 2003, antiwar demonstrations filled the streets of New York City.[66] The February 15 protests, which occurred about two weeks after the RNC had selected New York for its 2004 convention, was especially massive and abusively policed.[67] Plainclothes officers from the Intelligence Division, also known as Intel officers, interrogated those arrested at these demonstrations before they were released with appearance tickets while preventing lawyers from having access to the arrestees.[68] Arrestees were asked questions such as, "Why did you come to New York today?" "How do you feel about the war?" "Do you hate George Bush?" "Who did you come with?" "Do you go to school?" "Where?" "What do you study?" "Do you think anyone in Ithaca uses drugs?" "Do you know when the next peace rally will be?" "Where did you park your car?" "Why are you here at the demonstration?" "Have you been to any protests in the past? Where? When?" "At which website did you find out about the demonstration?" "What will you be doing and where are you going when you are released?" "Do you do any kind of political work?" "Where are you employed?" "What are your political affiliations?" "Are you staying with anyone?" "Don't you think it was necessary for us to get involved in World War II?" "Where have you traveled lately?" "What is your religion?" "Are you

Muslim?"[69] These questions indicated the use of police investigative powers targeted at First Amendment activities and associations and, in light of the question about employment, the potential for blacklisting.

As a consequence of the NYPD's immediate recourse to abusive investigations by engaging in political and argumentative interrogations of arrestees, Judge Haight required that the Patrol Guidelines incorporating the 2002 FBI guidelines become part of the Modified Handschu Guidelines and included within his "Order and Judgment" composing the modified consent decree. Under that order, the Handschu Authority remained almost entirely sidelined (except for after-the-fact investigations). The power to authorize investigations of those engaged in political activities was now placed under the authority of the deputy commissioner of the Intelligence Division, and all such investigations touching on political activity had to be conducted under the supervision of the Intelligence Division. Although the decree warned the NYPD that investigations must "not be based solely on activities protected by the First Amendment," investigations could commence with the "possibility of unlawful activity." A full investigation could proceed with a "reasonable indication" that an "unlawful act has been, is being, or will be committed," with the order reminding its readers that "reasonable indication" was "substantially lower than probable cause." Despite advising the NYPD that investigative techniques should take account of "the intrusiveness of the technique" and the "seriousness of the unlawful act," all investigations and the techniques utilized—including the use of undercover operations— would be governed by the Intelligence Division's discretion.[70] The only supervision of the Intelligence Division, aside from an after-the-fact inquiry by the declawed Handschu Authority or after-the-fact litigation, was a requirement that the head of Intelligence "periodically inform and advise the Police Commissioner concerning the status of any investigations pursuant to these guidelines."[71] Because New York law includes low-level, noncriminal violations of trespass and disorderly conduct (the latter boils down to inconveniencing the public on a street, sidewalk, or other public area as a demonstration might) that are the equivalent of a traffic or parking ticket, the change in the language of the Handschu Guidelines from "criminal" to "unlawful" acts lowers substantially the threshold for unleashing the NYPD's investigatory powers: as long as some connection to the possibility of a noncriminal legal violation can be made, a "preliminary inquiry," if not a "full investigation" or a "terrorism enterprise investigation," could now arguably be initiated.

The Patrol Guidelines and what little survived of the original Handschu Order together constituted the "2003 Modified Handschu Guidelines."[72] Set in place a year prior to the 2004 RNC, the 2003 Modified Handschu Guidelines defined the parameters for the NYPD's use of investigative powers until litigation arising from constant and groundless surveillance of New York City Muslims led to enhanced monitoring of the Intelligence Division in a March 13, 2017, ruling by Judge Haight.[73] As we have seen, the 2003 Modified Handschu Guidelines do not make adequate institutional provision for preventing abuse of police powers. These institutional failures would be borne out by what Judge Haight called the NYPD's "egregious" video recording of "quintessential 'political activity'" of a permitted march by the Coalition for the Homeless to the mayor's house December 4, 2005, and of a march from Marcus Garvey Park in Harlem to Central Park on March 19, 2005.[74] During the Coalition for the Homeless march, an affidavit describes the NYPD holding the video camera a few feet from the faces of the marchers, while making sure to capture the messages on the signs demonstrators were carrying. Affidavits note that in neither the Coalition for the Homeless march, nor the march from Marcus Garvey Park to Central Park, was illegal activity taking place.[75]

Perhaps the most notorious abuse by the NYPD—which led to Judge Haight's 2017 revisions to the Handschu Guidelines—was the discovery by Associated Press reporters that the NYPD systematically monitored mosques and Muslim groups all over New York with undercover personnel and informants through a disturbingly named department within the Intelligence Division—the Demographics Unit—that "took its cue from Israeli officers' methods of keeping tabs on military-occupied West Bank."[76] Just as alarming as the predictable incapacity of the 2003 Modified Handschu Guidelines to prevent abuse, and the NYPD's willingness to exceed its extensive permissible power under the Modified Guidelines, though, was the low standard for the acceptable deployment of the NYPD's investigative powers, as illustrated by Judge Haight's toleration of the video recording of Critical Mass bicyclists because some of them had ridden their bicycles through red traffic lights.[77] Since 2003, the smallest legal violations have been sufficient to trigger the enormous resources of the NYPD's Intelligence Division.

Although the changes to the Handschu Guidelines were made after the attacks of September 11, 2001, we should not be tempted to determine that negotiated management broke down as a response to those attacks by pointing to the changes the NYPD obtained to the Handschu decree (or that these changes were only for preparation for hosting the RNC). A perspective limited to the aftermath of September 11 misses how other cities and the federal government targeted political groups through the twentieth century and especially in the 1960s, how their power to target political groups was limited in the 1970s and 1980s as New York's was, and how they began efforts to loosen those strictures in the 1990s and early 2000s.

For example, the Handschu case in New York proceeded in parallel—indeed, in dialogue—with efforts to control the Chicago Police Department's Red Squad (while the consent decree regulating the activities of the Chicago Police Department's Red Squad was informed by the decree covering Memphis, Tennessee), which, in turn, worked in conjunction with FBI and Department of Defense surveillance of domestic "subversives."[78] Class action litigation began against Chicago in 1974—three years after the Handschu litigation began against New York—and a court order finalizing the consent decree between the parties to the Chicago litigation was formalized March 30, 1982—three years prior to the Handschu court order. While the Handschu order was modified in 2003, the Appeals Court for the Seventh Circuit ordered the district judge overseeing the Chicago settlement to accede to Chicago's request that she loosen the decree January 11, 2001—prior to the attacks of September 11.[79] By putting the modification of the Handschu Guidelines in relation to the modification of the Chicago decree, factors affecting the policing of protest beyond the attacks of September 11 become significant.

Adding to the importance of looking at broader forces to explain changes in protest policing, changes at the federal level regarding investigative powers and surveillance moved in parallel to the changes evident in Chicago and New York. Responding to the political culture of the 1970s outraged at government actions treating domestic political groups as if they were foreign enemies of the state, Congress held hearings on these abuses of power in 1976 and passed the Foreign Intelligence Surveillance Act (FISA) in 1978 to restrain such politically motivated exercises of power incompatible with a constitutional democracy. Then, anticipating shifts at the municipal level, Congress relaxed the limitations of FISA, reopening the door to broader uses of surveillance, by passing the Anti-terrorism and Effective Death Penalty Act in 1996—again, prior to the attacks of September 11—which, in turn, paved the way for the USA PATRIOT Act's passage in November 2001. With respect to federal law enforcement, in 1976 Attorney General Edward Levi established guidelines for FBI investigations to prevent the abuses that FBI Director J. Edgar Hoover condoned and encouraged by requiring suspicion of criminal conduct for an investigation to commence. After Ronald Reagan was elected president, his attorney general, William French Smith, modified those guidelines to permit FBI investigations where there was mere advocacy of crime in 1983, and Attorney General John Ashcroft loosened these guidelines still further in 2002.[80] The FBI guidelines are important for understanding some municipal police practices because they were made part of the Chicago decree and, since 2003, have become part of the New York decree, thereby embedding federal standards for investigations institutionally within local police practices.

Historical patterns of cities moving in parallel to establish, and then relax, limitations on municipal police investigations and surveillance, and evidence that these patterns move in parallel with shifts at the federal level, indicate that the legal policies of these different municipal governments and branches of the federal government are responding, in significant measure, to deeper shifts in political culture and political economy. The attacks of September 11 may have provided a window of opportunity making institutional changes easier to enact or enabled them to be deeper than they otherwise may have been. Likewise, preparations for the RNC allowed these changes to be thoroughly deployed and further developed through institutional practice.

*NYPD Mass Arrest Processing*

In preparation for the 2004 RNC, the NYPD changed how it would handle mass arrests. These changes facilitated preventative arrests that kept RNC protesters, potential protesters, and anyone who happened to be randomly in close proximity to someone who appeared to the NYPD to be, potentially, an RNC protester to be put in preventative detention during the RNC. The conditions of custody, as we shall see further below, were probative of a policy of extrajudicial punishment.

In New York City, there are three ways to arrest a suspect: issue a summons, issue a desk appearance ticket (DAT), or conduct a live arrest. First, the suspect can be issued a summons that charges the person with a violation and instructs the person to appear at a local criminal court at a certain date and time. Second, one can be arrested, taken into custody, and then issued a DAT instructing the person to appear in court at a certain date and time to be arraigned. In New York City, one might be in custody for four to five hours to have one's arrest processed with a DAT. In other jurisdictions, processing can be faster. For a live arrest, in New York City, one is taken to the Manhattan Detention Complex (also known as the Tombs) and Central Booking, which are adjacent to court facilities at 100 Centre Street. There, one is finger-printed, a mug shot is taken, and one is arraigned on an accusatory instrument before a judge. Under state constitutional law, this process should not take longer than twenty-four hours.[81]

The NYPD decided to implement a no-summons policy for RNC-related arrests and a policy to fingerprint all RNC-related arrestees, even those arrested for non–criminal law violations that are equivalent to a traffic or parking ticket under New York law.[82] The no-summons policy for demonstrators at the RNC expanded upon what originated as an unwritten policy to repress demonstrations at police headquarters protesting the police shooting of an unarmed black Guinean immigrant, Amadou Diallo.[83] This unwritten policy was in force between April 1, 1999, and April 30, 2001—a period that predated the attacks of September 11, 2001. The NYPD adopted a written no-summons policy for large demonstrations on May 1, 2001—again, prior to September 11.[84] The NYPD's no-summons policy for the 2004 RNC meant that all those arrested would be taken into custody and receive either a DAT or be, as the overwhelming majority of RNC arrestees were, fully booked as a live arrest.

Prior to 2004, the NYPD's institutional policy for managing mass arrests was to send approximately twenty arrestees (the capacity of an NYPD wagon for transporting those taken into custody) to different station houses so that no one station house would be overwhelmed. The policy reflected institutional thinking that processing a large number of arrestees from a mass arrest situation in any one station house would be "more than difficult."[85] The NYPD changed course from this line of thinking for the RNC.

As part of the planning for the RNC, the NYPD modified how it would process mass arrests in a manner incomprehensible from a perspective of bureaucratic efficiency. Rather than taking arrestees to precincts capable of processing arrestees—according to plaintiffs' lawyers in class action litigation against New York for its policing of the RNC, there were at least twenty such precincts in Manhattan alone—the NYPD decided to process RNC arrestees at a central location.[86] The NYPD would take arrestees by bus to a Post Arrest Staging Site (PASS) hastily constructed at Pier 57, a former Metropolitan Transit Authority storage and repair facility for city buses located on the lower west side of Manhattan that had been sitting empty and unused for about a year prior to the RNC.[87] This site, however, was a strange choice from a perspective of bureaucratic efficiency because it lacked fingerprinting equipment (and the NYPD had decided to fingerprint all RNC-related arrests). Therefore, arrestees would have to be transported from the PASS to the Tombs where they would be fingerprinted with Live Scan and photographed, and their data sent to Albany, New York, and then they would either wait for arraignment before a judge or be released with a DAT for a later arraignment.[88] The decision to bring arrestees to Pier 57, a location lacking fingerprinting capacity, while also deciding that all RNC-related arrestees should be fingerprinted, meant foreseeable delays in processing RNC-related arrestees. To emphasize: NYPD changes to the mass arrest process, in conjunction with its decisions not to issue summons for low-level violations, to require all arrestees to be fingerprinted, and to locate the PASS where fingerprinting capacity was lacking, meant NYPD RNC planning foreseeably extended the time spent in custody for RNC-related arrestees.

For mass arrests, a supervisor would assign five arrestees to an arresting officer.[89] Since the RNC, this number has been lowered to three as it is not plausible that one officer is likely to have personally observed five different people engaged in actions in violation of the law (let alone remember it months or a year later for a trial).[90] The arresting officer would then meet with a representative of the NYPD Legal Bureau who would provide the officer with assistance in filling out the paperwork. Only after meeting first with a representative of the NYPD Legal Bureau would the officer then meet with the Manhattan County District Attorney's Office, which would draw up the accusatory instrument that the officer would swear to on the penalty of perjury.[91]

A mass arrest for protest differs from an ordinary "turnover" arrest—an arrest in which the arrestee has been turned over to another officer responsible for filling out the paperwork where the latter is not the officer who personally observed wrongdoing. For an ordinary turnover arrest, the officer filling out the paperwork describes the wrongdoing—which the officer did not personally see—but the officer who did observe the wrongdoing will sign a statement corroborating the hearsay in the statement filled out by the officer who does the paperwork. In a mass arrest situation, the officer fills out paperwork indicating that he or she observed five (now three) persons violating the law, which, in fact, is not likely to be true as it was the supervisor who directed an arrest team to conduct arrests, and an arresting officer will be assigned to the arrestees at a later point in the process. Nevertheless, as a lawyer who defends protesters informed me, "We defense lawyers have a very hard time proving that, although sometimes it does happen, like when the cop is a block away and you have them on video when the person is getting arrested." The lawyer informed me regarding officers filling out paperwork about legal violations they did not personally observe: "It absolutely happens all the time."[92]

In an ordinary arrest, the arresting officer fills out paperwork at the precinct, perhaps with assistance from his or her sergeant. As a matter of course, the sergeant signs off on arrest paperwork. Then, the arresting officer goes to the prosecutor's office where a prosecutor interviews the arresting officer. The prosecutor will draft an accusatory instrument that the officer swears out on penalty of perjury, and it is signed by the officer. In a mass arrest, the "officers on the arrest teams are interviewed by lawyers from the Police Department's Legal Bureau before they write up the narratives in their memo books and in their other police paperwork about what they observed the defendants do. There's also polaroid photographs taken on the arrest scene and then more that are taken at the precinct. All of these extra steps construct the illusion that these officers assigned these arrestees actually observed them do something before they were assigned their arrests." The officer assigned these five (now, three) prisoners then writes up his or her paperwork. "And what your paperwork says is exactly what everybody else's paperwork says, except the names of your three people appear in it." The officers "sign off on these internal police reports and *then* they go to the DA's office." All of the narrative construction occurs at the mass arrest processing center before the prisoner is released and before police go to the prosecutors. "So by the time the cops go to the prosecutors," the lawyer continues, "their story is already constructed." Significantly, the lawyer emphasizes, "This is not something, as far as we know or were on to, that had been institutionalized before the RNC. None of us had heard of the Legal Bureau constructing these narratives and, really, coaching these officers. That's now a deeply institutionalized part of the mass arrest processing procedure."[93]

In the lead-up to the RNC, the NYPD wanted to be able fill out the accusatory instruments themselves, this defense lawyer informs me, but the DA's office would not go along with it due to past problems with the NYPD being able to verify truthfully the legal violations of arrestees. By having arresting officers meet first with NYPD lawyers, though, a legal narrative can be constructed that is likely to be facially sufficient for prosecution. So: "If you're a cop and you've got three Polaroid pictures and you can look at them and say, 'I remember the person with the green scarf 'cause that scarf was so memorable and she was part of a group of fifty people who were in the middle of the road, and two cars couldn't get by.' That's all you have to do. It's a pretty low-level lift in terms of test of lying."[94] Thus, the RNC was a significant landmark in terms of the NYPD modifying its mass arrest processing. By having arresting officers meet first with NYPD lawyers from the Legal Bureau, they hoped to produce simulacra for legally sufficient accusatory information for prosecution, if not truthful accusations. While the revisions may have made it more likely that the NYPD could keep track of its arrestees, the decision to create a centralized PASS in conjunction with a no-summons policy and a policy to fingerprint all RNC-related arrestees, however, foreseeably extended the length of time RNC-related arrestees would spend in custody at Pier 57.

## NYPD Institutional Development
## and Expressive Policing at the 2004 RNC

The NYPD's post-WEF preparations for the RNC would have important consequences for their policing of the RNC. The use of the NYPD Intelligence Division's (Intel) surveillance is connected to preventative arrests that policed New York's place branding associated with the RNC, that policed the image of prominent commodities associated with the city during the RNC, that disrupted the appearance of protesters as political subjects, and that targeted those even visually associated with protesters (e.g., those who were not protesters but who were nearby or were watching a demonstration). Detention incident to an arrest associated with protesting at the RNC was predictably excessive, and custody occurred under degrading—sometimes torturously so—conditions. The protest policing deployed at the 2004 RNC by the NYPD, unconstrained by legal violations, was at times symbolically or politically targeted while at other times seemingly indiscriminate. Both the selectivity and the seeming arbitrariness of arrests were acts of communication, and both led to an abusive and degrading process before an arrestee ever saw a judge. These are the institutional practices of a postlegitimation, post-democratic state formation dedicated to controlling post-Fordist symbolic production and disorganizing political agency on the part of the people. The NYPD's policing is an element of communicative capitalism, and the NYPD as an institution is affectively attached to its expressively violent conduct.

### Surveillance: Nothing Too Insignificant

The NYPD's Intelligence Division's surveillance, according to subsequent reporting in the *New York Times* by Jim Dwyer and Intel records ordered released to the *Times* and the New York Civil Liberties Union (NYCLU), was extensive and exhaustive. Seemingly, nothing was too small or insignificant for Intel to monitor and document. Although some Intel documents produced in preparation for the RNC did have legitimate public safety concerns, such as those directed to the illegal purchase of devices that can change traffic signals—a potential safety hazard—much of the documents released focused either on the possibility of nonviolent civil disobedience or on completely legal forms of expression.[95] Consistent with a commitment to avoid a Seattle WTO scenario, for example, Intel demonstrated a preoccupation with West Coast activists, closely monitoring activist Lisa Fithian's plans to appear at the RNC (she had participated at the 1999 WTO in Seattle), and compiled photos of dozens of activists for surveillance, some of which appeared on the evening news show *Nightline*.[96] Intel sources were behind luridly sensationalist tabloid stories of impending violence at the RNC that helped prime New York City residents for arrests of protesters, creating an aesthetics of consent for such arrests.[97]

The low threshold for Intel's use of undercover officers is evident in Intel documents and reporting based on them. College and university campuses around the country were monitored by the NYPD, and NYPD undercover officers were active in numerous states around the country, from Massachusetts to California, in addition to Montreal and Europe.[98] Undercover officers did not, however, merely monitor groups, but acted to influence events and occasionally endangered people with their actions. In one instance, a "sham arrest of a man secretly working with the police led to a bruising confrontation between officers in riot gear and bystanders." When an undercover officer attending a demonstration on behalf of the homeless was suddenly arrested, other demonstrators began chanting, "Let him go." In response, police arrested two other protesters. On another occasion, the same undercover officer was videotaped observing a movie being filmed that used actual demonstrations as its backdrop. At one point, the undercover officer appeared to be trying to agitate bystanders.[99]

Most of what Intel monitored, however, was planning for peaceful, nonviolent civil disobedience or were paradigmatic, if not mundane, First Amendment activities, and activities to monitor the police for legal or constitutional violations. Intel documented the ACLU's submission of a permit application on behalf of the Hip Hop Summit Network to protest the Rockefeller drug laws, the National Lawyers Guild's legal training to prepare legal observers, I-Witness Video's plans to compile video of protests to assist in the defense of those wrongly or abusively arrested, United for Peace and Justice's legal action appealing the city's denial of a permit for a demonstration at Central Park, the possibility of a Billionaires for Bush parodic flash mob noting how participants might be dressed ("formal clothing"), an "Anti-RNC" lecture at a church, a "Protest Related Party," and an "Anti-War Poetry Reading."[100] Occasionally, the documents displayed an inclination to inflate the possibility of a threat, for example, by implying an internet message was counseling violent retaliation when it responded to the possibility of police violence against protesters by stating people should respond by letting police know they are watching and to "give 'em hell."[101]

### Marking the Shift in NYPD Protest Policing

One New York City lawyer who defends protesters points to the 2004 RNC as marking a shift in how New York responds to protest.[102] The Critical Mass bicycle ride immediately preceding the RNC exhibits this shift. Critical Mass is a leaderless assembly of bicyclists who gather on the last Friday of every month in cities around the United States to go for a ride. The bicycle enthusiast organization Time's Up! often advertises the rides, which are an opportunity to experience the joy of riding with others, are safer than riding alone (bicyclists in a group are more visible), and are a call for cities to build infrastructure to support bicycling.

Prior to the RNC, either the Critical Mass rides would typically occur without police presence, or the NYPD would facilitate the rides by doing things like holding traffic at an intersection (which is called corking) until all the bicyclists had crossed safely, and by ushering riders through red lights. Critical Mass and Time's Up!, though, featured prominently in the NYPD's "Intelligence Documents" for the RNC, indicating they were being targeted.[103] Adding evidence to the claim Critical Mass was being targeted, a video of the April 29, 2004, Critical Mass ride, at which police blockaded riders and made arrests, showed an undercover officer captured on the video letting another officer know he was undercover during the arrests.[104]

On Friday evening, August 27, 2004, on the threshold of the RNC's opening, five thousand people participated in a Critical Mass bicycle ride. In the first mass arrest of the convention, 264 bicyclists were arrested when police pulled orange mesh netting across Seventh Avenue at two locations, trapping and arresting everyone on the block.[105] According to the NYCLU's report, *Rights and Wrongs at the RNC*, the ride began with cyclists following the instructions of the NYPD, and police were "facilitat[ing] the ride." As the ride proceeded, police broke the larger than normal group into smaller groups before blocking their path and, without a warning to disperse, conducted the arrests.[106] The factual circumstances of the event create the impression that the police were leading riders into a trap to be arrested.

Policing the neoliberal, post-Fordist city contributes to place branding, the appropriation of urban space, and the amplification of this symbolic production described by theorists of post-Fordist symbolic production.[107] The NYPD Intelligence Division documents display a preoccupation with protecting communicative capitalism while policing the symbolic value of New York's communicative production.[108] For example, Intel consistently documented MSNBC's plans to broadcast live daily from Herald Square Park, expressing the concern that such broadcasts could be disrupted by "spontaneous direct action protest."[109]

Intel closely monitored Joshua Kinberg as part of the NYPD's efforts to protect the symbolic value of New York's marketing and RNC communicative production. Kinberg is a graduate of the Parson School of Design who created a bicycle with an apparatus to accept text messages and reproduce them in water-soluble chalk on the pavement as the bicycle rides through the city. The project, Intel documented, had been featured in the August 2004 edition of *Popular Science*.[110] Intel described the bicycle in bold print as "having been *built for the sole purpose of protesting during the RNC*".[111] While being interviewed by Ron Reagan for MSNBC just prior to the convention, Kinberg was arrested. Kinberg spent twenty-four hours in the Tombs, but his equipment was confiscated for six months and his bicycle was never found. Though during the course of his arrest he can be heard asking the NYPD to be careful with his equipment, he later described finding it piled "behind a desk in the D.A.'s office."[112] Although he was interviewed upon his release from the Tombs by MSNBC, the confiscation of his equipment prior to the RNC prevented his planned exhibition of the art project during the convention with Bikes against Bush. Kinberg's appearance in Intel documents and the manner by which he was arrested—it occurred prior to the convention, with the NYPD appearing at his MSNBC interview to ask him for identification so the arresting officers could be certain they were arresting the person they had planned to arrest, and then they confiscated his equipment as part of the arrest—indicate the likelihood that Kinberg's arrest was planned and that he was targeted as part of the NYPD's policing of New York's visual appearance by preventing image production considered disruptive of New York's communicative goals in hosting a mega-event such as the RNC.

Despite the NYPD's concern that MSNBC's live broadcasts not be disrupted by protesters, they themselves disrupted an MSNBC interview for the purpose of arresting Kinberg. We can understand the NYPD not as maintaining order per se, but as policing a particular visual order while also producing a particular disorder visually. While helping to secure the image production of New York's hosting of the RNC as an urban mega-event, the NYPD acts to disorder and disrupt even the most minor visual appearance of people as political subjects within the city.

For instance, the NYPD Intelligence Division closely monitored the possibility for protest at Hummer of Manhattan.[113] On August 31, one woman, Georgianna Page, arrived at the Hummer dealership wearing a cardboard box shaped and colored to evoke a Hummer truck, with the word "Bummer" where "Hummer" would normally appear across the front. She held a sign linking gas-guzzling sport utility vehicles like the Hummer to the invasion of Iraq. She was the only person present on the public sidewalk, and could not plausibly be considered to be blocking traffic. She was arrested by an NYPD "white shirt" (a captain).[114]

### Producing Disorder by Disorganizing the People as Political Subjects

Intel closely monitored the War Resisters League, including where they would be and when. On August 31, 2004, the War Resisters League had planned a march at the World Trade Center toward Madison Square Garden, where the RNC was being held. On arrival at the Garden—or wherever they might be stopped—members of the group planned to hold a "die-in" to protest the wars in Iraq and Afghanistan. The group was tightly controlled by the NYPD, and confusion and disorder immediately resulted from the NYPD's interactions with the group. Police claimed to be "concerned about the possibility of violence and disorder," but the War Resisters League is an antimilitarism group that practices nonviolence, so a concern about violence would be unreasonable in this instance.[115] The ensuing disorder was caused by the NYPD themselves.

Although there was no permit for the march, NYPD Inspector Galati told one of the organizers that protesters should proceed only one or two abreast to avoid blocking the sidewalk. After announcing instructions about not blocking the sidewalk and to obey traffic laws through a bullhorn, Galati told the group to have a "safe march." As described by Federal District Court Judge Richard Sullivan, based on video evidence, almost as soon as the march began, NYPD Deputy Chief Terrence Monahan announced that if protesters continued to block the sidewalk they would be arrested. Officers on bicycles immediately blocked marchers by pinning them against a wall and placed them under arrest. Demonstrators were given no opportunity to comply with Monahan's warning and to continue the march. Shortly after Monahan's announcement, a woman approached the line of bicycle police and asked to leave but was not given a response and was not allowed to leave the group. At the same time as Monahan appeared to have decided marchers should be arrested, Galati was directing passersby to "get back into march formation *or* be subject to arrest."[116] While some effort was made to release journalists, Michael Schiller was not released, though he was filming the demonstration for an HBO documentary about the RNC protests.[117] In total, 227 were arrested.[118]

### Producing Disorder and Intimidation through Indiscriminate Arrests

A couple hours after the War Resisters League mass arrest, a crowd gathered to demonstrate without a permit around Union Square on August 31, 2004. With two marching bands, demonstrators attracted journalists and onlookers. Ann Maurer, a legal assistant at the ACLU, who "deliberately sought to avoid conflict with the police" and who tried to keep herself apart from the demonstrating group, and Hacer Dinler, who was on her way to work, were penned by the NYPD. The NYPD then conducted another mass arrest, trapping and arresting indiscriminately any who happened to be present at the time.[119]

The monitoring of individuals like Kinberg, the possibility for a protest at a Hummer dealership, or the monitoring of groups like the War Resisters League, and the conduct of preventative arrests in each of these instances show how the NYPD polices New York's branding conducted through its hosting of the RNC, and the communicative value of commodities like Hummer vehicles, contributing to their visual image and symbolic value. The NYPD, though, is also producing chaos and disorder with its unpredictable and indiscriminate arrests. Its production of disorder appears to be part of its psy-ops (psychological operations) dating back to the policing of the WEF to send a message of NYPD authority and to dissuade people from protesting, from becoming political subjects, or from being close to, or being perceived as associated with, protesters (as Ann Maurer and Hacer Dinler were).

### Lengthy, Degrading, and Torturous Postarrest Detentions

As discussed above, NYPD RNC planning decisions not to issue summonses to RNC arrestees for minor violations, to require all RNC arrestees to be fingerprinted, and to use Pier 57 as the PASS foreseeably would lead to lengthy detentions. How long were RNC arrestees detained? The NYCLU received reports on length of detention from 169 RNC arrestees, 111 of whom (65.7 percent) were detained longer than the state constitutional rule of twenty-four hours. Outrageously, thirty-eight were held between forty-five and forty-nine hours, and seven were detained longer than fifty hours.[120] Deirdre MacNamara, a teacher, spent fifty hours in custody "after she was arrested on her way to buy a Wendy's Milkshake."[121] When reports began to emerge about the conditions at Pier 57 and the length of detentions, United for Peace and Justice began to stage protests outside Pier 57 (which were monitored by Intel).[122] A state judge set deadlines for the city either to bring detainees to court or to release them during the last two days of the convention. The city failed to meet the deadlines, and the judge held the city in contempt of court. Another state judge issued an order requiring that defense attorneys have access to clients while they were being held in custody. The city refused to honor the court's order.[123]

Why were detentions so long? The city blamed the state, claiming that it took "five or six hours to get fingerprints from Albany." According to "state officials," however, "94 percent of the fingerprint reports" were sent to the city in "one hour or less," leading civil rights lawyer Norman Siegel to argue at the time, and lawyers in a class action lawsuit to echo later, that the city was engaged in "preventative detention" for the RNC.[124] Was it possible to process such large numbers of arrestees more quickly? In fact, during the negotiated management era, 1,691 people were arrested on June 14, 1982, at disarmament demonstrations in New York, which was 30 percent more than were arrested in conjunction with the RNC on any one day, and they were processed on the same day within "several" hours, "often within a few hours."[125]

Not only was the length of time that the NYPD forced RNC arrestees to spend in custody cruelly excessive, the conditions of their detention were degrading, and in some instances torturous. Arrested Critical Mass riders (along with others swept up in the mass arrest) were taken to Pier 57, the PASS, and then transported to the Tombs the next day for processing. Some were in custody for processing as long as thirty-six hours.[126] The conditions at Pier 57 were "terrible."[127] Arrestees were put into overcrowded fenced cages topped with barbed and razor wire. The floors were covered with motor oil, transmission fluid, and other hazardous chemicals.[128] With inadequate seating and no place to sleep, arrestees were forced to lie on the floor, exposed to the hazardous chemicals. Because of inadequate facilities, over the course of the convention, many were forced to relieve themselves on the floor.[129]

By the time the Critical Mass arrestees arrived at the Tombs (where they encountered Joshua Kinberg, who was detained for twenty-four hours after being arrested during his MSNBC interview), they were dirty from having spent the night sleeping on the floors covered with soot and hazardous substances at what they were now calling "Lil' Gitmo."[130] Since all they were wearing were their T-shirts and bicycle shorts from when they were arrested, there was little to limit their exposure to the hazardous substances on the floor, and they were already developing "serious skin rashes."[131] (After the RNC, at least forty officers stationed at Pier 57 complained of chemical and asbestos exposure.[132]) One rider considered the plan to bring arrestees to the dirty, crowded cages at Pier 57 with inadequate facilities to be an attempt to break people physically and mentally. At the Tombs for processing, police verbally degraded the riders for being dirty: "Why are you so dirty and crusty punks?"[133]

The RNC protesters were singled out for harassment and degradation in their interactions with NYPD in the streets, while at the Pier 57 PASS, and at the Tombs/Central Booking. One protester complained of being verbally abused by police for his anti-Bush shirt. Plainclothes officers riding unmarked scooters drove into a group of protesters, dangerously expressing their aggressiveness toward protesters. Officers at Pier 57 called a woman who had a partially amputated leg "crip." At Central Booking, Critical Mass riders were degraded for being dirty from their detention at Pier 57. Women complained of sexual harassment at Pier 57, and other arrestees at Central Booking were "repeatedly referred to" as "liberal scum."[134]

In addition to being debased, those requiring medical care during their detention were torturously discouraged, ignored, or denied.[135] One man with a corneal ulcer requiring a regimen of antibiotics and steroids was refused access to his medication. Another man with kidney stones who took prescribed pain medication should the stones begin to pass was refused his medication.[136] Women who were menstruating had no access to sanitary items.[137] Hacer Dinler, who was on her way to work when she was trapped in an indiscriminate mass arrest at Union Square, asked for medical attention repeatedly for two hours but was ignored. She was finally taken to the hospital when she fainted and experienced convulsions.[138] While the filthy conditions of the PASS in conjunction with being forced to relieve oneself on the floor and being denied sanitary items amounted to a degradation ritual, the exposure of protesters to toxic chemicals during their detention and the denial of medical care amounts to torturous treatment. Both are forms of extrajudicial punishment for protesting.

Over 90 percent of the cases involving RNC arrestees were either dismissed outright or conditionally or resulted in acquittals.[139] For example, the prosecutor declined to prosecute the 227 who were arrested at the War Resisters League demonstration.[140] In light of the lack of probable cause for so many of the RNC arrests, New York City was sued in class action lawsuits by numerous plaintiffs, including the War Resisters League, Hacer Dinler, Deirdre MacNamara, and many others.[141] In a "Memorandum of Understanding" reached in conference with Magistrate Judge James C. Francis IV dated December 9, 2013, the City of New York settled outstanding RNC cases with plaintiffs for $18 million (after having spent $16 million in legal fees fighting the lawsuits), the largest settlement for damages arising out of policing protest in U.S. history.[142]

From the perspective of technocratic risk management that functions as the premise for strategic incapacitation, one would expect such a significant settlement to be considered a costly risk of inefficient policing practices to be avoided by police and city managers in future calculations. The budgetary organization of New York City government, however, protects the NYPD from having to assume responsibility for these costs, thereby enabling, if not approving, such abusive policing regardless of its costs from a risk management perspective. While monetary damages arising out of civil litigation are subtracted from the Health and Hospital Corporation's budget in New York to encourage improved "risk and litigation management," damages arising out of successful civil rights suits are not taken from the NYPD's budget. Instead, damages come out of the City of New York's budget as a whole.[143] Therefore, the NYPD has no budgetary incentive to change the way it polices. More broadly, cities in the United States—or the RNC host committee itself, in the case of the 2008 RNC in St. Paul, Minnesota—purchase special insurance policies to insulate themselves financially from damages arising from the abusive policing of mega-events.[144] These are governmental arrangements designed to avoid the costs of inefficient risk management.

The organization of New York City government insulating the NYPD from budgetary consequences arising from abusive policing indicates that strategic incapacitation, the conceptualization of protest policing at mega-events which is situated in a broader understanding of policing as technocratic risk management, fails to grasp how abusive protest policing is not an exceptional or excessive deviation from otherwise coldly calculating police conduct.[145] This insight likewise undermines Wendy Brown's broader effort to theorize neoliberal government as solely an "economization" of the state, social policy, or law, a form of government where "economic metrics govern the institutions and practices of the state."[146] Clearly, economic metrics do not govern the NYPD or its protest policing. Abuses arising from the NYPD's protest policing are not ancillary to a primary goal of efficiently providing security services. The NYPD is integrated within a postlegitimation state formation that is affectively attached to post-democratic policing of protest. The abuses are part of their practice of policing protest.

### The Limits of Law and Courts

Should we nevertheless be consoled that civil litigation forced New York City to take responsibility for the NYPD's injurious policing at the RNC with a landmark settlement and, in litigation unrelated to the RNC, that Judge Haight modified the Handschu decree to enhance oversight of the Intelligence Division's surveillance with his March 13, 2017, order?[147] Considering that the financial settlement for violations of protesters' rights came more than nine years after the NYPD's abuses, and enhanced oversight of Intel's surveillance occurred after fifteen years of NYPD abuse, the accountability imposed by the courts is too little, too late to amount to political responsibility. Preventative policing of political demonstrations, in addition to unrestrained surveillance of city residents and visitors, foreclosed political possibilities that will never return. As conservative legal theorist Carl Schmitt, who facilitated the rise of the Nazis in Germany, observed, in "a race between the executive and the judiciary, the judiciary will mostly arrive too late."[148] Likewise, the judiciary has arrived too late to redress twenty-first-century political repression in New York.

Yet more disturbing, though, is what the judiciary has found to be acceptable policing by the NYPD. Consistent with post-democratic First Amendment jurisprudence described in chapter 1, Judge Sullivan, the federal judge responsible for the class action suits that would result in the settlement overseen by Magistrate Judge Francis, sustained the constitutionality of the 2004 RNC no-summons policy against First Amendment challenge. The no-summons policy forced RNC arrestees to endure a time-consuming, dangerous, and degrading Mass Arrest Processing Plan even when charged with the most minor, noncriminal violations.[149]

Sullivan acknowledged that the no-summons policy, applying only to those protesting the RNC, was content based and therefore would have to be subjected to the strictest judicial scrutiny. In his hands, however, strict judicial scrutiny became yielding deference to the NYPD. Sullivan found the policy to respond to the compelling interests of "preventing terrorist and anarchist attacks."[150] In his discussion of whether the no-summons policy was narrowly tailored to those interests, however, we can see how very broad concerns about "masses of demonstrators" coming to protest the RNC who could create "mass disorder" and "mass chaos" by functionally shutting down the city also motivated the policy.[151] NYPD "information," as well as "common sense," led Sullivan to conclude that people coming from out of town "for the sole purpose of protesting" the RNC were more likely to "repeat their illegal conduct," if not removed from the scene, than "street vendors who place their carts in a location that blocks traffic, or even City-based labor protesters seeking to temporarily impede traffic to have their views heard."[152] Because no "intelligence" suggesting RNC delegates or vendors, who also would have traveled to New York to demonstrate, wanted to disrupt the RNC or shut down the city, it would have been "overreaching, not to mention foolish, to apply the No-Summons Policy to them."[153]

In other words, Sullivan justified a policy that targeted anti-RNC protesters exercising First Amendment rights for a more onerous process when charged with minor violations than either commercial vendors not exercising First Amendment rights, or others exercising First Amendment rights unrelated to the RNC, or even those who might have also traveled to New York to demonstrate their views, but who were supportive of the RNC. By legally ratifying how the NYPD selected those exercising First Amendment rights criticizing Republican government's policies of neoliberalism, groundless war, torture, and internment camps for more onerous treatment based on their political views than those engaged in commerce or symbolic production to be circulated through the networks of communicative capitalism, Sullivan's ruling contributes one more case to the demise of the First Amendment's preferred position doctrine. It is another case indicating the emergence of a post-democratic First Amendment jurisprudence.

Sullivan also viewed the limited temporality of the no-summons policy favorably. Because the no-summons policy was "in place only for the brief duration the threat existed" (that is, while New York hosted the RNC), and because New York had "no 'viable alternatives' given the masses of demonstrators" coming to protest, Sullivan sustained its constitutionality.[154] By legally ratifying this exceptional, temporary decree targeting a substantive political viewpoint, Sullivan's ruling is doubly unsustainable from a perspective of legal legitimacy, indicating the legal rationalization of postlegitimation state practices.[155] Neoliberal, post-Fordist communicative production has superseded concerns with either democracy or legal legitimacy. Sullivan's judicial deference to the NYPD, in conjunction with the insulation of the NYPD's budget from financial penalty arising from its legal violations, therefore, suggests we might supplement Schmitt. Rather than merely arriving too late, at the end of the day, where the NYPD is concerned, the judiciary might not matter at all.

### A New Regime of Protest Policing

As we have seen, the NYPD's policing of the 2004 RNC was a product of institutional learning from how it policed the 2002 WEF, responding to weaknesses identified in Graham's "After Action Report" in intelligence and in managing mass arrests, on the one hand, and building on identified strengths, such as the use of undercover officers and exercises in intimidation of protesters, on the other. Graham also visited several other NSSEs to study "what the demonstrators did or didn't do," including the 2001 inauguration, the 2003 FTAA in Miami, the 2004 G-8 Summit on Sea Island, Georgia, and the 2004 DNC in Boston.[156] The process of hosting NSSEs and their repetition, then, has facilitated a vertical dissemination of security arrangements for policing protest, and has stimulated a post-democratic, postlegitimation model of policing protests that remains institutionalized within a city after the event, and becomes further developed by hosting subsequent events thereafter. The combination of post–fiscal crisis urban political economy and security planning materials deriving from the Department of Justice, in addition to preparation by observing how other cities police mega-events, means that factors producing post-democratic protest policing exceed a particular municipality's police department or locality's political culture.[157]

New York's hosting of the 2004 RNC is an institutional exhibition of the combination of factors contributing to post-democratic protest policing. The NYPD's particular inflection of these broader tendencies includes these elements: an expansive use of surveillance unhinged from reasonable suspicion of crime that targets even the most mundane First Amendment activities; an enhanced capacity for mass arrests; an institutionalized sense of guilt by association triggering often indiscriminate mass arrests; an institutional willingness to engage in preventative arrests; the use of trap-and-arrest tactics for large groups; the use of targeted and selective arrests informed by Intel's monitoring for individuals; and the establishment of an arrest processing system that lengthens time arrestees spend in detention under conditions that are both materially harsh and symbolically degrading to exercise extrajudicial punishment. Collectively, these aspects of NYPD protest polic-ing contribute to the city's image production while disordering the appear-ance of political agency.

New York City's bid to host the 2004 RNC allowed the NYPD to build an institutional capacity for post-democratic and postlegitimation protest policing. Why do it at all? Why police in a manner that is post-democratic and that is deaf to concerns regarding normative legitimacy? This question has at least two answers based upon the discussion in this chapter. First, neoliberal, post-Fordist urban political economy relies on hosting mega-events that are managed without disruption, as already discussed. There-fore, post-democratic, postlegitimation policing is the policing that develops from hosting NSSEs and viewing the production of mega-events as an urban imperative. The second reason can be sifted from the WEF reports, like Cap-tain Timothy Hardiman's praise of staging corrections buses with windows covered by metal grids for their "powerful psychological effect," Deputy In-spector Michael Shortell's enjoyment of police intimidation of protesters when he praised the staging of massive amounts of equipment for the effect it had on WEF protesters, or Graham's identification of "disorder helmets" as a "deterrent" and his positive assessment of proactive arrests for setting a "tone" with demonstrators: the NYPD enjoys post-democratic, postlegitima-tion protest policing.[158] This enjoyment, evident in the verbal abuse of RNC protesters by police on the street, in the Pier 57 PASS, and at Central Book-ing during the 2004 RNC, becomes yet more evident when we also consider officers telling antiwar demonstrators on February 15, 2003, to "go home," telling an injured demonstrator, "that is what you get for protesting," or call-ing demonstrators "FUCKING SCUMBAG" or "fucking cunt," in addition to the argumentative interrogations of those arrested at the February 15 anti-war protests.[159] In short, whether the NYPD is securing the symbolic value of New York City aesthetic production or enacting rituals of degradation upon protesters or those arrested for protesting, the NYPD's policing is ex-pressively communicative.[160]

The exercise of state power that is expressively communicative to engen-der fear and intimidation is similar to sovereign power terrorizing a popula-tion into submission with the spectacle of incalculably painful punishments during France's ancien régime described by Michel Foucault.[161] While tor-turous cruelties might maintain sovereignty, it comes at the cost of petty disorders (pickpockets working the crowd at an execution, labor lost in at-tendance of an execution) and the threat of revolt. Power that depends upon producing a fearful spectacle is at risk if the people interpret the spectacle as a sign of the sovereign's injustice. Then order becomes contingent on the superior might of armed forces and their capacity to prevent and put down a revolt. With respect to the contemporary state, recourse to extralegal intimidation of the people and cruel extrajudicial punishment indicates a state formation forsaking democratic or normative legitimation concerns, a rejection that erodes the public trust. This leaves order to be managed increasingly by control technologies that the state lacked during the escalated force era, and an armed capacity that is now superior to what the state possessed in the escalated force era. This is the post-democratic, postlegitimation state of neoliberal authoritarianism.

## Conclusion

This chapter describes how hosting the 2004 RNC affected NYPD protest policing. Determined to advertise recovery after the attacks of September 11, 2001, New York City bid to host several mega-events, succeeding in its 2004 RNC bid. In preparation, New York hosted the 2002 WEF. Learning from perceived weaknesses and strengths from policing the 2002 WEF, the NYPD expanded its capacity to monitor political activity within the Intelligence Division, and transformed its mass arrest processing. By instituting a no-summons policy for RNC demonstrators, by deciding to require all RNC arrestees to be fingerprinted, and by locating the postarrest staging site at Pier 57, which lacked fingerprinting capability but would dirty detainees and expose them to degrading and hazardous conditions, the NYPD foreseeably subjected protesters to unnecessarily long and unhealthy periods of custody after arrest. Although over 90 percent of all arrestees had their charges dismissed, the NYPD had already punished them with their postarrest process for the RNC.[162]

The surveillance of political activity prior to and during the 2004 RNC, in addition to the preventative arrests this surveillance facilitated, are consistent with the expectations of the strategic incapacitation model of protest policing and indicate that negotiated management has been superseded. The NYPD's efforts to intimidate and degrade protesters on the streets and in custody, however, are at odds with the premises of strategic incapacitation. Strategic incapacitation is an extension of the new penology's claims that policing and punishment are being arranged to manage the risk of unruly populations. The NYPD's affective attachment to expressive intimidation, and its enjoyment of cruelty in its protest policing, are not well captured by the new penology's depiction of police, prison, and parole institutions as technocratic managers of risk. Indeed, the NYPD is insulated from the costs arising from their legal violations. By focusing on efficient risk management, scholarship on policing of protest, scholars of policing and punishment, and theorists of neoliberalism miss the expressive dimensions of contemporary protest policing and the affective attachment to post-democratic, postlegitimation state practices.

The expanded capacity for surveillance, in conjunction with a proactive, prevention-oriented concept of policing exceeding mere law enforcement led to targeted arrests of individuals and groups during the 2004 RNC. In this regard, the NYPD plays a role protecting communicative capitalism, enhancing the symbolic value of the city's image and of capital's brands embedded within the city's landscape. Therefore, analyses should go beyond identifying the NYPD with order maintenance and guarding against disorder, no matter how minor. Indeed, both the NYPD's targeted arrests and their indiscriminate mass arrests produce disorder. They negate political agency, disorganize the appearance of the people as political subjects, and engender uncertainty, if not fear, corrosive of political solidarity necessary for any non-market-centered collective action. Of course it is subjectively unsettling to discover one has been monitored and selected for arrest on political grounds, and this can chill First Amendment activity. The NYPD's indiscriminate mass arrests, though, go further. Their indiscriminate arrests mean that someone like Deirdre MacNamara or Hacer Dinler can be on public streets either to buy a milkshake or to go to work and be at risk of arrest if, based on police perception, one appears associated with protesters. This can lead to behavior, like Ann Maurer's, to avoid being with a group or even perceived to be with a group, out of fear of being arrested. Such uncertainty of arrest not only chills political expression or mobilization. It chills even curiosity to listen to a speaker or to watch a demonstration out of fear of being associated with a political assembly the police may be targeting for repression.[163] Thus, while extrajudicial punishment enacted upon protesters by police is an attribute of a postlegitimation state, both the NYPD's selective arrests and their indiscriminate mass arrests are attributes of a post-democratic state. This is the security legacy the 2004 RNC left within the NYPD, and it would be deployed seven years later against Occupy Wall Street.

# Chapter Three

# Policing the Uprising
## Occupy Wall Street and Order Maintenance Policing

The effort to reclaim the city is the struggle of democracy itself.
—MICHAEL SORKIN, *Variations on a Theme Park* (1992)

Stop resisting!
—UNIDENTIFIED NYPD OFFICER (March 17, 2012)

POLICING PROTEST SCHOLARSHIP centering on international economic summits and other mega-events finds a more aggressive policing of demonstrations has superseded the negotiated management approach of dialogic interaction between police and protesters. Likewise, scholarship focusing on how more domestic or localized protests are policed in the United States finds negotiated management to be displaced by a more overbearing policing style informed by the "Broken Windows" concept of order maintenance policing. Whether the protest occurs at a mega-event classified as a national special security event (NSSE) with world or national leaders in attendance, or if it occurs under more everyday circumstances, negotiated management has been displaced by a more forceful police reaction to protesters.

This chapter elaborates how policing protest has become more aggressive, as illustrated by the quick resort to arrests and use of force, than the negotiated management model of protester-police interaction outlines by analyzing how the New York Police Department (NYPD) policed Occupy Wall Street (Occupy or OWS). In addition to the security legacy left behind after New York hosted the 2002 World Economic Forum (WEF) and 2004 Republican National Convention (RNC), we will see how the NYPD's commitment to the "Broken Windows" concept of order maintenance policing results in an aggressive, if not violent, approach to protesters. Although other scholarship also finds the "Broken Windows" approach to policing explains the NYPD's heavy-handed response to demonstrations, I expand on this scholarship by highlighting, as I did in chapter 2, the excessive, disorderly, and expressive dimensions of NYPD protest policing. These excesses indicate affective attachment to post-democratic neoliberal state practices. They also reflect the NYPD's efforts to pacify the people through the threat of cruelty or by subjecting protesters to postlegitimation state practices of extrajudicial punishment through a time-consuming, unpleasant, and degrading custody associated with arrest.

The current chapter uses personal or telephone interviews with activists involved with Occupy, and with lawyers who either served as legal observers at OWS demonstrations or defended activists. The interviews allow me to document not only forms of police conduct, but the effects of this style of protest policing on protesters exercising their First Amendment rights in New York.[1] This chapter also examines legal documents arising out of civil actions against the NYPD by protesters arguing their civil rights were violated. By attending to the results of motions to dismiss and motions for summary judgment in these cases, we can begin to understand which forms of police conduct are not judicially considered abuse of force, which forms of conduct may or may not be considered abuse of force—constituting a gray area for the use of force—and which are considered abuse of force. For a better apprehension of how the NYPD policed OWS, I also refer to press coverage, videos of actions, and books recounting the Occupy movement by participants or journalists.

Chapter 2's discussion of security preparations for, and policing of, the 2004 RNC and the current chapter's attention to the policing of OWS bring into focus how an increasingly authoritarian policing of protest taking shape since the late 1990s in the United States is the result of two institutional influences. It results, on the one hand, from the vertical dissemination of protest policing tactics that occurs when cities host mega-events. On the other hand, it results from the horizontal dissemination of the "Broken Windows" concept of policing through the movement of police managers among different policing agencies and private security consulting services, in conjunction with the symbolic significance of large urban police departments that have expressively adopted the "Broken Windows" concept of policing.[2] The aggressive policing of protest is, therefore, overdetermined, and its presence in New York City is especially evident as New York is well known both for the mega-events it hosts and for its early commitment to the "Broken Windows" theory of policing.[3]

By underlining the disorderly and expressive effects of contemporary protest policing, this chapter, like chapter 2, contributes to a more sophisticated understanding of the neoliberal state's power. Neoliberalism does not receive political support because of supposed technocratic efficiency or rationality. Demonstrations of its lack of efficiency or rationality by scholars and journalists have done little to weaken this state formation.[4] The policing of Occupy, which was notoriously expressive and disorderly at times, provides a lever to grasp how subjects become attached to neoliberalism and enjoy it. It exhibits the political basis of neoliberalism.

## Broken Windows and Policing Protest

### NYPD Command and Control Protest Policing

Alex Vitale's important work on policing protest addresses how different municipalities police protest distinctively—Miami polices protest more militaristically, while New York polices protest more in keeping with the NYPD's commitment to the "Broken Windows" theory of policing.[5] According to Vitale, the NYPD no longer adheres to the negotiated management approach to demonstrations. Instead, the NYPD follows a command and control style of policing protest.[6] Vitale characterizes command and control as the "hierarchical micro-management of demonstrations."[7] Command and control "sets clear and strict guidelines on acceptable behavior with very little negotiation with demonstration organizers." It utilizes "inflexible regulatory practices" in which "nothing is left to chance." Command and control has "zero tolerance" for even the most minor violations of the law or a permit, and will use force, if necessary, "even against peaceful protests," should any violation occur. Because command and control is the protest policing dimension of the NYPD's commitment to the "Broken Windows" concept of order maintenance policing, the NYPD's devotion to "zero tolerance," "quality of life," order maintenance policing means it has an institutional "aversion to disruption" and will "prevent demonstrations from interfering with the normal functioning of the city."[8] By micromanaging demonstrations, leaving nothing to chance, and by reacting with zero tolerance to even minor violations of the law or a permit, Vitale depicts the NYPD as an almost hyper-Weberian bureaucratic machine that coldly and ruthlessly enforces the law to its letter.

Vitale describes his portrait of the NYPD's protest policing as similar to that of John Noakes and Patrick Gillham, who argue that mega-event protests in the United States are now policed through "strategic incapacitation" based on risk assessments.[9] Analogous to the way that command and control is the protest policing expression of the "Broken Windows" concept of policing for Vitale, for Noakes and Gillham, "strategic incapacitation" is the protest policing expression of the new penology's "selective incapacitation philosophy of social control" that maintains a "utilitarian focus on preventing deviance."[10] The neoliberal new penology, in which command and control and strategic incapacitation are rooted, embraces a preventative, postrehabilitation risk management approach to crime and punishment.[11] The new penology's "affinity with a new 'actuarial' criminology," its emphasis on sorting, classifying, developing risk profiles, and "rationalizing the operation of the systems that manage criminals," highlights a mode of government that rationally calculates risk and technocratically manages it.[12]

This understanding of government is carried forward within both the strategic incapacitation and command and control models of policing protest. It is also carried forward in efforts to theorize neoliberal government more generally. According to Wendy Brown, the state, social policy, law, and rights undergo "economization" with the deepening influence of neoliberal reason.[13] Under neoliberalism's "steroidally charged form of Weberian instrumental rationality," this political reason "banishes nonmarket values and aims."[14] Therefore, Brown does not expect the neoliberal state to deploy "*excessive* uses of violence or extraconstitutional conduct," as economic metrics discipline government conduct to the most "efficient" or "prudent" courses of action.[15]

Vitale's concept of command and control protest policing, however, like Noakes and Gillham's depiction of strategic incapacitation at mega-events or Brown's theory of neoliberalism more generally, neglects the role of excess, indicating the significance of affective attachment to the NYPD's protest policing. By bringing forward that which exceeds utilitarian calculations in protest policing, such as affect, expressive policing, and the NYPD's role in New York's symbolic production, we will gain a more nuanced understanding of neoliberalism in terms of subjective attachment to the postdemocratic, postlegitimation state of neoliberal authoritarianism.

In the 1960s, conservatives fueled perception of a crime crisis in the United States. This crime crisis blurred conservatives' opposition to civil rights demonstrations with crime, riots, violence, and general lawlessness.[16] These conservatives preached obedience to authorities, advocated punishment, and urged a war on crime in response. For such conservatives, the Civil Rights movement was associated with crime, as was virtually any march, rally, protest, or assembly in a public place making visible grievances of the people.

In one well-publicized speech, former Supreme Court Justice Charles Whittaker complained that the Civil Rights movement, civil disobedience, demonstrations, and support for civil rights demonstrations by political leaders such as the secretary of state, the vice president, and even the president himself were spreading "mass lawlessness and violence" and were leading to riots and a "rash of crime." In response, he urged "swift, tough punishment."[17] Likewise, David Lawrence, editor of *U.S. News and World Report*, writing as the now-historic March on Washington was being planned, condemned President Kennedy for refusing to "deplore or discourage the coming 'demonstration' in Washington." He urged those who supported "law and order" to express it "at the polls in 1964."[18] In another essay, titled "The War against Crime," he asserted that the nation was suffering an unprecedented "crime wave" and referred to "street demonstrations" as putting a burden on police to "stop the violence of such mobs."[19]

Richard Nixon's 1968 presidential campaign famously used a Southern strategy to capture conservative, white Southerners—and white suburbanites—becoming disaffected from the Democratic Party for its support of civil rights legislation. Accepting the Republican nomination, he claimed to be responding to the voice of the "great majority of Americans" who were the "non-demonstrators" and who were "not guilty of the crime that plagues the land." By running for president on behalf of the "forgotten Americans," and by opening his acceptance speech by referring to "cities enveloped in smoke and flame," he reinforced the elision between crime, civil rights, demonstrations, and riots that knit together this new authoritarian political coalition around a nodal concern with "crime."[20] In his 1970 State of the Union address, Nixon asserted that the nation must declare a "war against the criminal elements" on behalf of "quality of life."[21] This conflation of civil rights, demonstrations, riots, and street crime indicates how crime represented more than an ordinary violation of the law in this conservative movement. Crime expressed resistance to civil rights, political democracy, and the aspiration that black people would count and have equal political voice in the United States. Crime exceeded ordinary criminality to suggest a political wrong.

The National Advisory Commission on Civil Disorders, better known as the Kerner Commission, issued its much-anticipated report on the 1960s urban riots in March 1968. Racial segregation, poverty, and racially abusive policing had produced seething frustration and anger in the black ghettos of American cities. This simmering discontent was stimulated further by rising expectations generated by important Supreme Court decisions and congressional legislation, on the one hand, and the recognition of a yawning gap between the promise of equality and the degrading material realities of life for black people in cities across the country, on the other. The report was exemplary of modernity's commitment to the human sciences, and the hegemonic social democratic orientation of the 1960s, with its efforts to identify the root causes of the disorder. The report recommended far-reaching action to close the gap between ideals and reality engendering a legitimation crisis for the state in the areas of education, housing, employment, and welfare. According to the report, as long as conditions of inequality remain, "a potential for disorder remains."[22]

The report became an overnight bestseller, and the basis of calls for the nation to make good on its democratic commitments.[23] According to scholars, reforms of policing that contributed to reducing the abuse of force by police were set in motion in the aftermath of the report's publication.[24] As part of these reforms of policing, the negotiated management style of policing protest in a less repressive manner also became established in the decades following the report's release.[25] Nixon's response to the release of the report from the campaign trail in New Hampshire, however, was deeply at odds with its hegemonic reception on network news or the pages of the *New York Times*. He complained that the report blamed everyone for the riots except the rioters.[26] The Nixon campaign was a wedge that managed to split not only the Democratic Party's northern and southern wings, but the hegemony of the social democratic horizon in U.S. political culture.

The 1970s were a decade of political disorientation in the United States. In the 1980s, Ronald Reagan revived not only Nixon's Southern strategy to become president, but street crime as a national preoccupation with his declared war on drugs (thereby directing attention away from crime in the corporate suites).[27] In 1982, the *Atlantic* published the essay "Broken Windows" by George Kelling and James Q. Wilson. In this enormously influential essay, "crime" concerning to the authors referred to the conduct of the poor in the streets. Much like for Nixon, crime exceeded ordinary legal violations for Kelling and Wilson. Kelling and Wilson, like Nixon and other conservatives, represented a reaction against conceptualizing policing as legally accountable law enforcement that the Kerner Commission had promoted. "Broken Windows," however, would not become a template for citywide policing in the United States until Rudolph Giuliani won election to become the New York City mayor in 1993 and appointed William Bratton as NYPD police commissioner. Bratton's appointment by Giuliani represented a victory for conceptualizing policing as order maintenance defending quality of life.[28] In other words, along with the proliferation of crime legislation that passed in Congress and in the states from the 1980s through the 2000s, and the massive growth in prison building in this period, Giuliani's victory, his appointment of Bratton as NYPD commissioner, and Bratton's embrace of the "Broken Windows" concept of policing represented important victories for political mobilization around a crime crisis. In conjunction with the neoliberal, post-Fordist response to the urban fiscal crisis of the 1970s, the response to the crime crisis produced transformations in policing at odds with tolerating political demonstrations of the people in the streets. The post-democratic shift in political culture corresponding to the crisis of democracy accommodated this more authoritarian approach to policing protest.

### "Broken Windows" Policing

Close attention to George Kelling and James Q. Wilson's essay, "Broken Windows," puts us on notice that its concept of order maintenance policing has investments that go beyond law enforcement, leading us to look for police behavior exceeding strict enforcement of the law and permits described by Vitale.[29] "Broken Windows" was published in 1982, when cities felt the effects of austerity measures associated with the disintermediation of cities from markets, the redirection of urban government away from meeting the social needs of city residents, urban government's attention to the needs of finance, insurance, and real estate, the redirection of urban infrastructures away from residents and toward tourists, and new city marketing efforts directed to potential visitors. "Broken Windows" makes police the primary agency responsible for addressing the growing number of urban residents with unmet social needs beginning in the 1980s. That is, "Broken Windows" expresses the neoliberal, post-Fordist state's concept of policing.

The authors of "Broken Windows" assert that disorder is associated with crime, and identify a fear of disorderly people to which order maintenance policing should respond.[30] Who are disorderly people? They are those with unmet social needs whom the neoliberal state governs distinctively in comparison with the social democratic state. According to Kelling and Wilson, they are disreputable or unpredictable people: "panhandlers, drunks, addicts, rowdy teenagers, prostitutes, loiterers, the mentally disturbed." As Kelling and Wilson admit, these people are not "violent, nor, necessarily criminals." The "Broken Windows" concept of policing is one that goes beyond law enforcement, strictly speaking, to address an ill-defined "disorder"—which they concede has "scarcely any legal meaning"—to make people "feel more secure."[31] In other words, the "Broken Windows" concept of policing is unmoored from the concept of legal legitimation; it is policing, as opposed to law enforcement.

"Broken Windows" functions to assist post-Fordist symbolic production. The "Broken Windows" concept of policing disorder is dedicated to the affective and aesthetic management of the urban environment. It makes people feel relieved and reassured by removing "undesirable persons from a neighborhood."[32] Its aesthetic management of the environment secures space for cultural production or consumer experiences.

Anticipating that some might question whether police behavior in accordance with Kelling and Wilson's advocacy could turn police into "agents of neighborhood bigotry," Kelling and Wilson concede, "We can offer no wholly satisfactory answer to this important question."[33] The "Broken Windows" concept of policing is a criminological expression of affective exhaustion regarding democratic commitments. "Broken Windows," therefore, is a template for post-democratic policing.

And what of the affective motivations of "Broken Windows"? Kelling and Wilson portray order maintenance policing as a response, in part, to the "urban riots" of the 1960s. Incited by poor and predominantly black frustration with existent urban material realities in contradiction with promises of democratic equality, to say nothing of the police brutality that often sparked the riots, order maintenance policing reacts to an expectation that police "do something." Kelling and Wilson hold out as a model for "doing something" the policing of a public housing project in Chicago. They quote one officer, who says, "We kick ass." Kelling and Wilson state that people approve of this, though they also concede this cannot be "easily reconciled with any conception of due process or fair treatment."[34] The "Broken Windows" concept of order maintenance policing, then, is also one that embraces a certain form of disorder and violence—one where police kick the asses of undesirable people. Motivated by an uprising of the poor and people of color, and by indicating that others approve of the police kicking ass, Kelling and Wilson's "Broken Windows" gives people and the police permission to enjoy postlegitimation, post-democratic policing targeting the poor and the mentally ill for abusive treatment and forced suppression.[35] "Broken Windows" provides important ideological support for the postlegitimation, post-democratic state formation of neoliberal authoritarianism.[36]

Because command and control protest policing is informed more broadly by the "Broken Windows" concept of order maintenance policing, the latter should lead us to be attentive not only to the NYPD's strict attention to minor legal violations or permits, but to its policing of protest that exceeds strict legalities, and how this policing of protest is part of a broader post-democratic orientation. The NYPD enforces the violation of disorderly conduct, for example, without attention to the First Amendment.[37] We cannot call this a strict enforcement of the law because it begs the question of which law ought to be enforced in particular circumstances.[38] Moreover, we should attend to occasions when the NYPD clearly exceeds law enforcement and acts arbitrarily, from a legal standpoint, when policing protest. Additionally, we should account for occasions when the NYPD tolerates, causes, or enjoys disorder when policing protest. Armed with an understanding of how the "Broken Windows" concept of policing exceeds law enforcement, Vitale's own insights become newly significant. He describes one of the NYPD's protest policing tactics as "shock and awe."[39] Shock and awe is a tactic that aims to demoralize one's enemies, to strike terror into their hearts and minds. As a tactic, it is powerful for expressive and affective reasons, in addition to providing an advantage of control due to the number of deployed officers in a particular location. Deploying the spectacle of awesome power to terrorize subjects is less an example of unyielding enforcement of legal minutiae than it is an act of extralegal intimidation that nests within, or helps create, a post-democratic symbolic field. It is the protest policing equivalent to the permission "Broken Windows" gives to enjoy the police kicking ass.

## Occupy!

Two thousand eleven. The year the people of the world revolted against neoliberalism. The year began with street demonstrations inspired by Mohamed Bouazizi's self-immolation leading to the Tunisian Revolution. Bouazizi was a street vendor who finally said "enough" to austerity and petty harassment from authorities. Events in Tunisia helped influence the uprising in Egypt against President Hosni Mubarak that included the occupation of Tahrir Square by tens of thousands.[40] By mid-February, thousands occupied the Wisconsin capitol for three weeks to protest Republican Governor Scott Walker's frontal assault on the collective bargaining rights of public sector workers and other austerity measures.[41] In June, New Yorkers opposed to Mayor Michael Bloomberg's proposed public sector layoffs and budget cuts to education and other social services occupied a location near City Hall in protest. Organized by New Yorkers against Budget Cuts, a coalition of educators, students, and union activists, the encampment lasted for three weeks and was the longest-running occupation New York had witnessed "in years."[42] In July, inmates in California's Pelican Bay "supermax," and throughout the California penal system, began a hunger strike protesting long-term solitary confinement policies.[43] Shortly after the protests of Bloomberg's budget cuts and public sector layoffs, *Adbusters* called for its readers to #occupywallstreet on September 17 ("bring a tent") with an image of a ballerina atop the Wall Street bull.[44] Galvanized by world events and Bloombergville, activists meeting at 16 Beaver Street helped organize an August 2, 2011, general assembly close to Wall Street. Among those assembled, someone held a homemade sign referring to Egypt, Greece, Spain, and Madison, Wisconsin.[45] General assemblies occurred thereafter on a weekly basis. With the Wall Street bull barricaded and Chase Manhattan Plaza closed off, on September 17, #occupywallstreet commenced.[46]

On September 17, a few thousand people converged on Zuccotti Park (also known as Liberty Plaza) in the Financial District, with a couple hundred spending that night in the park under the watchful eyes of the NYPD.[47] Zuccotti Park is classified as privately owned public space under the New York City zoning code, which presented certain legal advantages for the occupation. New York grants exemptions from certain zoning regulations to real estate developers on the condition that they dedicate some space under their ownership to the public.[48] While municipal park regulations typically provide for their closure at night, privately owned public spaces are presumptively open twenty-four hours unless the city permits the closure of such a public space, which it had not with regard to Zuccotti.[49]

Using a tactic once proposed by Martin Luther King Jr. to protest inequality in an urban setting (he called for a "camp-in" as a "middle road between riots and timid supplication of justice" to dislocate normal patterns "without destroying life and property"), Occupy Wall Street was an uprising against the inequality resulting from an economy that enriches the top 1 percent of society at the expense of the 99 percent.[50] It was also an uprising against the utter corruption of political institutions in the United States that not only block efforts to ameliorate such inequality but actively produce and entrench this order (represented by the infamous Supreme Court decision *Citizens United v. Federal Election Commission* in 2010 ruling campaign finance regulations unconstitutional for interfering with a corporation's free speech rights). Occupy sought to reinvigorate democracy with general assemblies and its critique of representational political institutions in favor of horizontal political organization.[51]

Occupy forced national and global attention to focus on economic injustice and political corruption under neoliberal conditions while maintaining its occupation of Zuccotti Park from September 17 until its eviction by the NYPD on November 15.[52] The OWS movement grew so fast in the United States and around the world that within a month it organized protests in over a hundred U.S. cities, and more than eighty countries, in a global day of action on October 15.[53] The occupation of public space enacted the social practices of meeting human needs while representing an insistent critique of contemporary political and economic institutions.[54] This articulation of meeting human needs with Occupy's political protests within public spaces around the United States and the world represented a fundamental critique of public space's closure to the people and their assembly. It also represented a critique of compelled participation within a neoliberal, post-Fordist state and its post-1970s juridical regime. OWS's symbolic practices of occupation represented the antagonism between neoliberal, post-Fordist government and the vision of democracy for which the movement struggled. Occupy expressed the people's right to be in public space, and the right to sharing in common requiring the organization of government and economy to meet the social needs of all rather than merely the few. Its social and symbolic practices were fundamentally at odds with order maintenance policing informed by "Broken Windows," and the broader state formation of neoliberal authoritarianism.

The significance of the politics of occupying public space against a neoliberal, post-Fordist state that cultivates the aesthetic environment for capital makes it easy to overlook OWS's important coalition work, and its identification of policy problems and proposed solutions to those problems for the well-being of the 99 percent. From its very first days, OWS made common cause with a variety of struggles against injustice and exploitation: on September 21, 2011, Occupiers marched, protesting Georgia's impending execution of Troy Davis as an example of the institutional racial injustice of policing and punishment in the United States.[55] Occupy held a vigil the night of his execution, and the next day, more than a thousand people marched in protest of Georgia's execution of Davis through the streets of New York in a "Day of Outrage." The protest gathered in Union Square to proclaim, "We are all Troy Davis," and marched to Zuccotti Park, where it joined in coalition with Occupiers encamped there.[56] On September 22, Occupy disrupted an art auction to call attention to the lockout of an art handler's union, and on September 27, OWS took a stand on behalf of postal workers.[57] After its eviction from Zuccotti Park, OWS practiced becoming more creative with its political actions in "spring training" during the winter and spring of 2012. Occupy working groups spun off numerous organizing efforts, such as Occupy Town Squares (to reclaim public space for common use), Strike Debt (to address the student debt crisis), and Occupy Homes (the foreclosure crisis), while forging coalitions to address numerous other injustices such as police brutality, climate change, labor rights, and immigrant rights. By fall 2012, its organizational capacity became integral to Hurricane Sandy relief efforts.[58]

Unfortunately, it is equally possible to tell the story of OWS through the NYPD's petty harassment, arrests, and violence against OWS. From the very beginning of the occupation, Occupiers were arrested. In the very first days of Occupy, the NYPD arrested Occupiers for wearing masks, or simply for writing on a sidewalk with chalk. One man was arrested when an NYPD officer claimed he jumped a barricade. *New York Times* reporters witnessed the event, however, and documented that he did not jump the barricade. The arrestee's charges were changed to disorderly conduct.[59] Tuesday, September 20, NYPD Captain Edward Winski arrested a schoolteacher for speaking into a megaphone. An Occupier holding a tarp in place over media equipment was arrested and dragged across the plaza, bloodying his hands. When it began to rain, officers removed the tarp covering media equipment, exposing it to the rain.[60] A few days later, police arrested eighty Occupiers returning from a march to Union Square. A small group of women penned by the NYPD's orange mesh were pepper sprayed needlessly by a white shirt (a high-level officer), Deputy Inspector Anthony Bologna, punishing them extrajudicially for protesting.[61] *New York Daily News* reporters were nearby, and video of the attack went viral.[62] Six Occupy protesters who were pepper sprayed by NYPD officers that day would settle their legal suits against the city for a total of $332,500.[63]

On Saturday, October 1, the two-week anniversary of OWS, the NYPD arrested over seven hundred marching from Manhattan to Brooklyn on the Brooklyn Bridge.[64] Two weeks later, the joint enterprise of Brookfield

*Figure 3.1* Occupy activists and legal observers described disproportionate uses of force by the NYPD to arrest protesters. Occupiers also perceived growing hostility on the part of NYPD officers toward OWS activists over time. The pictured arrests were made just after eviction, on November 17, 2011, a major day of action. PHOTO-GRAPHER: RAMIN TALAIE.

Properties and Mayor Bloomberg announced that Zuccotti Park would be cleared Friday, October 14 (the day before its global day of action), because it needed to be cleaned.[65] Occupiers worked through Thursday night scrubbing the park clean. Sympathizers flooded into the park to defend it early Friday morning—thousands were present—making the small park "full as it had never been before."[66] The eviction was called off. As OWS celebrated, the police "seemed especially vengeful."[67] Police Deputy Inspector Johnny Cardona was captured on video punching an Occupy protester on a march through the Financial District, and another officer ran over a legal observer's legs with a police scooter.[68]

The NYPD learned from its failure to evict OWS in mid-October. With two weeks of drills and training, orders to move forces to Lower Manhattan came at the "last minute" for what officers were told was "an exercise."[69]

According to someone speaking to the *New York Times* on the condition of anonymity, the "only people who were aware of them going into Zuccotti Park were at the very highest levels of the department."[70] Keeping tight control on information about the eviction plans within the highest echelons of the NYPD prevented officers from leaking the information to OWS so the NYPD could catch the Occupiers off-guard. At 1 a.m. on November 15, the NYPD assaulted the occupation with overwhelming numbers, klieg lights, and a prerecorded message booming from a public address system.[71] An LRAD was present.[72] As one Occupier described, "Eviction was huge. There were thousands of police there. I've never seen so many police in one place."[73]

Reporters and supporters were barred from the park. Members of the media were told they had to stay in a press pen; police vans obscured lines of sight; airspace above the park was closed to all aircraft but NYPD helicopters; and reporters discovered inside the park by police were treated roughly, with some getting either pepper sprayed or arrested.[74] One Occupy activist informed me that subway stops in Brooklyn were closed, as was the Brooklyn Bridge linking Brooklyn to Manhattan, which would have hindered OWS sympathizers from responding to a call for help and flooding the park with defenders as they had October 14.[75] The NYPD worked in conjunction with sanitation workers, who gathered protester belongings and other elements of the occupation, including the OWS library, for transportation "to the dump," symbolically associating the democratic political mobilization of OWS with

*Figure 3.2* One Occupier said she had never seen "so many police in one place" as she did when the NYPD evicted OWS from Zuccotti Park during the early morning hours of November 15, 2011. PHOTOGRAPHER: MARY ALTAFFER.

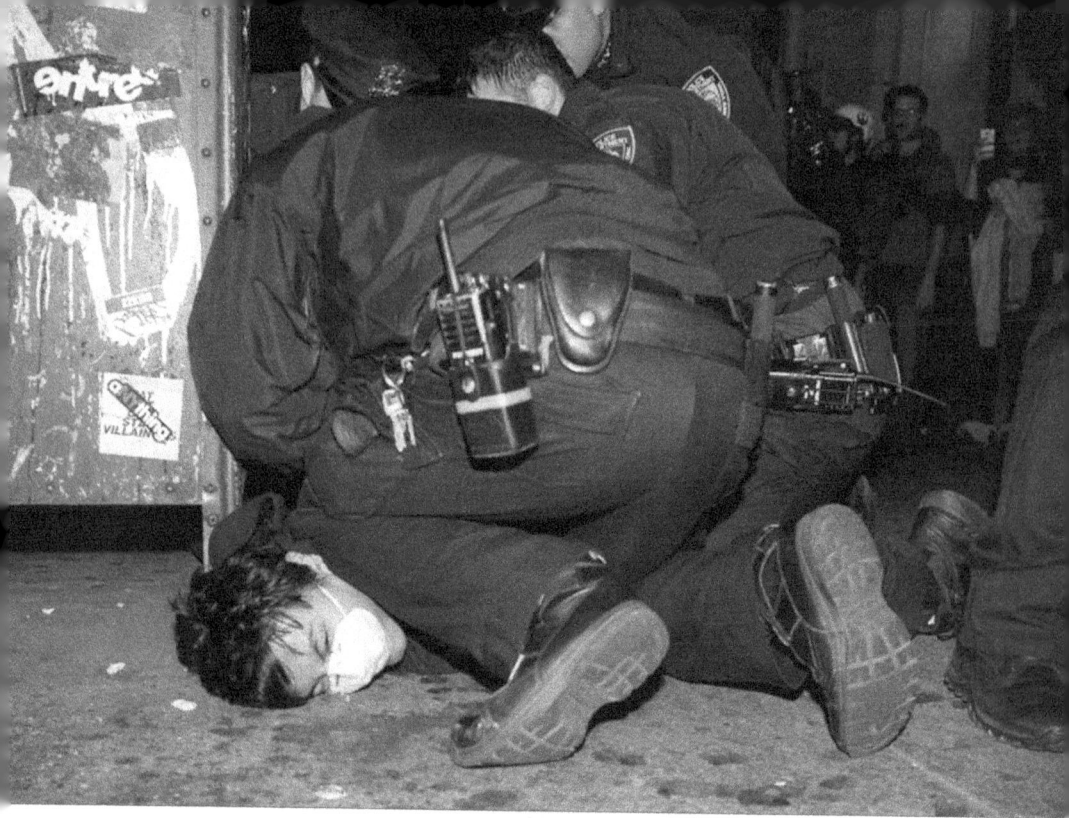

*Figure 3.3* The NYPD often uses multiple officers to conduct an arrest of a protester with overwhelming force, as shown here, where an activist is being arrested during the eviction of OWS from Zuccotti Park. PHOTOGRAPHER: DON EMMERT.

dirt or trash to be removed from the neoliberal, post-Fordist city.[76] The city would pay $350,000 to settle lawsuits stemming from the destruction of the People's Library, media equipment, and pedal-powered electrical generators during the eviction.[77]

At 3:30 a.m., the NYPD—some wearing riot helmets—began making arrests, and nearly two hundred people were arrested in total that night, including New York City Councilor Ydanis Rodriguez.[78] The NYPD established barriers around the park. Working in formation, they expanded the perimeter outward, yelling orders, threatening arrests, and using shields and batons to push Occupiers and those supporting them away from the park.[79] That morning, Occupiers flooded into an abandoned lot, owned in part by Trinity Church and in part by the city. Over twenty were arrested, including four journalists; among the arrested were reporters from the Associated

Press and the *New York Daily News*.[80] When Occupiers were finally allowed back into Zuccotti Park, they were forced to walk in single file through a "gauntlet" of officers. Those with tents or large backpacks were not permitted to enter the park, as if they were entering a high-security zone of an airport instead of a park formally open to the public.[81] (Throughout the winter, one could only enter this public park through a "check point," and those entering were subjected to a search of their bags.[82]) As New Yorkers observed at the time, Union Square was chock full of tents, generators, and food for consumers visiting its Holiday Market. The contradictory treatment of Zuccotti Park compared to Union Square marked the antagonism between Occupy's political speech and commerce in New York, and how commerce was privileged over speech.[83]

After forcibly ending the occupation of Zuccotti Park, the NYPD continued its abusive policing of OWS. On New Year's Eve, a small march in the

Figure 3.4 Hours after eviction, Occupy activists headed to Duarte Square, owned in part by Trinity Church and in part by New York City, located near Canal Street and Avenue of the Americas. Over twenty were arrested, including several journalists. PHOTOGRAPHER: BRENDAN MCDERMID.

East Village of about thirty Occupiers found themselves suddenly trapped by police on foot and on scooters (this is also known as kettling). Police accused OWS marchers of blocking traffic on the sidewalk.[84] Video showed that people using the sidewalk were able to walk past the marchers' procession, and that the sidewalk became blocked by the NYPD themselves when they trapped the marchers on it.[85] The NYPD ordered OWS marchers to disperse or face arrest, but by surrounding them, they had made dispersing impossible. Video showed Occupiers asking one officer where to exit, but once they made their way to where one officer directed them, another officer refused to allow them to exit. As disorder and confusion grew, an officer can be heard taunting the marchers, "Now you're all scared? Go home!"[86] The NYPD arrested at least fourteen that night. A legal observer was cuffed but later released.[87] Fourteen of the marchers sued the city for violating their First Amendment rights, and the city settled the case for $583,000.[88]

Interviews with Occupy activists disclose that the NYPD's most excessive brutality occurred on St. Patrick's Day, 2012—the six-month anniversary of Occupy Wall Street. One Occupier, "Catherine," recalled,

> There was one night, I guess it was March 17. . . . Those arrests were extremely brutal. We watched the cops come in [to Zuccotti Park]. . . . I was on the top . . . the northeast side of the park and we watched the cops come in in a formation. They had basically made three large single-file lines. . . . It was really threatening. It was really scary because we knew what [was] going to happen. You just saw that they were ready to like [smacks her hands together], you know, go at it. And so they came in and everyone was soft locked, and they just started grabbing people and hauling them off.[89]

Another Occupy activist, "Natasha," also described the police treatment of OWS on March 17: "The worst I ever saw the police was absolutely March 17, the six-month anniversary. That was the worst."[90] The barricades around Zuccotti Park from the eviction had finally come down. The day was warm; spring was coming, and people were celebrating and wearing green. There was joy among the Occupiers at being together in the park without the barriers again. During the evening, as it got dark, the crowd began to grow, not shrink, in part because the Left Forum had just ended its meeting around the corner. The police began talking about clearing the park shortly after midnight.

Natasha continued,

A bunch of friends of mine locked arms, and they sat down in the park to retake it. It was very organized, and very legible. . . . There was no threat. They were on the ground; the police were standing. They thought about the way it would look—they wanted it to look as passive as possible. . . . And the police came in batons *swinging*. Like swinging at the heads of my friends. . . . It was really horrifying to watch because even on the day of the eviction, they didn't come in swinging like that. . . . I've never seen them like this before. They were super rough with everyone. They arrested a ton of people. . . . It was disgusting.

She summed up: "All I know is I have never seen them as violent as that."[91]

Another Occupier, "Christine," echoed Natasha, recounting how there were some theatrical activities toward the back of the park when she heard someone yell from the front of the park that the police were surrounding it. She went with a group of people to the front and saw this was happening. "So we all sat down and locked arms," she recounted, "which I thought was amazing." Christine continued, "I really thought the police would just go away. Then one of them announced something on the bullhorn, and then suddenly they're sweeping into the line of people sitting on the ground with linked arms and just with batons flying and ripping kids up from the ground." Some people got frightened, and got up and tried to run, while others kept sitting. "They had one of the kids from Direct Action next to me, and they were choking him," she added. It was the most violent mass arrest she had seen up to that point. Christine described how the officers then grabbed her camera, and said, "Several cops had my arms, and like, my shirt was up. . . . And they sort of threw me to the ground and arrested me, and I was in a state of shock because I hadn't even planned on coming down, definitely not getting arrested, definitely not getting beat up."[92]

Another OWS activist arrested March 17 as part of the "soft lock" group in Zuccotti Park elaborated on the events Christine described. People were "sitting down, and locking arms, saying we aren't leaving this park, it is public space, it is our right to public space, and then they start arresting people." He recounted how the NYPD arrested him that night:

They grabbed me by my scarf [which had the effect of choking him] . . . and [I] got thrown to the ground, and this cop grabbed my thumb and bent it back. . . . We were locking arms, and we weren't making their job easier, and were sitting on the ground. And I did the going limp thing. But there was no need for him to really grab and bend my thumb, other than to inflict pain, because I had already been lifted away from someone else.

And then I screamed in pain and he did it again. . . . They really gang up and take six people to arrest one person. I was being kicked a bunch, and there was a cop standing on top of me with his boot on my head. . . . So it was incredibly violent.[93]

The police broke this Occupier's thumb when they arrested him that night. He was also bleeding from his ear due to blows to his head. After the arrests in Zuccotti Park, according to Catherine, "The remaining people took off and went up to Union Square. And there were just really brutal arrests. This one kid, the cops grabbed him and just slammed his head into an NYU building door. Out of nowhere. Just came up and grabbed him and threw him into the door."[94] At least seventy-three were arrested that night.[95]

As discussed in chapter 2, the report on the policing of the 1999 World Trade Organization (WTO) meeting in Seattle by the Citizens' Panel on WTO Operations criticized the Seattle Police Department for their treatment of protesters engaged in nonviolent civil disobedience, stating that their arrest should not be an occasion for summary punishment.[96] The exercise of extrajudicial punishment by the NYPD against those engaged in nonviolent civil disobedience—or the nonviolent assertion of their rights to public space may be a more accurate characterization of the soft-lock group in Zuccotti Park March 17—and the continuing retributive punishment of OWS marchers afterward indicate that negotiated management has been superseded in New York by a post-democratic, postlegitimation protest policing regime. The NYPD's brutality on the six-month anniversary of Occupy spurred OWS to lend their voice to those in New York who had been organizing against abusive policing for years, such as African American and Muslim groups, with a march against police violence Saturday, March 24, 2012, to criticize the NYPD's unconstitutional policing practices, such as stop and frisk and the surveillance of Muslims.[97]

Occupy's coalition-building efforts continued to be overshadowed by heavy-handed policing on May Day, May 1, 2012. The centerpiece of May 1 was a major solidarity march including labor, immigrant rights groups, and OWS, from Union Square south toward Lower Manhattan, ending in the Financial District. May Day events required significant organizing efforts, in part because Occupy believed that it ought not and need not ask for permission from governmental entities to use public spaces for First Amendment activities like speech, marches, assemblies, or the expression of grievances—that the people have a right to exercise these powers autonomously—and yet the main May Day march would be permitted by the City of New York.[98]

The day before May 1, police showed up at three different residences of OWS activists asking about May Day plans and about OWS leadership—an exercise of intimidation.[99] Another OWS activist was arrested in the evening of May 1 on a bogus warrant as a pretext to execute a sham arrest to take him into custody and question him.[100] Although a May 1 march in support of laborers' rights is traditional in New York, the NYPD was clearly preoccupied with policing OWS's participation in the day's events and issued an "event advisory bulletin" with six pages of OWS-associated warnings. The warnings were issued by NYPD Shield, the slogan of which is "Countering Terrorism *through* Information Sharing," illustrating how the NYPD conflated OWS with terrorism.[101] More than thirty demonstrators were arrested by the end of the day.[102]

An Occupy activist, "Sami," expressed his frustration with how OWS was policed during the May Day events. "May Day was one of the few moments in the movement's history where we chose to get for the main march a permit. You know what they did?" he asked. "They divided up. . . . They didn't follow the permit. The people followed the permitted routes, and they got separated and divided by the police. And that's when we took to the streets. They separated all the other groups from Occupy. So they're not playing fair." He contended this was an example of police efforts to separate OWS from the rest of the people.[103] By separating OWS from other marchers, the NYPD continued their practice, described in chapter 2, of disordering a visibly collective political agency, one that the May Day march sought to assemble through coalitional organizing.

Another Occupy activist described being harassed by members of the NYPD as part of a permitted event on May 1. He was the point person for the stage at the end of the march downtown near Bowling Green where there would be speakers and live music. During a sound check for one of the bands, a Community Affairs officer, known as "Hipster Cop" to OWS, began shouting at the Occupy point person. He complained that the sound was "too loud," though there was a permit that allowed amplified sound to a certain decibel level, which, according to the "sound guy," was not being exceeded. In other words, according to the legal permit, the sound was not too loud; it was only Hipster Cop's arbitrary opinion. For the Occupy activist, Hipster Cop's shouting felt like he was trying to create a false premise to arrest him, or he was "stepping in to show that he was going to be in control." The Occupy activist sought to pacify Hipster Cop, telling him, "If it is too loud, just let me know . . . and we'll turn it down," but Hipster Cop appeared "really irritated by me." Then he started shouting at the band to "play something" for him, not in a friendly way, but to bully them.[104]

Meanwhile, another white shirt was telling the Occupy activist that when the march arrived at the stage, they could not gather at the stage to listen to the music or speakers, but would have to keep marching past the stage, which "made no sense," since the very point of a stage with music or speakers is for people to be able to gather and listen. This added to his stress, particularly since he was not in possession of a physical copy of the permit (one of the unions had handled this), and he frantically began texting a lawyer (who sought to contact the union) to come downtown. Moreover, the permit was for a specific window of time, and the march was moving more slowly than planned, which added to the concerns of the OWS activist that time might run out on the permit. The OWS activist found another, older and calmer white-shirted cop, and tried to explain the situation to him, discussing the time limit. The officer said calmly but sternly that they would allow the rally to go fifteen minutes over the permitted time, but after that, they were "pulling the plug." The feeling the Occupy activist had, though, was that once the officer who would allow the rally to run fifteen minutes over walked away and Hipster Cop reappeared, everyone would get arrested. The OWS activist described the interactions with the NYPD over the event as "unpredictable." The dynamic changed when the lawyer and the union showed up, on the one hand, and thousands of marchers arrived, which included more institutionally recognized community and labor leaders, on the other.[105] As the appearance of the event shifted from the democratic rabble of OWS to more institutionally recognized civic and labor leaders, the feeling that arrests could happen at any moment receded. Hipster Cop's arbitrary commands, nevertheless, add weight to Sami's contentions that the NYPD and the city itself does not abide by the legal authorizations of the permits it issues.[106] This leads analysis beyond Vitale's description of NYPD protest policing that enforces permits strictly to their smallest detail, and toward a concept of postlegitimation policing.[107]

Demonstrators celebrated Occupy's birthday—or one-year anniversary—with numerous, simultaneous marches and protests throughout the Financial District on September 17, 2012. The NYPD responded by arresting 185 people associated with Occupy.[108] Goldman Sachs was especially well guarded by the NYPD. Five Occupiers sat down in front of the Goldman Sachs entrance, and, after a warning, the NYPD arrested them. Video showed plenty of space on the sidewalk for pedestrians to pass by or to enter the financial institution. In fact, the NYPD presence appeared to occupy more space on the sidewalk in front of Goldman Sachs than those representing the 99 percent.[109] Police also responded to the possibility of a "People's Wall" hindering access to the Financial District by erecting metal barricades across public sidewalks and streets, blockading the Financial District themselves. The NYPD required employee identification for access to barricaded blocks, causing "chaos" to Financial District traffic that day. The *New York Daily News* blamed the bankers' "Miserable Monday" on OWS, contradicting their own descriptions and photos of the "maze" of police barricades and identification requirements, as well as reports from other news organizations.[110] When the NYPD grabbed a man from the crowd on a sidewalk to arrest him, and he complained loudly that he had done nothing wrong as he was taken away, the NYPD pushed back journalists with batons, telling them no more photographs would be permitted, anticipating Donald Trump's hostility to news reporting.[111] Subsequent litigation arising from the policing of Occupy's one-year anniversary describes how Bishop George Packard, known as the "Occupy Bishop" for his ascent in flowing robes of a ladder to climb over the fence enclosing Duarte Square, a vacant lot owned by New York City and Trinity Church on December 17, 2011, led a group on a sidewalk by the New York Stock Exchange and Wall Street on September 17, 2012. The NYPD stopped him, and the "group was not able to proceed, nor was it allowed to turn back." He was arrested and spent eighteen hours in custody associated with the arrest, although his charges were later dismissed.[112]

This overview of how the NYPD policed Occupy between September 17, 2011, and September 17, 2012, lends partial support to Vitale's characterization of NYPD protest policing as command and control. We see how the NYPD strictly enforced regulations pertaining to a group wearing masks in public and to using an amplified sound system without a permit, and threatened to enforce the time period for the May Day permit strictly. We can add to Vitale's analysis, however, by attending to the more legally excessive aspects of the NYPD's protest policing. Bishop Packard's arrest on OWS's anniversary raises the question of which law the NYPD was enforcing strictly. By choosing to enforce the noncriminal violation of disorderly conduct, which is essentially the equivalent of a parking or traffic ticket, over the First Amendment to the U.S. Constitution, the right essential to the sovereignty of the people, we can characterize the NYPD's protest policing as post-democratic. This post-democratic orientation becomes more clear in light of the examples of NYPD protest policing that are legally groundless, such as the trap and arrest of OWS New Year's Eve marchers, the violent clearing of Zuccotti Park the night of March 17, and Hipster Cop's arbitrary harassment of the Occupy point person over the volume levels at the end of the May Day march. These examples illustrate the postlegitimation orientation to NYPD protest policing.

The post-democratic, postlegitimation orientation of the NYPD's protest policing is especially evident in instances where the NYPD is the cause of disorder, appears to enjoy the disorder it has caused, or exercises force expressively or vindictively to subjugate Occupy through violent acts that fall into the category of kicking ass. The NYPD is the cause of the disorder on the anniversary of OWS in the Financial District due to the maze of barriers it erected to bar public access to public sidewalks and streets out of desire to suppress Occupy. The NYPD is also the cause of the chaos deriving from its decision to kettle OWS marchers on New Year's Eve. The NYPD appears to enjoy the disorder, and the fear it apparently hoped to instill within protesters, when we consider the officer on New Year's Eve who taunts marchers by asking whether they were scared, and when he tells them to go home. The use of pepper spray on the women already barricaded within NYPD orange netting also exemplifies an expressive use of force. And the breaking of the peaceful Occupier's thumb is an instance of vindictive policing that uses extrajudicial violence as a tactic to intimidate subjects into submission. The legally excessive examples of NYPD protest policing going beyond the strict enforcement of minor violations discussed by Vitale bring into focus how NYPD protest policing is part of a post-democratic, postlegitimation state formation of neoliberal authoritarianism. They also allow us to understand neoliberalism as something more than the practice of utilitarian efficiency, as Brown depicts neoliberalism; they allow us to see affective attachment to neoliberalism, if not the conditions for subjective enjoyment of neoliberalism.

From September 17 through its one-year anniversary, OWS suffered heavy-handed policing. In the earlier days of the occupation, people would chant at the police, "You're part of the 99 percent!" and "Join us! Be with us!" But "the park changed in tone, definitely, in the days before eviction. It became a darker place." It became "a lot more confrontational" between Occupy and the police.[113] The "police started to seem resentful."[114] The persistence of Occupy engendered greater vindictiveness on the part of the NYPD, as seen with the March 17 arrests. Anything associated with Occupy became a target of excessive policing by the NYPD. Occupy activists described an instance in Bryant Park when there were about fifteen to twenty Occupy activists and thirty officers watching them. For a period of time in New York City, as this example illustrates, any event associated with Occupy would get an overwhelming police presence.[115]

Due to enduring petty or arbitrary police harassment, such as arbitrary arrests on public sidewalks, arrests for stepping off a sidewalk or writing with chalk, the removal of tarps protecting media equipment from the rain or the removal of generators as the weather got colder, in conjunction with experiencing more torturous forms of police brutality, the view of Occupy activists toward the police also shifted. One Occupy activist described how he got involved in OWS. He had been considering a move away from New York City and had been visiting the West Coast where he was watching Twitter one evening around a major OWS action in Times Square. He turned on the livestream and noticed that "tensions were building between the Occupiers and the police right at a barricade." The Occupiers then started chanting at the NYPD, "Over worked, under paid, we're doing this for you!" The Occupy activist said, "Something just clicked for me, I need to go down and check this out," and he returned to New York to become involved with OWS. After his experience with Occupy, however, he came to feel differently. He came to believe that the NYPD acted with "impunity." Referring to fast-moving events at a protest in a crowd, he described how it can be difficult to know which officer did what or to prove an officer committed a specific act of violence. He came to believe that the police are "not out there to protect the public." He had come to believe that the police were "terrifying." "It is interesting," he reflected, "because I started Occupy because of the chant, 'Overworked and underpaid, we're doing this for you,' but now I do not believe that police are people. They go through training and they go through a process of dehumanization in order to do their job."[116] Having witnessed and experienced the NYPD in an ongoing way with Occupy, he had come to view the police as a fearsome enemy.

### Chilling Effects, the Criminalization of Protest, and Occupy's Diversion

Lawyers who served as legal observers during the Occupy uprising described the NYPD's seemingly arbitrary policing, meaning demonstrators would have a difficult time knowing what the NYPD on a given day or in a given circumstance might permit, and what might make demonstrators subject to arrest.[117] This arbitrary policing of protest, in conjunction with excessive use of force to conduct arrests and overwhelming police presence at OWS demonstrations, created a chilling effect upon the exercise of First Amendment rights. This arbitrary, aggressive, and overwhelming police behavior also had the effect of diverting the Occupy movement away from its political purpose of protesting economic inequality to a preoccupation with the NYPD.

According to one legal observer, "Sally," sometimes the NYPD would "facilitate very, very actively the protests" and were sometimes "quite loose with their rules." Other times, though, they might police so "obsessively" that you could "put a *foot* on a street on a sidewalk march, and they might arrest you . . . a foot as in you are trying to avoid the garbage."[118] She speculated that this wide range in police conduct could be due to any number of reasons, from who was in command to the day of the week, the behavior of the protesters, where they were, or simply whether the police were tired.

Within a broader arc of the NYPD becoming more aggressive over time toward OWS, Sally found "frequent arbitrary rule application or changing the rules without explaining or any rational justification" on the part of the NYPD.[119] "So, sometimes it's unlawful to gather there, sometimes it's not unlawful to gather there. Sometimes you can bring in musical instruments to the park, sometimes you can't. Sometimes you can enter the park, sometimes you can't. Sometimes you can have a backpack, sometimes you can't. . . . There's so many examples like this where the rules just change." Sally observed that the NYPD's unpredictability left people feeling like "something fundamental about democracy is off." The constantly "changing rules" left protesters with a "really strong sense of injustice" that would get "reignited" every time they saw or experienced another example of arbitrary treatment.[120]

Another legal observer, "Allie," found the NYPD to act purposefully, even if it might appear to act arbitrarily to those without long-term experience observing NYPD protest policing. As a legal observer, she had seen NYPD control of protesters and their arrests of protesters "enough times to see it as policy, and not just an action that you see [on] a particular day." She speculated that an order would come from someone not present to clear a street, push protesters back, or to make arrests. Then, "you'd see a large cordon of police gather and start pushing the protesters back, and saying, 'if you don't leave this square block of pavement within the next minute, we're going to arrest you. . . . If you do x, y, or z things which are definitely not illegal in their own right, the threat would be real enough and enough people would get arrested in those contexts that people started backing away. . . . I've seen it many times." Nevertheless, she herself had gotten arrested on one occasion while legally observing. She mused, "It did show you the total arbitrariness of the situation and how easy it was to be in a situation where you are arrested and you have no power to get yourself out of that situation." Later in the interview, Allie described the NYPD's protest policing: "In some ways, it was totally arbitrary, and in other ways, it was very intentional."[121] Perhaps the arbitrariness Allie expressed is with respect to rules of law, and the purposefulness refers to the consistent post-democratic policing of Occupy.

The conditions of democracy, or the lack of democracy, are those experienced by protesters in the street during their acts of assembly and demonstration—this is the importance of looking at law "in action" or "on the ground," in addition to law "on the books," as Law and Society scholars urge.[122] The experience of OWS protesters, as described by Sally, was one of frustration at the contradiction between legal norms or democracy and the arbitrary treatment they experienced at the hands of the NYPD. Pointing to the significance of this, Sally explains how the frustration of Occupy activists was aggravated because there's "no way to really remedy [an officer's arbitrary rule application] in the moment."[123] Courts come too late to remedy the NYPD's preemption of constitutional rights in the streets; they come too late to restore the political possibilities suppressed by the NYPD's antipathy toward democratic mobilization or their active neglect of normative legitimation.[124]

A consequence of visibly arbitrary policing of protest, in addition to anger or a frustrating sense of injustice recounted by Sally, was that demonstrators would often try to be near her (legal observers wear bright green caps so they can be readily identifiable) so they would not be arrested, thinking that she either would know what the rules were or that she could help prevent their arrest. Although she kept her eyes "constantly peeled" in order not to be arrested for a variety of reasons, including the fact that a legal observer is not much good if she gets arrested, her arrest was ordered twice (though both times she was released without being charged or processed, which begs the question of whether she was being targeted by the NYPD and her arrests were for the purpose of intimidation). As she emphasized, if it is possible for someone "like [her], who has a really good sense of what's happening and is trying really hard not to be arrested, to get caught up, there's just no hope for anybody else."[125] In light of the unpredictable NYPD behavior—she described most of the OWS arrests as not due to civil disobedience, but due to police "grabbing people"—people would spend a march "wondering if they were going to be arrested," rather than focusing on the purpose and message of the demonstration.[126]

As an example of how anxiety about the NYPD can displace the substantive purposes of a protest or assembly, one Occupy activist told me about how she had been almost kettled without warning by the NYPD during an antiwar protest prior to OWS. Feeling "panic," she scrambled over the orange netting, which caused her to scrape her legs, and ran away to avoid arrest. She wanted to avoid arrest not only for the "hassle" but because she suffers from "health issues and anxiety issues." Describing how the NYPD polices protest, she told me, "You see, these things happen at random." Consequently, at marches she portrays herself as "vigilant and nervous at stuff," and tries to "keep an eye on exits, and on activity."[127] At demonstrations, her attention is anxiously preoccupied by the NYPD.

Added to the arbitrary behavior of the NYPD with respect to OWS was the overwhelming numbers of police dedicated to OWS demonstrations. According to Sally, the police presence at Occupy events could be "so excessively large, that it was really difficult to understand why, and it seemed unbelievable—like, I wouldn't believe it unless I had seen it for myself and had video of it." She elaborated, "You could have a situation of twenty, thirty protesters, entirely peaceful . . . on the sidewalk and you would have squads of scooters, senior officers who surely have better things to do, police officers with their batons out, large numbers on foot, squad cars following them. . . . And the proportionality of the police presence versus (a) the number of protesters, and (b) the behavior of the protesters was so excessive, it was difficult to describe without looking at video of how it happened." According to Sally, the excessive numbers of police at OWS events "was itself very intimidating for people, and especially intimidating for people who wouldn't necessarily call themselves 'Occupy protesters,' but who were in agreement with some of what Occupy was doing at certain points." People could find the overwhelming police presence to signal that this was not a safe environment in which to be, or one might believe that "there must be something illegal going on if there are all those police." She added, "It creates an appearance of wrongdoing, and stigmatizes the people who are involved in First Amendment–protected activity."[128] The NYPD police response to demonstrations or marches visually criminalized OWS, disqualifying their collective expression of grievance.

Sally also highlighted not only the large number of arrests of OWS protesters that occurred "basically every day," but the constant threats of arrest that framed OWS protests. Constant warnings, such as, "If you do this, you'll be arrested, or if you don't move from the sidewalk, you'll be arrested," aggravated the stress of an Occupy demonstration where the arbitrariness of police behavior was already enough to keep protesters on edge. Moreover, the visibility of arrests—to bystanders or their appearance in the media—in conjunction with "arbitrary rule application," produced an environment that

*Figure 3.5* The NYPD policed OWS marches by pinning the demonstrators to the sidewalk with officers on police scooters, accompanied by officers on foot and in patrol cars. This protest policing tactic separates protesters from other people. When the number of police is disproportionate to the number of demonstrators, this can create a visual criminalization of the march for onlookers or the experience for protesters of being criminalized for exercising First Amendment rights. Here, OWS protesters are marching on October 15, 2011, to Times Square. PHOTOGRAPHER: DAVID KARP.

could be experienced as "unpredictable for your own safety."[129] The NYPD created an environment in their policing of OWS that amplified the visible criminalization of protest in New York.

Aggravating the visible criminalization of protest was the violent and disproportionate manner in which the NYPD conducted arrests when responding to the "slightest infraction." From the legal observer Allie's perspective, aside from the Community Affairs Unit, the NYPD seemed to find it "desirable, from a policing perspective, to be seen as aggressive." Allie describes observing an OWS protest and seeing one person participating in the march who "literally puts one foot into the street." As soon as he does so, "he gets kicked by the cops, thrown to the ground, and within a minute, is into a police van."[130] The legal observer Sally summarized the consequences of this visible criminalization of protest by the NYPD, in conjunction with arbitrary rule enforcement, the constant threats of arrest, and the disproportionate police response to OWS: in addition to stigmatizing OWS and intimidating onlookers, NYPD conduct made it likely that many others would simply stay home for their own safety, or because they had to go to work the next day, or because they had children, or because they were not U.S. citizens, deterring the exercise of First Amendment rights.[131]

In addition to the chilling effect the NYPD produced in those who might exercise First Amendment rights, and the condition of anxiety the NYPD engendered in others, some Occupy activists became increasingly angry with the NYPD's protest policing.[132] People who were present at OWS "a lot," according to Sally, not only suffered from "constant anxiety" in protests about getting "pushed by a cop," "arrested," or seeing "someone violently arrested," but also "a lot of anger." As a result, some people she knew either "wouldn't go at all" to protests, or "stopped going because of how negative it felt for them."[133] As one Occupy activist put it to me, she feels "fired up" when she sees cops "beating up people." That's why "I don't attend protests, because I can only be there for a limited time before I feel *so* angry."[134]

As described by these legal observers and supported by interviews with other Occupy activists, NYPD protest policing has a chilling effect upon the exercise of First Amendment rights. For those Occupiers still courageous enough to protest, though, the aggression and violence of the NYPD's protest policing supplanted OWS's political purposes. Underlining Sally's observation that anxiety regarding whether one was going to get arrested distracted protester attention from the message of the demonstration, Allie also described how the police response to OWS diverted the Occupy movement. The NYPD's policing "became the focus of the attention of the protesters." The OWS activists found themselves "demanding [the] right to protest rather than pushing forward with whatever claims the protesters would be making."[135] Or, as Sami put it, "the key story ends up being not that they were protesting Wall Street; the key story is that they had an altercation with the police."[136] This points to the antagonism between marches, demonstrations, and assemblies as components of democratic practices, on the one hand, and NYPD protest policing, on the other, as a dimension of the neoliberal, post-Fordist state. It points, that is, to a distinctive state formation of neoliberal authoritarianism.

The NYPD's postlegitimation, post-democratic policing—which contributes to certain forms of disorder—rather than strict enforcement of legal minutiae, links the NYPD's protest policing to its general zero tolerance, quality of life, order maintenance policing informed by "Broken Windows." In both their general approach to city policing and in their approach to protest policing, as we have learned through interviews with Occupiers and legal observers of OWS, the NYPD polices less in accordance with law enforcement, strictly speaking, and more in accordance with their perceptions of who or what counts as disorderly. This converges with legal evidence regarding the NYPD's policing more generally. In statistics Judge Shira Scheindlin cites in *Floyd v. City of New York*, finding the NYPD's stop and frisk practices unconstitutional, between 2004 and 2009, "the percentage of stops where the officer failed to state a specific suspected crime [in his or her UF-250 arrest paperwork] rose from 1% to 36%."[137] Precinct recordings capture supervisors telling the rank and file to arrest first and worry about justifying the arrest legally later.[138] We can understand the statements of OWS legal observers describing legally arbitrary protest policing by the NYPD, then, to be part of a broader post–legal legitimation orientation to NYPD policing practices.

As we also know, Judge Scheindlin ruled that the NYPD's stop and frisk practices were unconstitutionally racially disproportionate.[139] The racially unequal NYPD stop and frisks criminalizing and symbolically degrading the racialized poor are police practices inconsistent with the democratic principle of equal citizenship. The visual criminalization and stigmatization of OWS protesters exercising First Amendment rights, then, is also a subset of the NYPD's broader post-democratic police practices: in both instances, the NYPD polices in a manner incompatible with democracy.

We see, as well, that the affective attachment to postlegitimation, post-democratic protest policing is part of the NYPD's broader affective attachment to policing unhinged from legal constraint or commitment to democratic principles of equal citizenship. At routine roll calls, the NYPD is exhorted in affective terms to exhibit contempt for local residents. In one instance, a supervisor sought to motivate the rank and file during roll call by stating, "They might live there, but we own the block. All right? We own the streets here." In another instance, an officer urged his fellow officers to "crush the fucking city."[140] The NYPD's general conduct might be legally arbitrary, but it is systematically directed to the control of space. This systematic effort is discursively expressed in terms that represent the resident population as if it were the enemy, and that motivate affective attachment to extralegal policing practices. The NYPD's affective attachment to postlegitimation, post-democratic protest policing, then, is a subset of a broader dedication to the policing depicted by Wilson and Kelling in "Broken Windows." As the officer quoted by Wilson and Kelling put it, "We kick ass."

In addition to the influence of the "Broken Windows" concept of policing upon NYPD protest policing, there is the legacy from hosting mega-events like the 2002 WEF and the 2004 RNC. We can complement Vitale's attention to the way that the NYPD's protest policing is determined by its commitment to the "Broken Windows" concept of policing with attention to how NYPD's institution building from 2002 and 2004 is layered on top of this longer-standing commitment to order maintenance policing. The NYPD protest policing regime, therefore, is the institutional result of zero tolerance policing of the streets sensitive to the mere appearance of disorder combined with its legacy of mega-event security preparations that react against nonviolent political demonstrations by treating them as if they were an illegitimate threat to the state. We can see the institutionalization of the NYPD's mega-event security legacy in the continuing use of the Intelligence Division (Intel) with respect to the ordinary First Amendment activity of OWS, the targeting of specific OWS activists for interrogation or arrest based on Intel surveillance, the use of extrajudicial punishment, including verbal harassment and more torturous physical punishment, of OWS protesters, and the deployment of a Mass Arrest Processing Plan (MAPP) against OWS modeled upon the 2004 RNC institutional paradigm, causing extended periods of time in custody for OWS arrestees.

*The Intelligence Division and OWS*

Numerous OWS activists were under surveillance by Intel. For example, the NYPD staked out one activist's apartment in the East Village "for weeks, photographing visitors as they came and went."[141] Another's home in Brooklyn was staked out while organizers discussed a demonstration planned for December 17, 2011.[142] After being arrested in conjunction with a motorcycle gang assault on an SUV driver, Detective Wojciech Braszczok admitted to spying on OWS as part of Intel. He was described as "omnipresent," the kind of person who would "show up at your birthday party, sleep on the street, and get arrested at a demonstration." Braszczok attended "every major action and some of the minor ones." He monitored not only political organizing or demonstrations for Intel, but Occupy Sandy relief efforts as well.[143]

As discussed above, the NYPD arrived at three different apartments the day before May Day protests with pretextual warrants to interrogate the activists.[144] Intel surveillance also led to targeted, preemptive arrests of Occupy activists, much like the use of Intel led to targeted, preventative arrests during the RNC. For example, on the evening of May 1, the NYPD used a bogus warrant to arrest an OWS activist. While he was in custody, Detective McDonnell, an officer with Intel, interrogated him.[145] On November 15, after eviction from Zuccotti Park, Sami—who was involved in planning meetings at an apartment under surveillance—had been attempting to negotiate OWS access to Duarte Square when he was brutally arrested by a group of officers. He had been on his telephone while standing next to a police detective. The detective put his arm around Sami and told him not to make a scene. Suddenly, the detective put him in a headlock, and officers surrounded him, punching him and kneeing him in the back while he was on the ground. Sami described the officers as "angry" with him. The detective told him that he would be going in for "a very long time." He was in custody in conjunction with this arrest for approximately two days, although the charges were later dismissed.[146] Other Occupy activists were completely "shocked" at having witnessed Sami's brutal arrest, and their concern deepened when they could not locate him in the system afterward.[147] As Sami described in an interview, "We were all under surveillance. We knew that."[148]

On November 17, 2011, a major day of action, an Occupy activist was buying coffee and found herself suddenly surrounded by approximately thirty officers, indicating she had been under surveillance.[149] Members of Intel arrested her and her three friends waiting for her in a nearby car, preemptively— arrested without a legal basis—recalling numerous arrests during the 2004 RNC (based on perceived successes of the 2002 WEF). They were strip searched, denied requested legal representation, and detained for approximately twenty-four hours. While in custody, she was questioned by Intel officers about "her personal history, her relationship with other protesters, the nature of Occupy Wall Street and plans for upcoming protests."[150] The charges against her and her friends were later dropped by the Manhattan District Attorney's Office. She and two others then sued the city, and she settled her case for $15,000.[151] Because it is unclear what happened to the fourth person in the car, it is possible that this person was either an undercover officer with the NYPD or an informant.[152]

Certain key OWS activists appear to have been targeted for especially lengthy detentions in conjunction with their arrests. Christine, who had been violently arrested on the March 17, 2012, six-month anniversary of OWS in Zuccotti Park, was involved with media for OWS. Previously arrested as part of the mass arrest on the Brooklyn Bridge and again on December 17 when Bishop Packard ascended the ladder over the fencing enclosing Duarte Square, she was in custody in conjunction with her March 17 arrest for fifty-six hours. The Occupier whose thumb was broken by the NYPD on March 17 helped organize Occupy actions. He was in custody in conjunction with his March 17 arrest for over forty hours. As mentioned above, Sami had been attempting to mediate between OWS and the police at Duarte Square November 15 when he was grabbed and beaten by numerous NYPD officers. He was in custody for approximately two days.[153]

*Extrajudicial Punishment of OWS: Verbal and Physical Abuse*

Considering the arrest process to which the NYPD subjected Occupy activists, we can identify not only a targeted use of extended detentions, but verbal abuse and physical brutality. As we learned above, the NYPD verbally taunted a small group of Occupiers after trapping them on New Year's Eve. It also verbally abused journalists who covered OWS. One reporter, whom the NYPD violently arrested while he was covering a demonstration on the one-year anniversary of OWS, was subjected to verbal degradation and ridicule while in custody.[154] When he was released, the NYPD told him not to return to New York to cover more protests.[155]

The NYPD also used violence as extrajudicial punishment against OWS. In addition to a group of NYPD officers jumping and beating Sami in Duarte Square November 15, the NYPD targeted the Occupier whose thumb it had broken in Zuccotti Park March 17 for particular abuse. One officer, whom the Occupier with the broken thumb identified as Officer Perez, yelled at him in a crude attempt at intimidation while he was in custody. Perez screamed, "You motherfucking protesters, every time you come back to that park, we're going to kick your ass!"[156]

Perez also continued the physical abuse of this Occupier whose thumb was broken while he was in custody. Perez removed the splint on his thumb and threw it in the trash when fingerprinting him. When the Occupier was waiting to be photographed with others, a friend (who was also an arrestee) offered him a sandwich, which he accepted since he hadn't eaten in some time. Once he took a bite, Perez charged across the room, grabbed his injured thumb, and raised it above his head, screaming in his face, "I thought I told you not to fuck with me!"[157] Perez's verbal and physical abuse of this Occupier expresses his affective attachment to punishing Occupy activists and to defeating Occupy, indicating a postlegitimation, post-democratic orientation to policing that understands OWS to be a political enemy.

*Marom v. City of New York*, a federal civil rights action arising out of the violent March 17, 2012, arrests in Zuccotti Park, shows the legal latitude within which the NYPD can use force in the process of an arrest as a form of extrajudicial punishment. We can define these parameters by comparing the legal claims that federal court judge Castel dismissed to those he refused to dismiss.[158] Castel dismissed one male plaintiff's and one female plaintiff's excessive force claims. The male Occupier was tightly handcuffed for several hours, but there was no evidence that he complained at the time to an officer of physical injury to his wrists. Castel considered being handcuffed for "several" hours to be an insufficient duration of time to constitute excessive force.[159] The female Occupier was grabbed by two male NYPD officers by her arms and violently thrown to the ground, ripping her jacket. As she was on the ground facedown, one officer kept telling her, "Stop resisting," although she was not resisting. Customarily, NYPD officers yell "Stop resisting" when they are engaged in the abuse of force, simulating the acceptable use of force when they have reason to believe that they are being witnessed or captured on video.[160]

After telling her, "Stop resisting," the officer told her to "just relax." She responded, "Fuck you, don't tell me to relax." At that point, the officer said, "Fine, fuck you then," and, according to the complaint, "twisted her arm up her back as he placed plastic flexcuffs on her." The officer yelled at her to "get up," but she could not. As she was unable to get up on her own because she was cuffed with her arms up her back while lying face down on the ground, the NYPD officers dragged her "by her hair and pulled her up onto her feet." Her cuffs remained tightly on her wrists for four hours.[161] Although the manner in which this woman was arrested was rough and degrading—the officer was rougher than was necessary to conduct the arrest by throwing her to the ground, as extrajudicial punishment for the Occupier's verbal response to the officer's baseless order for her to "stop resisting" and to "just relax," and she was symbolically degraded by being told to get to her feet when she could not and then pulled to her feet by her hair—Castel dismissed her claims of excessive force because being cuffed for four hours was an insufficient duration of time to constitute excessive force, and because she presented no evidence that she had sustained any physical injuries from her arrest. Therefore, Castel characterized the force used to arrest her as "minimal."[162]

Castel allowed a third Occupier's charge of excessive force to proceed.[163] When he was arrested March 17, this Occupier was thrown violently face down on the ground. While he was lying on the ground, an unidentified NYPD officer hit him "at least ten times in the face" while telling him, "Stop resisting." Due to the beating he sustained by this officer when he was arrested on the six-month anniversary of OWS, his face was "swollen and painful for around a week" (the judge characterized these injuries as "slight").[164]

Comparing the claims of excessive force that were dismissed to the claim that survived a motion to dismiss, we can identify the parameters within which the NYPD can operate to use the arrest process to punish protesters extrajudicially. The NYPD can operate somewhere in between punching a helpless arrestee in the face at least ten times, which is considered potentially excessive if it leaves evidence of lasting physical injury, on the one hand, and using gratuitous force unnecessary to conduct the arrest by throwing someone to the ground, pulling them to their feet by the hair needlessly, and keeping them cuffed in a painful manner for four hours, as long as the rough treatment does not result in a lasting physical injury, on the other.

*Extrajudicial Punishment of OWS:*
*Mass Arrest Processing and RNC Security Legacies*

The NYPD used Mass Arrest Processing Centers (MAPCs) to manage OWS arrestees.[165] These mass arrest policies emerged from the NYPD's decision to refuse to issue summonses or desk appearance tickets in response to demonstrations protesting the "police shooting of Amadou Diallo in 1999," and this decision was formalized in writing May 1, 2001.[166] A MAPP was fully developed in anticipation of mass arrests during the 2004 RNC.[167] Likewise, when conducting arrests at Occupy demonstrations, the NYPD would put the arrestees through a centralized process at MAPCs similar to the one described in chapter 2 for RNC arrestees, "even if the numbers did not necessitate" the use of a MAPC. The NYPD's use of MAPCs for processing OWS arrestees meant that arrestees would be in custody for longer periods of time than someone processed more conventionally at a local precinct.[168] Moreover, if the arrest was for a noncriminal violation of disorderly conduct or trespassing, the NYPD could have issued a summons that may not have resulted in significant time spent in custody for the arrestee. Mass arrest processing also meant that arresting officers would be assigned to arrestees, as described in chapter 2. The arresting officer, therefore, was unlikely to be the officer who actually witnessed the conduct alleged to be a legal violation or who made the actual arrest, although this officer would sign off on paperwork stating that he or she did witness the alleged violation.[169]

In a related civil rights suit arising out of the March 17, 2012, arrests, *Caravalho v. City of New York*, also assigned to Judge Castel as *Marom* was, the MAPP resulted in none of the plaintiff arrestees being charged, and all being released "out the backdoor of 100 Centre Street without any paperwork" after serving about the same amount of time in custody—approximately twenty-eight hours.[170] Nevertheless, Castel dismissed all of the false arrest claims. He argued the NYPD had probable cause to arrest all of those in Zuccotti Park that night because a few people had erected tents, hung banners, or stood in flowerbeds, in violation of park rules promulgated by Brookfield Properties, and because a "risk" of disorderly conduct could have been "inferred."[171]

In addition to extending time spent in custody, the MAPP practice of assigning arresting officers to arrestees aggravates the potential for NYPD extrajudicial punishment of protesters. Because the arresting officer may not be the officer who physically arrested the protester, it can be difficult for protesters to know who used force abusively against them in the course of making the arrest, and thereby hold the officer(s) accountable in a subsequent civil rights suit (particularly if NYPD officers who may have engaged in such abuse, or witnessed such abuse, do not come forward and testify to what they did or witnessed during the discovery phase of a civil action). For example, in *Caravalho v. City of New York*, Occupiers experienced or witnessed numerous acts of police brutality.[172] One plaintiff saw police "hit demonstrators with batons and kick them as they were being arrested."[173] Other plaintiffs complained of being kicked in the ribs while being arrested, having their right arm twisted, being kicked in the abdomen several times, being dropped on the sidewalk, requesting medical attention and not receiving it, being hit by a baton on the left shoulder, having an officer "ramming his knee" into their back, having an officer press their face into the concrete with his foot, and being thrown to the ground despite screaming at police, "I'm not resisting arrest. Jesus Christ, I'm not resisting arrest."[174] Many complained of plastic handcuffs placed on their wrists too tightly and kept on for too long, and of suffering numbness and marks for up to three months.[175] Despite the physical abuse these Occupiers (and other Occupiers involved in this civil rights suit) suffered at the hands of NYPD on March 17, all of their excessive force claims were dismissed (with one exception) because, after a year and a half of discovery, no one could ascertain which officer had physically assaulted them.[176]

In addition to its excessive force claims, *Marom v. City of New York* challenges the NYPD's use of MAPCs as a federal civil rights violation.[177] Judge Castel's rulings raise legal questions about the NYPD's MAPP even as they show the difficulty in demonstrating the NYPD's systematic intention to punish OWS extrajudicially by utilizing a particularly punitive process for OWS arrestees. Judge Castel allowed claims to proceed for false arrest by OWS protester plaintiffs contending that their arresting officers never witnessed the alleged conduct of plaintiffs, fair trial claims associated with the false arrest claims, First Amendment retaliation against plaintiffs, and an instance of excessive force.[178]

Dismissed claims arising from the NYPD's use of MAPCs likewise highlight the broad legal parameters within which the NYPD is free to operate and to make the arrest process punitive. For example, Judge Castel dismissed claims that the MAPC constituted a civil rights violation for the Occupiers' duration of custody due to the varying lengths of time each of the plaintiffs spent in detention associated with their arrest (meaning, for Castel, no systematic ill will toward OWS protesters), and because federal jurisprudence sets a forty-eight-hour limit on custody incident to an arrest (as opposed to the stricter New York State standard of twenty-four hours).[179] The three plaintiffs in the action were in custody, respectively, for forty or more hours before arraignment, twenty-four or more hours before arraignment, and thirty or more hours. Additionally, in *Marom*, Castel rejected civil rights claims contending that the NYPD's MAPP was an unconstitutional municipal practice or that the NYPD failed to train its officers regarding their legal obligations, finding that plaintiffs had not demonstrated a "history of the NYPD mishandling mass protest situations on a scale that could be reasonably construed as setting out a pattern or practice of constitutional abuse."[180]

To conceptualize the significance of the NYPD's refusal to issue summonses for minor violations and instead to use MAPCs for OWS arrestees, we should consider how the NYPD's policing of OWS extends from its refusal to issue summonses for minor violations during the 2004 RNC and to put RNC arrestees instead through a time-consuming, dangerous, and degrading MAPP. Federal Judge Richard Sullivan sustained the constitutionality of the 2004 RNC's no-summons policy in conjunction with its MAPP against First Amendment challenge by referring to the compelling interests of "preventing terrorist and anarchist attacks."[181] In his discussion of whether the no-summons policy was narrowly tailored to those interests, however, we can see how very broad concerns about "masses of demonstrators" coming to protest the RNC who could create "mass disorder" and "mass chaos" by functionally shutting down the city also motivated the policy.[182]

In chapter 2, we saw how Judge Sullivan justified a policy that targeted anti-RNC protesters exercising First Amendment rights for a more onerous process when charged with minor violations than either commercial vendors not exercising First Amendment rights or others exercising First Amendment rights either unrelated to, or supportive of, the RNC. Such political favoritism is contrary to the most basic sense of legal legitimacy, and in the context of First Amendment analysis, the singling out of anti-RNC protesters for such burdensome treatment makes legal illegitimacy a state practice of political illegitimacy. We also saw how Sullivan justified the no-summons policy, used in conjunction with the MAPP, because of its limited temporal duration.[183] These policies were permissible as a kind of NSSE exception to First Amendment legal doctrine, and presumably the law would return to normal at the conclusion of the RNC. Inspired by the 1999 protests against the NYPD shooting of Diallo and a haunting specter of black insurrection these protests evoked, then expanded and institutionalized as an exception during the RNC, the NYPD's no-summons policy in conjunction with its use of MAPCs has clearly migrated beyond the limited temporal duration of the RNC. Judge Castel's refusal, in *Marom v. City of New York*, to allow civil rights claims to go forward against the NYPD policy of using MAPPs for OWS arrests shows judicial acquiescence to the NYPD's institutionalization of MAPCs when faced with a political uprising. In other words, rather than viewing the use of a MAPP during the RNC and its legal validation afterward for both the RNC setting and more general use as an exception, we should view the NYPD's use of MAPCs and their legal validation by courts as indicative of a distinct state formation that is postlegitimation and post-democratic: neoliberal authoritarianism.

The NYPD's and Judge Sullivan's recognition that the sheer numbers of anti-RNC protesters threatened to overwhelm the city without a mechanism for removing protesters from the streets for lengthy periods of time sufficient to prevent disruption to the RNC expresses a deep paradox insurrections present to a liberal legal order that Isaac Balbus identified in the early 1970s. In Balbus's study of responses to rioting in the 1960s, he found that city governments were able to suppress the immediate disorder through repressive power, such as mass arrests often lacking evidence, excessive bail, or slow administration of the bail process. Cities suppressed the immediate disorder, however, at the cost of sacrificing normative legal legitimacy, a sacrifice that later, more lenient legal processes sought to remedy.[184] In the context of the RNC, the evidence shows New York made a similar calculation to sacrifice normal legal processes to the exigency of hosting the RNC in the face of widespread and deeply felt political opposition. This illustrates how enforcing the logic of neoliberal, post-Fordist political economy driving cities to host mega-events, particularly when the event itself is deeply controversial, can be conducted against mass opposition only at the cost of legal and political legitimation.

The institutions developed for post–legal legitimation repression of political dissent have not, however, remained historically confined to the 2004 RNC mega-event. As *Marom v. City of New York*, among other civil rights actions arising out of OWS, and the interviews and other data described here show, the NYPD redeployed processes and institutions developed to maintain order during the 2004 RNC against the Occupy uprising challenging the neoliberal, post-Fordist state's democratic—its political—legitimacy. Rooted in an NYPD reaction to contain those protesting police violence against black residents, further developed in 2004 for an exceptional, discrete event and justified by reference to threats of terrorism, violence, and masses of persistent anti-RNC protesters flooding New York from out of town, these mass arrest processes and institutions have become part of the normal protest policing apparatus within the NYPD: they have been used for arrests of Critical Mass bicyclists during and after the RNC, and now against OWS. The MAPCs have become a normal institution to repress nonviolent New Yorkers (and others) who have had enough of neoliberal inequalities, authoritarianism, and the closure of public spaces to the people's assemblies.[185]

In the civil rights suits arising out of OWS or Occupy-related movements, several of the later civil complaints do not merely contend that individual members of the NYPD violated civil rights in a particular instance. They argue that New York should be liable as a municipality because it is New York's policy to suppress or deter the exercise of First Amendment rights.[186] In one such legal action before federal judge Analisa Torres, she dismisses this claim, in part, by minimizing the cases cited to establish a pattern or practice of suppressive conduct by the NYPD, observing, "all but one involved the specific context of Occupy Wall Street protests."[187] Torres implies the OWS uprising was a sort of exception that necessity dictated be suppressed. Yet the OWS protests build upon the exceptional mobilization against the RNC. The accumulation of exceptions suggests, instead, the emergence of a distinctive state formation.

In this section, we have seen how New York, faced with a political insurrection, responded with political repression—a response that exceeded normal legal processes of legitimation—by relying on Intel, a no-summons policy, MAPCs that are distinguishable from typical arrest processing, extended periods of custody for activists, and extrajudicial (and torturously violent) punishment of protesters to suppress the Occupy movement. In the previous section, legal observers and OWS protesters described how the NYPD's tactics criminalized the Occupy movement. In this section, we have seen how the NYPD sought to repress, intimidate, and defeat Occupy.[188] New York's response to the Occupy movement is a hybrid, one that mixes the criminalization of protesters with a response that represents OWS as a political enemy constituting a threat to the state. "Security" captures this hybridity between crime and politics. The NYPD is neither an institution of law enforcement nor the military, strictly speaking. The hybrid response to Occupy indicates the NYPD functions increasingly as a security force, one that not only criminalized OWS but sought to repress it.

By acting not as a law enforcement agency but as a security force dedicated to criminalizing and defeating OWS, the NYPD exhibits the investments and constraints of the contemporary state structure. The NYPD's excesses in defeating OWS lay bare the political commitments of neoliberal authoritarianism enacted by postlegitimation, post-democratic state practices. With this post-democratic formation, state and civil society institutions are now either unwilling or incapable of mediating political conflict and responding to unmet social needs. Thus, NYPD excesses exhibit an intensity of politics as the people are increasingly forced to confront the state and capital directly.

## Conclusion

In this chapter, I show how the NYPD's commitment to policing informed by "Broken Windows" results in aggressive and violent protest policing, indicating that the negotiated management model of dialogic protester-police interaction has been superseded. The discussion of "Broken Windows" adds to chapter 2's elaboration of how hosting mega-events, like the 2002 WEF and 2004 RNC, pushed New York protest policing in a more abusive direction. Together, these chapters establish that the increasingly abusive policing of protest that has developed in the United States since the 1990s results from the vertical influence of hosting NSSEs in conjunction with the horizontal dissemination of the "Broken Windows" concept of order maintenance policing.

While Vitale's scholarship also demonstrates how NYPD protest policing is indebted to the "Broken Windows" concept of order maintenance policing, and is distinctive from negotiated management, Vitale's hyper-Weberian depiction of NYPD protest policing strictly enforcing legal minutiae to the letter cannot account for the NYPD's excesses in its confrontation with OWS, excesses indicating the NYPD enjoys its abusive policing of Occupy. These excesses include the NYPD's expressive acts of intimidation, its baseless arrests, its exercises of unnecessary, and at times expressively cruel, force, and the use of targeted, excessive, and punitive postarrest detentions of OWS activists. Close attention to the "Broken Windows" essay, however, points us toward an incitement of affective attachment to police kicking ass. This is an affective attachment shared by the NYPD, as represented not only by the *Floyd v. City of New York* ruling on stop and frisk, but also by Officer Perez screaming at the Occupier in custody with a broken thumb that every time OWS returned to the park, the NYPD would "kick your ass!"[189] This expanded understanding of "Broken Windows" policing, in turn, leads us to a better grasp of the neoliberal state. In contrast to those, such as Brown, who do not expect the neoliberal state to deploy "*excessive* uses of violence" in its pursuit of "efficient" courses of action, the NYPD's excesses direct attention to the way political subjects become affectively attached to the neoliberal state not despite its excesses, but because of them.[190]

Though it appears excessive when considered from the perspective of either law enforcement or economic efficiency, NYPD protest policing is governed more by a political investment in the post-democratic state of neoliberal authoritarianism. Therefore, this chapter characterizes NYPD protest policing as a hybrid, one that both criminalized OWS and sought to defeat it politically. Strictly speaking, the NYPD is neither a law enforcement agency nor a military force. For this reason, I represent the NYPD as a security force to acknowledge this hybridity. On the one hand, the NYPD does not appear bound by strict legalities, as shown by its arbitrary enforcement of permits, the noncriminal violation of disorderly conduct, or its neglect of the First Amendment as a fundamental right. On the other hand, some OWS activists experienced the harsher, more political side of this security force when they were pepper sprayed, punched, had their thumb broken, were preemptively arrested, or were targeted by Intel.

This hybridity of the NYPD also finds its roots in Kelling and Wilson's "Broken Windows" essay. By urging police to target an ill-defined disorder caused by those who are disreputable, Kelling and Wilson embrace a concept of policing that goes beyond mere law enforcement. It is a concept of policing delinked from legal legitimation. "Broken Windows" is also motivated as a continuing reaction against the urban riots of the 1960s. That is, it is oriented to the political purpose of preventing or suppressing those rising expectations of the 1960s that the lives of black, brown, and poor people matter, that they count. In this regard, the political commitments of "Broken Windows" are post-democratic. Transformed by the "Broken Windows" concept of order maintenance policing, the NYPD polices protest as a post-legal legitimation, post-democratic security force.

During the 1970s and early 1980s, theorists depicted capitalist democracies (i.e., Keynesian or social welfare democracies) as suffering a "legitimation crisis."[191] According to Claus Offe, these states faced a structural dilemma that capital required bourgeois democracy to legitimize its inequities. Commitment to democracy, however, meant these states had to regulate capital and enact policies to promote equality, the core value of democracy, or risk a loss of legitimacy and face a political uprising. Yet, if the state went too far in the pursuit of democratic legitimacy, this could cause capital to rebel if its profit margins became unacceptable.[192] The dilemma seemed at the time to be intractable, but the growth of inequality since 1970s in the United States has not engendered the kind of crisis of the state anticipated by these theorists. Why not?

The significance of the argument presented here provides a partial understanding of why this crisis failed to materialize. Cities became fundamentally transformed by their disintermediation from markets—neoliberalism—in the wake of the urban fiscal crisis of the 1970s. This transformation was encouraged by the perception of an excess of democracy overloading governments, was facilitated by a growing preoccupation with crime, and was structurally imposed by federal and state governments, on the one side, and the financial markets that refused to buy urban debt (like New York City's), on the other.[193] By orienting infrastructure and outreach to markets, rather than to residents, urban governments invested in capital and divested themselves of concern for many of their residents; indeed, emergency austerity measures have repeatedly coincided with the suspension of representational government since New York's fiscal crisis in the 1970s. This mutual investment between the state and capital has also occurred at the national and global levels, to the detriment of the people's needs and democratic accountability.[194] The state depicted by crisis theorists was one that sought to balance antagonistic interests: capital on the one side and the people's social reproduction and their political commitment to popular sovereignty on the other. Today, the state does not balance these interests. Instead, the relation between the neoliberal state and the people is one increasingly of antagonism. The build-out of municipal police forces, like the NYPD, driven by a reaction to a crime crisis in the 1980s and 1990s, and thought to be necessary for mega-event security, provides the state with enormous repressive power unchecked by legitimation norms.

In sum, this chapter documents the presence of a postlegitimation, post-democratic state formation of neoliberal authoritarianism by focusing on protest policing. This state is no longer constrained by normative legitimation concerns in the way that the state checked by mass organizations with social democratic commitments, and oriented to the horizon of social democracy, was.[195] On the one hand, the affective attachment to this state's violent suppression of OWS expresses the postlegitimation, post-democratic attachment to neoliberal authoritarianism by this state's political subjects. On the other hand, OWS expresses the neoliberal authoritarian state's bankruptcy in terms of normative legitimation, much as #BlackLivesMatter does.

# Chapter Four

# Violent Appearances and Neoliberalism's Disintegrated Political Subjects

New rages dissolved old rules of decorum.
—RICK PERLSTEIN, *Nixonland* (2008)

FIFTY YEARS AGO, police and mobs reacted violently against Civil Rights activists marching to protest racial segregation and disenfranchisement. The images of cruelty shocked the nation's conscience, creating pressure for stronger enforcement of constitutional rights to equal protection, to vote, and for freedom of speech, association, and assembly. More recently, police have reacted to demonstrations at major economic summits and major party conventions, as well as antiwar protests, Occupy Wall Street (OWS), and #BlackLivesMatter with intimidation, arrests, violence, and excessive postarrest custody. Videos and photos of police violence circulate widely on the internet. Reviews of these events have been conducted and reports written; there have been civil rights suits; and numerous, and sometimes very substantial, monetary damages have been paid to settle civil litigation. Nevertheless, intimidating and abusive policing of protest is repeated in the United States. The repetition of excessive police violence against protesters is counterintuitive if one theorizes the neoliberal state and neoliberal law as having been rendered economized, responsibilized, and efficient by market-based metrics to "eschew *excessive* violence or extraconstitutional conduct."[1]

The repeatedly abusive policing of protest in the United States since the late 1990s is also unexpected if we theorize police as concerned with legal liability because they have adopted a "normative model" of "legalized accountability" that should discipline police departments to "make rights real."[2] So why do police repeatedly react violently against protesters?

In this chapter, I argue that the normative force of legalized accountability has been eroded by what scholars familiar with the work of Michel Foucault might call a deeper, postdisciplinary shift in contemporary society. Other scholars more oriented to psychoanalytic theory, such as Slavoj Žižek or Jodi Dean, might describe a collapse in the symbolic order that has produced a decline in symbolic efficiency. With the meaning of words or legal norms now in flux (hence they function less efficiently), the collapse of the symbolic order results in a weakened hold of legal norms upon subjects. These distinct theoretical perspectives converge to describe a condition where the power of norms is weakened. Instead of a strong normative orientation, subjects have a reflexive understanding of infinite communicative possibilities and the communicative equivalence of all opinion. Therefore, images of police violence against protesters do not shock the conscience by violating an important social or legal norm as they might once have. Instead, they add one more frame to a universe of infinite communicative potential. Some enjoy their participation in communicative production and the potential for plural interpretive experiences. They are not shocked by the appearance of police brutality, and respond with a cynical, bemused, or slightly bored "whatever." Others enjoy it.

### Making Rights Real

Charles Epp, in *Making Rights Real*, describes how police during the 1960s were poorly trained and abusive, and legal rules, such as the fleeing felon rule, accommodated their violence. But as journalists treated the police increasingly critically in the wake of events such as the 1968 Democratic National Convention (DNC) in Chicago, and "in the context of growing litigation against the police," sociolegal conditions shifted from enabling or acquiescing to police abuse of force, to constraining and penalizing their violence.[3] Epp argues that through "interaction between activist pressure for law-based reform and conflict within managerial professions," such as police departments, legalized accountability grew.[4]

Several vectors would converge to facilitate this change, including developments in law, increasing activism against police abuse of force, and changes within the profession of policing. Legal changes included Supreme Court decisions such as *Monroe v. Pape* (1961), which revived Section 1983, a provision of U.S. civil rights law, enacted by the Civil Rights Act of 1871, that allows government officials to be held responsible for violating federal rights in the course of their official duties, and plaintiffs to receive monetary damages; *Monnell v. New York Department of Social Services* (1978), allowing municipalities to be found financially liable for a "policy or custom" that caused violations of federal rights; and *Tennessee v. Garner* (1985), finding the rule permitting police to shoot a fleeing felon to be unconstitutional.[5] Liability lawsuits by activists, media coverage of that litigation, and work by the National Association for the Advancement of Colored People (NAACP) and the National Lawyers Guild proved important in supporting this litigation. The Lawyers Guild, in particular, organized panels and workshops on tort litigation, reported on civil liberties and civil rights cases through its "Civil Liberties Docket," and produced a legal guide on police misconduct.[6] Litigation, and media coverage of the litigation, provided useful levers for reform-minded police chiefs and policing experts, such as Patrick Murphy and James Fyfe, to push the policing profession to reform.[7] By the mid-1980s, even the slow-moving International Association for Chiefs of Police (IACP) was producing training materials and had convened a panel, composed of police chiefs from around the country, on preventing the abuse of force and how to train officers in accordance with this professional norm.[8]

In terms of police violence's "big picture," the number of police departments adopting new rules regarding shootings increased between 1970 and 1984. Epp reports that "the number of police shootings in major cities declined by about a third, and the racial disparity in the rate of shooting whites and blacks was cut in half."[9] He contends, in agreement with other scholars, that these results "strongly suggest" that "rule-based reforms made the difference." Scholars who replicated, in the late 1990s, the study on police violence conducted between 1970 and 1984 likewise observe a "significant reduction in police violence toward disrespectful citizens," which they believe is due to "the growing legalization of police departments."[10]

Of course, policing in the United States is highly decentralized, and Epp studies the uneven nature of reform, identifying factors associated with the adoption of the legalized accountability model (and factors associated with police departments being less likely to adopt the model). Whether or not a police department adopts the legalized accountability model is greatly influenced by (1) "the relative vibrancy of local support structures for police misconduct litigation," and (2) "how closely departments are connected to broader professional police networks (and employ internal legal advisers)."[11] In other words, the institutionalization of the legalized accountability model is associated with (1) the existence of resources (activists, organizations, lawyers) that can be mobilized to enforce compliance by police departments, and (2) how well integrated the members of the police department are within professional networks that would disseminate professional norms, knowledge, and support with respect to training and compliance mechanisms. Strikingly, being sued does not matter as much as these two factors.[12]

Nevertheless, fear of legal liability drove police departments to adopt the legalized accountability model, and the IACP to hold training sessions on how to avoid liability and to publish articles in its magazine, *The Police Chief*, on the threat of liability.[13] Epp's survey of police departments indicates that concerns regarding employee morale, media coverage of a lawsuit, and the effects of litigation on a department's public image all were more significant factors leading police departments to control the abuse of force than liability's effect on a department's budget or a police manager's job security. Thus, litigation's "reputational sanction is significantly greater than [its] financial sanction." Because of the emergence of a "public and professional norm in favor of careful regulation of force," litigation threatens the "public legitimacy and credibility" of police departments.[14]

In other words, because of the significance of norms—legal norms, ethical norms, or norms regarding police conduct in a democracy—and the way that liability represents a contradiction between the normative basis for police authority as a public institution and the actual conduct of police in particular, concrete situations, the threat of litigation compels efforts among police managers for institutional compliance with the norm against police abuse of force. Police manager concerns regarding morale within the department, media coverage, and the public image of the department, moreover, show that police are conscious of, reflective about, and influenced by how the public perceives them—how they appear to the normative gaze of a generalized other or, in the language of psychoanalytic theory, the "big Other." Finally, police departments achieve compliance with the norm against police abuse of force by adopting specific rules, by training recruits in the proper use of force, and by institutionalizing "mechanisms of internal oversight."[15] By highlighting the significance of the norm, concern for how others perceive one's relation to the norm, and the implementation of training and constant oversight with respect to normative conduct, Epp's research describing how police have reduced abuses of force not only depicts the fundamentals of liberal legal order with its emphasis on harnessing the use of force to the law while ensuring that police are legally accountable for their conduct, it closely resembles Michel Foucault's depiction of disciplinary power (though how a department might institutionalize training and oversight, or why they are driven to manage their public reputation, might differ from some of the specific elements of disciplinary power).[16]

## Discipline and Democracy

The transformation of governing institutions from medieval law and the ancien régime of monarchical sovereign power to liberal law and republicanism is accompanied by the rise of what Michel Foucault refers to as disciplinary institutions.[17] The prison is the institution Foucault uses to express the diagram of discipline with the greatest intensity, though it is the part that stands for the larger whole in his representation of modernity more broadly as a society of discipline.[18] Human subjectivity likewise experiences a transformation whereby subjects internalize the normative gaze of the generalized other due to the spread and increased power of disciplinary logics within and beyond institutions.[19] Foucault describes the institutional processes whereby the normative gaze of the other—a prison guard, a factory manager, a teacher, a military commander, or professionals wielding forms of expertise—becomes progressively installed within subjects. Discipline bears on the "soul."[20] It "acts in depth on the heart, the thoughts, the will, the inclinations."[21] Discipline is the "technical transformation of individuals."[22] Through discipline, subjects acquire useful habits, improve their utility, or gain particular aptitudes.[23] With respect to Epp's discussion of policing and violence, then, a disciplined police officer might acquire an aptitude for de-escalating tension, rather than allowing emotions to escalate a situation such that it becomes a violent confrontation.

How do these disciplined subjects emerge? They develop through education, training, repeated exercises, and surveillance.[24] Exercises are repeated, schoolchildren trained, and whether we are referring to classrooms, factories, the military, or prisons, supervision keeps order and enables assessments of rank.[25] Training (or punishment) is corrective. In the educational context of students, for instance, it is the "means of advancing their progress by correcting their defects."[26] "Disciplinary writing" enables documentation, comparison, classification, and the determination of averages, deviations, and distributions within a given "population."[27] Epp's depiction of police departments that have more successfully institutionalized the legalized accountability model expresses key elements of disciplinary power as described by Foucault due to their use of training and mechanisms to monitor compliance.

As is well known, disciplinary power is oriented toward a norm. Disciplinary power is the power of normalization.[28] It coercively produces proletarians, standardizes humans, represses or hierarchizes diversity, and constitutes the frontier of the abnormal.[29] Foucault treats the power of the norm critically. As he reminds his readers at more than one juncture, "the Roman reference [at the Enlightenment] transmitted, somewhat ambiguously, the juridical ideal of citizenship and the technique of disciplinary methods."[30] Discipline, for Foucault, is the "dark side" of the "parliamentary, representative régime" and its "formally egalitarian juridical framework."[31] Of course a prison's purpose is to punish, but it is unfair to punish an offender for who they might be ("legal punishment bears upon an act; the punitive technique upon a life"), and it is both wrong-headed and unjust to impute "instincts, drives, tendencies, character" to "quasi-natural classes" in the criminological construction of the "delinquent."[32] Is it possible, nevertheless, to tease out of Foucault's work a more positive valence to discipline and the power of a norm?

As Foucault himself notes at several junctures, formally egalitarian legal rights and representative parliamentary regimes coemerge, premised on the sovereignty of the people supplanting monarchies, on the one hand, and disciplinary power, on the other.[33] Discipline, or, to use Foucault's synonyms for discipline, education and training, improves collective aptitudes and abilities.[34] It helps constitute subjects more capable of self-government, that is to say, democracy or exercising the power of popular sovereignty. In its formal orientation to equality, it is not necessarily for the already privileged or against the poor, but inclusively and equally oriented to a "defence of society" or, in Foucault's more derogatory expression, to a "homogeneous social body."[35]

We can contrast disciplinary power to Foucault's discussion of the ethical practices of the ancients. He describes these ethical practices as managing oneself "as a governor manages the governed."[36] The art of living is a "training of oneself by oneself," and the ancients carried notebooks, or "training books," to assist themselves in this project of the self.[37] To become the subject of one's aspirations, one must train or exercise oneself. One who cannot govern himself cannot govern others because he cannot control himself—he will be a "slave of his appetites"—and will therefore abuse power as a tyrant.[38] Foucault distinguishes the ancients' ethical practices of the self from modern discipline, in part, on the ground that such practices were "reserved for a few people in the population." They were a "personal choice" limited to a "small elite."[39] As the disciplinary techniques of training and education become socialized and democratized after the Enlightenment, then, we could likewise say that the capacity for self-government is socialized and democratized. No longer limited to the few who will take up their "rightful" position in the community, the eighteenth-century emergence of the people as sovereign political subject corresponds to the extension of disciplinary power throughout society, and the extension of collective capability. By favoring the elite practice of "training of oneself by oneself" of the ancients over disciplinary power of modernity on the grounds that the ancients' practices of the self occur on an individualized basis for a minority while discipline involves the socialization of such training and education more broadly, we can identify a point where Foucault's work, if not Foucault himself, may accommodate neoliberalism and provide impetus to the corrosion of social institutions crucial for supporting and improving the democratization of human capabilities.[40]

In *Discipline and Punish*, Foucault states, "The ideal point of penalty today would be an indefinite discipline: an interrogation without end . . . a procedure that would be at the same time the permanent measure of a gap in relation to an inaccessible norm and the asymptotic movement that strives to meet in infinity."[41] Here, Foucault places disciplinary power in a critical light. Of course a literal interrogation without end would be torturous. Yet the asymptotic relation between norm and practice also expresses the discontinuity between an incalculable qualitative norm expressing an important value of justice, and practices within an empirical plane. The Enlightenment project and the project of democracy are an interrogation without end of present circumstances in relation to norms of human dignity, equality, and justice. It is a project that grapples with a "lasting hiatus" or "incommensurability" between norm and reality, between a rule and its application.[42] This is the space constituting a condition of possibility for judgment, critique, and antagonism. In the more mundane terms of Epp's study of policing, it is the space between the norm that government may not use unauthorized force and the reality of policing in the United States where critique, protest, and civil rights litigation occur.

Epp's study refers to the important role that the Kerner Commission— and other national commissions—played in spurring legalized accountability.[43] These reports are informed by a normative orientation underlining values of justice, democracy, and equality. They highlight the role of norms as part of the assessment and critique of policing in the late 1960s. These reports evaluating policing of the 1960s critically against normative standards would inspire reforms in the use of force Epp describes and the emergence of negotiated management's relation of police to demonstrators that protest policing scholars discuss.[44]

Press accounts published in anticipation of the Kerner Commission's release prepared readers for the report's normative orientation. One *New York Times* article stated that the commission would "recommend measures that it deems essential to racial peace and justice without reference to their cost impact on other political or economic demands on the nation's resources."[45] Another warned that the "commission's members are aware of the political implications that could be attached to their findings in an election year. They have decided to recommend what they think needs to be done regardless of the war in Vietnam or budgetary limitations."[46] As expected, concrete as many of the report's recommendations were, they represented a broader, normative vision. "The nation has substantial resources—not enough to do everything some might wish," the commission acknowledged, "but enough to make an important start on reducing our critical 'social deficit,' in spite of a war and in spite of current requirements."[47] Anticipating criticisms, such as those Richard Nixon or Georgia's segregationist governor Lester Maddox would make, the report expected that there would be "those who oppose these aims as 'rewarding the rioters.'" The commission responded on normative grounds that such critics would be "wrong," arguing, "We propose these aims to fulfill our pledge of equality and to meet the fundamental needs of a democratic society."[48] Though perfection is impossible where justice, equality, or democracy are concerned, the commission argued that present realities showed how much room for improvement there was, and how much better we could be doing with available resources regarding these normative ideals.

We can understand policing protest as a subset of broader policing practices. In this light, the Task Force on Demonstrations, Protests, and Group Violence (operating as part of the National Commission on the Causes and Prevention of Violence) critiques the repressive reaction to protest in a manner consistent with the Kerner Commission's critique of policing in many major cities. The response to protest should be "within a democratic framework," where police operate "within the framework of due process of law" and use "the minimum force required." Moreover, the failure to reform "fundamental problems" and instead respond to protest with violence produces a "cycle of hostility." Not only does the "escalation of violence" result in "increasing resistance," but a one-sided emphasis on social control outstrips "democratic values." "Little by little," according to the task force, "we move toward an armed society which, while not clearly totalitarian, could no longer be called consensual."[49] Values of due process, human dignity, justice for all, and democracy are used to critique protest policing and compel reform.

More broadly, analyses of the Civil Rights movement characterized the appearance of contradiction between reality and norms of justice, equality, and democracy as engendering a crisis for legal and state legitimacy.[50] Because of the symbolic power of the norm (and organizational strength in producing the contradiction), state actors responded by pressing forward egalitarian changes. Legitimation concerns among state actors drove efforts to reduce the gap between the promise of justice and the realities of racial inequality in the United States.

But without normative power, if norms function less efficiently or if their functioning is understood to have collapsed, then progress—movement toward closing the gap between the empirical conditions of existence and norms of human dignity, equality, or justice—through critique or protest is not possible. Therefore, there is a progressive orientation to disciplinary society, to education, to the training and correcting, to unromantic modernity's endless interrogation of the present and its orientation to the horizon of social democracy. The work of some theorists and criminological scholars, however, questions the continuing significance or symbolic power of norms. Instead, we are experiencing normative decline, a weakening of disciplinary power, and the disintegration of institutions criminologist David Garland refers to as composing "penal modernism." Without critique, a felt responsibility for avoiding a legitimation crisis for public institutions likewise diminishes. The social and political commitment to the better realization of dignity, equality, and justice collapses if the commitment to those values is thought to be duplicitous, self-interested, or a sham. Today, we are experiencing "the decay or 'the decadence' of the idea of progress," the diminished power of norms, the "death of the social," and the decline of disciplinary power.[51] These broad transformations affect policing and punishment in general, policing protest more particularly, and subjectivity itself.

### The Decline of Discipline and the Rise of Control

According to Michael Hardt and Antonio Negri, today, disciplinary institutions of civil society are in crisis and are withering. This means not only that these institutions cannot mediate between social forces and the state, or transmit grievance upward toward the state for resolution—hence the increased significance of protests, demonstrations, and assemblies such as Occupy Wall Street (OWS)—but these institutions cannot produce legitimacy for state policies in society. Moreover, because these institutions are withering, they fail to shape normatively oriented subjectivities the way they once did.[52]

Disciplinary society is socially integrative. Discipline is integral to social democracy because social democracy presupposes a mentality of social security, the idea that we are all better off if risk is socialized and shared by all. To defend society means providing a basis for social security. On the one hand, this means subjects having the capacity and knowledge to govern themselves and their relations with others. On the other hand, this means creating institutions that engender and support these practices of self-government while providing mutual security against the risks immanent to human existence of old age, illness, accident, poverty, and other forms of misfortune. The disciplinary prison, at least diagrammatically, seeks to rehabilitate the prisoner (it is a correctional institution) so the prisoner can be reintegrated as a productive member of society.[53] The social welfare state and the modern prison as an institution of correction are two sides of the same coin of social democracy in their orientation to social integration.

As President Lyndon B. Johnson's July 27, 1967, address to the nation, in which he announces the formation of the Kerner Commission, makes clear, crime prevention, for those oriented to the horizon of social democracy, is achieved by attacking "the conditions that breed despair and violence. All of us know what those conditions are: ignorance, discrimination, slums, poverty, disease, not enough jobs."[54] For those concerned with the "defence of society," attacking social problems and promoting social integration are both normatively right and a practice of crime prevention. This paradigm is what Garland refers to as "penal modernism."[55] This is the paradigm that collapsed due to the crisis of democracy and the growing perception of a crime crisis in the wake of the riots. Control would come to replace penal modernism's ideals of correctionalism, social welfare, and self-government.

Hardt and Negri follow Gilles Deleuze by arguing that there has been a transformation from disciplinary society to "societies of control."[56] Control technologies substitute for debilitated disciplinary institutions. Control technologies operate through new communications technologies and digitalization. Control functions through passwords, digital passcards coding bodies to spaces, barcodes, RFID chips, biometrics, and the trackable traces, data, and built-in surveillance these digitalized movements or actions produce.[57] For example, for a mobile phone to work, the position of the phone must be known to the network. Surveillance is a necessary condition for the phone to function.

Significantly, these control technologies do not bear on the soul. One's soul remains untouched when one is digitally enclosed. For example, DVDs would be encoded so they would operate on DVD players in one region but not others. Electronic book readers control how long we can choose to lend a book to a friend or prevent us from reselling that book to a used book dealer. They also produce data from which books one reads, or which passages one highlights, to improve how the person is targeted for future book purchases. Thus, control technologies do not require subjects to internalize the normative gaze of the generalized other. Regardless of one's good habits, intentions, or purposes, the technology will not allow us to lend the book to a friend for too long if we possess the book only in an electronic format. One does not police oneself (as the panopticon encourages one to do); one is policed through a code that operates in accordance with its corporately dictated and programmed logic, irrespective of any self-reflection or training of the subject.

Control technologies can also supplement diminished capabilities, weaknesses, or indiscipline on the part of the subject. Cars may stop automatically if the driver did not notice that something was in the path of the vehicle (or if people fail to look both ways before crossing a street or driveway), or the car can now parallel park itself. The technology does away with the need to watch where one is going or to learn how to park a car. Control technologies substitute for training in these examples. With the weakening of disciplinary power, and the disintegration of disciplined subjectivities, control technologies accommodate and encourage a process of desubjectification and decapacitation.

Hardt and Negri find the rise and proliferation of control technologies to be closely related to the emergence of post-Fordism. Transformations in capitalism from Fordism to post-Fordism have contributed to the substitution of control for discipline. Worker resistance pushed capitalism from a Fordist phase of disciplined, unionized factory production to post-Fordism.[58] Under post-Fordism, automation allows for production with fewer workers, making capital less reliant on labor. New communications technologies coordinate production from multiple sites. They also allow goods to arrive just in time, permitting capital to employ workers only when necessary. Production occurs through networks, and computer networks are embedded within production processes. Communications networks also mean that production is not limited to an eight-hour work day within the enclosures of the factory's walls; productive activity begins whenever workers receive the email, phone call, or text message. As sociologist Zygmunt Bauman portrays postdisciplinary work under conditions of neoliberal globalization, the "pressure today is to dismantle the habits of permanent . . . regular work," forcing workers into a more economically precarious position and to become more flexible and more responsive to "whatever."[59] Control technologies count keystrokes of office workers, keep track of the websites they visit, govern their warehouse activities, and monitor the location of delivery workers. Control technologies marginalize the role of labor, manage labor by substituting for their lack of discipline, or bring supervision to forms of work previously not easily supervised otherwise. Control enhances exploitation beyond disciplinary power, and regardless of the socialization, training, docility, or normative orientation of the subject.

Under post-Fordism, production is more responsive to consumer preferences thanks to communications technologies, and post-Fordist marketing can target ever more narrow market profiles.[60] On the one hand, post-Fordist commodities communicate these profiles. On the other hand, consumer purchases and internet browsing patterns produce data that allow more finely tuned surveillance, marketing, and exploitation. Thanks to the trackable traces of prior choices, Amazon.com can tailor its marketing to us more closely, websites can individualize the appearance of webpages (and their advertising) to us, and Google can personalize "information" to our interest profiles when we use its search engines. In this way, we are increasingly digitally enclaved and enclosed. (And this, in turn, is homologous to the increased segmentation and segregation of lived geographic space.) Rather than being oriented to social norms, subjective experience under neoliberal, post-Fordist conditions is increasingly narcissistic, enclosed, and self-referential, like a market niche. It also becomes ungrounded and disoriented.

### Consequences for Punishment and Policing

What have been the consequences of control superseding weakened disciplinary institutions and norm-oriented subjects for punishment and policing? Prisons and policing are institutions that nest within a broader lattice of political institutions, social organization, and cultural sensibilities.[61] Disciplinary institutions oriented to the socialization of education and training contributed to the democratization of aptitude and capacity. The decline of disciplinary institutions Hardt and Negri describe was triggered during an era of broader crisis in the wake of the 1960s and 1970s. In the United States, these crises instigated a crisis of democracy, an urban fiscal crisis producing transformed urban political economies neglectful of human dignity, equality, and social reproduction, and a crime crisis that weakened social solidarity and encouraged reactionary support for repressive state actions against the despised and disparaged. That is, these crises set in motion institutional and cultural transformations useful for neoliberal authoritarianism.

As mentioned in chapter 3, Nixon pointedly rejected the conclusions of the Kerner Commission from the campaign trail in 1968, fracturing its hegemonic reception.[62] He complained that its normatively oriented report, articulating concern for the legitimation crisis contemporary institutions faced in light of the glaring injustices it documented, blamed everyone except the (black) rioters for civil disorder.[63] This, and his conflation of riots, crime, and protest, would produce a profound shift in political culture, directing attention away from questions of normative legitimacy and toward a crisis engendered by too many taking democratic commitments at their word.[64] The political, social, and cultural supports for social democracy and penal modernism collapsed like "a house of cards" in the wake of the crisis of democracy, the urban fiscal crisis, and the crime crisis. The joint "collapse of faith" in penal modernism and the deeper horizon of solidaristic social democracy as a normative standard for society's institutions was like a reaction to, or a reaction that causes, a "stock market crash."[65]

*Prisons*

The consequences for prisons and punishment in the United States were dramatic. Incarceration rates increased steadily, exponentially, and without relation to fluctuations in crime rates.[66] Racially, prison populations became increasingly black and Hispanic due to extreme racial disparities in admissions between the late 1970s and 1990s.[67] The relation of the prison to society also changed from the diagram of discipline, where the prison's function was corrections and rehabilitation with an eye to reintegrating the offender as a productive member of society, to the postliberal, post-democratic logic of incapacitation or "waste management" of those deemed "too risky" to be permitted within society.[68] Carceral control also extended beyond the enclosures of the prison. Those sentenced to non-prison-based detention, in addition to probation or parole, would now be monitored through control devices such as ankle bracelets or other communicative hardware.[69] This transformation from discipline to control, though, is nowhere more apparent than in the frenzy of prison building that focused on secure housing units (SHUs) for long-term solitary confinement.

No supermax is more notorious than Pelican Bay in California.[70] The story the institution tells itself to justify itself is that it is built in reaction to black revolutionaries like George Jackson, a member of the Black Guerrilla Family (BGF), a prison-based group with ties to the Black Panthers.[71] Jackson was an inmate who pleaded guilty to a minor robbery (despite protestations of his innocence to family and friends) in exchange for what he expected would be a short jail term. Instead, the judge sentenced him to "one year to life," and he was repeatedly denied parole. At San Quentin, Jackson studied radical political theorists. From the perspective of correctional officers (COs), those who read radical political theory or who were associated with BGF were gang members. In the late 1960s and early 1970s, black prisoners were killed with impunity by white guards, and white guards were sometimes killed in retribution. The retaliatory violence by guards in such events could be extreme, and went unpunished. Prison administration officials fingered Jackson for murder after a white guard plummeted to his death off the third tier of a cell block, and Jackson himself was killed by guards under highly mysterious circumstances in 1971. Surviving members of the BGF, or anyone believed to have been associated with Jackson, were kept under permanent lockdown, and the supermax became the institutional expression of the permanent lockdown.[72]

Jackson remains a mythic figure for California prison officials and their justification for the supermax.[73] For example, according to Carl Larson, who served as a CO at San Quentin in the 1960s, became "warden of new prison design and activation" in the mid-1980s, and would claim credit for having designed Pelican Bay, "'the national revolutionary movement that culminated in George Jackson' was pivotal to understanding why California built a supermax."[74] California's first supermax was Pelican Bay, and Pelican Bay has served as the model for supermaxes around the country, including the first federal facility in Colorado and for the isolation units in the U.S. military prison at Guantanamo Bay, Cuba.[75] According to criminologist Keramet Reiter, "nearly every state that experienced [prison] riots and lockdowns eventually followed California's lead, building a supermax prison to institutionalize lockdowns."[76]

Pelican Bay represents the transition from discipline to control with extreme intensity. At Pelican Bay, like other supermaxes, inmates are kept in solitary confinement twenty-three hours a day, seven days a week, with no human contact, and with nothing to do except legal work, or tasks and hobbies of the inmate's own devising. Meals are served on a tray through a slot in the door, and the tray is returned the same way. Correctional officers control cell doors electronically from a guard booth, where they monitor prisoners using video cameras.

Indiscipline proliferates in Pelican Bay. Although the doors to two different cells should never open simultaneously (since inmates are to be kept in solitary confinement and thus denied human contact), this does happen from time to time. Guards at Pelican Bay in the 1990s were known to encourage "gladiator fights"—fights between inmates—for their own amusement.[77] Their history of torturous treatment of inmates is medieval. One mentally ill prisoner was placed in a bath of scalding water: "You could smell my skin burning. I was cooking."[78] In an attempt to break a leader of a hunger strike during the 2010s, COs put the hunger striker in a "suicide watch" cell covered with human feces.[79] Rather than receiving treatment, the mentally ill in the California prison system are placed in isolation, though research shows that even a few days in isolation causes psychological deterioration.[80] According to estimates, 33–50 percent of all prisoners in isolation are mentally ill, and 50–73 percent of all suicides in the California system occur in isolation. Prison officials are said to have difficulty distinguishing "mad from bad prisoners."[81]

The use of isolation and control technologies causes a disintegration of subjectivity for inmates.[82] Many are now released from the SHU at the end of their sentences, but they are released directly from isolation into society, begging the question of why such prisoners were in isolation to begin with: in California, prisoners deemed by the system to be too dangerous for the general prison population are now driven to a bus stop and left there. Those released from the SHU must rely on meager social services, family members, or others to help them to resocialize (e.g., learn how to be in public again) and rehumanize themselves (e.g., learn how to speak or smile again).[83] Those who survive isolation do so by resisting this antisocial, subjectively disintegrative institution by applying a highly disciplined daily regimen to themselves for years on end.[84]

For Foucault, the prison was a particularly intense site of disciplinary power expressing a broader disciplinary logic at the heart of modernity. If we apply similar reasoning attentive to the way the contemporary prison is likewise situated within a complex of complementary institutions, then the supermax is an especially intense site of control causing disintegration to human subjectivity, one representing a broader tendency of institutions in control societies to function in antisocial, socially and subjectively disintegrative ways.[85] More disturbingly, it is an institutional site where COs enact torturous cruelties with impunity out of callousness or for their own entertainment, and it is the site of degrading cruelties that society enjoys knowing exists.

## Policing

Policing, like punishment in the United States, has been transformed in reaction to the riots and broader political changes of the 1960s and 1970s. Though Epp describes the growth of the legalized accountability model in policing as having been influenced by the response to the riots represented by the Kerner Commission and other reports that urged reforms on police to control their abuse of force and violations of due process, the "Broken Windows" concept of zero tolerance, order maintenance policing was also motivated in part as a reaction to the riots of the 1960s. That is, Epp describes one arc of institutional transformation that grew out of the 1960s, one that sought to make police more like a law enforcement agency. A decade after the initial emergence of police reform, George Kelling and James Q. Wilson, the authors of "Broken Windows," helped advance a different arc of institutional development for policing in response to the 1960s, one that encouraged less legal accountability and more discretion for police. The institution of policing was divided—as Epp's research implicitly acknowledges—and while Epp highlights one side of this split where police became more legally accountable, "Broken Windows" represents the other side of this split, one where institutional pressure enables and encourages police to be less legally accountable.

As I've discussed in chapter 3, Kelling and Wilson refer to the "urban riots," thereby invoking the specter of black insurrection, in addition to "urban decay," to set the scene for their discussion of developments in policing.[86] They recount the shift in policing from order maintenance to crime fighting. Police used to make arrests on grounds of "'vagrancy' or 'public drunkenness'—charges with scarcely any legal meaning." "Once we begin to think of all aspects of police work as involving the application of universal rules," Kelling and Wilson observe with disapproval, it becomes impossible to define an "undesirable person," leading to the decriminalization of disorderly behavior that does not harm others (like public drunkenness or being homeless). Though the Supreme Court struck down as unconstitutional such vague laws enabling unconstrained police discretion, and the police became conceptualized as a law enforcement agency, for Kelling and Wilson, this is not an advance, but a "mistake." Police lost the tools they needed for their order maintenance function. The changes to policing in the 1970s making the institution more legalized neglected the role police played in order maintenance—a role that Kelling and Wilson, by the 1980s, believe neighborhoods want police to play and which they believe will prevent crime.[87]

The "Broken Windows" concept of policing contends that the focus on law enforcement that emerged from commission reports of the 1960s disabled police from maintaining order, leading to urban decline.[88] The "Broken Windows" concept of policing urges reempowering police discretion to address problems of "deviant behavior" and "disorder" encouraged by the judicial recognition of individual rights.[89] Rather than social welfare institutions or the helping professions addressing "root causes" of poverty, addiction, or homelessness, "Broken Windows" advocates for more and better police as a response to social problems or social disorganization.[90] "Broken Windows" policing manifests the split in policing, representing those in conflict with the advocates of legalized accountability and the practices Epp depicts as "making rights real."

Other developments within policing and criminology reinforced the unhinging of policing from law enforcement that "Broken Windows" advocated. Fueled, in part, by the expansion of "mass private property," the private security sector grew in comparison with public police forces, and by the 1970s and 1980s would increasingly outnumber municipal or state police.[91] One of the primary characteristics of private security was the way it sidelined the legal process to privilege prevention and to minimize costs.[92] By the 1990s, some criminologists pointed to private security as modeling the "future of policing."[93] Private security was an example that public police were "beginning to recognize" by demonstrating to public police "the inherent limitations of their justice-based approach."[94] Developments in policing and criminology occurring concurrently with advocacy of the "Broken Windows" concept of order maintenance policing bolstered the trend away from law enforcement as the purpose of policing, further unmooring policing from legal accountability.[95]

The consequences of perceiving the solution to social problems as more policing, unshackled police discretion, and an institutional neglect of legal norms are represented in Judge Scheindlin's 2013 decision in *Floyd v. City of New York* ruling the New York Police Department's (NYPD) stop and frisk policy unconstitutional. The factual findings of that ruling show institutional patterns of racial bias unconstrained by legal norms. In 83 percent of NYPD stops, the person stopped was either black or Hispanic, and in only 10 percent of cases was the person white. Weapons were found only in approximately 1 percent of all stops of black and Hispanic people, and contraband other than a weapon was found in less than 2 percent of cases (weapons or other contraband were more likely to be found in stops of white people). Rather than individualized suspicion, people were stopped by NYPD because they were black or Hispanic.[96] According to Scheindlin, there was "no evidence . . . that the quality of stops in the sense of their *constitutionality* receives meaningful review" by the NYPD.[97] Without legal constraint, race determines those whom the NYPD targets as potentially disorderly or criminal.

The growing use of control technologies, in conjunction with the collapse of the social democratic horizon, contributes to post–legal legitimation, post-democratic policing. The NYPD is well known for developing CompStat, a computerized mapping process keeping track of local crimes and police activity. At weekly CompStat meetings, NYPD Chief Esposito and his assistant chief would evaluate a unit based on the number of stops they performed. Commanders were pressured to increase stops, and they conveyed this pressure down the line to other NYPD personnel: between 2002 and 2011, the NYPD increased stops by about 700 percent.[98] Indiscipline and conduct unhinged from legal normativity grew. The number of stops without legal justification increased from 1 percent to 36 percent between 2004 and 2009, and "*every* patrol borough . . . failed *every* annual audit of activity log entries corresponding to stops for the last decade," prior to Scheindlin's ruling.[99]

Advocates of "Broken Windows" urge police to focus on minor, quality of life violations and to treat them with zero tolerance. This becomes an opportunity to see if any warrants appear in the system for the suspect. It also becomes an opportunity to enter this person into the system. The zero tolerance approach to policing reflects the theory that some are too risky (or evil) to be tolerated in society, so getting them off the street for a minor violation prevents more serious crimes. This is where the shift in penology from corrections to incapacitation links up with the shift in policing from law enforcement to order maintenance. Homologous to the way control technologies amplify the subjectively disintegrative effects of incapacitation penology, Katherine Beckett and Steve Herbert's study of the Seattle Police Department (SPD) demonstrates how control technologies amplify the ease and effects of the "Broken Windows" concept of policing in removing the poor or racially disparaged from valorized urban space.

While on patrol, the SPD will look for people who appear "out of place."[100] The SPD will then stop the person and run their name through the communications system. In Seattle, "Stay Out of Drug Area" (SODA) and "Stay Out of Areas of Prostitution" (SOAP) are common conditions for probation or parole. If the SPD determines that the person has such an order, then they can be arrested if they are found in designated drug or prostitution zones. Moreover, the Seattle legal code authorizes police to issue "park exclusion orders" for those in violation of park rules. The violation of the park rules is noncriminal, and the order is civil in nature. Violating the exclusion order, however, is a criminal offense. Likewise, the SPD has arrangements with some of Seattle's landlords who have delegated trespass authority to the police. This allows police to issue trespass admonishments to "suspicious" people on otherwise open properties, the violation of which, again, is a criminal offense. The legal hybridity of the last two orders—they are a civil-criminal hybrid—vastly expands police power. The evidentiary burden of the civil order is basically the word of the police officer, and in a remarkable 59.8 percent of trespass admonishments in the authors' sample, no reason was given for the trespass admonishment.[101] The consequences for violating the order, however, are criminal.[102] As Beckett and Herbert observe, it is hard to think of an easier arrest than stopping someone based on their appearance in conjunction with where they are located, running their name, and seeing if the name registers in the system.[103] In fact, the SPD are so dependent on the computer terminals in their cars accessing databases that when the system is down, they can be at a loss for what to do.[104]

Because much of downtown Seattle is in a SODA or SOAP area, and because downtown public parks are closely patrolled, these four legal tools empower the SPD to control the appearance of downtown Seattle. Those who bear the brunt of this policing, though, are the poor and racial minorities. Beckett and Herbert estimate that between half and two-thirds of those who receive trespass admonishments are homeless. The number of black people receiving park exclusions is five times greater than their percentage of the Seattle population. Native Americans receive ten times more park exclusion orders than their proportion of Seattle residents should merit.[105] The "Broken Windows" concept of policing, the legal tools Seattle provides police to enable this concept of policing, and the amplification of the effects of this policing through control technologies produces consequences at odds with legal normativity. Homeless veterans or Native Americans—especially if they are drinking—are at risk of being banished from downtown Seattle. They are undesirable people from the perspective of neoliberal, post-Fordist urban political economy. Tourists picnicking in a city park with wine coolers, or drunken tourists stumbling off a cruise ship, are not similarly at risk of exclusion or arrest.[106]

The SPD polices urban aesthetics with discretion unshackled from legal constraint, and the control technologies upon which they rely exacerbate the race-based and class-based discrimination contributing to Seattle's place-based aesthetic production. In addition to the subjective degradation from the status of equal citizenship experienced by those targeted, this policing is subjectively unhealthy for those banished from safer parks in more centralized locations where their friends or other people also congregate. Moreover, this form of policing is positively Kafkaesque for those subjected to SOAP or SODA orders who suffer from substance abuse problems, or who have a right to other forms of disability support, because many of those services are located in areas subject to SOAP or SODA orders.[107] In other words, this form of policing is not legally accountable and has disintegrative effects on those subjected to it in terms of their civil status and their mental and physical health.

Policing is further transformed by the digitalized semiotic traces of our activities becoming exchange value to be bought and sold by commercial data brokers or communicated and gambled upon by finance capital.[108] Not only does this deepen economic exploitability of human subjects by capital, it expands the reach and capacity of the state to disintegrate the social and the subject. Subjects are disintegrated—dividuated—into bits of digital data to be communicated, mined, and communicated again by commercial surveillance, state surveillance, and state surveillance that is enhanced and extended by commercial data or those who provide data aggregation and integration platforms (such as Palantir Technologies).[109] As police are increasingly inserted into communications networks providing access to noncriminal data, or they increasingly purchase or otherwise obtain access to databases compiled by commercial data brokers, we can expect the effects of policing undisciplined by legal norms to become intensified.[110] Such communicative policing simulates and projects criminal suspicion based on consumer behavior, geographic location, other associative characteristics, or police-initiated communicative activity. In some data aggregation systems, one police query becomes data influencing the results of other police queries.[111] Furthermore, when police use commercial data, policing assesses risk and probability based on consumer behavior and socioeconomic inequalities.[112] In other words, legal norms of due process and equal protection are further eroded and are displaced by market-based inequalities or police bias repackaged in a technocratic veneer of risk analysis and data analytics.

Because "many of the resources for developing big data analytics come from federal funds," criminologist Sarah Brayne expects police departments will continue to use big data regardless of its utility for reducing crime because the federal funds available for these technologies are becoming a routinized part of their budgets.[113] Elsewhere, I have expressed a similar expectation as commercial entities become stakeholders lobbying for the continuation and expansion of state reliance on their data and data analytics for state security practices.[114] We should recall, though, that Congress stimulated policing's integration within the networks of control technologies in reaction to the riots of the 1960s. The Safe Streets Act of 1968, passed in reaction to the riots, provided money not only to enhance police hardware but also to build communications systems networking police departments and creating the capacity for local police departments to interface with data sources through the National Crime Information Center. Using these funds, states began creating electronically accessible databases of criminal histories, and Congress further facilitated state development of computerized intelligence systems to analyze the potential for civil disorder, conflating dissenter with terrorist.[115] Thus, like prisons geared to incapacitation rather than corrections, the specter of black insurrection set in motion important transformations in policing.

## Policing Protest

Let's carry forward the integration of policing within communicative networks, and its embrace of control technologies, by considering how it has affected the policing of protest. The policing of protest could not remain unaffected by the emergence of the "Broken Windows" concept of policing emphasizing zero tolerance for minor violations to maintain order. And it wasn't. Negotiated management might be considered the highest expression of penal modernism due to its embeddedness within disciplinary power, its commitment to social integration, and its normative orientation.[116] By encouraging dialogue between police and protesters, negotiated management promotes social integration and the reduction of physical violence, both important aspects of disciplinary power. Moreover, negotiated management presupposes a clear hierarchy of value, where people are more important than property. Finally, by recognizing the fundamental constitutional right to assemble and demonstrate to redress the people's grievances, negotiated management is normatively oriented to the horizon of social democracy. Negotiated management encourages restraint on police arrests, and thus tolerance for minor violations, so that antipathy toward disorder does not submerge more primary commitments to democratic practices to remedy injustice.[117]

The "Broken Windows" concept of policing, by urging zero tolerance for minor violations, institutionalizes an antithetical model of policing that is fundamentally at odds with negotiated management. As we have seen, its commitment to "kicking ass" encourages and enjoys police perpetrating petty, violent cruelties upon protesters. Moreover, by hosting mega-events, cities operate within national constraints regarding security and operate according to neoliberal, post-Fordist urban political economic incentives to prevent disorder and to encourage controlled communicative participation in the event. The growing integration of control technologies within order maintenance policing to target the economically disadvantaged and the racially disparaged is also used to control and displace protesters in urban space.

The capacity for control has grown since the NYPD's Intelligence Division trolled internet websites to prepare for policing the 2002 World Economic Forum and 2004 Republican National Convention (RNC). Police monitor, sometimes using the services of social media intelligence firms, those posting under selected hashtags. Moreover, police and marketers will contract with social media intelligence firms promoting geofencing capabilities, such as Geofeedia, to "track and collect users' posts as soon as they are disseminated within a bounded" geographic area.[118] By tracking and collecting protester social media data, Geofeedia provides police "situation awareness" of protests (this technology is also useful for marketers because it allows them to push social media advertising at targeted groups). This use of control technology has been used to target #BlackLivesMatter protests in particular.[119]

Not only do police track and collect protester social media data, police have also shut down or interrupted cell phone and internet service to disrupt protests. For example, Bay Area Rapid Transit shut down cell phone and internet service at its San Francisco stations to derail demonstrator plans to protest the police shooting of a homeless man.[120] Arrested Trump inauguration protesters had their phones seized to search and obtain their social media activity in 2017.[121] These developments in the area of police use of control technologies are increasingly significant because First Amendment jurisprudence has permitted growing burdens on demonstrations in public space. Courts justify displacing demonstrations from the target of the protests to marginal spaces, located far from an intended audience, on the grounds that "modern communications," including the internet, allow protesters to reach their audiences even if they cannot address them firsthand.[122] Clearly, the oligopolistic economy of media ownership reduces the likelihood that ordinary people's disintegrated communications will reach as far as the amplified communications of those promoting a mega-event, reducing the effective political and social voice of protesters.[123] By forcing protesters to rely on social media to have any voice at all, though, contemporary First Amendment jurisprudence coerces protesters into situations where police can completely silence protesters by shutting down communications services. It also requires demonstrators to communicate through a medium vulnerable to police surveillance, and vulnerable to police acquiring all their communicative content for later communicatively creative use.

In sum, Epp's important scholarship exploring how police came to control better the abuse of force highlights the institutionalized growth of the norm of legalized accountability, due, in part, to the commission reports of the 1960s that were written in the wake of the riots. By seeking to explain what makes a police department more or less likely to adopt the legalized accountability model, Epp's scholarship evinces a split within policing by accentuating factors leading to legal accountability's development, while also identifying factors negatively associated with a police department's adoption of legalized accountability. I also acknowledge the split within policing in the United States, but I have accentuated institutional developments at odds with legalized accountability on the other side of this split within policing.[124]

The developments I have accentuated were also set in motion by the riots of the 1960s, but as a reaction against conceptualizing the police as law enforcement. In addition to spotlighting the turn away from legal normativity, I have underscored how prisons and police institutions came to function in a socially and subjectively disintegrative manner by building on the work of those finding that Foucault's important insights on the normalizing power of modern disciplinary institutions are being superseded by distinctive logics of power operating within the state and economy that are no longer oriented to social integration or the normative horizon of social democracy. The disintegrative, post–legal legitimation, post-democratic tendencies of control societies are further exacerbated by communicative capitalism.

## Communicative Capitalism

Communicative capitalism aggravates the erosion of disciplined and normatively oriented subjectivity, and the effects of social and subjective distintegration produced by control technologies. Communicative capitalism is capitalism as communicative production such that communication comes to incorporate, mediate, arrange, fragment, and communicate virtually all spheres of life.[125] In this mode of production, communicative capitalism is sustained, in part, through communicative production and uncompensated labor producing "content," communicating communication, and the experience of communicativity and communicative potential.[126] For example, oligopolistic media and their media products rely on viewers retweeting and recirculating their communications, sometimes with an added, creative, and communicative twist.

Because markets are, theoretically, relations of sellers responding to preferences out of self-interest, under communicative capitalism, the social or symbolic power of expertise is diminished because every piece of communicated advice or information is considered by the user as self-interested or as preference rather than knowledge based or truth oriented. Here, communicative capitalism contributes to the erosion of disciplinary institutions of professional knowledge.

This postfact, posttruth experience of communicative capitalism is heightened through reflexivity. Online news sites adjust the presentation of news stories based on hits or what consumers of the site want to see.[127] Ads and information are adjusted to one's search histories, cookies stored on one's browser, or one's activities and associations on Facebook. Such personalized informational experiences, or filter bubbles, mean that shared social standards, professional metrics, or legal or ethical norms by which one can compare better or worse, progress or regress, truth or falsity, are lacking under contemporary conditions, thereby undermining conditions sustaining expertise, legal normativity, public institutions, and democratic deliberation.[128] Moreover, in a condition of reflexivity doubled, to the extent that internet users are aware of these algorithms and systemic reflexivities producing market niches and distinctive, disintegrative experiences for diverse users, one can react either with a detached "whatever" to that which one encounters, or decide that one's opinions, preferences, or affective attachments are as good as anyone else's.

Longtime Fox News anchor Shepard ("Shep") Smith visually presented the communicative embeddedness, the communicative equivalences, and the communication of communication under conditions of communicative capitalism when he introduced the Fox News Deck to viewers.[129] The News Deck moves from screens where sports appear to celebrity news, or perhaps a story about another mass shooting or genocide, or a political announcement, each appearing on equivalent screens, encouraging the viewer to experience the flow of images as communicatively equivalent regardless of content. Those subjected to communicative capitalism encounter the communicative equivalence of all opinion along a common denominator of communicativity, cultivating a condition of reflexivity without normativity. Whether one is a religious fundamentalist, a doctor, or a political strategist, no one's opinion is "truer" than anyone else's.

Communicative capitalism forces us to grapple with the changed role of communication in comparison with Jürgen Habermas's discourse ethics. The communication of communicative capitalism does not easily fit into Habermasian categories of normatively acceptable discourse or rational-technical means-ends utility for administrative or scientific efficiency. Communication has become a component of economic production, further blurring the distinction between economic base and political-legal-ideological superstructure. The News Deck exhibits contemporary mediality producing news. This synergy created by users of social media and oligopolistic media manifests communicative capitalism: when we communicate, or when the digital traces of communication are mined from us, it is now a relation or an input of capitalist production. As part of economic production, on the one hand, and as part of normatively ungrounded market exchanges, on the other, the sincerity and normative orientation of communication matter less because communication is not functioning toward the production of consensus governed by principles of normative universalizability or the discovery of truth. Instead, communication is a force or relation of production, embedded in exchange value relations, or is a vehicle for affective association and expression within a niche (or under a hashtag).

## Communicative Capitalism's Political Subjects

This experience of disintegrated mediality corresponds to a manner of subjectivity at ease with the communication of communicativity beyond meaningful semantic content. We can call this subjective orientation "whatever being." Whatever being is a subject at ease with the no longer hidden mediality of communication, with communication expressing communicative potential unfixed from content-based meaning, and with interpretive pluralism—the communication of whatever. Communicative capitalism therefore amplifies a connection that Michael Hardt draws between the experience of control societies and Giorgio Agamben's concept of "whatever being."[130] Control, according to Hardt, "functions on the basis of the 'whatever,' the flexible and mobile performance of contingent identities, and thus its assemblages or institutions are elaborated primarily through repetition and the production of simulacra."[131] Hardt is the translator of Agamben's *Coming Community*, where Agamben describes whatever being as singularity exposed "as such."[132] Whatever being is a "perfect exteriority" of humans experiencing "their own linguistic being—not this or that content of language, but language *itself*, not this or that true proposition, but the very fact that one speaks."[133] It is the communication of communicability and the exhibition of mediality as such.[134] This sharing of the communicative experience in itself occurs without presupposition, foundation, or condition of belonging. This is communication without revelation.[135] It is a communication of . . . whatever.

Viral memes can illustrate whatever being's communication of communicability, communicative potential through repetition, the exhibition of mediality, and communication without revelation. An internet meme is an element of media that spreads through creative and repetitive transmission.[136] The meme could be generated from a funny YouTube video of two children ("Charlie Bit My Finger"), something absurd (a prairie dog appearing to be a chipmunk looking over its shoulder dramatically), a gesture utterly common that simultaneously expresses singularity (person blinking), or a quirky gesture. They often exhibit their own mediality, or they are used to communicate reflexivity, such as when a reaction meme is used to communicate "I am communicating that I am reacting." For instance, a photo of Kim Kardashian West advertising sneakers became a viral meme. She has an oddly blank stare and is in an awkward position on a bed. The image of her was quickly Photoshopped and inserted into a variety of absurd and amusing situations or backgrounds that were widely communicated, and the event of the image-becoming-meme itself was communicated.[137] An image of an awkward Kim Kardashian West lying among the toys from *Toy Story*, or appearing to win the San Francisco Marathon with an awkward gesture, means whatever though it exhibits its own mediality and communicability. Whatever being is at ease with this communication of communicability.

Images of police subjecting protesters to violence have also become viral memes. For example, a video of campus security officer John Pike pepper spraying University of California–Davis students seated on the ground in protest went viral as one of the top memes of 2011. Some of these reworked images seem to be political, like Pike pepper spraying the Declaration of Independence or the Constitution. Others use Pike reflexively to express the internet's affinity for memes by having him pepper spray keyboard cat. Some were artistic, such as the image of Pike pepper spraying rendered as a Banksy painting. Others seem random, like Pike's pepper spray appearing as light through a prism from Pink Floyd's album cover for *Dark Side of the Moon*.[138] The "Casually Pepper Spray Everything Cop" (also known as "Pepper Spray Cop") meme gallery posted on KnowYourMeme.com seems literally endless.

*Figure 4.1* Images of police subjecting protesters to violence can become viral memes. The image of campus security officer John Pike pepper spraying peacefully seated University of California–Davis students became the "Casually Pepper Spray Everything Cop" ("Pepper Spray Cop") meme. Here, the image of Pike is rendered as a work of contemporary street art in a style evoking the artist Banksy.

These remixes express the infinite communicative potential of whatever through an associational mode of thought as necessary to the arts and to branding as it is to the recirculation of memes.[139]

Control technologies and communicative capitalism are complementary concepts. At a basic level, both are enabled by communicative production, the mining and aggregation of the digital tracks of life increasingly embedded within communicative networks, and the marketing of access to this communicative universe. Additionally, they both utilize a logic of associative reason. Much like becoming meme strengthens the Kim Kardashian brand (and the brand of sneakers she was wearing) through multiplicative association, rather than a central meaning or principle, or the way that the shapes and color scheme of an iteration of the Pike pepper spray meme evoke the NBA trademark or an album cover, likewise, one becomes suspicious and risky through Palantir or Geofeedia or other social media intelligence platforms by associative reasoning. Who are you associated with? What is your credit rating? Where do you live? What hashtag did you tweet under? Who did you retweet? Where were you located at that time? Who was near you? What political views did you express?

More significantly, both cultivate a flexible, communicable, or disintegrated subjectivity. Hardt describes the subjective effects of control technologies as whatever being. The worker under neoliberal, post-Fordist conditions must be flexible and open to whatever. Likewise, Dean uses whatever being to designate the subjective effects of communicative capitalism.[140] The subject flexibly receptive to the pluralization of interpretation, or the diversity of purposeless communicative expression for its own sake (means without end), is not a disciplined subject. The subject open to whatever is the opposite of a subject trained to certain purposes or educated to discern better from worse—ideally, a judge, for example, discriminates between better and worse legal interpretations rather than merely reveling in the multiplicity of interpretation.

Connected with cultivating the subjectivity of whatever, both control and communicative capitalism engender the corrosion of norms. Control technologies enable policing neglectful of legal norms while enabling or amplifying the use of nonlegal factors to direct police activity by affective association, including race, visible poverty, and communicated markers of economic precarity. With respect to communicative capitalism, an openness to whatever, again, is the opposite of norm-oriented practice. Norms collapse with the demise of subjects capable of sustaining them or the emergence of subjects who fail to recognize norms as such.

Here, Žižek's and Dean's use of psychoanalytic theory to express the collapse of the symbolic order, its consequences for subjective identities, and how this leads to a decline in symbolic efficiency may be useful. The symbolic order refers to belief, what one believes others believe, or what one must express for the "big Other." It is the domain of language, legal norms, public institutions, and public appearances. When someone acts a certain way or says something because it is expected, or when one believes and acts as if the judge's ruling has authority regardless of how one feels about the judge as a person, this is evidence of the symbolic order.[141]

The symbolic order also anchors symbolic identities as one performs before the gaze of the big Other or one's ego ideal. The subject asks, Who am I (for the big Other)? How do others see me? With respect to the question of desire, the subject will ask, What do I want? What is wanted of me? What should I want? What do others desire that I should desire? Desire "addresses itself to the symbolic big Other, it seeks active recognition from it."[142] Of course, there cannot be a final answer or resolution to this question of desire for the subject—there will always be something missing. Each thing attained will not quite be it or the Thing the subject seeks to fulfill his or her fantasy. This is why desire is ultimately open and never to be finally fulfilled, even as the subject strives to maintain one's desire.

The symbolic order also sustains the efficient functioning of language, law, and norms. The law has "symbolic efficiency" when "everyone" knows what it means and acts to carry out its rulings (or recognizes legal transgression). Within communicative capitalism, however, the proliferation of communication and the communicative equivalence of everyone's opinion exacerbates the erosion of the symbolic order, and we experience the "decline of symbolic efficiency" with particular intensity.[143] This unraveling of the symbolic order is apparent in broader society when a member of Congress becomes so overcome with emotion that he fails to respect the "Office of the President" by yelling "You lie!" while the president delivers a speech before Congress or when Donald Trump fails to recognize judicial authority and opines that a judge cannot judge because he is "Mexican."[144]

With the erosion of symbolic authority, recognized (by the big Other, by everyone) symbolic identities are weakened. For example, because of the diminished authority of medical expertise, we are told to "go online" to "get information" about our diet or health. Of course, there are limitless views online, many of which are contradictory, so we are told to choose "what is right for you." Choosing the information that is "right for you" not only speaks to the decline of symbolic efficiency of medical knowledge (choose what you like), it also manifests the decline of symbolic identities and the corresponding significance of the imaginary.[145] Because someone's self-image might change with the encounter of new information (perhaps because of its associations), Dean shows how identity has become more unstable, insecure, or more open to whatever under conditions of communicative capitalism.

The mobility and flexibility of communicative capitalism, openness to whatever, and encouragement of expression accommodates and aggravates the collapse of the normatively hegemonic horizon of social democracy that Nixon's response to the riots set in motion. Communicative capitalism also accommodates and facilitates another mode of political subjectivity—whatever being's doppelganger—also set in motion by Nixon's response to the riots. Nixon punctuated this collapse of the social democratic horizon during his 1968 campaign by refusing the very premise, or place of enunciation, of the Kerner Commission's report in his response to its release.[146]

Nixon failed to recognize the legitimacy of the Kerner Commission's presupposed audience; he did not recognize the credibility of its recommendations, did not interpret himself as being obligated by its recommendations, and, because he was not interpellated by the commission's authority, the reasons it gave for its recommendations did not register with him as meriting response or engagement.

We can describe the Kerner Commission as acting within the parameters of disciplinary society by the nature of its inquiries: Why did the riots occur? What is the meaning of the riots for society and the state? Based on this knowledge, how can we prevent civil disorder? The Kerner Commission produced evidence of a contradiction between accepted democratic norms and material inequalities in conjunction with racially abusive policing. It pointed to a crisis of legitimacy for the United States and its democratic commitments. Nixon, however, simply blamed the rioters for rioting, unperturbed by the gaze of the big Other, who might judge him poorly for his neglect.[147] Indeed, his political biographer, Rick Perlstein, demonstrates how Nixon achieved political gains by being judged poorly by "liberals," the "elite," or the "media," because such blame only built his political appeal among those whose voices had no credibility according to the social democratic norms then determining legitimacy.[148]

In 1968, many in the South (and northern cities) left the Democratic Party to vote for Wallace, and many in the suburbs (and the South) did the same to support Nixon. A task force report to the National Commission on the Causes and Prevention of Violence in 1970 (distinct from the task force that studied protests for this national commission) sought to understand the violent potential or support for violence expressed by these emergent voices and affective energies in a study and character portrait of what they called the "Forgotten Man." The "Forgotten Man" repeated an identifier Nixon used for his supporters, whom he also called "non-demonstrators," at the 1968 RNC.[149] As characterized by the task force, the Forgotten Man (and Woman—the task force's report also referred to interviews with women) is antigovernment but supports police cracking down on rioters, Civil Rights demonstrators, and college protesters. The Forgotten Man (and Woman) are distrustful of authority; they don't "trust or believe." They are prone to conspiratorial thinking and using the N-word to refer to black people, though they don't perceive themselves as "bigots." One interviewee liked Franklin Delano Roosevelt, and John, Robert, and Ted Kennedy, but didn't like Johnson or the War on Poverty, believing that black people "like being on welfare." She voted for Nixon because she didn't want to throw her vote away by voting for Wallace. An interviewee from West Virginia, however, extended his populism, as the task force noted, "without embarrassment" or "overemphasis," to "our black brothers." Another interviewee is stockpiling weapons and ammunition. The report characterizes the Forgotten Man and Woman as a "receptive potential audience for racists and super-patriots." The task force assesses them, in the condescending tones liberal experts use, as lacking the "high level of educational sophistication and ego security" necessary for "acceptance of the norms of democracy." The Forgotten Man and Woman are portrayed as both "prey of the extremists" on the far right and, using Nixon's felicitous phrase, as the "silent majority." According to the task force, their most prominent attributes are that they suffer from resentment, envy, disappointment, and uncertainty, believing their power has been "stolen" by "blacks and their liberal allies" (or their spokesmen). With their power stolen, they yearn for a return to America's "good old days."[150]

The task force's portrait of the Forgotten Man (and Woman) anticipates the logic of Žižek's concept of "theft of enjoyment," which he uses to explore ethnic violence in Eastern Europe during and after the fall of the Soviet Union: America would be unified, enjoying prosperity and security, just like the good old days, if blacks and their liberal allies had not taken equal citizenship at its word. Or, my enjoyment of my citizenship has been stolen or tainted by those now enjoying the rights of citizenship long denied them even more than I do (or can). As Žižek observes, however, stolen enjoyment ultimately refers to the subject's own excess of enjoyment or hatred of the subject's own enjoyment. For the Forgotten Man and Woman, this means that their excessive enjoyment of citizenship derives precisely from performatively relegating black people to second-class status (I enjoy my citizenship insofar as black people are subjected to degradation and do not enjoy equal citizenship).[151]

The portrait of the Forgotten Man (and Woman) registers movement, flux, and confusion, as previous political allegiances—structured by the New Deal coalition—have become unsettled by the Wallace campaign and by Nixon's Southern strategy. The distrust of authority and the refusal to believe, reported by the task force, exhibit the collapse of the symbolic order. Moreover, the Forgotten Man's (and Woman's) affective attachment to a loss of power and victimhood at the hands of black people and liberal elites, expressed through resentment, envy, disappointment, and uncertainty, will be repetitively politically mobilized by Republican campaigns from the 1980s onward. It would provide one potential channel directing the political anger of those coming to experience increased economic precarity resulting from the growing intensity of neoliberal inequalities. Significantly, no political victory, no capture of Congress, the presidency, the judiciary, or state governments, no policy victory—such as ending welfare in 1996, increasing budgets for police departments, racially disproportionate uses of police violence, or stunning increases of black and Hispanic people in prisons—and no capture of media outlets, or desegregation decrees ended, will make this political subject feel any less like they have been taken advantage of by blacks and their liberal allies. Despite winning office or media attention by expressing antipathy—and enjoying expressing antipathy—toward black people, Hispanic people, women, and those who are gay or trans, they claim they are punished by the politically correct. They remain victims, and they remain stuck within the political coordinates of 1968.[152]

This stuckness in resentment regardless of political victory, increased economic or environmental precarity, or destructive effects of their policy victories on broader society (the social bond) is an effect not of desire, but of what psychoanalytic theory calls drive exceeding the pleasure principle. Drive is "inert" and "non-subjectivized."[153] It is "where questioning stops."[154] It is a "destructive force, which endlessly undermines the points of support that the subject has found in the symbolic universe. . . . There is no longer any identification, there is only *jouissance* [enjoyment]."[155] Drive is a "constant pressure . . . a painful satisfaction" that is "indifferent" to the symbolic order or "the way it will affect social life."[156]

Communicative capitalism captures, feeds, and feeds off drive. According to Dean, drive is the "compulsive shape of networked media as they enact the loss of symbolic efficiency."[157] As it does for whatever being, communicative capitalism provides a rich ecology for whatever being's doppelganger. Nonlinear associations appearing in constituent letters quoted by Perlstein, where blacks, civil rights, federal bureaucracies, loss of freedom or civil rights for whites, liberalism, welfare, taxes, whites being made into "suckers," riots, socialism or communism, and crime are keywords that trigger another association to another keyword and become, under communicative capitalism, one link that associatively links to another.[158] As Dean writes, "I enter; I click; I link; I poke. . . . The circulation of contributions in the networks of communicative capitalism suggests a . . . structure, one characterized by drive."[159] Communicative capitalism amplifies nonlinear associative reason, sustaining and stimulating the doppelganger's enjoyment while expressing resentments.

Drive is like the "flow of water into multiple tributaries and canals."[160] For Žižek, modern science—or its subfields—is one such canal. Science "follows its path . . . heedless of cost," where satisfaction is "provided by knowledge itself," or by contributions to knowledge.[161] Communicative capitalism, as Dean shows, is also such a canal. Likewise, within communicative capitalism, media platforms such as Breitbart.com, which captures and repeats substantive elements composing the Forgotten Man (and Woman), canalize and become the vehicle for enjoying anger and outrage at progressives who tell the doppelganger that, due to demographic changes in America, his or her way of thinking is dead.[162] The doppelganger repeatedly communicates personalized affective expression unconstrained by the norms of impersonal, legitimate public discourse. In a mutually reinforcing relation, on the one hand, communicative capitalism accommodates the expression of anger by whatever being's doppelganger in one of its niches, and, on the other hand, the expression of anger adds contributions to the communicative universe— communicative contributions to be retweeted, condemned, forwarded, or enjoyed for the expression of that opinion, which is equivalent to all the others.[163] Communicative capitalism sustains, feeds, and is fed by the doppelganger as it is by whatever being.

### Violent Appearances

Since 1999, the policing of protest has been visibly violent. Abusive policing of protest occurred at the 1999 World Trade Organization (WTO) protests; the 2000 DNC in Los Angeles and RNC in Philadelphia; the 2000 International Monetary Fund/World Bank (IMF/WB) protests in Washington, DC; the 2002 IMF/WB protests, and antiwar protests in Washington, DC; the 2003 antiwar protests in New York City, Chicago, and Oakland; the 2003 Free Trade Area of the Americas (FTAA) protests in Miami; the 2004 RNC in New York City; the 2007 May Day protest in Los Angeles; the 2008 RNC in St. Paul, Minnesota; the 2009 G-20 protests in Pittsburgh; the 2011 OWS protests; and the 2014 uprising in Ferguson and subsequent #BlackLivesMatter protests. This repeatedly abusive policing of protest has resulted in civil litigation producing significant settlements, as the following sample indicates: $1.8 million for the 1999 WTO; $4.1 million for the 2000 DNC; $13.7 million for the 2000 IMF/WB; $8.63 million for 2002 IMF/WB/antiwar protests; $11 million for Chicago antiwar protests; $1.5 million for 2003 Oakland antiwar protests; $1.5 million for the FTAA; $18 million for the 2004 RNC; $12.8 million for 2007 May Day; and civil rights cases still remain open arising out of OWS protests around the country, as well as #BlackLivesMatter protests.[164]

Significantly, over the last twenty years, abusive policing of protest in the United States is repeated. This repetitive series of aggressive and violent policing of protest indicates that the normative model of legalized accountability Epp describes may have been superseded, particularly insofar as many of these abusive events have occurred in cities where we would expect many of the factors positively associated with the emergence of legalized accountability to be present, like Washington, DC, or New York City. Importantly, this repetitive series of violent appearances indicates the negotiated management model of protest policing has been superseded.

The global interurban competition for visitors, attention to urban branding deriving from the post-Fordist context of urban political economy, and the incentives post-Fordist urban political economy creates for cities to market themselves through mega-events all encourage efforts to prevent disruptions when hosting major events. This leads to the post-democratic treatment of protest by rendering it the communicative equivalent to any other potential disruption a city might face, like crime, terrorism, or a natural disaster, when considered from the perspective of managing a city's image. The growing influence of the "Broken Windows" concept of order maintenance policing makes post-democratic and abusive treatment of protest more likely because "Broken Windows" is self-consciously a post–legal legitimation reaction against understanding policing only in terms of law enforcement. Moreover, "Broken Windows," by encouraging not only a zero tolerance approach to minor, quality of life violations, but also an enjoyment of police who "kick ass," is a model of policing incompatible with encouraging tolerance and disciplined self-restraint that the negotiated management relation of police to protesters requires. Since the 1980s, transformations in policing at odds with the legalized accountability model in conjunction with transformations in urban political economy reinforce each other to produce an aggressive approach to policing protest.

Although an aggressive approach to policing protest is overdetermined, why don't police departments seem to care about the consequences of the aggressive treatment of protesters with respect to their public image in the media, as Epp's research suggests they do, or did? The answer may lie in the way that control technologies substitute for disciplinary social organization, and the emergence of communicative capitalism. As described above, we have witnessed the erosion of the force of legal or social norms, a decline in symbolic efficiency, and in place of disciplined subjects, or subjects concerned with how the big Other might view or judge them, we have subjects who enjoy self-expression within networks of communicative capitalism without much concern for any normative gaze of a generalized other. In other words, rather than a hegemonic recognition of the normative wrongfulness of police violence against protesters, rather than subjects whose collective consciences will be shocked at the violation of this norm or who will judge police critically, and rather than police who care what a generalized other may think of their conduct, we have the displacement of a generalized other, whose gaze was filled by the ideological content of social democracy, by whatever being and its doppelganger.

KnowYourMeme.com has embedded a documentary segment within the webpage for the "Casually Pepper Spray Everything Cop" meme. In it, the meme of an expert on memes concludes the embedded video segment with two open questions. The expert on memes asks, "Does the quick spread of these images serve to raise awareness of the alleged police brutality, or do they turn the situation into a joke," inviting further comments from viewers.[165] The first question describes the gratuitous pepper spraying of peacefully seated demonstrators as alleged police brutality. The video thereby suggests that what should appear to be obvious police violence against protesters could be interpreted in different ways, eroding norms against police brutality by inciting reflexive receptivity to multiple interpretations of the scene. Moreover, the video continues to erode norms and normatively oriented subjects by pointing to the benefit of a meme as raising awareness. Under conditions of communicative capitalism, raising awareness is an incitement to recirculate, retweet, and forward. It is not, however, a denunciation, an identification of a wrong, or an experience where one's conscience is shocked by a contradiction between legal norms and police brutality. Awareness of an event is merely to be aware that it happened, or that it was communicated and shared. Likewise, the invitation to comment is another communicative incitement. KnowYourMeme.com transforms an instance of police abuse of force into the communication of whatever.

KnowYourMeme.com's second question is whether the recirculation of the meme of "Casually Pepper Spray Everything Cop," through a plurality of niches and multiplicity of communicative encounters, could be interpreted by some, along the way, as a joke. Here, KnowYourMeme.com highlights how communicative production and recirculation occur without a hegemonic norm in place, one that would identify abuse of force as wrong. KnowYourMeme.com acknowledges that some may enjoy watching protesters getting pepper sprayed.

We can observe the prominent presence of whatever being and its doppelganger communicatively coexisting with—if not overshadowing—the remains of the mode of subjectivity that sustained the social democratic horizon, its legal norms, and its norms regarding justice, in responses to the pepper spraying of protesters. Photos and video of NYPD Deputy Inspector Anthony Bologna needlessly pepper spraying female OWS protesters while they were detained within NYPD orange mesh netting went viral in 2011, and videos of the event are posted on YouTube. One of the videos of the event (this version has been slowed down at certain junctures so the viewer can see Bologna emerge from the crowd of NYPD, spray the women, then turn and walk away) has almost a million views and more than 3,500 comments.[166] Another video of the event has more than 1.6 million views and almost 8,600 comments.[167]

The YouTube comment thread of Bologna pepper spraying the OWS women will disappoint liberals and deliberative democrats, as it will disappoint advocates for a socially recognized (or hegemonic) legal norm of legalized accountability for police departments, though remnants of this mode of subjectivity are still evident in the posted comments. For example, someone writing with the handle Feminazi Frequency responds to other comments, "She [one of the OWS women who were pepper sprayed] didn't break the law . . . how would you feel if I walked up to you in the street and maced you? You'd probably have me arrested! If you think the police should be allowed to brutalize citizens for legally protesting, as their constitutional rights allow, you are part of the reason America is becoming a fascist state!"[168] Blake30615, who identifies himself as a former member of the NYPD, asserts that Bologna committed assault in the third degree and should have been arrested. DYoung2112 registers the contradiction between Bologna's conduct and the social democratic horizon by criticizing the hypocrisy of "US authorities" who "hailed" the "democratic aspirations of Arab Spring," but who then authorize the suppression of their own people when they "make PEACEFUL protest about the abuses and corruption going on in government and Wall Street." These commenters are subjects who continue to denounce police abuse of force violating legal norms and democratic practices. As Mia summarizes, "Those poor girls . . . those. poor. girls."

Among the comments is evidence of whatever being, its receptivity to communicative potential, its capacity for communicative productivity generated through associational reasoning, and a tendency to suspend visual moments or gestures for their communicative potential freed from normative purpose or other interpretive limits.[169] Cynicism facilitates communicative generativity, because once norms are deflated as hypocritical, then subjects are unleashed from their constraints, and communication is free to follow whatever vector. The thread includes several cynical commenters. Pauly Walnuts writes, "She was at a protest. From what i see, it didn't look like she was doing anything but exercising her right to do so. The cop came over there just spraying the fuck out of anything that moved. Lol. I really could care less. I mean, the protest isn't going to change anything in the long run. . . . Its always been that way. Nothing new." Others proceed unconstrained by norms. Tommy Weber says, "hahahahahahahaaha!!!!! yeah Tosh.o needs to see this." Christopher A. S. H. associates the video with the communicative productivity of memes, asking, "Where the fuck is the keyboard cat to play this out!?!?" ShyGuy1919 exhibits receptivity to the communicative potential of interpretive pluralism, observing, "They dont show whats leading up to it." Being unconstrained by norms, or other potential constraints on interpretation, engenders receptivity to visual moments that might otherwise pass unnoticed as insignificant. Several commenters, flexible to the communicative possibilities of whatever, communicate a moment in the video where a man passes in the foreground across the camera frame: "Black guy at 108 [1:08 mark in the video] is lookin fly." Another writes, "nice fro, bro," and another is yet more expressive: "at 1:12 I Screamed 'AFRO DUDE!!!!!'" Cynicism and distraction instigate communication where points of normative orientation become obscure. In response, 247robme asks commenters to be clear because "sarcasm" makes comments "more difficult to understand." Whatever being is "aware" of the video, using it as a resource for further communicative production unmoored from normativity.

Many of the responses exhibit deeply authoritarian dispositions. For some, police give orders that people must obey—regardless of the legal legitimacy of the order—and if people fail to obey such orders, they can expect to be punished by force. Other responses express an authoritarian orientation not far from an attachment to slavery, stating that if the women had been at work, then they would not have been punished by police.

As KnowYourMeme.com anticipates, though, many commenters find the video to be a joke, responding "HAHAHAHA," or "LOL." These commenters get a kick out of the women being pepper sprayed. For instance, CrosseyedTenFour writes, "Haha. Stupid hippies," or as Matt K responds, "This made me happy." RiFFRaFF is more enthusiastic: "AWESOME!" CrimsonSpectre summarizes this disposition, writing, "I could watch this video over and over and over again ..and laugh every time :D." The satisfaction these commenters express indicates enjoyment without reference to the legal norm against police abuse of force.

Unfortunately, some commenters express an even more enthusiastic enjoyment of watching protesters getting pepper sprayed. LigerSupremacy "really enjoyed the girl screaming @ 1:21. I love watching protesters get pepper sprayed." Others also enjoyed the image of the women protesters in pain, like Luke who, in apparent response to an earlier commenter who says he would have pepper sprayed them "twice," says, "I would do it three times, just to make sure the scum are hurt." Don Collier summarizes the enthusiastic enjoyment of watching the protesters suffer from being pepper sprayed by the NYPD: "I love it. Few things make me happier than pepper spray and protesters." After being criticized by another commenter as "sick" and "disgusting" for taking pleasure watching others suffer, he responds, "Do I enjoy watching these people suffer? I revel in it."

While the enjoyment for some derives, as it does for Jose Vega, in identifying Bologna's image for them as a "bad ass" (which may be rooted in the gendered image produced by Bologna's performance of masculinity as punishing women), the enjoyment for many others circles back to the Forgotten Man, a being stuck within the coordinates of 1968 and an aversion to social democracy. A Johnson states, "Mace all this hipsters who think that they deserve everything in life, go out and fucking earn your living you pansy hippies." For AllStringsAttached, "Those fucking commies deserve more than just pepper spray. I hope they all burn in hell." HEADSHOTZ1120 would also go further than pepper spray, saying, with evident enjoyment, "oh my god i want to shake that guys hand they should just get the military down there and kill them all -_- fucking hippys." The association with race and civil rights, deriving from the infamous image of Bull Connor attacking Civil Rights marchers with dogs and fire hoses in the 1960s, however, becomes more clear in those comments wishing that a "fire hose" would have been used on the protesters. As Steffano Ducati, who echoes the *New York Post*'s repeated references to OWS as "bums," summarizes, "I say bring out the dogs, water cannons and batons and send a message to the fringe that they wont forget."

This comment thread's different strands exhibit the more general tendencies of communicative capitalism that have eroded a broader recognition of legal norms against the abuse of force in protest policing. Forbalance, a commenter on a photo published in the *Portland Oregonian* of a Portland police officer pepper spraying an Occupy Portland protester directly into her open mouth as she is yelling, encapsulates this moment. "One thing I do like about the photo," this person writes, "is that it can be interpreted in so many different ways. . . . Some can look at it and imagine police brutality, others can see someone's daughter who became an idiot." A video communicating police violence becomes another moment in the communication of communicability, a moment of reflexivity regarding communicative multiplicity, or a moment of enjoyment to revisit one's affective attachments. It no longer reveals a wrong or inspires collective outrage.[170]

This is the subjective and associative media environment within which the policing of protest occurs.[171] Disturbingly, but perhaps not surprisingly, the NYPD exhibits similar tendencies that enjoy the environment of communicative capitalism where mashups and the reflexive relation to multiple interpretive possibilities thrive. It also enjoys, as we have seen in previous chapters, its abuse of protesters. Corresponding to communicative capitalism's rich ecology for remixes conducive to the enjoyment of memes, trials of demonstrators from both the 2004 RNC and OWS have produced evidence that the NYPD mashed up their videos to create the misleading impression that protesters had committed crimes.[172] On the one hand, the NYPD video mixes indicate the weakened effects of legal norms, or the gaze of the big Other, on policing. On the other hand, when police and protesters release competing videos of protest arrests, the overall effect is a disintegration of symbolic efficiency and a heightened sense that everyone is biased, so express your bias and let the market or whoever is better armed decide (which may be why some express enthusiasm for an individual right to bear arms today).[173] Within this broader reflexive environment of media remixes and incitement to affective communication, the NYPD's enjoyment of intimidating protesters, abusive policing of protesters, or affective attachment to defeating protesters is less constrained by legal legitimation, democratic sensibilities, or norms for conduct of public authorities. Instead, the NYPD protest policing is expressive of its communicative niche. The NYPD enjoys its anger at protesters. It enjoys its self-image of kicking OWS's ass, and whatever being's doppelganger enjoys watching video of this abusive policing on YouTube. Rather than shocking the conscience, it is enjoyed.

The comment thread for the YouTube video of Bologna pepper spraying the OWS women, then, chimes with themes and associations present in the broader environment of communicative capitalism. It indicates a media environment contributing to a weakening of the norm of legalized accountability through the disintegration of subjects committed to such norms, on the one hand, and manifests the disintegration of the subject of social democracy, on the other hand. Beside the subjective dispositions of liberal legal accountability and social democracy, along a plane of communicative equivalency, we have whatever being, its doppelganger, and a culture of policing that enjoys the abuse of protesters.

## Conclusion

Since the late 1990s, police have treated protesters abusively, whether the demonstrations occur at a mega-event likely to be classified as a national special security event or at a more domestic protest event. Moreover, the abusive policing of protest has occurred repeatedly. In light of Epp's *Making Rights Real*, these repeated instances of police abuse of force are surprising. In response to experts' reports on the riots, media criticism of protest policing (for instance, press criticisms of the Chicago Police at the 1968 DNC), court rulings establishing legal norms constraining the abuse of force, civil litigation holding police departments accountable for civil rights violations, and media coverage of the litigation, in addition to the efforts of reform-minded police managers inside policing, many police departments established mechanisms to control the abuse of force. A norm of legal accountability for policing became legally and socially recognized, and training and oversight geared to compliance with those norms—the policing model of legalized accountability—became institutionalized. Significantly, Epp finds that police concern about the effects of litigation on a department's public reputation in the media is more important than the financial sanctions of litigation for constraining abuse of force. Because of the proliferation of photographs and video capturing and recirculating police abuse of force against protesters, and the civil litigation producing significant settlements, the importance of a broadly recognized norm against police abuse of force, and institutional concern for public criticisms of abusive policing, appear to have weakened. This weakening of legalized accountability also corresponds with the weakening of the negotiated management model of police-protester interaction.

As legalized accountability and negotiated management became institutionalized within police departments, another movement within policing and penology was taking shape in conflict with legalized accountability. Also influenced by the urban riots, Kelling and Wilson, in "Broken Windows," urged police to go beyond mere law enforcement to reembrace an order maintenance function that, they acknowledged, would be at odds with legal legitimation—at odds, that is, with policing that would be fully legally accountable. Extending the "Broken Windows" concept of policing to target the appearance of disorder, policing has increasingly integrated control technologies within its practices. Policing has become progressively delinked from legal standards like probable cause, due process, or equal protection, as police managers urge the rank and file to meet quantitative goals for stops, or police patrols target the mere presence of the disadvantaged and racially disparaged to see if the targeted person can be associated with a file in a database.

The legalized accountability model of policing relies on subjects trained or socialized to recognize norms against police abuse of force. Social and political theorists, however, have described a long-term weakening of disciplinary institutions that might educate such norm-oriented subjects, on the one hand, and a decline in symbolic efficiency resulting in weakened public recognition of such norms, on the other. Order maintenance policing untethered from legal norms is accommodated, if not facilitated, by such postdisciplinary developments.

The repetition of abusive policing of protest, and the viral circulation of such images of police violence against protesters, suggest that police are less concerned about detrimental consequences for their reputations when such abuse of force appears in the media than Epp's work would lead us to expect. Legalized accountability—and the tolerant, dialogic relation of police and protesters known as negotiated management—is being superseded by a more aggressive and violent style of policing protest that is supported and facilitated not only by postdisciplinary developments in policing and punishment but by communicative capitalism. Communicative capitalism splinters the normative gaze of the generalized other, making it less forcefully felt by subjects. It engenders and amplifies a subjective sense that either the norms were not norms—a flexible openness to whatever—or it provides a vehicle for those who enjoy the appearance of violence against protesters.

Earlier chapters establish that members of the NYPD either police protest with little regard to the normative gaze of a generalized other, or that they enjoy the abuse of force against protesters. Internal memoranda circulated in the aftermath of the 2002 World Economic Forum show NYPD managers enjoying the intimidation of protesters.[174] Human rights reports regarding the policing of the 2003 antiwar demonstrations and the 2004 RNC and resulting civil litigation document how officers enjoy verbally abusing protesters and how the NYPD is at ease with the torturous and degrading treatment of protesters in custody.[175] Interviews with Occupiers and civil litigation that emerged from the NYPD's abusive policing of OWS detail how the NYPD enjoyed its abuse of force against OWS. In *Caravalho v. City of New York*, for instance, one plaintiff saw police "hit demonstrators with batons and kick them as they were being arrested."[176] Other plaintiffs complained of being kicked in the ribs while being arrested, having their right arm twisted, being kicked in the abdomen several times, being dropped on the sidewalk, requesting medical attention and not receiving it, being hit by a baton on the left shoulder, having an officer "ramming his knee" into their back, having an officer press their face into the concrete with his foot, and being thrown to the ground despite screaming at police, "I'm not resisting arrest. Jesus Christ, I'm not resisting arrest."[177] As Officer Perez screamed at one Occupier in custody whose thumb was broken by the NYPD during his arrest for protesting in Zuccotti Park, "You motherfucking protesters, every time you come back to that park, we're going to kick your ass!"[178] Such verbally and physically abusive policing seems to be institutionalized due to the rote repetition of the phrase, "Stop resisting," when NYPD inflict violence on protesters, their Mass Arrest Processing Plan making it difficult for protesters to know which officer harmed them, and the way New York City absorbs civil damages arising from abusive policing into the citywide budget, rather than holding the NYPD financially accountable for their policing.

The NYPD's abuse of force against protesters does not shock a collective conscience that might experience a sense of contradiction between norms of law or justice and the NYPD's protest policing that would be damaging to the NYPD's reputation. Although the comment thread for the video of Bologna pepper spraying the OWS women includes some who are shocked and outraged at the needless and painful use of force, it also includes many other relations to those images. The comments include those who are receptive to the possibility that the video's images could be interpreted differently (or those who encourage alternative interpretations, claiming, for instance, that the women are "crisis actors" who signaled the NYPD to pepper spray them so they could generate sympathy for OWS), those who associate the video images to memes or other aspects of internet culture, or who cynically declare that abuse of force is nothing new. The comment thread also includes, disturbingly, many who enjoy and derive satisfaction from watching the image of Bologna pepper spraying the protesters.

Under conditions of communicative capitalism, there is a disintegration of the social, the image, and the subject. As discussed in chapter 1, First Amendment jurisprudence has become reshaped under neoliberal, post-Fordist conditions to allow the zoning of demonstrations to locations far from (or invisible to) what one seeks to protest. The neoliberal First Amendment is satisfied as long as demonstrators can "express" themselves, perhaps utilizing "modern communications" like the internet, to participate in the production of communicative multiplicity without contradiction, along a plane of communicative equivalence.[179] Homologous to this disintegration of the social, repeated acts of police using excessive violence against demonstrators appearing in news reports or in YouTube videos do not compel normative outrage or changes to police practices the way they did in the 1960s. It adds one more icon to communicative dispersal as the image of police violence is disintegrated and recombined associatively to become a meme. Likewise, there is a disintegration of the subject before whom the image of police abuse of force against protesters appears. The subject of social democracy—the subject of the Kerner Commission's report—persists, as does the liberal subject who might demand legal accountability from policing. Alongside these subjects are those who respond to images of police violence by recirculating them, remixing them into a meme, subjects who enjoy the communication of interpretive multiplicity, or who respond with the cynical boredom of whatever because this expresses nothing new. And there are those who enjoy the images of police use of violence against protesters. With the disintegration of the social, the image, and the subject under conditions of communicative capitalism, police violence against protesters merely appears. Like the protests.

The forms of disintegration encouraged by communicative capitalism help to deflect the problematic legitimation crisis that preoccupied social and political theory in the 1970s and early 1980s.[180] Without a generalized or hegemonic understanding of normative standards for the legitimacy of public institutions, there can be no crisis for a state that fails to meet such standards. The potential for a legitimation crisis of the state, or for the institution of policing, is defused if there is no contradiction between norm and actuality, if protest produces no antagonism. There may be no sense of institutional legitimacy, but crisis can be avoided if abusive practices represent nothing new. Or if abuse is enjoyed.

# Political Antagonism #BlackLivesMatter and the Postlegitimation, Post-Democratic State

I can't breathe. . . .
—ERIC GARNER (2014)

Not a big deal.
—LT. CHRISTOPHER BANNON, New York Police Department (2014)

THE AGGRESSIVENESS AND BRUTALITY OF the New York Police Department's (NYPD's) reaction to Occupy Wall Street (OWS) displaced efforts to mobilize action redressing injustices produced by the excessive and growing inequalities of neoliberalism. Media attention incited by OWS, and the attention of OWS, became preoccupied instead with how authoritarian policing has become in the United States—a problem that had long concerned those who had actively challenged the constitutionality of the NYPD's stop and frisk practices. Growing economic inequality and policing that keeps the people disempowered and disorganized have developed into the state formation of neoliberal authoritarianism. Neoliberal authoritarianism emerged and persists, in part, through the exercise of force unconcerned with questions of legitimacy, and, in part, through political subjects who either displace and dismiss questions of legitimacy with their cynical enjoyment of interpretive or communicative multiplicity for its own sake, or who turn their backs on questions of justice and enjoy class or racial resentments. Today, those particularly subjected to neoliberal authoritarianism's violence have refused to take it anymore. "We Can't Breathe!"[1]

As prior chapters have discussed, a series of institutional reactions to the protests and riots of the 1960s and early 1970s have constellated as the post-legitimation, post-democratic state formation of neoliberal authoritarianism. For analytical purposes, we have identified three interlinked crises, the reactions to which have produced this state: a crime crisis, an urban fiscal crisis, and a crisis of democracy. The reactionary responses to these crises have superseded and displaced the efforts called for by the Kerner Commission to address the social ills its report described as leading to the urban riots of the 1960s.

What are the findings of the Kerner Commission with regard to the causes of the urban riots of the 1960s, and what are their recommendations? The Kerner Commission states, "We have cited deep hostility between police and ghetto communities as a primary cause of the disorders surveyed by the Commission. In Newark, in Detroit, in Watts, in Harlem—in practically every city that has experienced racial disruption since 1964—abrasive relationships between the police and Negroes and other minority groups have been a major source of grievance, tension and, ultimately, disorder."[2] The Kerner Commission bases this assessment on demeaning and hostile policing strategies, such as stop and frisk, as well as verbal and physical abuse, that resulted in practices "inconsistent with the basic responsibility and function of a police force in a democracy."[3] Its "Recommendations for National Action" urges the nation to ameliorate material inequalities urban residents suffered in such areas as employment, education (including efforts to eradicate de facto segregation), welfare, and housing.[4] In effect, this 1968 commission report understands these material inequalities, and the abusive policing practices inflicted on those urban dwellers particularly affected by these inequalities, as contributing to a legitimation crisis for the state.[5]

How did the reactionary crisis responses identified in earlier chapters turn policies and politics in a direction diametrically opposed to the Kerner Commission's recommendations? First, the political perception of a crime crisis incited support for zero tolerance, quality of life, order maintenance policing inspired by "Broken Windows." It also led to the growing militarization of policing. Political investment in policing and punishment arrested the impetus to render police more legally accountable and compatible with democracy by the 1990s and 2000s.

Second, the Ford administration turned the urban fiscal crisis into an opportunity to make a broader example of New York City and the support it provided for social reproduction by forcing its residents to submit to harsh austerity measures.[6] Subsequent cuts to urban programs, and limits upon local revenue raising, forced cities to become more entrepreneurial by competing against each other in the marketplace for visitor-based revenue, and by providing a favorable environment for finance, insurance, and real estate (FIRE) industries.[7] Federal and state governments disintermediated cities from markets, and urban government became neoliberal as a result.[8]

Third, protests and riots of the 1960s represented a crisis of democracy for reactionaries, rather than a legitimation crisis for the state. This reactionary perception of a crisis of democracy singled out the political mobilization of black people to portray an excess of democracy, thereby deflecting criticisms of policies aggravating, rather than ameliorating, material inequalities in the decades following the publication of the Kerner Commission's report.[9] For example, Harvard University's Samuel Huntington contended the United States was suffering from an "excess of democracy" caused by "marginal social groups, as in the case of blacks," who were "now becoming full participants in the political system." Their political participation was "overloading the political system."[10] The political culture of the decades following the Kerner Commission's report expressed exhaustion—if not antipathy—toward democratic commitments.

As I argue in previous chapters, the vectors of institutional change set in motion by the crime crisis, the urban fiscal crisis, and the crisis of democracy led to the post-democratic state formation of neoliberal authoritarianism. These reactions are haunted by the specters of black insurrection. As previously discussed, the authors of "Broken Windows" refer to the "urban riots" of the 1960s as one of the concerns motivating their call for police to respond to "disorder" exceeding ordinary crime.[11] In this light, we can understand the vectors of institutional change set in motion by these three crises as emerging through the political question of black lives mattering, but in antagonistic relation to this normative political claim. Neoliberal authoritarianism takes shape by expressing a political will to negate the claims and victories of mid-twentieth-century black political mobilization, and the political orientation that would have gone further still toward a social democratic horizon.

This hauntology of black insurrection also shapes how police relate to protests today.[12] The more tolerant and dialogic police-protester relations of negotiated management are at odds with a broader zero tolerance orientation to policing.[13] The two cannot coexist, and they haven't. Negotiated management has withered and become displaced by more aggressive and violent police responses to protests. This more aggressive policing style represses—where it fails to control or prevent—the appearance of political antagonism incompatible with neoliberal, post-Fordist urban imperatives to host mega-events without disruption so cities can brand themselves and market themselves in interurban competition. The postlegitimation, post-democratic political culture does not register the preemption, control, or repression of protest as a contradiction with normative principles, but takes it as an opportunity to communicate whatever or resentfully to enjoy the appearance of police violence inflicted upon protesters.

The figure of black insurrection, then, is politically significant for neoliberal authoritarianism insofar as the institutions of this state formation have been built upon the premise of repressing this figure's appearance.[14] Moreover, with the corrosion of civil society's capacity to transmit grievances to the state, negotiate public policy, and legitimate state power, as well as the corrosion of subjectivities receptive to accepting political representation, protest also becomes more politically significant. In this light, protest demanding that black people count politically, that black lives matter, expresses the antagonism between democratic commitments (which presuppose the conditions necessary for social reproduction) and contemporary material realities in uniquely powerful symbolic terms.

Policing protest has been transformed with the development of neoliberal authoritarianism. Alex Vitale's scholarship on protest policing distinguishes between the NYPD's style of policing protest indebted to the "Broken Windows" concept of policing and a more militarized approach other departments have used to police protest. In contrast, I build here from my argument in earlier chapters demonstrating how policing is unmoored from law enforcement and has become a more hybrid institution of security that both criminalizes those it perceives as disorderly, on the one hand, and responds in a more militarized manner to the disorderly, on the other.[15] Policing as a practice of security means that there is a continuum within policing between zero tolerance, quality of life policing sensitive to the most minor signs of disorder and a force that responds in a more spectacular, politically expressive manner with military garb, weaponry, and violence.

I argue in this chapter that with negotiated management's demise, and within the broader context of policing as an institution of security, protest policing is developing two postlegitimation, post-democratic tendencies. One of these tendencies is in the direction of greater use of militarized responses to protest. The other tendency is one that, in conjunction with the

spatial zoning of protesters, relies more heavily upon postdisciplinary control technologies to track and manage protesters. Both tendencies go beyond
a law enforcement function of policing: the excesses of a militarized response
express a political effort to defeat an enemy, while the second tendency seeks
to disorganize and manage "dividuals," preventing their emergence and assembly as political subjects.[16] These two tendencies can be understood as
tactics of a postlegitimation state insofar as the first tendency is unhinged
from law enforcement by utilizing displays and exercises of force beyond a
simple arrest for a legal infraction, while the second governs by profiling in
advance of any legal infraction. Further, both are dedicated either to preventing the appearance of political antagonism (the second) or to its defeat
(the first). In this regard, they are both tactics of a post-democratic state
hostile to the sovereignty of the people. Finally, both tactics have either been
used against #BlackLivesMatter (BLM) protesters in such different localities (and by such different police forces) as Ferguson (or St. Louis County)
and New York City, or are held out as recommended tactics for managing
protest. Protest policing's contemporary logic, indicated by these twinned
postlegitimation, post-democratic tendencies, exhibits how the development of neoliberal authoritarianism in the United States is set in motion by
the figure of black insurrection.

### Crime Crisis

In the wake of protests and riots that shook the United States in the 1960s,
the National Advisory Commission on Civil Disorders, better known
as the Kerner Commission, was formed and its report was published in
1968. The report found that deep-seated frustration over economic and
racial injustices became riotous when triggered by instances of excessive
use of force by police.[17] Economic and social decay in cities, in addition
to rural poverty, threatened democratic values. Consequently, the Kerner
Commission recommended a "greatly enlarged commitment to national
action" that would be "massive and sustained" and backed by "will and
resources" to redress the nation's "social deficit."[18] As mentioned above,
the report singled out education, employment, housing, and welfare as
areas meriting particular action.[19] It may be difficult to imagine today, but
the report attracted the nation's attention and became a best seller. When
leaders thought the Johnson administration was not moving quickly enough
to implement the report's recommendations, a bipartisan call was made for
the administration to redouble its efforts. Economic and racial inequalities

represented a crisis of legitimacy for the state oriented to the horizon of social democracy.[20]

Another disposition, however, was also taking shape in the 1960s.[21] From the perspective of segregationists and their allies, the Civil Rights movement's use of nonviolent civil disobedience in demonstrations to draw attention to, and protest, persistent segregation was nothing more than criminal activity on an organized mass scale.[22] As the now-historic March on Washington was being planned, *U.S. News and World Report* editor David Lawrence complained that "minority groups" were "pretending that they cannot express their will effectively except through marches in the streets or 'lie down' and 'sit in' demonstrations." "Why," he asked, "have so many Negro ministers become active leaders and managers of street 'demonstrations' that have resulted in disturbance of the peace, arrests, bloodshed, and death?" Lawrence counseled "law and order" as an antidote.[23]

The reaction to the crime crisis arrested social democratic momentum and displaced legitimation concerns arising from the gap between democratic promise and the realities of material inequalities. Richard Nixon's "Law and Order" campaign of 1968 marked the loss of hegemony for the social democratic orientation of the Kerner Commission's report. By claiming his victory was on behalf of the "forgotten Americans," the "non-demonstrators" who are "not guilty of the crime that plagues the land," Nixon, like Lawrence, elided protest with crime.[24] The crime of the crime crisis was always more than ordinary crime. It was a reaction against the crime of political equality. Illustrative of how the three crises were interlinked, this orientation would see in the demonstrations and riots of the 1960s not a legitimation crisis, but, as Huntington urged in the mid-1970s by referring to black political mobilization, a crisis of democracy.

Historian Jefferson Cowie describes the 1970s as a period when the United States was moving "vigorously left, right, and center at the same time"; a "bridge between epochs."[25] The social democratic paradigm, though persisting, was collapsing. Beginning with the Reagan administration, and continuing with the Bush and Clinton administrations, neoliberal authoritarianism became hegemonic. The Reagan and Bush administrations fueled the perception that the country was experiencing a crime crisis and required a war on drugs. The Clinton administration, with its support of the 1994 Violent Crime Control and Law Enforcement Act, and the 1996 Anti-terrorism and Effective Death Penalty Act, accepted and promoted this premise.

The line between law enforcement in a constitutional state and military action directed against a political enemy of the state became increasingly blurred. The 1984 expansion of asset forfeiture at the federal level encouraged state and local police to ask the federal government to adopt an asset seized for conduct in violation of federal law (typically, drug cases) in exchange for police keeping up to 80 percent of the assets thereby forfeited. This transformed policing by creating in police departments a vested interest in revenue raising from a source not subject to civilian oversight through formal legislative appropriation.[26] These revenues allowed departments to purchase military-grade equipment and armaments. Changes in federal law, regulatory rules, and, later, the availability of Department of Homeland Security grants, further facilitated access by state and local police to military armaments and equipment.[27] Militarized units now regularly policed hot spots, or performed ordinary warrant work, in areas of racialized poverty.[28]

Politicizing racial resentments, harsh crime legislation passed in even-numbered—that is to say, election—years. These harsh crime laws arrested penal modernism and its correctionalist disposition and replaced it with aggressive efforts to incapacitate evil.[29] The state now tasked the prison, as Malcolm Feeley and Jonathan Simon once put it, with a waste management function for a postliberal, post-democratic era.[30] Theoretically speaking, we can say that the prison's transformation to manage lives neoliberalism rendered disposable heralded a postdisciplinary era of control.[31]

We should note, however, that the crime crisis was targeted at people in the streets. It was not targeted at crimes that occurred in the "suites."[32] Indeed, the 1980s onward witnessed the deregulation of corporate wrongdoing, whether we are speaking of hindering the right to unionize, workplace safety, public health, the environment, or the financial industries. Policing was directed away from corporate malfeasance. The poor and racialized, however, experienced an intensified policing of their lives in terms of being monitored at work, burdensome conditions placed upon more paltry unemployment benefits or public housing, or the right simply to be in public: using public streets or sidewalks secure in one's basic legal rights and equal civil status.

The conceptual driving force for intensified policing of the streets was the article "Broken Windows" by George Kelling and James Q. Wilson, published by *The Atlantic* in 1982.[33] As discussed in prior chapters, the authors of "Broken Windows" urged police to do more than address crime. They argued that police should focus on "disorder" so that people would "feel relieved and reassured." The article is haunted by the riots of the 1960s. It is also written as cities experienced an urban fiscal crisis due to the combination of manufacturing relocating to suburbs, Southern states, or other countries, the loss of the middle class to the suburbs, cuts in federal aid to cities, and the transformation of urban economies to focus on the FIRE industries or the production of affectively managed urban environments for the entertainment of conventions, tourists, and shoppers. The essay took neoliberal inequality as its premise to advocate that police target, among others, the homeless, panhandlers, or the mentally ill—the "disreputable"—so that others would "feel more secure." The role of police was now to address "the fear of being bothered by disorderly people." Kelling and Wilson urged police to go beyond crime to control "disorder," but not all disorder merited control. As highlighted in chapter 3, one officer the authors quoted described how he polices public housing: "We kick ass." As Kelling and Wilson noted, "None of this is easily reconciled with any conception of due process or fair treatment."[34] "Broken Windows," a concept of policing also known as zero tolerance, quality of life, or order maintenance policing, was part of the state's postlegitimation transformation.

As emphasized in previous chapters, the "Broken Windows" concept of policing is not, strictly speaking, an example of law enforcement. It goes beyond the law to target the perception of disorder. It is resonant with post-Fordist urban economies that privilege attention to aesthetics and the management of image and affect. Not only does it urge police to produce an affective sensibility of safety for the privileged, it receives affective support from those who enjoy police kicking the asses of the poor or racially disfavored—those whose lives have been disqualified by neoliberal authoritarianism. The "Broken Windows" concept of policing and the militarization of policing with the growth and institutionalization of paramilitary police units within police forces are part of a continuum of postlegitimation, postdemocratic policing. Much as "Broken Windows" encourages an excessive form of policing—a mode of policing in excess of law enforcement—so also are dramatic displays of military force on a patrol, or for ordinary warrant service, excessive. These elements of excess dramatize the truth of this mode of policing. In their excess, they express the purpose of this mode of policing as subjugation while the support it receives indicates how subjects are affectively attached to this mode of policing—how subjects are attached to neoliberal authoritarianism that not only neglects, but enjoys its neglect of, legitimation concerns.

Theoretically speaking, the significance of the insight that subjects are affectively attached to the neglect of due process, equal protection, and police kicking ass is that we fail to grasp neoliberalism politically if we limit ourselves to pointing out its inefficiencies with respect to public goods or equitable distribution or the various ways that markets are prone to failure. For example, if we consider the United States today with respect to the recommendations of the Kerner Commission, we find that the unemployed face substantial probabilities of incarceration, and manufacturing industries, in which those with little education can work while earning a decent wage, have abandoned cities, making poor city residents even more economically precarious than they were in the late 1960s; funding for public education has stagnated relative to policing and prison, and since the 1980s, public education has grown progressively more, not less, segregated;[35] rather than being expanded, welfare was cut, then ended and replaced with Temporary Aid to Needy Families, and its support levels have become more inadequate so that its recipients cannot subsist on its payments and must work in the informal economy to survive (and/or borrow money), making them vulnerable to zero tolerance, quality of life policing of minor infractions;[36] and public housing and other housing programs have been cut substantially in comparison with government investments in prisons.[37] Developments in political economy since the late 1960s, and particularly since the presidential election of 1980, have been in the exact opposite direction of that recommended by the Kerner Commission. Neoliberalism is not politically entrenched despite the inequalities that have been produced. Neoliberalism is politically entrenched because of the inequalities that have been produced.

### The Killing of Eric Garner and Michael Brown

Reading Judge Scheindlin's opinion in *Floyd v. City of New York* (2013) on the NYPD's stop and frisk practices, one experiences an ex post facto premonition of Eric Garner's homicide. New York City was an early adopter of the "Broken Windows" concept of policing. Former NYPD police commissioner William (Bill) Bratton introduced it as chief of New York City's Transit Police in 1990. The "Broken Windows" concept of policing became policy for all of New York City when Rudolph Giuliani was elected mayor in 1993 and appointed Bratton commissioner of the NYPD. As described in chapter 4, the NYPD's institutionalization of "Broken Windows" policing unmoored it from legalized accountability. This is represented by the steep increase in the percentage of stops lacking documentation of a specific suspected crime that would have given cause for the stop, from 1 percent to 36 percent between 2004 and 2009.[38] New York City's population is slightly more than 50 percent black and Hispanic, yet blacks and Hispanics make up about 84 percent of those stopped in 2011.[39] Between January 2004 and June 2012, in 88 percent of all stops, there was no further law enforcement action.[40]

Indicative of the use of race rather than reasonable suspicion in NYPD stop and frisks, between 2004 and 2012, it took 143 stops of black people to lead to one seizure of contraband, 99 stops of Hispanic people to lead to one seizure, and 27 stops of white people to lead to one seizure.[41] In other words, stopping a white person was substantially more likely to lead to the seizure of contraband, yet white people constituted only 10 percent of all stops.[42] Additionally, the higher a precinct's black population, the less likely a stop would result in a sanction, indicating the greater likelihood in such precincts that black people were being stopped based on race rather than reasonable suspicion.[43] Force was also 14 percent more likely to be used against stopped black people than against stopped white people.[44] Supervisors told rank and file: "We own the streets here." Or, "If they're on a corner, make them move. They don't want to move, you lock them up. Done deal. You can always articulate later." Rank and file were urged on by supervisors at an affective level to "go crazy," to "get those numbers," and to "crush the fucking city."[45]

When Eric Garner was killed by NYPD officers on July 17, 2014, he was known to sell loose cigarettes in Staten Island, which the NYPD considered to be a quality of life violation.[46] Zero tolerance for quality of life violations drew the NYPD to confront Garner. Police escalated the situation as they were more accustomed to kicking ass than to deescalating conflict, and force was used, as it is disproportionately against black people in New York City. The result was Garner's death, marked by the expiration of his last breath, which he used to whisper with as much force as he could muster, "I can't breathe. . . ." When an NYPD Staten Island commander, Lieutenant Christopher Bannon, was informed by text message that Garner was "most likely DOA" (dead on arrival), he responded, "Not a big deal."[47]

Reading the Department of Justice's *Investigation of the Ferguson Police Department*, or the Arch City Defenders' "White Paper" on Ferguson, one also experiences the sense that black teenager Michael Brown being shot multiple times and killed by Ferguson police officer Darren Wilson on August 9, 2014, seemed a death foretold. Like New York City, Ferguson's policing disproportionately targets those poor and black. According to collected data, between 2012 and 2014, black people were subject to 85 percent of vehicle stops, 90 percent of all citations, and 93 percent of all arrests made by Ferguson police officers, though only 67 percent of Ferguson's population is black. Black drivers are twice as likely as whites to have their vehicles searched by police, yet are 26 percent less likely to be found in possession of contraband in comparison with white drivers. Between 2011 and 2013, black people represented 94 percent of all "Failure to Comply" charges, and black pedestrians accounted for 95 percent of all "Manner of Walking in a Roadway" charges—the initial reason why Wilson confronted Michael Brown and his friend in the incident that resulted in Wilson shooting Brown numerous times. In many of the "Failure to Comply" cases examined by the Justice Department, there is no reasonable suspicion of a crime that would permit a police officer to stop someone in conformity with the Constitution. African Americans account for 90 percent of all documented instances where police used force, and 100 percent of all instances of a canine bite.[48] According to the Justice Department, Ferguson officers are quick to escalate a situation and to resort to force.[49] Often in these situations, the initial stop lacked a legal basis. Ferguson police aggressively ticket those whom they have stopped (who are disproportionately black) for minor violations where the penalty is a fine. Then, its municipal court aggressively issues warrants for those so ticketed if they fail to appear for court dates or are unable to make fine payments.[50] This enables police to put someone they encounter with a warrant in jail in order to coerce payment of the fine (checking for warrants, rather than reasonable suspicion of criminal activity, is one of the main reasons for stops in Ferguson).[51] Of those admitted into the Ferguson jail for an outstanding warrant, 96 percent are African American.[52] Often, punitive fines that accumulate against those too poor to pay the original fine result in payments well in excess of the original penalty. The fines are impoverishing in themselves and in the way that warrants can affect one's employment and housing.[53] Nevertheless, almost 25 percent of Ferguson's fiscal year 2015 budget was expected to come from fines and fees disproportionately extracted from those poor and black, and there was constant communication between different parts of the municipal government to meet, if not exceed, revenue targets.[54]

Considering the racial humor that circulates among municipal workers over email, and the verbal abuse to which black people are subjected at the hands of Ferguson police during interactions, Ferguson city employees and police appear to enjoy their racism.[55] Ferguson's police practices are not rational with respect to public safety. The racially extractive nature of Ferguson policing, combined with the vulnerability of black Ferguson residents to police acting arbitrarily, and using excessive force with impunity, results in a racial caste system, with black people being economically expropriated while having politically disqualified lives. Police reinforce this disqualification of black lives discursively. These elements of excess indicate the points of subjective attachment to neoliberal authoritarianism. Meanwhile, the use of racial extraction (a form of primitive accumulation) at the hands of police and courts to fund government, rather than formal appropriations through a representative and popularly accountable legislative body, points to the postlegitimation, post-democratic structure of neoliberal authoritarianism as a state formation to which these political subjects are attached.[56]

## Beyond the Criminalization of BLM Protests

Given how Ferguson is actively producing a racial caste system through racial expropriation and dispossession to fund its municipal government, on the one hand, while encouraging a racial authoritarianism in its police force and court system on the other, it is hardly surprising that Brown's death served as a trigger for the eruption of simmering, yet forcefully suppressed, anger on the part of the people.[57] The police response to those protests exemplified a model of policing protest as paramilitary pacification. Ferguson and St. Louis County police sought to repress, if not punish, protesters with an overwhelming display of military force, such as the use of tear gas, flash-bangs, rubber bullets, Long Range Acoustic Devices (LRADs), military-grade weaponry including "semi-automatic weapons that were pointed at demonstrators," riot gear, armored personnel carriers, and military tactics like an "overwatch" police sniper monitoring the crowd through a rifle sight, in addition to issuing legally arbitrary orders like curfews, dispersal orders, restricted assembly areas, orders to "keep moving" on threat of arrest, snatching people from a crowd for arrest, and arresting and hindering journalists covering these events.[58] Internal mission briefings used by the Missouri National Guard, which was deployed to Ferguson, referred to protesters as "enemy forces" and "adversaries," before officers were commanded to refer, instead, to "criminal elements."[59] The militarized response to their protests illustrated vividly the grievances of Ferguson's black and poor residents.

Yet Ferguson and the St. Louis County police are not uniquely militarized. For thirty years, national politicians have mobilized political support by facilitating the militarization of state and local police. Moreover, Ferguson's residents share a more generalized experience with other black and poor Americans in being subjected to quotidian degradation rituals—if not deadly violence—when using public streets and sidewalks by police who enjoy impunity, and who are supported by political subjects who enjoy their enjoyment of impunity. Ferguson therefore crystallizes for the country and the world the postlegitimation, post-democratic state formation of neoliberal authoritarianism.

The uprising in Ferguson was extraordinary. No longer could anger at neoliberal authoritarianism, or a sense of justice, be contained, individualized,

*Figure 5.1* A member of the St. Louis County Police is positioned on the roof of its Tactical Operations Unit vehicle in an overwatch position during the uprising to protest the killing of Michael Brown by Ferguson police officer Darren Wilson on August 13, 2014. "Overwatch" refers to a military tactic where the overwatch provides cover for the advance of friendly units against enemy forces. PHOTOGRAPHER: SCOTT OLSON.

criminalized, and displaced with a "Failure to Comply" charge. Ordinary routines were ruptured. Ferguson residents poured defiantly into public streets and onto public sidewalks. The occupation of public space by Ferguson residents was a visible condemnation of their systematic political disqualification. Ferguson residents forced the antagonism between neoliberal authoritarianism and the political qualification of black lives and the poor into the open, into political registration. Not only in Ferguson but in cities throughout the United States, people of color and the poor collectively demanded that they should count and be accounted for, legally and politically.[60] They insisted that #BlackLivesMatter.

Not only did New Yorkers protest Garner's killing by the NYPD during the summer of 2014, they traveled to demonstrate solidarity with Ferguson residents after the killing of Brown. And NYPD detectives followed them. According to then-NYPD commissioner Bratton, the NYPD detectives were there to "help out in terms of intelligence we have on some of the professional agitators who are involved in these types of activity." The NYPD was also there to learn what they could in preparation for potential reaction to a Staten Island grand jury that had yet to return a decision on the indictment of NYPD officer Daniel Pantaleo, the officer who placed Garner in the chokehold responsible for his death.[61]

When the grand jury declined to indict Pantaleo, major protests erupted in New York City and around the country on December 3–5, 2014. People poured into the public streets. Protesters marched and came together chanting, "I can't breathe," performed die-ins, and disrupted ordinary routines by blocking traffic.[62]

As BLM activists called for justice—for instance, at Grand Central Station—protesters began to suspect that they were under surveillance. One protester

*Figure 5.2* Illustrating the militarized response to the Ferguson uprising protesting the killing of Michael Brown by Ferguson police officer Darren Wilson, heavily armed police wearing battle dress uniforms, and masks to protect them from gas, patrol the streets of Ferguson on August 11, 2014, to drive protesters from the business district. PHOTOGRAPHER: SCOTT OLSON.

*Figure 5.3* Protesters conduct a die-in at Grand Central Station, December 5, 2014, after a Staten Island grand jury did not indict NYPD officer Daniel Pantaleo for killing Eric Garner by using a chokehold to arrest him. PHOTOGRAPHER: ANDREW BURTON.

at Grand Central Station noticed "uniformed and plainclothes police officers regularly and openly recording events as they were taking place."[63] The activist filed a Freedom of Information Law (FOIL) request under New York State law, concerned that the NYPD might be violating limits on political surveillance imposed by the Handschu consent decree. The NYPD responded by denying documents responsive to the FOIL request existed or by denying access to other requested material. The protester appealed the denial, and the NYPD denied his appeal. This activist then sought an Article 78 judgment under New York State law to compel the NYPD to obey the law and release the requested documents. Under the threat of contempt, the NYPD complied by releasing a limited number of documents, forcing the protester to recommence legal proceedings against the NYPD to obtain the remainder.[64]

At a demonstration on Martin Luther King Jr. (MLK) Day 2015, an attorney joined a small group of protesters who had decided to engage in an unplanned march to Grand Central Station. About twenty-five minutes later, "the group ran into NYPD officers blocking their way."[65] There were "more cops . . . than protesters." Since the group was so small, it was unlikely if not impossible that a uniformed member of the NYPD could have overheard the decision to march toward Grand Central Station. Had the small group been under surveillance?[66]

Organizers with Millions March NYC, a multiracial group that organized a march protesting the failure to indict the police officers who killed Eric Garner and Michael Brown attended by over seventy thousand people, experienced "repeated problems in using their cell phones to organize and publicize protest activities."[67] One activist's phone shut down when the person was trying to record an event, indicating it was out of battery power though it had been fully charged. Others lost reception, were prevented from posting on the group's Twitter account, or received messages "indicating the possibility of interference with their messages sent and received on Signal, a secure communication tool." Was Stingray technology (Stingray is a brand of cell site simulator—technology that mimics a cell tower to intercept or interfere with cell phone communications—manufactured by the Harris Corporation) being used to intercept or interfere with their communications?[68] When arrested for disorderly conduct while protesting, two organizers taken to 1 Police Plaza witnessed members of the NYPD making copies of their arrest records and overheard conversation that a copy would be placed in "movement files." In another instance, they overheard "comments from police officers indicating that they are monitoring social media accounts of activists."[69]

The Millions March NYC organizers filed a FOIL request. The NYPD responded with a very partial disclosure and claimed that the remainder of the requested documents, "if in existence, are exempt from disclosure." In response to an appeal, the NYPD repeated what is known as a Glomar response in the context of federal law.[70] A Glomar response refers to protections the Central Intelligence Agency enjoys from being compelled under federal law to obey Freedom of Information Act requests for documents pertaining to counterintelligence operations out of consideration for national security and foreign diplomatic interests (powers the U.S. Constitution delegates to the federal government).[71]

Initial releases of documents pertaining to the surveillance of Grand Central Station protests by the Metropolitan Transit Authority (MTA) and the Metro-North Railroad, and obtained by *The Intercept*, revealed surveillance by counterterrorism agencies and undercover police. Although the NYPD had been unresponsive initially, documents produced by the MTA and Metro-North revealed the participation of NYPD officers who were undercover, associated with the Counterterrorism Division or with the Intelligence Division (Intel). The documents showed that the police agencies themselves found the BLM demonstrations to be "peaceful" and "orderly"—"The usual routine." Nevertheless, Adam Lisberg, a spokesperson for the MTA, defended the police response because their transportation networks "have been persistently targeted by terrorists." One MTA document included the head of the NYPD's Counterterrorism Division sharing photos of an activist in an email claiming the document was for "deterring, detecting, and preventing terrorism." In January 2015, then–NYPD commissioner Bratton had justified the creation of the new Strategic Response Group (SRG), a unit dedicated both to disorder control and counterterrorism, stating it was "designed for dealing with events like our recent [Eric Garner] protests, or incidents like Mumbai or what just happened in Paris," thereby associating protests and BLM with terrorism. The police mobilization in response to a peaceful BLM demonstration confirmed, institutionally, Lisberg's and Bratton's discursive elision between protest and terrorism.[72]

As BLM mobilized, assembled, and marched, the NYPD continued its institutional practice of targeting those it perceived to be key activists for surveillance, intimidation, and grueling arrests that it had established in its policing of Occupy Wall Street (OWS) described in chapter 3. Documents released in response to FOIL requests show police agencies circulating photos of those they perceived to be key BLM activists, naming them where possible and documenting their activities (e.g., did they lead a "mic check"?), and even noting silent supporters. Sometimes NYPD officers would address protesters by name, letting the protester know that they were known to the NYPD.[73]

Some BLM protesters may have been targeted for assault due to being known to the NYPD as BLM protesters.[74] The NYPD also appears to have targeted known BLM activists for arrest. Deputy Inspector Andrew Lombardo, a "high-ranking officer within the Strategic Response Group," and someone who was also part of the military chain of command at Abu Ghraib when it functioned as a site for the United States to torture Iraqis, arrested the head of the New York chapter of Cop Watch, an active participant in BLM protests, at a march commemorating the anniversary of Michael Brown's death. The arrest was for use of amplified sound without a permit (the activist was holding, but not using, a megaphone when Lombardo arrived). Lombardo told the activist that he was going to be taken "somewhere no one can find you," a threat that proved to be accurate. Rather than take the activist inside the NYPD's Forty-Second Precinct—the protester was arrested in front of that precinct house by Lombardo—or to one of the precincts used for mass arrest processing, he was taken in an NYPD SRG vehicle to "one of the northernmost precincts in New York City, the 50th, just south of Van Cortlandt Park." Similar to the way that Occupy activist "Sami" could not be located after his brutal arrest in Duarte Square, neither jail support nor the National Lawyers Guild could determine where the NYPD was holding this BLM protester, and it was not until his release that his whereabouts became known.[75]

One former NYPD detective and a professor at John Jay College, Joseph Giacalone, was not surprised that key BLM activists were identified and their photos circulated in police surveillance documents: "If you take out the biggest mouth, everybody just withers away, so you concentrate on the ones you believe are your organizers." He continued, "Once you identify that person, you can run computer checks on them to see if they have a warrant out or a summons failures, then you can drag them in before they go out to speak or rile up the crowd."[76] The linkages between surveillance and politically based targeting of activists for intimidation or a grueling arrest—to say nothing of the use of the SRG for the policing of peaceful protesters—that are described in reporting on BLM protests and BLM surveillance documents extend a disturbing pattern of politically based policing by the NYPD that also appeared in the NYPD's policing of the 2004 RNC and of OWS.

As we have seen, the NYPD has resisted producing its surveillance documents of BLM despite disclosures from other New York–based police agencies that had already revealed its integral participation in surveillance of this political movement. One state judge threatened the NYPD with contempt of court if it continued to refuse to produce requested documents.[77] Another state judge rejected the NYPD's Glomar response to the request asking whether the NYPD has monitored or interfered with the phones of BLM activists in New York.[78]

Those records that the NYPD has released show that the NYPD has infiltrated groups of BLM activists—whether through undercover officers, confidential informants, or both. Emails within the NYPD included pictures of organizers' group text message exchanges.[79] These emails show that surveillance of BLM was coordinated with Intel Chief Thomas Galati, in addition to Galati's Deputy Chief Paul Ciorra, Intel Inspector William Viscardi, Deputy Inspector of Field Intelligence Operations within the Criminal Intelligence Unit of Intel Roberto Rios, and Deputy Inspector Paul Mauro, the executive officer of the Intelligence Operations and Analysis Section.[80] Concerns that the NYPD was surveilling BLM—including small groups of BLM protesters like the one intercepted by the NYPD on its way to Grand Central Station on MLK Day 2015—were confirmed.[81] Recalling Detective Wojciech Braszczok's infiltration of OWS, the precedent of the NYPD's policing of OWS laid the institutional groundwork for BLM's infiltration.[82]

Released emails have shown that the NYPD's Organized Crime Control Bureau (OCCB) oversaw much of the BLM surveillance conducted on the streets.[83] The bureau's handlers organized undercover surveillance teams that would keep tabs on BLM demonstrations, marches, and other actions. These OCCB undercover teams would stake out various locations where BLM protests were anticipated, or where the NYPD appeared to be concerned that BLM would use the site for protest. Undercover teams monitored the size of BLM demonstrations,[84] the movements of protesters,[85] protesters' activities,[86] whether protesters were orderly and peaceful,[87] locations where traffic was blocked, or if there was a die-in at Bryant Park or near Barclays Arena.[88] Photos of perceived leaders or speakers were shared, as were photos of the messages on protesters' signs or those they expressed in their chants.[89] Flyers announcing meetings or future actions were also photographed and circulated.[90]

The NYPD's surveillance of BLM kept a particularly close eye on parks—presumably to prevent an OWS-style assembly and occupation—in addition to important sites for New York City tourism, place branding, and city marketing. Surveillance teams monitored parks before, during, and after BLM protests. For example, on December 15, 2014, at 9:07 p.m., Undercover Team 2 reported, "all quiet @ US [Union Square], no protesters."[91] At 12:41 a.m., however, this undercover team reported, "app[roximately] 20 protesters in US at 17 and US w[est]. They are now standing up and orderly."[92] When the protest at Union Square broke up at 12:48 a.m., the undercover team reported this activity, informing handlers that protesters were now "leaving in diff[erent] directions."[93] Similar to Intel's surveillance of RNC 2004 protesters, the NYPD kept locations like Times Square under tight observation—even if there was only one protester—as well as the Barclays Center in Brooklyn where the Nets professional basketball team plays.[94] The Wall Street Bull was also watched.[95] Communications with undercover surveillance teams show NYPD policing of BLM was anticipatory and preventative. This close monitoring of parks and sites dedicated to tourism or spectacle demonstrates a political authoritarianism complementary to a project of securing a neoliberal, post-Fordist political economy from potential disruption.

Does the NYPD surveillance of BLM constitute a violation of the Handschu decree? The Handschu consent decree sets legal limits and establishes institutional processes governing NYPD investigations involving political activity. Perhaps the maintenance of records on BLM activists for approximately four years constitutes a violation of the Handschu decree. As urged by the authors of "Broken Windows," the NYPD has been reshaped to address disorder in excess of legal violations. Therefore, and much like its stop and frisk practices, technical violations of Handschu should be treated as another instance of postlegitimation policing, indicating how the NYPD is dedicated to disorder control whatever its nature. Faced with the political challenge of BLM, then, the NYPD responded informally using customary practices to suppress this political mobilization.

Of equal or greater concern, however, is the lack of evidence that high-level NYPD managers even considered the possibility that the NYPD's surveillance of BLM could have been a violation of the Handschu decree at all. On the one hand, the relatively minor legal infractions of traffic laws, or the potential violation of city park curfews, may be legally sufficient for the mobilization of Intel's vast resources, including undercover officers and their constant monitoring of BLM. On the other hand, the perception of a crime crisis and the reshaping of the NYPD informed by the "Broken Windows" concept of policing, as we have seen, were reactions against the protests and nonviolent civil disobedience of the Civil Rights movement, and were haunted by the trauma of the 1960s riots. The crime that inspired the reactionary crime crisis was always more than ordinary unlawful activity. The crime crisis reaction was inspired by what many perceived as the political crime of the claim that black lives matter, that black people count politically and ought to be taken into account through a process of sharing power in the United States. Haunted by the terror of #BlackLivesMatter, the fear of riot—in sum, the figure of black insurrection—and as manifested by the inclusion of key NYPD leaders in email chains, the surveillance of BLM may express the core of the state formation of neoliberal authoritarianism by being considered integral to an ongoing terrorist enterprise investigation.[96] That is, the NYPD, using formal bureaucratic practices set in motion by the specter of black insurrection as much as by concrete BLM protest activities, responded to suppress the political threat BLM represented.[97]

Was the NYPD's surveillance of BLM a lawless response driven by customary practices? Or did the NYPD perceive BLM to be a terrorist enterprise and therefore believe the surveillance was legally justified as part of a terrorist enterprise investigation permitted by the Handschu decree? Whether informal or formally legal, the NYPD responded to BLM as a political threat. Lawless or a bureaucratic response driven by potential terror? Either way, the NYPD reaction to BLM represents a postlegitimation, post-democratic institutional orientation exceeding normative expectations for a legally accountable law enforcement agency.

When the NYPD confronted the small BLM march to Grand Central Station on MLK Day 2015, it outnumbered the group, producing a visual criminalization of the BLM protest much as the number of NYPD officers deployed had overwhelmed OWS protests to create a visual criminalization of the Occupy movement. The NYPD had also responded to OWS as a political enemy by its use of Intel and undercover surveillance of Occupy activists, and by targeting specific OWS activists for arrests based on Intel surveillance, to say nothing of their extrajudicial punishment of OWS activists. Similarly, the use of Intel, undercover officers, and counterterrorism assets, the targeting of key activists and organizers, and the institutional maintenance of these political files for several years in conjunction with making every effort to avoid being governed by New York State FOIL on security grounds suggests that the NYPD, like the Ferguson Police Department (FPD), St. Louis County, and the Missouri National Guard, has responded to BLM like a political enemy. Much like the evidence with respect to its policing of OWS, the NYPD's policing of BLM migrates from its criminalization of the movement to its treatment of the movement as a political enemy of the state to be defeated.

The NYPD's policing of OWS and BLM protests shows it is a hybrid institution. I have tried to represent this institutional hybridity by depicting the NYPD as a security force, one that mixes criminalization with militarization. Less than war, but exceeding that of policing ordinary crime, the modality of the NYPD's response to OWS and BLM has been more in the manner of a low-intensity conflict. Unconstrained by ordinary processes of law enforcement in a campaign to contain or defeat a political movement, security represents a postlegitimation, post-democratic institutional development of the state.

## Urban Fiscal Crisis

Ferguson addresses its urban fiscal crisis through fines and fees rooted in an expropriating, post-democratic mode of government and political economy structured in racial domination. New York City addresses its urban fiscal crisis by creating a favorable environment for investments by the FIRE industries and through neoliberal, post-Fordist symbolic production, one component of which is to host mega-events. As I observed in chapter 2, New York hosted the 2004 RNC to prove it was recovered from the attacks of

September 11, 2001, and was coming back. To prepare, the NYPD expanded the capacities of Intel in relation to demonstrators, and it created a Mass Arrest Processing Plan that included a no-summons policy inspired by their repressive policing of those protesting the NYPD killing of Amadou Diallo between 1999 and 2001.[98] It also acquired two LRADs.[99]

Also known as sound cannons, LRADs are acoustic weapons. Developed for the U.S. military in the wake of the attack on the USS *Cole* off the coast of Yemen in 2000, LRADs can warn off boats and ships that approach a U.S. vessel. If those warnings are not heeded, then the weapon has an "area denial" function whereby it emits sound at a "dangerously high level" that can cause pain and permanent hearing damage to those targeted.[100]

According to then–NYPD spokesman Paul Browne in 2004, the LRADs acquired by the NYPD might be used for communicating to crowds and directing them to safety "following a terrorist attack or other calamity" or for communicating with protesters regarding "where they're allowed to march and rally." At the time, NYPD representatives stated that the device would only be used as a loudspeaker to communicate with crowds, and that its "warning tone" capacity would not be used.[101] Since the 2004 RNC, all known NYPD deployments of LRADs have been at demonstrations and First Amendment assemblies (it was not used during Hurricane Sandy). For example, it was deployed during the eviction of OWS from Zuccotti Park in November 2011. The NYPD's first known use of the LRAD firing its warning tone was against those protesting police brutality November 28, 2014. Its deployment against those protesting police brutality and demonstrating on behalf of BLM became routine around December 2014.[102]

During the evening of December 4, 2014, and into the early hours of December 5, protests occurred around New York City in response to the refusal of a Staten Island grand jury to indict NYPD officer Pantaleo in Garner's death. Around 1:00 a.m. December 5, at the intersection of Fifty-Seventh Street and Madison Avenue, police began making arrests.[103] A chain of NYPD officers kept demonstrators away from the arrests. Demonstrators, members of the media, and onlookers watched, and occasionally called for the police to let go those being arrested, but they did not interfere. Some claimed to have heard what sounded like a glass bottle break, but no one was injured. Then, without warning, NYPD officers began discharging pepper spray.[104] Demonstrators and observers "began to run in different directions" and police ordered them to "return to the sidewalk."[105] "Seconds later," according to Robert Katzmann, the chief judge of the U.S. Second Circuit, "the wail of a high-pitched alarm began pulsing through the streets." The NYPD had "activated the LRAD's area denial function." No order to disperse preceding the use of the LRAD is audible on video of the event, and plaintiffs say they never heard such an order.[106]

"After several bursts from the alarm tone," Judge Katzmann continued, "Lieutenant Maguire and Officer Poletto, both members of the Disorder Control Unit, began broadcasting commands." Orders not to interfere with vehicular traffic continued to be interspersed with LRAD alarm tones for about three minutes.[107] This deterrent tone was "employed between fifteen and twenty times," a rate that was "almost continuous."[108] Though "many people in the LRAD's path 'were already fleeing on the sidewalks,' the officers followed close on their heels, sometimes from fewer than ten feet," pointing the LRAD directly at the demonstrators and observers while firing the weapon.[109] The back of the LRAD has an image of a sound cone labeled with the warning: "DO NOT ENTER WITHIN 10 METERS DURING CONTINUOUS OPERATION."[110] When the Disorder Control Unit tested the LRAD model purchased prior to the 2004 RNC, it did not take any sound level readings within 320 feet of the front of the LRAD, calling it a "potential danger area" and "not tested."[111] Plaintiffs subjected to the LRAD at the demonstrations of December 4 and 5, 2014, filed a lawsuit for the violation of their civil rights caused by the NYPD's "gratuitous and unlawful use of force."[112] Plaintiffs in the suit all experienced physical injuries, including "ear pain, prolonged migraines, vertigo, and ringing in the ears." One suffered hearing loss and nerve damage due to the extreme level of the noise pushing a bone in his ear inward. Several of the plaintiffs are now afraid to attend protests.[113]

The NYPD's LRAD use is an example of the security hangover or legacy that follows from hosting national special security events (NSSEs). Weapons, vehicles, institutions, and other forms of security infrastructure—for instance, closed-circuit TV cameras—stay within the police agencies and the host cities of NSSEs, becoming part of a host city's built environment, after the NSSE has concluded. Likewise, the NYPD's use of the LRAD, acquired for the exceptional circumstance of the 2004 RNC, became routinized against protesters by December 2014.[114] In this regard, it joins the build-out of Intel and the no-summons policy developed in conjunction with Mass Arrest Processing Centers, which have also been used against protest movements opposed to neoliberal authoritarianism in New York City after the conclusion of the 2004 RNC and despite the record monetary damages paid to protesters whose rights were violated during the 2004 RNC. Such a security legacy is a major driver of institutional processes leading to the policing of protests with more aggression and violence since the late 1990s.

The NYPD has only used its LRAD against demonstrations. This indicates how the NYPD is a postlegitimation, post-democratic institution. The LRAD is postlegitimation because it necessarily functions in a manner producing indiscriminate pain and suffering for those subjected to it. Its use is post-democratic insofar as its only deployment by the NYPD has been against protesters and those engaged in First Amendment activities. How should we make sense, though, of the fact that the occasion of its routinized use has been the mobilization against police abuse of force and in solidarity with the normative claim that black lives matter—to repress, that is, BLM?

*Antagonism: Ontological or Political?*

Frank Wilderson III's work provides one lever for making sense of the NYPD's unique deployment of the LRAD against BLM. For Wilderson, onto-logical anti-Blackness is a constituent, antagonistic element establishing the underlying structure for political conflicts in the United States.[115] As part of a growing body of scholarship known as "Afro-pessimism," Wilderson ar-gues that the modern imaginary for the Human, Whiteness, the state, and civil society are all "parasitic on the Middle Passage."[116] Slavery is a condi-tion of social death—the Slave is "generally dishonored," "void of a kinship structure," and is "perpetually open to gratuitous violence."[117] The practice of enslaving the Black established, by negative relation, a world; it consti-tuted being. Slavery expresses, therefore, an ontological positionality. The ontological conditions necessary for slavery that emerged to constitute the modern world consist of a structural prohibition on the extension of Human empathy to Blacks by banning the Black, strictly speaking, from ontology (from being).[118] This ontological condition of the modern world also, then, creates the "position against which Humanity establishes, maintains, and renews its coherence."[119] Humanity emerges through a constitutive negation of the Black where the latter represents a "human void."[120]

Why engage with this intervention regarding ontological anti-Blackness here? By arguing in ontological terms, Wilderson's Afro-pessimism is mak-ing claims about the essential qualities of being and Blackness—about what is essential to being or Blackness as an originary or first principle.[121] On the one hand, Blackness is a void outside of history, political conflict, and civil society. On the other hand, history, politics, and civil society are structured in negative relation to Blackness. Whether or not such simultaneous claims are philosophically plausible, Afro-pessimism leaves other questions unan-swerable that are central to the analysis here. Wilderson acknowledges that the period between 1968 and 1980 differs from the period that precedes it, and which follows it, in terms of Black political power and its production of political discourse.[122] At the level of ontology, such distinctive periods are either inexplicable or insignificant. Is it possible to acknowledge the forms of violence and exclusion to which black people are subjected (to say nothing of expropriation or exploitation), on the one hand, and also comprehend and attribute significance, on the other, to movements and political successes that have helped produce periods of reduced police abuse of force or greater social well-being for black people, among others? What, then, are the stakes of deciding to pursue inquiry guided by first philosophy (ontology) versus political philosophy? By displacing thought from the political register to the ontological, by depoliticizing analysis, Wilderson leaves us without the necessary conceptual tools for comprehending how such institutional changes were produced that reduced violent policing or improved social well-being, and how they were lost in the face of reactionary countermovements.

To grasp the power of Wilderson's contributions to Afro-pessimism, and how they force us to confront seriously the violent subjugation of black people, let's return to the thread of his argument. As "socially dishonored," "natally alienated," and thus "devoid of kinship structure," Blacks in America are positioned outside social relationality, as having no relations that require recognition or incorporation.[123] According to Wilderson, "Afro-pessimism explores the meaning of Blackness not—in the first instance—as a variously and unconsciously interpellated identity or as a conscious social actor, but as a structural position of noncommunicability in the face of all other positions."[124] Blackness is therefore positioned beyond the symbolic order, using the terms of Jacques Lacan's theory of psychoanalysis, for which "subjectivity is a discursive, or signifying process of becoming."[125] Social death "bars the slave from access to narrative."[126] As incommunicable nonsubjects "zoned beyond the pale of speech," from the perspective of civil society, "the Black is neither protagonist nor antagonist." Thus, "the Black can be placed *on* film but cannot be positioned *within* the frame."[127] Blackness may appear, but Blackness remains speechless nonsubjectivity.

As a manner of social death perpetually open to "gratuitous violence" (as opposed to the Human who may be the victim of contingent violence), Blackness is an absolute Other to civil society.[128] While the subaltern or others who enjoy recognition within civil society are dominated in the first instance by hegemony and the construction of consent, and then only secondarily, in the face of symbolic transgression, are subjected to violence, for Blacks, consent is beside the point. "Blackness," Wilderson argues, "is constituted by violence in the ontological first instance."[129] Instead of violence as contingent upon a transgression, as it is for members of civil society, gratuitous violence as a defining feature of Blackness means violence is an ontological condition of (non)existence.

Afro-pessimism, as explained in conversation between Saidiya Hartman and Wilderson, then, may be conceptualized as a sort of visual ontology inspired by Frantz Fanon's expression of Blackness in the phrase, "Look! A Negro!" It is the ontology of a primary despotism where "despotism manifests itself visually" as the structurally necessary condition for human being, civil society, and subjectivity.[130] Wilderson contends, "the spectacle of Black death is essential to the mental health of the world."[131] Therefore, the "ultimate stabilization is the spectacle of violence against Blacks." It produces a sense of "ontological presence," if not "communal pleasures" or enjoyment.[132]

From the perspective of Afro-pessimism, then, the NYPD's routinized deployment of the LRAD against BLM is symptomatic of the broader ontological conditions where Blackness is without social relationality, is outside of symbolic authority or recognition, is beyond intra–civil society discursive relations or communication, and is constitutively nonsubjectivized and thus beyond Human empathy. As theorized by Afro-pessimism, Blackness is perpetually exposed to gratuitous violence, and its social death is the condition of possibility for the state and civil society. The violence Blackness suffers is constitutive of the American imaginary. Here, the NYPD's routine deployment of an LRAD against BLM, much like the spectacular deployment of military force in Ferguson, is an ontic manifestation of a more fundamental ontological condition of being American.

The NYPD's deployment of an LRAD against nonviolent BLM protesters is an excessive, gratuitous exercise of violence. The LRAD is also a weapon developed initially for the military. Likewise, police deployments in Ferguson confronting BLM protesters appear in military dress, outfitted with battlefield weaponry, and supported by vehicles and weaponry (including an LRAD) also more typically deployed against a foreign enemy on the battlefield. The militarized response to the BLM uprisings in New York and Ferguson indicates that BLM is comprehended by U.S. governments more like an enemy than as domestic citizens with equal civic standing before the law and fundamental constitutional rights not to be treated as a foreign enemy on the battlefield.

The importance of militarized responses to BLM by the NYPD and Ferguson police agencies centers on the meaning of antagonism or negation. Wilderson theorizes the relation of antagonism between the state and Blacks in ontological terms where the negation of Blackness is constitutive of Human being.

However, BLM seems to appear to police in New York and Ferguson as a political enemy in an antagonistic relation to the state if we note the militarized response to BLM that exceeds normal police responses to crime in both of those cities. As is well known, in *The Concept of the Political*, Carl Schmitt argues that the friend-enemy distinction expresses the essence of politics. It is the "most intense and extreme *antagonism*, and every concrete *antagonism* becomes that much more political the closer it approaches the most extreme point, that of the friend-enemy grouping."[133] In such a concrete situation representing the potentially "extreme case," possibly manifesting in war or revolution, political participants in that situation must "judge whether the adversary intends to *negate* his opponent's way of life."[134] Could the antagonism between police and BLM—evident in the excessive, militarized responses to BLM protests—represent a political antagonism or negation rather than an ontological relation? If so, rather than Blackness manifesting a human void, nonbeing, or nothingness, police would perceive BLM protests as representing a threat to their way of life, as would those who associate themselves politically with policing antagonistically related to BLM. In other words, to the state formation of neoliberal authoritarianism—shaped by (and thus haunted by) its negation of the figure of black insurrection—BLM would represent the threat of a political enemy, the materialization of the spectral figure of black insurrection.

Politics, or, in the extreme case, war or revolution, implies relationality and subjects who struggle. For Wilderson, structures of power and positionality, such as the exploitation of workers or the Native American loss of sovereignty—relations where subjects are in conflict with each other—presuppose a prior ontological antagonism of anti-Blackness.[135] Blacks can be neither protagonist nor antagonist.[136] The political enemy, though, is not an ontological void of nonrelation, as ontologically defined Blackness is. The political friend and enemy are related through their mutual enmity. One addresses one's friend or friends; one addresses one's enemy or enemies (through a declaration of war, a shock-and-awe display of military force, or simply by wearing a military uniform on the battlefield to announce one's status and be identified under the laws of war as a legal combatant). Whether making common political cause or responding with force to political antagonism, political subjects share relationality, including some manner of communicative relationality as enemies comprehend each other as mutually hostile. Such forms of relationality, of course, can change over time. Making friends risks making enemies. The proximity of the practice of making political common cause to making enemies is exemplified by the case of civil war where friends or brothers turn on each other to become enemies.[137]

Jacques Rancière further explores the significance of communicative relationality for political action, particularly when political relations occur within a stabilized speech situation that is nevertheless an order structured by inequality and domination.[138] On the one hand, for Rancière, even under such conditions of inequality where one gives commands and subordinates fulfill those commands, those who obey "must understand the order," and they understand that they "must obey."[139] On the other hand, the one giving the orders must assume that the subordinates "understand what he is saying."[140] To follow orders, one must be the equal of the one who gives orders in terms of capacity for reason and language, and the one giving orders "must presume the equality of speaking beings," contradicting a structure that presupposes a natural or inherent inequality among human beings.[141] According to Rancière, this necessarily presupposed equality of reason and linguistic potential among humans even in situations of structured inequality "gnaws" at the order.[142]

Politics, for Rancière, occurs when those who do not count within the order, the part of no part who nevertheless identify themselves with the whole, assert rights or claim a wrong that cannot be acknowledged, that is "incommensurable," within the order as it stands.[143] Those who interrupt the order with their "fundamental dispute" are both heard and not heard as the partition of the perceptible rests on their invisibility and nonspeech among those who count even as their equality is, contradictorily, presumed.[144] Political activity "makes visible what had no business being seen, and makes heard a discourse where once there was only place for noise."[145] Rather than the more or less of labor-management contract negotiations, for instance, political activity "reconfigures the relationships that determine the workplace in its relation to the community."[146] It makes manifest a split, gap, division, or antagonism by expounding a wrong that cannot be processed by the order as presently constituted, thereby forcing a shift in the field or, indeed, the world itself.[147]

Should we understand the antagonism between the NYPD and BLM in terms of ontology or politics? Should we understand this antagonism as nonrelationality and incommunicability, or as joined in relation, relations of enmity? While Wilderson insists on the primary importance of ontological anti-Blackness denying Blacks social relationality, subjectivity, or communicative relationality, Rancière insists on "deontologizing" the miscounting of the part of no part in order not to associate the "miscount to an originary difference."[148] Although an ontological claim cannot be simply proven or disproven by empirical evidence, we can, nevertheless, explore how well an ontological claim fits with events or empirical conditions. Bearing in mind the distinctive registers of ontology and social science or political theory, we can still ask: Do the police and black city residents or BLM communicate?

### Communicating Mutual Enmity

Policing expert and criminologist Jerome Skolnick opens "The Police in Protest," a chapter from one of the numerous presidential commission reports on violence, riots, and protests of the 1960s, with a long excerpt from James Baldwin's *Nobody Knows My Name*.[149] Skolnick quotes Baldwin: "The only way to police a ghetto is to be oppressive. . . . [The policeman] is facing, daily and nightly, the people who would gladly see him dead and he knows it. There is no way for him not to know it: There are few things under heaven more unnerving than silent, accumulating contempt and hatred of a people. He moves through Harlem, therefore, like an occupying soldier in a bitterly hostile country; which is precisely what, and where he is."[150] After describing studies finding "overwhelming evidence of widespread, virulent prejudice by police against Negroes," astonishing to Skolnick because the evidence for such racism on the part of police was often produced voluntarily in front of observers without restraint, he notes in response to Baldwin's 1962 characterization of policing Harlem: "Today the situation is even more polarized."[151] While the Kerner Commission was careful to note as significant factors contributing to the urban riots the broad grievances with respect to racial discrimination and social and economic conditions, both the Kerner Commission and Skolnick's study of policing protest clearly identify the mutual enmity communicated between police and black urban residents during the 1960s as posing a crisis of legitimacy for the state. As these presidential commission reports depict, police and black residents communicate; they communicate enmity expressing a political antagonism, and this political antagonism is publicly understood.

The Kerner Commission found "contemptuous and degrading verbal abuse," stripping black residents of their dignity, contributed to "abrasive relationships between police and Negroes and other minority groups" that were a "major source of grievance and, ultimately, disorder."[152] It also found that stop and frisk policies requiring officers to file a minimum number of reports aggravated tensions producing disorder.[153] As I have already argued, we can understand the "Broken Windows" concept of policing as a reaction against developments spurred by the Kerner Commission to render police more legally accountable.[154] We can observe further that Judge Scheindlin's legal decision in *Floyd v. New York City*, finding stop and frisk as practiced by the NYPD to be unconstitutional, reaffirms what the Kerner Commission found forty-five years earlier: excessive, racially disparate, and legally groundless stops and searches engender mutual enmity.

One of Scheindlin's examples illustrates how this mutual enmity is communicated. David Ourlicht, a twenty-five-year-old male of mixed background, was walking on the street when an officer, Christopher Moran, drove past him on a police scooter from behind. They made brief eye contact, and when Ourlicht reached the intersection where Moran was stopped, the officer asked him what he was doing in the area and where he was going. Moran asked Ourlicht for identification, to which Ourlicht responded, "why are you stopping me?" After Moran had recorded Ourlicht's information, Ourlicht said, "now that you have my information do you mind if I take down yours?" Moran said "sure." Ourlicht made it clear to Moran that he was reaching into his pockets to get pen and paper, and recorded Moran's badge number, nameplate, and scooter number. Moran had radioed for backup, and a patrol car pulled up. Moran "then said, 'okay now you're going to get the full treatment, get up against the wall.'"[155] The description of the stop suggests that it was a result of Ourlicht making eye contact with the officer, and its escalation by the NYPD was in response to Ourlicht communicating that he and Moran were coequal citizens by insisting on his right to record Moran's information, and the NYPD's hostile reaction to the relations implied by such a claim. The NYPD escalated the stop as part of the mutual communication of enmity.[156]

The Department of Justice's *Investigation of the Ferguson Police Department* found numerous instances of racially degrading and abusive speech, in addition to needless threats of violence, on the part of the FPD directed to black Ferguson residents.[157] Such instances of racial abuse—and the racial disproportionalities of investigatory stops produced by police departments that embrace such stops as part of a preventative policing strategy informed by the "Broken Windows" concept of policing—have documented effects similar to those of degradation ceremonies.[158] A degradation ceremony functions performatively through communicative work to reduce the symbolic status of someone or of a group in the social order—to degrade their current status to a lower status or to reinforce through such repetitive communicative work (backed by force in the case of the police) a status that otherwise could be interpreted as equal to that of the dominant group asserting their status over those whom they aim to degrade.[159] Insofar as the FPD's policing practices (or stop and frisk more generally in light of broadly similar racial disparities in different localities) can be likened to systematic degradation ceremonies, they are symbolic (communicative acts) and material (acts that deprive subjects of freedom, acts of financial expropriation, acts of physical force) practices of degradation representative of a political antagonism.

When Ferguson residents rose up to protest the abusive and degrading treatment they had endured at the hands of the FPD and Ferguson municipal government for so long—when they politicized policing practices of an unequal order—they encountered efforts by police to impede their protests, assemblies, and speech. Police required protesters to keep moving or risk arrest for "refusal to disperse," a rule that was arbitrarily enforced, and enforced without regard to whether individuals had any intent to violate the law. The rule rendered protesters vulnerable to arrest through their mere presence in public space, whether they had stopped marching to catch their breath, to obtain information, to gather and listen to a speaker, or to raise their collective voice. According to the observations of an Amnesty International delegation, on the night of August 19, and with the curfew lifted, police arrested demonstrators for a failure to disperse. When Amnesty observers asked different officers why arrests were occurring, they received inconsistent answers, from "I don't know," or "I can't answer that question," to being directed to other officers, to a response from one officer who "characterized the protest as 'a riot situation.'"[160] A belatedly created Protester Assembly Zone was located out of sight from the hastily created Media Staging Area, and was without water or restroom facilities. Very few used the Protester Assembly Zone except to rest when they became exhausted from continuous walking.[161] Protesters believed the rule prohibiting them from standing still in public was an effort to tire them out so they would cease protesting.[162] The police response to the Ferguson uprising targeted its expression of political antagonism.

As I have already described, when Ferguson residents protested, police forces responded with excessive displays of militarily force. The excesses of this spectacle of military force are its communicative dimension. Police deployed this excessive force in response to the protests—a political response to political protest.

Police also responded with an excess of force against journalists covering the Ferguson protests. One St. Ann Police Department officer pointed an "AR-15 semi-automatic rifle at a group of journalists and threatened to kill them."[163] Between August 13 and October 2, 2014, "at least 19 journalists and members of the media were arrested by law enforcement with others subjected to tear gas and the use of rubber bullets. Reporters for CNN, Al Jazeera America and other outlets report[ed] being harassed or physically threatened."[164] This excessive threat and use of violence manifested an effort to enforce the partition of the perceptible through which black residents of Ferguson can be expropriated without such expropriation registering symbolically as a wrong. Rather than incommunicable nonsubjects, police targeted Ferguson protesters, and those who sought to report on their protests, as political subjects for their speech acts and communicable relationality—for forcing a contradiction with the partition of the perceptible by making political antagonism appear. Rather than ontological nonbeing or an ontological void, the Missouri National Guard honestly framed the relation of protesters to police when the Guard referred to protesters as the "enemy."[165]

## Blue Lives Matter

The emergence of Blue Lives Matter is a powerful indication that #BlackLivesMatter registers as a political enemy. Blue Lives Matter responds to BLM protests, and the normative claim that black lives should matter, should count, by communicating hostility to this normative claim. The enmity Blue Lives Matter demonstrates to the claim that black lives should matter is exhibited on its website, on Facebook, on Twitter, and in legislation passed by Louisiana and proposed in the U.S. Congress.

Blue Lives Matter was founded after a man with a history of mental illness shot his girlfriend in Baltimore (she survived), and then traveled to New York and killed two NYPD officers, Wenjian Liu and Rafael Ramos, before committing suicide on Saturday, December 20, 2014. His posts on social media implied the officers were targeted in retaliation for the police killings of Eric Garner and Michael Brown.[166] When New York mayor Bill de Blasio, who had praised the work of police officers while stressing the right of BLM protesters to express themselves and who had described publicly how he had "instruct[ed] his biracial son . . . to 'take special care' during any police encounters," arrived at the hospital where Liu and Ramos had been pronounced dead, officers turned their backs on de Blasio. The president of the Patrolmen's Benevolent Association, Patrick Lynch, stated, "There's blood on many hands tonight." He added, "That blood on the hands starts on the steps of City Hall, in the office of the mayor."[167] At the hospital, one

*Figure 5.4* The Blue Lives Matter Twitter banner, "Sometimes there's justice; sometimes there's just us," represents a postlegitimation orientation to policing. Screenshot: November 20, 2019.

officer exclaimed, "It's f—ing open season on us right now."[168] On the Sunday after the officers were shot, former NYPD police commissioner Ray Kelly, on *This Week*, criticized de Blasio for his statements about training his son to be careful in police encounters, commenting, "I think that set off the latest firestorm."[169] Former New York mayor Rudolph Giuliani condemned de Blasio, in addition to U.S. Attorney General Eric Holder and President Barack Obama, for fueling "intense, anti-police hatred."[170] When de Blasio spoke during the funeral for Ramos, officers in attendance turned their backs on the mayor again.[171]

An article in *Time* magazine described "criticism of cops by public officials" as "taboo."[172] Nevertheless, protests against police violence associated with BLM forced what had been an implicit prohibition constituting the premise for normal political discourse in the United States, premises for speech unspeakable by public officials, into public discourse. Blue Lives Matter, a pro-police media company, reacted to this fissure in the partition of the perceptible by forming in December 2014.[173]

■ Blue Lives Matter was founded based on the need of law enforcement. On August 9 2014, Ferguson PD Officer Darren Wilson was doing his job as he stopped Michael Brown, who had just committed a robbery of a local convenience store. Brown attacked Officer Wilson in an aggravated assault. Officer Wilson was forced to defend his life by shooting Brown. In the months that followed, agitators spread outright lies and distortions of the truth about Officer Wilson and all police officers. The media catered to movements such as Black Lives Matter, whose goal was the vilification of law enforcement. Criminals who rioted and victimized innocent citizens were further given legitimacy by the media as "protesters." America watched as criminals destroyed property, and assaulted and murdered innocent people, and they labeled these criminals as victims. Personal responsibility for one's actions went away, replaced by accusations of racism and an unjust government. It seemed that almost every media organization was spreading the absurd message that people were being shot by law enforcement simply because of the color of their skin. Our political leaders pandered to these criminals and helped spread this false narrative, with no thought of the consequences.

On December 20, 2014, NYPD Officer Rafael Ramos and Officer Wenjian Liu were ambushed and murdered by a fanatic who believed the lies of Black Lives Matter, the media, and politicians. While reporting on the murder of these heroes, the media continued to spread the false narrative of Black Lives Matter.

Even the big law enforcement media companies, who purport to be all for the police, helped spread misinformation through re-posting articles written with an anti-police bias. This highlighted that these companies weren't run by law enforcement, and they only cared about saving time and money "reporting" the news.

The officers who founded this organization were motivated by the heroic actions of Officer Darren Wilson, and many others, and decided to create this organization in the hopes that it could prevent more officers from being hurt.

Blue Lives Matter formed and gathered supporters of law enforcement on Facebook to distribute information which accurately reflected the realities of law enforcement. Feeling the limitations of being contained to Facebook, the Blue Lives Matter news website was launched to provide accurate coverage of law enforcement, from a law enforcement perspective.

In 2016, after an unprecedented number of ambush attacks on law enforcement officers, the founders decided that we could be doing more to help the officers who are getting attacked in the streets. The Blue Lives Membership was created so that citizens who aren't afraid to support law enforcement could become actively involved in providing law enforcement officers with lifesaving equipment and training, and providing financial support for the families of heroes killed in the line of duty.

Blue Lives Matter will continue to support law enforcement in any way when there is a need that we can fill.

SOURCE: *Blue Lives Matter, "History," n.d., accessed November 20, 2019, http://archive .bluelivesmatter.blue/organization/.*

The Blue Lives Matter narrative of its origins not only points to the political antagonism between BLM and Blue Lives Matter, it manifests Rancière's depiction of the political claims of the unvalued and uncounted as being heard and not heard at the same time—as expressing a wrong incommensurable with the dominant order, and thereby exposing a fundamental dispute. The Blue Lives Matter organization's "History" (available in an archive of its website) begins by describing how Ferguson police officer Darren Wilson was "forced to defend his life" by killing Michael Brown. The parallax view of the Ferguson protests is unmistakable in the Blue Lives Matter organizational autobiography: while condemning the protests in Ferguson after Brown's death as a moment when "personal responsibility for one's actions went away," it remains blind to the possibility that Wilson should be personally accountable for killing Michael Brown. Similarly, it refers to the protesters as "criminals" engaged in the "vilification of law enforcement," while recognizing angrily that they were "given legitimacy by the media as 'protesters.'" Affectively attached to the racial resentments mobilized and expressed by the crime crisis that began to constellate in the 1960s, a double vision regarding victimhood also appears as the text refers to Brown attacking Wilson (i.e., Wilson was the victim, not Brown), and it elides protest, crime, and riots when it condemns the protesters ("Criminals," in the words of Blue Lives Matter) for having "victimized innocent people" with their protests. Nevertheless, the media "labeled these criminals as victims." The black and poor residents of Ferguson had stolen the whitened, melodramatic halo of victimhood from police and those who enjoy abusive policing of black people, assisted by the media and "political leaders" who "pandered to these criminals and helped spread this false narrative with no thought of the consequences," victimizing police and the Forgotten Man (and Woman) yet again. Blue Lives Matter's investment in an order in which police enjoy impunity and black lives do not matter is clearly communicated by their faulting the media and public officials for failing to consider the consequences of acknowledging the black and poor residents of Ferguson as political subjects who count (protesters whose claims merit consideration).[174]

The following paragraph in the Blue Lives Matter history addresses the deaths of officers Liu and Ramos, complaining, "the media continued to spread the false narrative of Black Lives Matter," and how even "big law enforcement media companies" contributed to "anti-police bias."[175] The association of the deaths of Liu and Ramos with BLM protests is a racial association activating a leap from one mentally ill black person who killed police officers to BLM as a movement out to kill police officers. The first Blue Lives Matter law, passed in Louisiana, codified such racial fears by representing legislatively the status of police as victims by treating felonious acts against the person or property of police officers as a hate crime and subject to hate crime sentence enhancements.[176] Because policing does not rank even among the top ten most dangerous jobs, according to the Bureau of Labor Statistics, and because fatal shootings of police officers have fallen steadily since the 1970s (from about 127 per year to 41 in 2015, in comparison with 1,146 people killed by police in the United States in 2015 according to The Guardian's collection of police shootings data in The Counted, with black people more than twice as likely to be shot as white people), this legislative action is motivated less by an existential threat to police than by the haunting, spectral figure of black insurrection.[177]

Although Blue Lives Matter characterizes BLM as criminals, something more than ordinary criminality is implied. This excess is apparent in its reference to Officer Darren Wilson's actions as "heroic." Often, a hero is one who demonstrates bravery by saving or defending another by putting themselves at risk of harm. How is killing an unarmed teenager heroic? If we contextualize this narration within an imaginary of war and mutual enmity, however, the Blue Lives Matter history makes more sense: Wilson killed a political enemy, or one who evoked the specter of the enemy.[178]

From the NYPD's mobilization of Intel and Counterterrorism assets against BLM protests in early December 2014, or its deployment of an LRAD against BLM throughout the month, to the militarized response by St. Louis County and the National Guard to the Ferguson uprising, BLM protests are the occasion for a hybrid discursive and institutional response, one that migrates from crime to war. This reaction to BLM makes questionable the ontological assertion of Black incommunicability from the perspective of the Human, and Blackness as a void of relationality. The protest of BLM is that the current order in the United States rests on a fundamental wrong. This protest triggers, in response, a hostile reaction of antagonism and negation: the expression that Blue Lives Matter, not black lives. The very claim that black lives matter registers and provokes the public appearance of mutual enmity. Blue Lives Matter produces communicative expression of affective attachment to neoliberal authoritarianism. It also expresses branded affective attachment to the political negation of the very claim that black lives matter. Blue Lives Matter hears the claim. And it enjoys rejecting it.

*Political Antagonism and the Securitization of Protest Policing*

Scholars have documented how policing in the United States became increasingly militarized in the 1980s and 1990s.[179] This increased militarization of policing is linked to an increasingly militarized culture of policing more disposed to use military-grade weapons or to resort to lethal force.[180] Though created for exceptional circumstances, the deployment of paramilitary police units has become normalized and is often used for warrant service or neighborhood patrols—particularly in areas of racialized poverty.[181] Because the acquisition of military accoutrements makes their use more likely, militarized responses to protest became possible and probable. Protest policing at major economic summits in the United States during the late 1990s and early 2000s actualized this potential by showcasing militarized displays of force and utilizing violent responses to protesters, including the use of an LRAD when Pittsburgh hosted the G-20 meetings in 2009.[182]

I add to the literature on the militarization of policing by highlighting how neoliberal, post-Fordist urban political economies stimulate the militarization—or more accurately, the securitization—of policing protest. Presidential Decision Directive 62, issued by President Bill Clinton in 1998, created the NSSE classification, the highest security designation in the United States.[183] Examples of NSSEs include international economic summits, major party conventions, presidential inaugurations, presidential funerals, and significant sporting events such as the Olympics and the Super Bowl. Due to neoliberal, post-Fordist incentives for cities to host such mega-events for purposes of place branding and urban marketing to potential visitors and conventions, the planning process to prepare security arrangements for NSSEs, and federal aid available for such security arrangements, hosting mega-events produces a multiplier effect spurring the securitization of policing and urban environments. Exemplifying how hosting mega-events produces lasting security legacies in the host city, the NYPD acquired its LRAD in conjunction with hosting the 2004 RNC, albeit with assurances that it would be used only in its public address function. Despite such assurances, the NYPD is normalizing LRAD deployments, though only when policing protest.

More disturbingly, the only known NYPD use of an LRAD in its area denial capability at this writing—and the routinization of such exercises of military force—has been against those protesting police abuse of force, claiming that black lives matter. Although such violence may be understood by Wilderson as manifesting an anti-Black ontological antagonism, I propose we may better understand this antagonism politically. The violent excesses of the NYPD's routine deployment of an LRAD to suppress nonviolent protests against police abuse of force mobilized under the banner of BLM, and the spectacularly militaristic reaction against the BLM uprising in Ferguson protesting police violence, racial degradation, and financial expropriation, represent an intense political antagonism. Responding to this political antagonism, police seek to restore the order of neoliberal authoritarianism by resorting to military force as an instrument of violence, and as an expressive spectacle of intimidation, both of which produce order through subjugation.

My analysis here enables a theoretical appreciation for events not well explained by Wilderson's commitment to ontologizing racial subjugation. Wilderson acknowledges how political movements destabilized relations of domination in the late 1960s, and how these relations of domination became reestablished in the 1980s.[184] These events should be considered mere, incidental facts from the perspective of his broad ontological sweep, though viewed in terms of politics, this periodization reflects the power of mobilizations oriented toward or beyond a social democratic horizon, on the one hand, and their defeat, on the other. This periodization—problematic from an ontological standpoint—points to what is lost when questions of politics are displaced onto ontological grounds.[185]

Jacques Derrida's concept of hauntology troubles analyses determined and enclosed by ontological premises.[186] Hauntology expresses the idea that we learn to live from others, others who may no longer be present.[187] Their ideas about living, their spirits, remain with us, informing, haunting, or inspiring how we live. Being, therefore, entails being-with others, others who may have passed but whose traces remain, nevertheless, with us now. It is a mistake, then, to think life in terms of an essentially unified contemporaneous presence. This critique of ontological presence means that time is always out of joint because specters of the past, of others, continue to haunt or inspire the present. We continue to be haunted today, perhaps by the desire for a lost future that would entail living better than we do (living that surpasses mere life).[188] Or some may be haunted in the present by the specters of an enemy thought to have been defeated in the past—in their present encounters they see ghosts of enemies past, or perhaps they are driven persistently to remain attached to the specters of past enemies.[189] The state of neoliberal authoritarianism's institutions and political subjects remains haunted in this latter manner by the protests and riots of the 1960s.

Not only do we see a tendency toward increasingly militarized responses to protest by police, we also see a growing use of control technologies.[190] Control technologies use "dividuated" data produced by communicative capitalism.[191] Reflexive systems of fragmentation, collation, or probabilistic or possibilistic association enable control technologies to monitor, construct patterns, modulate, and incapacitate. Some may enjoy access—whether to movement, instruments basic to living in one's environment (such as a car or phone), institutions, accounts, data, websites, care, or communicability—if they can provide accepted communicative signals. Some may receive conditioned access or certain levels of access; some may be denied access or experience their access incapacitated. Control technologies also enable other actors or systems to monitor, modulate, or incapacitate those made communicatively visible.

On the one hand, control technologies complement more lethally militarized weaponry with their tracking, guidance, surveillance, and associative capacities. For example, Stingray technology was developed in a military context for use in tracking those to be targeted by drone strikes, complementing U.S. counterinsurgency (COIN) operations.[192] On the other hand, control technologies function similarly to more lethal weaponry as they control, disintegrate, or incapacitate subjects (or their communicability), representing a continuity between control technologies and more lethal weaponry when compared to disciplinary power. Today, we see a growing integration of control technologies and lethal weaponry as drones are developed with lethal capacity that can be flown without direct guidance from human pilots, and are increasingly able to identify their targets independently of human pilots.[193]

Policing's deployment of control technologies is at odds with freedom of speech as part of a practice of democracy, a practice of the sovereignty or rightful power of the people. As Justice Douglas writes in the Supreme Court decision *Terminiello v. Illinois*, sometimes freedom of speech serves its highest purposes when it invites "dispute," when it "induces a condition of unrest, creates dissatisfaction with conditions as they are, or even stirs people to anger."[194] In other words, freedom of speech as part of a practice of democracy must have the potential capacity to be disruptive of oppressive, unjust conditions—speech acts and assemblies must be linked to the power of the people. The Supreme Court's decision and its reasoning in *Terminiello* would be repeated to reverse breach of the peace convictions of civil rights protesters in the 1960s whose demonstrations provoked gatherings of sometimes disgruntled, if not angry, onlookers.[195] Technologies of control track users and can condition or incapacitate their access to spaces and institutions. They disassemble, or disrupt, collective action, with their orientation to the preemption of disorder or even the appearance of antagonism. They have the capacity to disorganize efforts to organize political subjects and political action in the name of security by creating potential or possible criminalized associations, or by treating political subjects as political enemies to be monitored, contained, thwarted, or incapacitated. This conflict between technologies of control as situated within the security paradigm of policing and freedom of speech as a democratic power is exemplified by the way the Memphis Police Department (MPD) has policed Black Lives Matter actions and activists.

### BLM, the Memphis Police Department, and the Specter of Black Insurrection

Memphis residents sued the city on February 22, 2017. They complained of surveillance by the MPD when it videotaped their demonstrations, and of its creation of a "blacklist" of eighty-one persons who could not enter City Hall without a police escort to their destination in the building. Activists involved with BLM were heavily represented on the list. They also complained of the city's use of Geofeedia software.[196]

Memphis, like Chicago and New York, was one of several city police departments discovered to be keeping political intelligence and "blacklists" of "radicals," "reds," or "subversives" for the purpose of destroying the left during the 1960s.[197] As the "negotiated management" paradigm of protester-police relations superseded the "escalated force" era, such surveillance and actions of political disruption by police were recognized as incompatible with a constitutional democracy, and these cities were barred from engaging in political surveillance, political disruption, and keeping or circulating blacklists. Memphis, Chicago, and New York police were prohibited from engaging in these activities by judicial consent decrees, with Memphis becoming the first of these cities to become subject to such a consent decree, known as the *Kendrick* Consent Decree.[198] Unlike the Chicago and New York decrees, the Memphis decree had remained unchanged since 1978 when activists filed their action against the city in 2017. Therefore, activists charged Memphis had violated its consent decree, and sought to have it enforced.

As their case proceeded, activists and the American Civil Liberties Union of Tennessee learned that MPD monitoring of BLM was much more far-reaching than they had initially believed. Although the MPD's Office of Homeland Security (OHS) focused on counterterrorism when it was created, evidence produced by the litigation demonstrated that OHS had become "refocused on political intelligence."[199] Time devoted to terrorism threats had diminished, only occupying about 35 percent of OHS time, while "protests involved much of [OHS] time" between 2016 and 2017, according to officer testimony.[200] Therefore, federal judge Jon McCalla found Memphis to be in violation of the *Kendrick* Consent Decree because it conducted forbidden political intelligence practices and "Operated the Office of Homeland Security for the purpose of political intelligence."[201] Judge McCalla also found Memphis to be in violation of *Kendrick* because it intercepted electronic communications and infiltrated groups using a fake Facebook account; failed to familiarize MPD officers with the decree; did not create an approval process for criminal investigations that could implicate First Amendment rights; disseminated information the MPD collected to individuals outside law enforcement; and recorded and maintained a database of protest attendees.[202]

Why did OHS institutional resources become redirected away from counterterrorism to protests? Evidence shows that OHS became retooled to focus on political intelligence in response to the events of Ferguson.[203] The redirection of OHS resources was also in response to protests targeting the MPD due to an MPD officer having killed Darrius Stewart, a teenaged African American male, who was a passenger in a car pulled over for a broken headlight in July 2015.[204] The OHS became the MPD's organizational hub for targeting the BLM movement in Memphis.

The OHS produced and disseminated between one and three Joint Intelligence Briefings (JIBs) daily.[205] The JIBs circulated information on police shootings/deaths, riots/protests, BLM, and officer safety.[206] The JIB circulation broadened "exponentially" over time and was forwarded beyond its circulation list.[207] The list's recipients included not only different components of the MPD, but Shelby County officials, the U.S. military, U.S. Department of Justice, Tennessee Department of Homeland Security, Arkansas Fusion Centers, Memphis Gas & Electric, Shelby County Schools, FedEx, Autozone, and St. Jude. Events included public protests, events on private property, a rumored event that turned out to be a hoax, and a BLM activist's complaint about police harassment. The JIBs included "Sensitive/Classified" information like driver license profiles, juvenile arrest records, mental health histories, and photographs.[208]

Michael Rallings, MPD director, instructed OHS to create and maintain a database of protests and demonstrations. The database included protest events with as few as four people. Only two recorded events resulted in any arrests, and none produced any damage.[209]

The OHS captured private communications of Memphis residents active in BLM, and OHS created a dummy Facebook account under the name "Bob Smith" to "catfish" activists and convince them to friend the account.[210] Tim Reynolds, who was one of the key officers in the OHS monitoring of BLM, also obtained an undercover phone from the Organized Crime Unit to allow him to communicate surreptitiously with BLM activists by call or text message about planning, preparation, and events so the MPD could become more "proactive" with respect to BLM demonstrations.[211]

To support its political intelligence gathering, OHS enlisted the Real Time Crime Center's (RTCC's) resources. The RTCC has a "bank of approximately 30–33 computers on the floor," staffed by officers who work in three shifts.[212] The officers in the RTCC monitored live video feeds from cameras posted throughout Memphis, mobile cameras, and a drone. They would manually search social media, and they used social media collators Geofeedia and NC4 to search and monitor social media chatter in public posts regarding protests in the Memphis area, and reported findings back to OHS.[213] The OHS would then disseminate this intelligence to precinct commanders and would make sure that protests were covered by officers either in uniform or in plainclothes.[214]

Officers in the RTCC would use analysis software, such as Accurint LE Plus and i2 Analyst's Notebook.[215] Accurint assists police by creating a visual image of "complex relationships" and uses identifying information to locate other identifying information (such as telephone numbers or photos), property assets of suspects, and information about potential financial distress that police can use in their investigations.[216] The i2 Analyst's Notebook is a "visual analysis tool" that performs "social network analysis." It creates "network visualizations" by constructing "connections" and organizing them either spatially or temporally.[217] Officers in the RTCC would use the i2 package to create a document mapping events and Memphis residents to each other, scoring the relationships thereby created in terms of their closeness. The document is titled "Black Lives Matter.pdf."[218]

The construction of the blacklist at issue in the complaint against Memphis exhibited this logic of association integral to the use of control technologies embedded within preventative policing. The list began with the names of those who conducted a die-in protest at Memphis mayor Jim Strickland's residence, December 19, 2016. There were no arrests at the protest, but MPD director Michael Rallings instructed that the MPD respond, and the response resulted in the City Hall Escort List and an Authorization of Agency (AOA).[219] The AOA was a delegation of trespass authority to the MPD so that if the MPD encountered members of the list on Strickland's property, for example, the MPD could arrest and charge these persons with criminal trespass without Strickland needing to be present. The list was not limited just to those who participated in the die-in protest. It extended to "associates in fact"—those deemed to be associated with the protesters through social media contacts, whether they were seen with an individual the MPD had identified as a key activist, or if they had been at other protests, either with the group that organized the die-in or the key individual. The logic of control technologies—like other weaponry such as LRADs—functions through an illiberal logic of guilt by association more compatible with combating a political enemy than conducting enforcement in the context of civil society.

In fact, the slightest mention of BLM drew MPD attention and was sufficient for dissemination for further monitoring, flagging, or more proactive intervention by MPD organizational resources—a process that created an ever-extending web of association. For example, an email from Officer Bradley Wilburn to Officer Timothy Reynolds in OHS with the subject heading "Protest Monitoring" observes, "Tami Sawyer is active with Steve Cohen, post below." Steve Cohen is a member of Congress representing Memphis, and the post in question stated that Cohen called for "cultural training" for police and said that "Black Lives Matter is doing important work."[220] When asked about the email during his deposition and why that social media post might have been sent to OHS, Wilburn responded, "Probably because of the mention of Black Lives Matter."[221] Another email, from Officer Jessica Grafenreed, includes an attachment titled "BLM event." In her email, she describes why she forwarded the attachment: "Due to the 'black lives matter' on the flyer wanted to pass it along."[222] When MPD got wind of a church hosting a community-police dialogue, it contacted the bishop to make sure that the forum would be "pro-police."[223] A memorial service for Darrius Stewart was also monitored by MPD, observing "known individuals" in the crowd and other details until it concluded and attendees left.[224]

#BlackLivesMatter also became elided with "black," as "Black Owned Food Truck Sunday" did not escape MPD notice.[225] The MPD prevented black BLM protesters from entering Graceland during Elvis Week in 2016, keeping them enclosed behind barricades and separated from tourists.[226] Meanwhile, a group of mostly white BLM protesters were free to enter this major annual tourism event in Memphis.[227] Could one not be both a supporter of BLM and a fan of Elvis? Local lawmakers articulated concern that the MPD's policing of the event was not "content neutral" because it allowed free movement and expression to those celebrating Elvis but not to perceived BLM speakers.[228] While Elvis Presley Enterprises later released a statement communicating support for inclusion and hospitality, the MPD's policing during Elvis Week sought to separate BLM from Elvis Week celebrations—segregating actions where the exercise of First Amendment rights overlapped significantly with race.[229]

The MPD's use of control technologies not only to monitor but to construct lines of association linked to potential criminalization as part of a practice to preempt protest demonstrates a logic of post-democratic policing. Nevertheless, as these lines of association become almost absurd in their breadth—and narrowness—they can tell us something about the state formation of neoliberal authoritarianism through this state's practices of protest policing. The MPD's reaction to BLM is so excessive—it is experienced by Memphis residents as harassing, intimidating, chilling the exercise of First Amendment rights, and as paranoid behavior—that it expresses core elements of this state formation.[230]

A PowerPoint presentation created by OHS represents the MPD's frame of reference for BLM. Titled "Blue Suede Shoes," it addresses BLM protests and MPD intelligence regarding leading protesters. The presentation opens by referring to "the social climate in the 1960's and the 1970's," and the title of its second slide is "2016: A Year of Social Unrest Reminiscent of the late 1960's and early 1970's."[231] The MPD is haunted by the specter of black insurrection.

Like *U.S. News and World Report*'s editorials on the Civil Rights movement in the 1960s conflating nonviolent sit-ins and protest with crime and violence, or Richard Nixon's speeches during the 1968 campaign conflating crime, protests, and riots, "Blue Suede Shoes" and depositions of MPD officers conflate protest, violence, and riots or civil disorder. The PowerPoint reports that a BLM protest during Elvis Week could be used to "incite" and "escalate the violence." "Smaller radical groups" in "metropolitan areas all across the United States," the PowerPoint informs its audience, are using "peaceful demonstrations to use violence and destruction to promote or advance their own agendas." One slide identifies a woman arrested for standing at Elvis's gravesite one night at approximately 10:30 p.m. yelling, "Black Lives Matter!" When she refused to leave, she was arrested and charged with "Disorderly Conduct, Inciting a Riot, and Criminal Trespass."[232] When asked about the database of demonstrations in Memphis, the director of the

MPD responded by characterizing demonstrations as "civil disturbances," a term typically used to describe a riot or insurrection, until conceding it was "very rare" that "law enforcement had to do anything other than just kind of be there to keep everybody safe."[233] Institutionally, the MPD comprehends BLM as an insurrection.[234]

If the MPD understands BLM to represent a political insurrection, then the use of control technologies for surveillance, intelligence gathering, databases, mapping, and weighting possible associations among residents and events, the MPD briefings and deployment of institutional assets begin to make more sense. So also does the "Blue Suede Shoes" PowerPoint and MPD Detective Tim Reynolds's deposition, which express concern that activists are using (or "hijacking") "legitimate community organizations to advance a radical agenda," such as "embarrass[ing] law enforcement in order to undermine the bond between law enforcement and the community."[235] As the Army field manual *Counterinsurgency* instructs, the struggle between insurgents and counterinsurgents is a struggle for popular support.[236] To undermine popular support for insurgencies, the field manual recommends, "Insurgents Must be Isolated from Their Cause and Support" so that "the people [will] marginalize and stigmatize insurgents to the point that the insurgency's claim to legitimacy is destroyed."[237] The field manual also advises, "When insurgents are seen as criminals, they lose public support."[238] Much like COIN operations conducted by U.S. armed services, the MPD seeks to criminalize BLM, separate BLM from community organizations perceived as popular, and control police-community dialogues in order to protect the popularity of their own brand's image while preempting potentially damaging associations. Whether compiling an AOA, separating BLM demonstrators from Elvis fans, arresting a woman who is chanting a slogan that is antiviolence ("Black Lives Matter!") for inciting a riot, or contacting a faith leader to receive assurances that the community dialogue to be hosted would be "pro-police," and like the NYPD's preemptive arrests of protesters or its effort to keep OWS separated from more established civic organizations on May Day 2012, policing in the United States increasingly incorporates the COIN principles of the armed services.

## BLM and Resistance to Neoliberal Urbanism

Neoliberal, post-Fordist urban governments face legitimacy challenges distinctive from social welfare states of the mid-twentieth century. For instance, the latter needed capital to profit sufficiently to produce tax revenue that could be used by the state to support social reproduction and maintain democratic legitimation without taxing to the extent of imperiling capital's capacity to provide necessary revenue or risking an investment strike by capital.[239] Neoliberal, post-Fordist urban governments are invested in capital, whether through partnerships for both governmental and commercial purposes, for their urban branding, or to maintain credit ratings for favorable access to bond markets.[240] Neoliberal, post-Fordist urban governments rely on successful symbolic production in the realm of city marketing, branding, and governance that appears appealing and can circulate to relevant markets.

Neoliberal, post-Fordist success, then, can mean that urban governments exist in an uneasy, if not conflictual or even antagonistic, relation with resident populations. Residents may suffer under "Broken Windows" order maintenance policing targeting those who appear disorderly or who might make tourists feel fearful. And mega-events and other forms of symbolic production must not be disrupted by protests. In the context of neoliberal, post-Fordist urban political economy, policing represents the forward edge of a state that is postlegitimation from the perspective of meeting the needs of all its residents for social reproduction. The disproportionate use of often lethal violence by police to which black people are disproportionately subject, and BLM as a movement, expresses this relation of political antagonism.

We see this relation of political antagonism in the MPD's targeting of BLM, but this targeting also goes beyond BLM. When being deposed, OHS detective Timothy Reynolds is asked what is meant by "legitimate" in the "Blue Suede Shoes" PowerPoint where "radical groups" are seeking to advance their agenda by using legitimate community organizations. Reynolds eventually states that "legitimate" means "widely supported."[241] Asked what was meant by "radical agenda" in "Blue Suede Shoes," he answers, "Disrupt commerce."[242] The PowerPoint and Reynolds refer simultaneously to BLM and something more.

The PowerPoint includes a BLM protest shutting down the Interstate 40 (I-40) bridge on July 10, 2016, and identifies BLM as a political problem in COIN terms for undermining "the bond between law enforcement and the community."[243] Memphis Police Department email characterizes BLM protests as "encounters" the MPD must "mitigate."[244] In these instances, the relation of political antagonism is between the MPD and BLM. Yet Reynolds does not limit his depiction of "radical" to those who want to make "the police department . . . look bad." Radicals might target "the city or somebody else."[245] To this end, the MPD PowerPoint "All Shook Up," produced by Reynolds at OHS, focuses significantly on a group called Memphis Coalition of Concerned Citizens (CCC), a coalition that includes those who support Palestinian rights, Fight for $15, the Sierra Club, and several other organizations.[246] It also supports opponents of a proposed pipeline to the Valero Memphis Refinery (and those arrested on MLK Day in 2017 protesting the proposed pipeline were added to the blacklist).[247]

Memphis CCC is the group that organized the die-in protest at Mayor Strickland's house—the protest triggering the compilation of the blacklist and AOA composed not only of die-in protesters but the "associates in fact" produced by Reynolds on orders from MPD director Rallings at the center of this litigation. The "associates in fact" were also identified as people who might "cause problems" at the Elvis birthday celebration on January 8, 2017—a major tourist attraction and, in conjunction with Elvis Week every year in August, a major element of post-Fordist symbolic production for Memphis and Elvis Presley Enterprises.[248]

On Strickland's lawn, CCC protesters pretended to be dead, and an activist and key target of the MPD stated, "That's what he [Mayor Strickland] wants. He wants us to die." In a comment to Memphis television news station WREG, he elaborated, "The discomfort we have been feeling from poverty, poor education, bad police-community relations—we just wanted him to feel that same discomfort in some way." The group criticized how "Elvis Presley Enterprises (EPE) and the City of Memphis colluded in the violation of the First Amendment rights of many citizens by not allowing them passage on a public . . . street," stating that the MPD had acted as "private security" for EPE by preventing access of some citizens to Elvis Presley Boulevard. In addition to castigating the militarized response to the BLM I-40 bridge protest, CCC also condemned EPE for not paying its employees a "livable wage" and fueling a "cycle of poverty," asking satirically if it would be better that they died to reduce the "surplus population."[249] Although policing is one problem CCC identifies with the Memphis government, policing is only one part of CCC's broader denunciation of neoliberalism and neoliberal urban government where the state and capital function as a joint enterprise against the social reproduction of city residents. In other words, CCC's grievances are with a neoliberal political economy, and with the post-democratic state formation of neoliberal authoritarianism as enmeshed and invested in this political economy in which the people themselves don't count.[250]

In sum, the policing of the OWS movement's challenge to neoliberalism's inequalities—particularly the enrichment of the 1 percent and growing impoverishment of the 99 percent—caused its message to become diverted, and ultimately superseded, by abusive protest policing on the streets of New

York and elsewhere between 2011 and 2012. Shortly thereafter, BLM became prominent with the police killings of Eric Garner and Michael Brown— among many other instances in 2014 and 2015 of police killing black people in police-initiated encounters—and quickly grew into a movement bringing police abuse of force and impunity to broad attention. Yet to discuss the breadth and depth of injustices that policing, prosecution, and punishment cause and perpetuate became impossible without reference to the economic injustices identified by OWS—indeed, policing and punishment have become adjuncts of a broader economy of immiseration, and are politically implicated in the affective enjoyment of cruelty that attach some political subjects to this economy and its postlegitimation state.[251]

As we have seen in the civil litigation brought against the City of Memphis, the use of control technologies within the MPD was part of a broader, post-democratic politicization of the MPD at odds with the *Kendrick* Consent Decree. The MPD mobilized these control technologies to secure "legitimate" events like the Elvis birthday celebrations or Elvis Week. This policing indicates BLM is an important nodal point of antagonism with respect to neoliberal authoritarianism. The breadth of the associations produced by MPD control technologies proves the impossibility of redressing the injustices identified by BLM without a political encounter with the neoliberal state and political economy, as OWS urged. Yet the way that BLM framed the MPD's policing, and how the slightest mention of BLM (or even blackness) would trigger deployments of the MPD's institutional resources, demonstrate how the spectral figure of black insurrection continues to haunt political investment in the post-democratic, postlegitimation state of neoliberal authoritarianism.

### Best Practices

Lawyers for the City of Memphis justify the MPD's conduct using a narrative strikingly similar to that of Blue Lives Matter. After Ferguson, not only are protest and violence against police associated, but Memphis implies that BLM protests cause violence against police. They explain, "as the number of these oftentimes violent protests increased, so did violence against law enforcement," referring to the shooting of NYPD officers Luis and Ramos.[252] Memphis describes rallies or demonstrations they have not permitted as "threats," and they characterize the "risk of violence or public harm" posed by such gatherings as "high."[253] Although Memphis's risk analysis suffers symptomatic distortions, such distortions are not, as we have seen, unique to the city or its police department. They are shared, for example, with the NYPD.

The MPD's use of control technologies, preoccupation with social media, and their drive to accumulate political intelligence on neoliberal authoritarianism's adversaries is also not unique among police departments in the United States. During the litigation, the MPD released a statement from Director Rallings arguing, "Monitoring these public social media posts is simply good police work."[254] After Judge McCalla ruled that the MPD had violated the *Kendrick* Consent Decree in terms of political intelligence gathering and ordered a trial on other questions, Memphis submitted a legal motion asking that the MPD be relieved of its obligation to the consent decree. In its motion, Memphis contended the "forty year old document" was "impractical" and "not suited to today's world of social media activity driving protest and counter-protest" where "activities must be monitored" for "public safety." "The Consent Decree's . . . prohibition against modern methods of surveillance," Memphis continued, "is dangerous and untenable in today's world."[255] Memphis's motion was stayed.[256] Nevertheless, Memphis is correct to observe that the use of control technologies, and far-reaching political intelligence gathering going beyond law enforcement in the name of proactive policing, are considered by many today to be best practices, as we can see from the federal after-action review of the response to the Ferguson protests and reports on emerging issues or best practices issued by the Department of Justice's Community Oriented Policing Services (COPS) or the Police Executive Research Forum (PERF).

The *After-Action Assessment of the Police Response to the August 2014 Demonstrations in Ferguson, Missouri (AAA)*, produced under the auspices of the COPS Office, finds several aspects of the joint response to the Ferguson protests to be excessive or counterproductive. The AAA criticized many of the militarized elements of the response for escalating tensions, for frightening or angering citizens, as "causing greater animosity toward police," or as likely to be interpreted as an effort to "intimidate."[257] The AAA does not, however, fault St. Louis County's use of an LRAD; it only faults the use of an armored vehicle as its platform, which can create a "negative public image."[258]

Regarding "Use of Intelligence," the AAA finds "intelligence personnel had learned a great deal about threats associated with the Ferguson mass gatherings, particularly from some special-interest groups with an intention to create havoc."[259] The AAA goes on to report, "Groups and individuals for which a criminal predicate had been established in other areas of the country, representing both supportive and antagonistic positions to demonstrators, were traveling to Ferguson."[260] The level of communicative vacuity of this passage (and its communicative equivalences) means we can only speculate to whom this passage might refer. Other reporting finds that the NYPD followed New York–based activists to Ferguson ("professional agitators," to use Bratton's terminology), so one wonders if Occupiers, or those associated with Occupy, were being considered "special-interest groups with an intention to create havoc" or among those "for which a criminal predicate had been established in other areas of the country."[261] Interviews with officers involved indicate their perhaps emblematic difficulty distinguishing "protesters from criminals."[262] As for "Lessons Learned," although the AAA recommends policing agencies have a "protocol for identifying the type of information intelligence units can collect," it urges them to "proactively leverage the resources and expertise of fusion centers in response to a critical incident such as that in Ferguson."[263] The AAA exhibits neoliberal cynicism when it reduces political concern regarding police abuse of force against black people to the self-interest of "special-interest groups," a cynicism that is compatible with the discursive parameters of Nixon's 1968 "Law and Order" campaign or the affective attachments of the Forgotten Man (and Woman). In a post-democratic vein, it also perceives the mobilization of local and national solidarity regarding the disproportionate police use of force against black people to be a "threat."[264] In its orientation to the threat that protesting police abuse of force poses, though, the AAA strikes chords remarkably similar to Memphis and the MPD.

With respect to social media specifically, the AAA recommends hiring "technologically savvy personnel" capable of using social media both to "share information and to collect intelligence."[265] This enthusiasm for monitoring social media echoes other professional iterations of policing's best practices. Leading police executives are urged, and urge each other, to "tap into the social media system."[266] The COPS Office and PERF put forward the NYPD's Intel Division, which includes a unit dedicated to monitoring social media, as exemplary for the way it "studies information about mass demonstrations and protests," and puts officers from Intel "on the ground before and during events" (as we saw with Intel's monitoring of BLM protests).[267]

In its study of the policing of Ferguson's protests, the AAA also recommends creating a "First Amendment free speech zone" that is "clearly marked" and "accessible to the media."[268] Rather than public space being available to people for their assembly as a fundamental right, the AAA's political imaginary is one where police control protester expression. Such zoning of demonstrations enables police to contain the potential political force of the people by using the COIN tactic of separating protesters from the public and from symbolic productions in which urban governments are invested. Police zoning of protest displaces and controls the appearance of political antagonism; it disassembles the people. Expression becomes personalized and disarticulated from practices of collective democratic power, reformatting First Amendment rights in terms more compatible with neoliberalism.

Court decisions permit cities to zone protests to marginalized locations based on the presumption that demonstrators can still express themselves using "modern communications" like the "internet."[269] By preemptively zoning demonstrations, courts and police compel protesters to rely on communicative capitalism to express themselves, making them invisible from the perspective of urban public space or the target of their protests, but visible to control technologies, while also rendering them susceptible to further monitoring, containment, diversion, preemption, or even incapacitation. For example, on August 11, 2011, after a Bay Area Rapid Transit (BART) police officer shot and killed a homeless man in a subway station, BART thwarted an expected protest by shutting down wireless communication services in its downtown San Francisco stations.[270] The action itself engendered protests and unfavorable comparisons with authoritarian regimes that shut down access to the internet or cellular services as a means to maintain state power without legitimation from citizens.[271] Nevertheless, this example points to the way judicial tolerance for limits on demonstrations in public forums to enhance security—particularly when a city is hosting a mega-event—can interact in the future with police acquisition and deployment of control technologies. Displaced into marginalized spaces, protesters are separated from the people and public space. This displacement from public space coerces protester expression into the circuits of communicative capitalism, reducing the power of the people to disintegrated signs legible only to those already searching for them or those who randomly stumble upon them (and rendering these signs susceptible to whatever association). Or protesters may be at the mercy of police capacity to incapacitate their communicability entirely, either by shutting down access to the internet or, perhaps, by interference from a Stingray.

Control technologies are increasingly being embedded within urban infrastructures and are becoming capable of subsuming entire urban environments. For example, when cities host mega-events like the RNC, the DNC, or the Super Bowl, they become eligible for federal money to enhance security. Cities use this money to acquire weapons and vehicles—including armored vehicles—and to increase the number of security cameras in their cities. These cameras remain in the city after the mega-event is over.[272] While many cities are working to integrate private security cameras into police networks, most stored video from security cameras is "never watched." Additionally, watching live video feeds is "mesmerizing," and experts find that after twenty minutes of monitoring, attention levels decline "well below acceptable levels."[273] Because of significant improvements in computer vision due in part to a dramatic decline in the time needed to train a computer to recognize images, however, we can foresee the substitution of machines for humans as monitors of video feeds, substantially amplifying the density of control technologies.[274] A partnership between the NYPD and Microsoft gives Microsoft access to New York's vast network of security cameras to further develop its video analytics system, which it then plans to market to other cities.[275]

Aerial surveillance allows police to preempt protests. For instance, during the 2004 RNC, the NYPD used a blimp to obtain live video of protesters. The NYPD's helicopters were also outfitted with video cameras feeding into their command centers, enabling the NYPD to "monitor where groups are moving" and allowing the NYPD to "cut off groups of protesters and keep them away from delegates. We could tell where people were going before they got there."[276] Aerial surveillance developed to enable the U.S. military to monitor large areas, and then rewind and fast-forward footage to track insurgents, was deployed in Baltimore during the uprisings over Freddie Gray's death at the hands of Baltimore police. Offered by Persistent Surveillance Systems and funded by a private donor, the system can capture an area of thirty square miles and send real-time images to analysts on the ground for up to ten hours a day. The system is described as like "Google Earth with TIVO capability."[277]

Memphis and the MPD are correct, then, to observe that maximal monitoring using control technologies for proactive policing that can contain, preempt, or even incapacitate protests is the forward edge of contemporary policing. They are also correct when they identify the conflict between contemporary policing's best practices and the values represented by the *Kendrick* Consent Decree over forty years ago. The decree represents an important victory against politically repressive policing inconsistent with constitutional democracy, one that paved the way for similar decrees in cities like Chicago and New York, and which was part of the movement toward more dialogic and less violent protester-police relations known as negotiated management. Memphis's and the MPD's discomfort with, if not political opposition to, the values of *Kendrick*, and their approval of contemporary policing's best practices, represents the tendency toward postlegitimation, post-democratic policing integral to neoliberal authoritarianism. Neoliberal authoritarianism permits "community" to express itself when subsumed within community policing or place branding, or when subsumed within the joint symbolic productions of the state and capital, but views the assemblies or grievances of the people increasingly as a threat to be contained, disintegrated, or incapacitated.[278]

## Conclusion

Protest policing is becoming more militarized and increasingly uses control technologies to monitor, disassemble, preempt, or incapacitate protests. The policing of the BLM movement shows both tendencies. The use of militarized or control technologies reflects how protest policing in the United States may be characterized as a practice of security—an institutional practice treating protesters as something more than criminals, while functioning short of total war. In this regard, the policing of BLM protests proceeds like a low-intensity war or a practice of counterinsurgency. In its excesses, this policing of BLM protests exhibits a haunting, the haunting of the spectral figure of black insurrection.

The reaction to BLM protests indicates a relation of political antagonism. By treating BLM like a political enemy, protest policing provides insights upon debates within political theory. Instead of ontologizing the condition of blackness in America, by conceptualizing the relation of BLM to the state of neoliberal authoritarianism as one of political antagonism, we can better appreciate the gains of past movements of the 1960s and 1970s—gains reflected in consent decrees of the 1970s and 1980s in cities like Memphis, New York, or Chicago to prevent police from operating units dedicated to the surveillance and destruction of political enemies—and what the demise of these consent decrees represents. Their demise points to the neoliberal state as post-democratic and postlegitimation: it is a state that, when faced with political movements seeking redress of impoverished conditions of social reproduction, responds to contain, disintegrate, or incapacitate those political movements. The relation of enmity between police and BLM expresses this political antagonism, crystalizing the authoritarianism of the neoliberal state.

While militarized responses are geared to defeating an enemy threatening a state's interests (or way of life, as Schmitt put it) materially and performatively, control technologies prevent or minimize potential threats or damage a system or network may face. The former overtly and expressively displays declared enmity, while the latter manages favorable or negative image-based associations as it responds to associative probabilities, possibilities, or proximities. The former recognizes a political subject in order to defeat or destroy it, while control technologies seek to disintegrate the subject, which may involve constructing and targeting associative aggregations. Both responses, though, remain caught between the existential political claims of BLM and the specter of black insurrection in their excesses.

A state that responds to BLM's protests with a logic of security situated somewhere between crime and war, with military weaponry, dress, dramaturgy, and the kind of surveillance typically reserved for enemies of the state, on the one hand, and control technologies to monitor, guide, disassemble, preempt, or incapacitate, on the other, is not a state concerned with the root causes of protest. An interest in root causes is a focus of the human sciences accompanying the rise of disciplinary power, as well as being an interest central for democratic aspirations. The AAA lays out better practices for policing in Ferguson (by not using armored vehicles as platforms for LRADs, cities can avoid negative images), while the Department of Justice's *Investigation of the Ferguson Police Department*—as important as it is—displays little of the concern of the Kerner Commission for normative legitimation and none of its sensitivity to the way inequalities in education, housing, employment, and degrading conditions of welfare thwart social integration, making state legitimation impossible.

The security footing of the neoliberal state blocked OWS's grievances regarding social reproduction and economic inequality as aggressive and violent protest policing displaced and overwhelmed their expression. #BlackLivesMatter directly confronted the authoritarian nature of policing in the United States—its exercise of violence with impunity—and triggered a response that simultaneously remained deaf to this concern and identified BLM as threatening to the very core of the state for evoking the haunting figure of black insurrection. The MPD proved how spectral this haunting figure is, as it seemed to appear in CCC's performative critique of Memphis's investments in neoliberalism on the mayor's front lawn or as it became associated with pipeline protesters.

In sum, people cannot bring grievances regarding poverty, inequality, social reproduction, or climate change without taking on the problem of police abuse of force raised so urgently by BLM. Correspondingly, BLM's concerns are indissociable from crises concerning poverty, gendered inequality, social reproduction, and climate change—injustices raised by OWS. The post-democratic, postlegitimation state of neoliberal authoritarianism produces and exhibits insecurity as it continues to be haunted by the spectral figure of black insurrection.[279]

# Policing Protest and Neoliberal Authoritarianism

My deputies won't be palace guards.
—DAVE MAHONEY, Dane County sheriff (2011)

NEGOTIATED MANAGEMENT, a model of police-protester relations that emerged in the 1970s and persisted into the 1990s, and that conceptualized the role of police as helping to protect First Amendment rights of demonstrators, is no longer the dominant paradigm for protest policing in the United States. Beginning in the late 1990s, a more aggressive and violent style of protest policing took shape and has superseded negotiated management. The policing of protest since the late 1990s not only criminalizes protest, but reacts to protests with increasing militarism bent on defeating protesters where it fails to prevent or disassemble political mobilization critical of growing economic inequalities and political authoritarianism by utilizing "technologies of control."[1] "Security" captures the institutional hybridity of contemporary protest policing that goes beyond ordinary law enforcement, yet stops short of total war. Security is the protest policing arm of the distinctive state formation called neoliberal authoritarianism.

The reactions to three interrelated crises of the 1960s and 1970s converged by the 1990s to institutionalize this new mode of policing protest that is remarkable for the hostility it displays to demonstrations. Richard Nixon's

1968 presidential campaign, in which he elided protests and crime, made apparent a crisis of democracy. His presidency gave political power to an expressive antipathy regarding democratic practices. Samuel Huntington, a leading voice of those perceiving a crisis of democracy, argued that increasing political participation of marginal social groups, such as black political mobilization, was overloading the U.S. political system. He contributed to an emergent post-democratic political culture that reacted to the political mobilizations of the 1960s—particularly black political participation—as representing an excess of democracy and as causing a crisis of democracy. Nixon's four appointments to the Supreme Court gave legal force to this political sensibility increasingly averse to democracy, as long-standing legal doctrines thought key to a constitutional democracy, such as the preferred position of the First Amendment to commerce, fell into disuse. Law marginalized the significance of rights to free speech and assembly, and the political culture cultivated by the reaction to a crisis of democracy accommodated repressive policing of protest.

Significantly, the perception of a crisis of democracy eclipsed concerns that the state faced a legitimation crisis. Those oriented to social democracy identified the gap between democratic norms and material inequalities as indicative of a legitimation crisis. For instance, the National Advisory Commission on Civil Disorders created by President Lyndon Johnson, also known as the Kerner Commission, not only pointed to abusive policing as leading to the urban riots of the 1960s. It also pointed to deep social inequalities as threatening democratic values, and as creating conditions contributing to the anger expressed in the civil disorder that shook the nation in the 1960s. The Kerner Commission's efforts to inspire the political will to reduce the gap between democratic norms and the unequal realities of American life were overtaken by the crisis of democracy and a political culture marked by growing exhaustion, if not animosity, toward democratic norms or practices.

Second, the reaction to the urban fiscal crisis of the 1970s resulted in cities reorienting their infrastructures away from residents and their social reproduction, and toward the finance, insurance, and real estate industries, on the one hand, and toward tourists and conventions, on the other.[2] Cities were forced to govern in accordance with market logics and to become market actors themselves. Urban government was compelled to become neoliberal.

In this neoliberal mode of urban government, cities would invest in cultural and symbolic production, and would host mega-events to brand and market themselves to potential visitor markets. Producing cultural experiences, though, relies on governing the aesthetics of the urban environment and minimizing potential disruptions to urban environments designed to enhance a city's cultural productions. Likewise, mega-events must be produced without disruption to fulfill their function as spectacle for attendees and potential audiences, whether such disruptions are crime, a disaster, or a protest. Therefore, the neoliberal, post-Fordist turn in urban political economies since the 1970s depends on policing that prevents disruptions to the production of cultural experiences or mega-events, whether such a disturbance comes from the visibly poor, crime or disaster, or a protest.

Third, conservatives perceived in the civil rights demonstrations of the 1960s a crime crisis as they conflated civil rights demonstrations with crime, riots, or the violence of those defending racial apartheid. Or, perversely, they considered peaceful civil rights demonstrations as causing violence or even considered peaceful civil rights demonstrations to be violent.[3] Nixon's Southern strategy in pursuit of the White House echoed the calls for law and order aimed against the Civil Rights movement by racial reactionaries, and he accepted the Republican Party's 1968 presidential nomination on behalf of "non-demonstrators" who were "not guilty of the crime that plagues the land."[4] The "crime" of the crime crisis always exceeded ordinary crime in its reaction against black political mobilization and political equality. The crime crisis spurred affective attachment to expressive policing and punishment, if not vengeance.[5]

George Kelling and James Q. Wilson's concept of "Broken Windows" policing reacted against the Kerner Commission's efforts to reform racially abusive policing and to render police legally accountable. For Kelling and Wilson, a law enforcement model of policing neglected the importance of order maintenance. Kelling and Wilson urged policing to target the perception of disorder. In so doing, they exhibited an enjoyment of police who "kick ass" while being haunted by the riots of the 1960s. With William Bratton's appointment as police commissioner by newly elected mayor Rudy Giuliani in 1993, the "Broken Windows" concept of policing became policy for the New York Police Department (NYPD). Meanwhile, policy changes at the federal level propelled the militarization of policing at the state and local levels. Zero tolerance, order maintenance policing, and police patrols with dramatic displays of military dress, weaponry, and vehicles were developments increasingly at odds with negotiated management's concept of police tolerating, if not enabling, the exercise of First Amendment rights by interacting with protesters through dialogue, rather than by force. Negotiated management could not coexist with zero tolerance policing, and it hasn't, as a security model of policing protest has superseded negotiated management.

Vertical and horizontal forces push protest policing to become more aggressive and violent. There is a vertical dissemination of security influences into police departments and urban space when cities host mega-events. If a mega-event is classified by the federal government as a national special security event, training materials and security preparations shape local policing institutionally. Weapons, security cameras, and armored vehicles acquired for policing the event remain in the city as a security legacy, deepening the securitization of the urban environment long after the spectacle is over. The influence of police executives circulating from the NYPD (or other cities that embrace the "Broken Windows" concept of policing) through other major city police departments or private security firms disseminates zero tolerance, order maintenance policing horizontally. These vertical and horizontal forces overdetermine the transformation of protest policing to become more hostile to demonstrations, assemblies, and the meaningful exercise of First Amendment rights.

Each of the reactions to the three crises of the 1960s and 1970s contributing to more forceful policing of protest was haunted by the spectral figure of black insurrection. First, the crisis of democracy was a reaction against black political mobilization. Second, the punishing effects of austerity upon urban residents that resulted from the urban fiscal crisis reflected the racialization of cities and the racial resentments of those who imagined black people living off welfare at their expense, even after welfare had been ended and replaced by Temporary Aid to Needy Families.[6] Third, the crime crisis conflated civil rights demonstrations with crime, violence, and riots. Where many perceived the pursuit of justice, reactionaries simply saw crime. The crime crisis mobilized and politicized affective attachments to the spectacle of police who kicked ass.

The policing of #BlackLivesMatter (BLM) crystalizes the institutional forces set in motion by the reactions to the crisis of democracy, the urban fiscal crisis, and the crime crisis. It exhibits the leading tendencies of protest policing. Today we see, on the one hand, a growing militarization of protest policing and, on the other, the growing use of control technologies. If the latter fails to prevent or disassemble the organization of a political subject antagonistic to neoliberal authoritarianism, then the former is deployed to defeat it.

Neither the tendency toward a militarized response to protests nor the use of control technologies is compatible with the principles of a constitutional democracy, which rejects interference with freedom of speech, political organization, and political participation.[7] Nor are these tendencies compatible with the most basic conditions of normative legitimation. The excess of a militarized response, such as the NYPD's use of a Long Range Acoustic Device (LRAD) against BLM demonstrators, is disproportionate to absent or minor legal violations. Likewise, the Memphis Police Department's ever-widening mapping, monitoring, catfishing, and blacklisting of those associated with peaceful BLM protests is an example not only of disproportionate policing but of how control technologies can function as tools of preventative policing unmoored from any grounding in legal violations. Both LRADs and control technologies target or punish based on association—either shared geographic location or the constructions of a software platform's associative logic set in motion by the specters of black insurrection haunting police suspicion. The spectacle of militarized intimidation (shock and awe) and the disintegrative effects of technologies of control are both aspects of preemptive policing—policing that intervenes prior to a legal violation based on predetermined strategic goals of the police. These tendencies in contemporary protest policing are post-democratic and postlegitimation, and, as such, they are components of an increasingly authoritarian neoliberal state formation.

The policing of Occupy Wall Street (OWS) and the policing of BLM expose the qualities of neoliberal authoritarianism. Occupy's grievances regarding economic precarity and the corruption of political processes engendered by corporate power were derailed by the NYPD's authoritarian policing. The NYPD's authoritarian policing, though, has long been a concern for human rights campaigns opposed to its stop and frisk policies. Shortly after OWS's assemblies and marches protesting economic and political inequalities, BLM catalyzed national attention regarding degrading and deadly policing in the United States. The institutions of policing and punishment in the United States, though, are not only exercises of violence and symbolic degradation; they are also deeply impoverishing.[8] To make good on the aspiration of black lives mattering requires nothing less than addressing impoverishment resulting from a state formation politically committed to eviscerating programs necessary for social reproduction. The policing of OWS and BLM, then, is a product of a political economy of immiseration, a state that maintains its commitment to this political economy in the face of growing illegitimacy through its dependence upon authoritarian practices like the security model of protest policing, and a state that is politically motivated to maintain its commitment to this political economy because it is afflicted by an affective drive to resist the haunting figure of black insurrection.

Must protest policing be aggressive and violent, and express hostility toward demonstrators? Must it function in the modality of security? When Wisconsin governor Scott Walker introduced a "Budget Repair Bill" in February 2011 that would impose deep measures of austerity on the people of Wisconsin and gut collective bargaining rights for public employees (except police and firefighters), union members and their supporters protested the attack on social reproduction and democratic organization by occupying the Wisconsin State Capitol Building.[9] During the most intense period of this uprising, from February 14 through early March 2011, between eight thousand and ten thousand protesters occupied the capitol around the clock, and the numbers of demonstrators outside the capitol surged at weekend rallies to well over 100,000. These were the largest demonstrations in Madison history and among the largest prolabor demonstrations in U.S. history.[10] There were, however, virtually no arrests (though right-wing radio hosts Glenn Beck and Rush Limbaugh represented the demonstrations as a "riot" or "chaos in the streets").[11]

Charles Tubbs, chief of the Capitol Police, had a goal of seeing through the demonstrations with "zero arrests."[12] Noble Wray, chief of the Madison Police Department, approached the demonstrations similarly: "Our job is to create an environment for democracy to take place."[13] According to Dane County sheriff Dave Mahoney, "We're setting an example of how to maintain a democracy."[14] In stark contrast to evidence in the NYPD's "After-Action Assessments" of its policing of the World Economic Forum in 2002, which show NYPD officers enjoying the effects of their intimidating appearance to demonstrators, riot or hard gear was not used during the Wisconsin uprising. Inside the tightly packed capitol building, Tubbs walked among protesters and police, and met regularly with representatives of protesters. Tubbs and his deputy chief, Dan Blackdeer, did not want officers to appear intimidating. Tubbs did not want officers even to stand with "their hands on their guns . . . or batons," because of the signals that could be sent to demonstrators. He tried to prevent officers from wearing black gloves. He did not want officers coming into the capitol building looking like they were "ready to go to war with citizens" and encouraged manners, respect, and professionalism in conversations. "Our position was to let them [the demonstrators] know we were here to provide one thing," he explained, "public safety."[15]

The major Madison-based police agencies responded to Wisconsin's mass political mobilization with negotiated management. These principles had been introduced into the Madison Police Department in the early 1970s by Chief David Couper, and they remained institutionally embedded in Madison-based police departments in 2011.[16] In addition to creating an "environment for people to . . . petition the government," Madison police chief Noble Wray underscored negotiation, dialogue, using minimal amounts of force, and, like Tubbs, the importance of officers at a demonstration not appearing to be intimidating. Instead, Wray wanted police appearance to signal an intent to facilitate the exercise of First Amendment rights. For Wray, this is part of a broader, trust-based philosophy of policing that is at odds with zero tolerance policing. According to Wray, the zero tolerance focus on numerical goals (How many stops? How many frisks? How many arrests?) can lead to police neglecting the quality of their service. Zero tolerance "moves you away from why you joined [the force] in the first place."[17] Speaking in 2011, Dave Mahoney, the Dane County sheriff, elaborated further that the University of Wisconsin's police, the Dane County sheriff, the Capitol Police, and the Madison Police Department all shared the protest policing philosophy that police are present to protect personal safety first, then freedom of speech, and that property is at the "very bottom of the list."[18]

With principles that people take precedence over property firmly institutionalized in Madison area police departments, and by training to these principles repeatedly over time, when trouble arose, Wray and Mahoney were ready. In a secretly recorded phone call, Walker stated he had "thought about" planting troublemakers among the peaceful demonstrators. Wray responded by issuing a statement asking for an explanation of "what was being considered by state leaders," reiterating how police sought to ensure that people could demonstrate safely, and expressed concern that "anyone would try to undermine these relationships."[19] When the state closed the capitol and wanted assistance from the Dane County sheriff to keep demonstrators out of the capitol building, Mahoney refused, famously asserting, "My deputies will not be palace guards."[20] As he later explained, there had been a court order to open the capitol, and he was an "officer of the court." Moreover, he viewed the capitol as the "people's house," and they needed the "ability to assemble in the place of government," where state officials were eliminating collective bargaining. The cuts being proposed would affect people's lives in a "multitude of ways." People needed to be able to "air their grievances." To shut the people out while doing all this, he argued, could have increased the likelihood of violence because people then would have seen that they were "shut out of government and they have no voice in their government."[21]

Wray and Mahoney confronted Walker with their statements and their refusal to participate in illegal state practices. These statements show that being law enforcement officers can mean needing to stand up to state actors like the Koch-backed governor whose conduct violated standards of legal legitimacy. They also show how constitutional commitments mean that a law enforcement officer requires political commitments to democratic practices in the face of a political antagonism with neoliberal authoritarianism. The appearance of political antagonism in Madison was slightly disruptive of ordinary routines, but not violent. Order was mutually maintained through dialogue and negotiation. Any acts of intimidation or violence by police could have resulted in massive disorder and the likely endangerment of public safety. Protest policing, as shown by the uprising in Madison, does not have to be abusive of demonstrators; negotiation and dialogue with demonstrators is superior for both freedom of speech and public safety.

### Abusive Protest Policing Is Integral to Neoliberal Authoritarianism

Mahoney observed that shutting people out of political processes affecting their lives may lead to anger potentially threatening to peaceful conditions. We can go further and note how shutting people out of policy making, designed to weaken their political voice, health, and social and economic well-being, can lead to anger and the threat of disorder. These observations indicate why neoliberal authoritarianism relies on protest policing hostile to the demonstrations and assemblies of the people, whether this hostility is exercised through displays of military force or through technologies of control.

Neoliberalism has a distinctive relation to legitimacy in comparison with social welfare democracies. The latter publicly claim to enact public programs, policies, or regulations for the direct benefit of the people, and one dimension of their legitimation deficit arises in the gap between promise and reality. The beneficiaries of the neoliberal state's actions, however, are markets, or specific market actors, in the first instance. The people are not directly benefited by neoliberal policies, or are only implausibly benefited, or are never mentioned at all due to a myopic state focus upon markets.

Constituents of the neoliberal state, self-interested property owners, and market actors (also known as stakeholders) may either enjoy state benefits or become resentful if they were not the market sector or market actor benefited by a particular program. Viewed through the lens of market behavior, state decisions—and the competition to become their beneficiary—are rooted in particularistic preference and interest; they are not rooted upon more universalistic and impersonal grounds of legitimacy and justification (such as the public good, common good, good of the people, or the use of public reason). Furthermore, the neoliberal state becomes functionally (or actually) invested in the economic well-being of particular market actors, and the prospects of the neoliberal state are dependent upon whether certain markets or market actors look favorably upon this state. For example, the question of whether, say, Amazon will locate its next campus in any given city leads to that city's dependence on the private profitability of Amazon if Amazon should choose that city. Or the question of a city's creditworthiness in the perception of bond markets indicates the dependence of that city on bond markets. Therefore, from a legitimation perspective, the neoliberal state is fundamentally compromised. At some point, the conditions of possibility for the well-being of the people become compromised as well. The people's protests express this antagonism between the neoliberal state and the people's well-being.

Wisconsin under Walker manifested the tendencies of neoliberal authoritarianism. When fourteen Democratic state senators fled the state to prevent the quorum necessary for the Budget Repair Bill to be voted upon, the antiunion provisions were stripped from the bill, turning it into nonbudgetary legislation (or so claimed its supporters) that could be voted on and passed by the remaining Republicans.[22] The legislation was moved to a conference committee and passed under an uncertain procedure in violation of the state's Open Meetings Law requiring twenty-four hours of notice before public meetings (there was less than two hours of notice before the conference committee meeting).[23] Many filed formal complaints that the votes were illegal.[24] The Wisconsin State Journal editorialized, "Hasty Action Violates Public Trust."[25] Some called for a general strike in response, while others began preparations for recall elections of Republicans.[26]

Was the bill a law? Dane County circuit judge Maryann Sumi issued a temporary restraining order, preventing the secretary of state, Doug La Follette, from publishing the law, which was necessary for the law formally to take effect, due to irregularities in the legislative process of enactment and lack of compliance with the Open Meetings Law.[27] Then the Legislative Reference Bureau published the law on the legislature's website. The director of the Legislative Reference Bureau doubted that posting the act on the legislature's website made the bill effective. La Follette insisted that, because the bill had not been published in the Wisconsin State Journal, the official state newspaper, as required for a legislative measure to take effect, and because he had not ordered the *State Journal* to publish it, it was not law. Wisconsin State Senate majority leader Scott Fitzgerald, however, did not care. He considered the website posting to have published the law, regardless of legal formalities.[28]

Such fundamental disagreements over law repeated an incident that had occurred at the doors to the capitol a couple weeks earlier. Dane County circuit judge Daniel Moeser ordered the capitol to be opened during business hours. The capitol should have been opened to the public, but protesters were not being allowed in. Mahoney had pulled his deputies from the capitol doors, refusing to act as a "palace guard" under these illegitimate conditions, but other police enforced the assertion of state power against demonstrators. Protesters read from a temporary restraining order to police guarding the doors, "to no avail."[29] A couple days later, another judge would order the capitol opened no later than 8:00 a.m. the following Monday, contending that the state had closed access to the capitol "impermissibly."[30] The scenes outside of the capitol, and the conduct by Republican legislators inside the capitol, pointed to the extralegal authoritarianism being used to push through neoliberal changes in Wisconsin.

State practices appeared increasingly irregular. Discipline was breaking down throughout the state. Wisconsin elects its state supreme court in formally nonpartisan elections, and there was a four–three conservative majority on the court when one of the seats was up for election in the spring of 2011. The incumbent judge, Justice David Prosser, was known as a conservative. On election night, the challenger, a relatively unknown liberal, JoAnne Kloppenburg, declared a slim victory over Prosser.[31] The results changed, though, when a Waukesha County clerk revealed that she had failed to include fourteen thousand votes in the vote count she reported to the Associated Press election night, turning a 204-vote victory for Kloppenburg into a 7,500-vote victory for Prosser.[32] Prosser would later resign from the state supreme court in 2016 without offering a reason in the middle of his term after battling ethics charges from the Wisconsin Judicial Commission.[33] The charges arose from Prosser having called the chief justice of the state supreme court, Shirley Abrahamson, a "bitch," and threatening to "destroy" her.[34] He also placed his hands around the neck of fellow state supreme court judge Ann Walsh Bradley, in a "chokehold," during an argument regarding the case arising from whether Walker's antiunion bill was a valid law.[35]

Fundamental disagreements on facts and law deeply eroded grounds for legal legitimacy as the state supreme court addressed whether the antiunion Budget Repair Bill had been properly enacted and was law. A majority of the court acknowledged that notice of the conference committee was posted an hour and fifty minutes before its meeting, not following the notice provisions of the Open Meetings Law. Nevertheless, the majority stated that it "declines to review the validity of the procedure used to give notice of the joint committee on conference." It justified this refusal on the grounds of separation of powers. The majority did not want to "intermeddle" with the legislature by reviewing whether or not it had complied with its own procedural rules while enacting legislation, characterizing such questions as "purely legislative concerns."[36]

Dissenters present a completely different picture of the case's facts, law, and whether the court itself was in violation of its own procedures for the way that it had handled the case. Regarding court procedure, dissenters observed that the majority of the court stated that the case was being heard not on appeal but in the state supreme court's original jurisdiction (original jurisdiction means a supreme court not only answers questions of law but becomes a trier of fact). Yet no party petitioned the court to hear the case in its original jurisdiction! Although there are mechanisms within the court's procedures for developing a factual record in its original jurisdiction, they were not used in this case. Therefore, by considering the case as one of original jurisdiction, the majority could ignore the factual record that had been developed in a forty-eight-page circuit court ruling.[37]

Regarding the facts of the case, Justice Patrick Crooks provided examples where either the majority or concurring opinions state "facts" that either do not appear in the limited record before the state supreme court or are directly contradicted by the factual record developed at the circuit court level.[38] With respect to the majority's refusal to exercise judicial review of whether the legislature enacted the Budget Repair Bill in accordance with the Open Meetings Law, Crooks found that the Open Meetings Law was enacted to comply with and implement the state constitutional requirement that the "doors of each house shall be kept open except when the public welfare shall require secrecy." The Wisconsin legislature further "directed courts to enjoin or void actions taken in violation of the Open Meetings Law," yet this clearly did not happen in this instance as a majority of the court declined to review the process of enactment. Crooks then identified numerous legal questions and questions of judicial precedent that the state supreme court ought to have addressed, discussed, and resolved, but which the majority neglected in its haste to, in the words of Chief Justice Abrahamson, reach a "pre-determined conclusion not based on the facts and the law."[39] This neglect of the court's own procedures, facts, and the law undermined the decision's legitimacy and the state supreme court's legitimacy, bred contempt for the law, and undermined the legitimacy of the legislative process and the "legitimacy of our government," according to the dissenters.[40]

Walker's inspiration for pushing through the Budget Repair Bill was President Ronald Reagan's firing of the striking air traffic controllers in 1981. At a February 7, 2011, dinner meeting of his cabinet in the governor's mansion, Walker "held up a photo of President Ronald Reagan" and called the Budget Repair Bill "our time to change the course of history."[41] As historian Jefferson Cowie described Reagan's war on the Professional Air Traffic Controllers Organization (PATCO), "it was the size and drama of Reagan's response that shocked." Not only did Reagan fire the striking workers, he went further by "smashing the entire organization designed to represent both employees' interest and public safety, and, ultimately giving the nod to business to declare open season on organized labor."[42] Striking workers at the time remarked on the excesses of the response. One striking worker stated, "I'm really surprised at how bloodthirsty they've been." Describing the "rage" he felt at seeing a fellow protester being taken away in "chains and leg irons on television," he continued, "it's such overkill—they brought in the howitzers to kill an ant." He pointed to the postlegitimation, post-democratic aspects of Reagan's attack on them, saying, "Don't sit down and talk to people like human beings, just bring in the howitzers and wipe them out." "I feel scared of a system of government," he asserted, "that turns me off as a human being and says, 'O.K., if you don't play the game our way, you're a nonentity.'"[43] Reagan firing the striking PATCO workers was a key moment in building the state formation of neoliberal authoritarianism.[44] Afterward, not only did the number of strikes plummet, but the number of corporate violations of the National Labor Relations Act "skyrocketed" in the 1980s and 1990s.[45] Reagan's actions signaled acceptance of postlegitimation, post-democratic, lawless corporate practices, and they incited, with their excesses, affective attachment from Walker and neoliberal authoritarianism's political subjects.

The Walker administration in Wisconsin impoverished social reproduction with its cuts to public school funding, cuts to the Department of Health Services (while rejecting more than $9 million in grants from the Affordable Care Act for drug and alcohol abuse), instituted rules preventing localities from making up the losses in state funding by raising local property taxes, and cut corporate taxes.[46] There was one state spending increase Walker supported: increases for tourism marketing.[47] During the Walker years in Wisconsin, income inequality would grow to its highest levels since the onset of the Great Depression in 1929.[48] A comparison of the Minnesota and

Wisconsin economies at the end of the Walker administration showed that job growth was higher in Minnesota; wages grew faster in Minnesota; gender wage gaps had declined more in Minnesota; median household income grew more in Minnesota than Wisconsin; and Minnesota made greater strides in reducing poverty, while the poverty rate in Wisconsin continued to be about the same as it had been during the Great Recession. People were moving out of Wisconsin, but Minnesota experienced population growth during the same period.[49]

While they were imposing austerity on Wisconsin residents, Walker and Republican state legislators also enacted changes suppressing voter participation and radically gerrymandered legislative districts in favor of Republicans. In 2011, Wisconsin enacted one of the most restrictive voter identification laws in the country (though due to court challenges, it would not be used in a statewide election until 2016).[50] According to statistical estimates, approximately 11.2 percent of eligible voters in Dane and Milwaukee counties were deterred from voting in 2016 due to either confusion or the lack of acceptable identification. Low-income and black voters were disproportionately affected.[51] Additionally, Republican-led redistricting in 2011 was so extreme that Walker lost his reelection bid for governor in 2018, but analyses of results showed that he won sixty-four out of ninety-nine Wisconsin State Assembly districts.[52] (The U.S. Supreme Court ruled in the summer of 2019 that partisan gerrymanders were no longer justiciable by federal courts, no matter how unrepresentative they may be.)[53] The political regime of Scott Walker and Republicans in the state legislature enacted policies that simultaneously immiserate Wisconsin residents while insulating elected officials from the grievances of the people by restricting the capacity of the people to hold their representatives politically accountable through formal processes.

The use of negotiation and dialogue between police and protesters during the Wisconsin uprising shows that the policing of protest does not need to be aggressive, intimidating, and violent. The imposition of austerity and impoverishment upon Wisconsinites in conjunction with the severe constriction, or active destruction, of representative processes and democratic organization in Wisconsin, however, suggests that the security mode of protest policing is an integral component of neoliberal authoritarianism, a state formation that is post-democratic and postlegitimation. The breakdown of the most minimal conditions for state legitimacy in Wisconsin during the winter and spring of 2011 indicates how neoliberal authoritarianism may need to rely on postlegitimation, post-democratic protest policing as even the pretense of legitimacy, representative democracy, and respect for democratic political organization are subordinated to authoritarian political mechanisms driven to produce greater exploitation, expropriation, and an authoritarian reshaping of state structures.

Is the security mode of protest policing determined to become an entrenched extension of neoliberal authoritarianism by enforcing our enclosure within a perpetual present of material hardship and political hopelessness? Are we doomed to a state formation that polices protest with hostility and violence when faced with the slightest objection to the destruction of conditions necessary for social reproduction? A longer view of political history in the United States shows unevenness in state formations. The state is not unitary or completely coherent in all its institutions. For example, the escalated force model of violent and undisciplined police reactions to protests was inconsistent with other, more hegemonic orientations toward social democracy in the 1960s. At the time of the Wisconsin uprising of 2011, the persistence of negotiated management in Madison was in tension with hostility to protesters exhibited by police departments in other major cities. It was in tension with broader tendencies toward neoliberal authoritarianism that would become dominant in the 1990s and 2000s across the United States. The state can be out of joint as developments in one institution lag behind developments in another, or anticipate developments in another. The state can be subject to periods of convergence between institutions, and periods of coherence can unravel as change occurs in one state institution in response to political forces, but perhaps not in others (or not yet in others).

Policing in the United States can also be uneven if one compares any particular department with more dominant paradigms or more general institutional trends. Major urban areas are becoming deeply securitized and divided spaces of concentrated wealth and poverty. Perhaps we can leverage space for voices and assemblies where those dispersed by these garrisons gather. Perhaps we can leverage space in smaller cities, or in rural areas, in addition to continuing creative and insistent appearances in urban centers manifesting the wrongful divisions of inequality. Militarized and control-based protest policing is not necessary. Yet it seems to be. This discontinuity in perspective expresses the antagonism between the neoliberal authoritarian state and the well-being of the people. Perhaps this is the fissure that we can use to open a space where we can begin assembling to determine a better life for ourselves.

*Introduction*

1  "City to Pay $18 Million to Settle 'Wrongful' Arrests during 2004 RNC," *CBS New York*, January 15, 2014, https://newyork.cbslocal.com.

2  Dunn et al., *Arresting Protest*.

3  "Scott Olsen, U.S. Vet Nearly Killed by Police Beanbag at Occupy Oakland, Settles Lawsuit with City," *Democracy Now*, March 21, 2014, https://www.democracynow.org.

4  Julia Carrie Wong, "Dakota Access Pipeline: 300 Protesters Injured after Police Use Water Cannons," *The Guardian*, November 21, 2016, https://www.theguardian.com.

5  Alleen Brown, Will Parrish, and Alice Speri, "Leaked Documents Reveal Counterterrorism Tactics Used at Standing Rock to 'Defeat Pipeline Insurgencies,'" *The Intercept*, May 27, 2017, https://theintercept.com.

6  Schweingruber, "Mob Sociology and Escalated Force."

7  Skolnick, *Politics of Protest*, 207–8.

8  Schweingruber, "Mob Sociology and Escalated Force"; McCarthy and McPhail, "Institutionalization of Protest"; McPhail, Schweingruber, and McCarthy, "Policing Protest in the United States"; Epp, *Making Rights Real*.

9  McCarthy and McPhail, "Institutionalization of Protest," 96–100; McPhail, Schweingruber, and McCarthy, "Policing Protest in the United States," 51–64; Soule and Davenport, "Velvet Glove, Iron Fist"; Rafail, Soule, and McCarthy, "Describing and Accounting."

10  MacNamara v. City of New York, U.S.D.C. S.D.N.Y. 04 Civ. 9216, "Second Amended Class Action Complaint" (January 29, 2008), 25.

11  McCarthy and McPhail, "Institutionalization of Protest," 83–84, 102–4.

12 Tim Elfrink, "'It's Still a Blast Beating People': St. Louis Police Indicted in Assault of Undercover Officer Posing as Protester," *Washington Post*, November 30, 2018, https://www.washingtonpost.com.

13 Gillham, "Securitizing America." In the years following the attacks of September 11, 2001, several scholars theorized the repression of human rights in the United States in terms of a logic of sovereign decisionism. See Butler, *Precarious Life*; Agamben, *State of Exception*.

14 Vitale, "From Negotiated Management to Command," 295–98.

15 Honig, *Emergency Politics*, chap. 4.

16 Huntington, "United States," 114.

17 Habermas, *Legitimation Crisis*.

18 National Advisory Commission on Civil Disorders, *Report of the National Advisory Commission*, 305, chap. 17. As the *New York Times* editorialized: "On the urgent need of a gigantic attack against urban slums . . . there can no longer be debate." "The Urban Programs" editorial, *New York Times*, March 9, 1968, 28; Henry Raymont, "Riot Report Book Big Best Seller," *New York Times*, March 14, 1968, 49.

19 "Social democracy" refers to the recognition that social rights, in addition to civil and political rights, must be protected to fulfill the promise of equal citizenship. Social democratic states are typically understood to be Keynesian (or state-regulated capitalist) democracies. On the value of "equal citizenship," see Marshall, "Citizenship and Social Class." The social democratic orientation forms a crucial context for discussions of a legitimation crisis. See Offe, *Contradictions of the Welfare State*, 79, 148.

20 "New Controversy in the Wake of the Kerner Report," *New York Times*, March 10, 1968, 2B.

21 Richard Nixon, "Address Accepting the Presidential Nomination at the Republican Convention in Miami Beach, Florida," August 8, 1968, American Presidency Project, https://www.presidency.ucsb.edu/documents/address -accepting-the-presidential-nomination-the-republican-national-convention -miami.

22 David Lawrence, "What's Become of 'Law and Order'?" *U.S. News and World Report*, August 5, 1963, 104.

23 Kohn, *Brave New Neighborhoods*.

24 Moody, *From Welfare State*; Phillips-Fein, *Fear City*. My understanding of "social reproduction" is broad. It refers to that which is needed to reproduce society and a society oriented to doing justice to the needs of all. I am informed by Silvia Federici's concern that today, there is a "profound crisis of social reproduction." See Federici, "Social Reproduction Theory"; Silvia Federici and Marina Sitrin, "Social Reproduction: Between the Wage and the Commons," *ROAR Magazine*, no. 2 (n.d.), accessed September 14, 2019, https://roarmag.org/magazine/social-reproduction-between-the-wage-and -the-commons/.

25 Foucault, *Birth of Biopolitics*, 117–19, 148.

26 Eisinger, "Politics of Bread and Circuses"; Lester Spence, "Corporate Welfare Is Draining Baltimore," *Boston Review*, May 14, 2015, http://bostonreview.net.

27 Greenberg, *Branding New York*.

28 Connors, *Planning and Managing Security*.

29 Beckett, *Making Crime Pay*, 30–32, 41–43; Perlstein, *Nixonland*.

30 Nixon, "Address Accepting the Presidential Nomination."

31 Blumenson and Nilsen, "Policing for Profit"; Kraska and Kappeler, "Militarizing American Police." For a more international perspective on the militarization of protest policing, see Wood, *Crisis and Control*.

32 Chambliss, "Policing the Ghetto Underclass." For discussions of how responses to the crime crisis reshaped the state more generally, see Simon, *Governing through Crime*; Wacquant, *Punishing the Poor*.

33 George Kelling and James Q. Wilson, "Broken Windows," *The Atlantic*, March 1982, http://www.theatlantic.com.

34 Parenti, *Lockdown America*.

35 Wacquant, *Prisons of Poverty*.

36 Vitale, "From Negotiated Management to Command."

37 Dean, "Networked Empire"; Dean, *Democracy and Other Neoliberal Fantasies*.

38 Agamben, *Coming Community*; Hardt, "Withering of Civil Society," 32; Dean, *Blog Theory*.

39 Wilderson, *Red, White, and Black*, 58. I follow Wilderson's use of capitalization for significant ontological categories.

40 Wilderson, *Red, White, and Black*, 11.

41 Schmitt, *Concept of the Political*, 29.

42 Schmitt, *Concept of the Political*, 27.

43 Martinot and Sexton, "Avant-Garde of White Supremacy."

44 Wilderson, *Red, White, and Black*, acknowledges how the period from 1968 to 1980 differs from the period that precedes it and supersedes it (5–6, 30, 139, 142).

45 For a critique of essentialism in the discourse of Black Lives Matter, see Johnson, "Panthers Can't Save Us Now." For a theoretical discussion of Afro-pessimism, see Gordon et al., "Afro Pessimism."

46 Deleuze, "Postscript on the Societies."

47 Crouch, *Post-Democracy*.

48 Habermas, *Legitimation Crisis*, 107–8.

49 Brown, *Undoing the Demos*, 63, 140–41. For similar approaches to neoliberalism, see Bourdieu, *Acts of Resistance*; Crouch, *Strange Non-Death of Neoliberalism*.

50 Brown, *Undoing the Demos*, 150, emphasis in original.

51 Others also make affective concerns key to comprehending neoliberal government: Dean, *Democracy and Other Neoliberal Fantasies*; Anker, *Orgies of Feeling*; Kotsko, *Neoliberalism's Demons*.

52 "What We Know About the Death of George Floyd in Minneapolis," *New York Times*, December 9, 2020, https://www.nytimes.com.

53  Larry Buchanan, Quoctrun Bui, and Jugal Patel, "Black Lives Matter May Be the Largest Movement in U.S. History," *New York Times*, July 3, 2020, https://www.nytimes.com.

54  Kishi and Jones, "Demonstrations and Political Violence."

55  Andy Mannix, "Charges: Boogaloo Bois Fired on Minneapolis Police Precinct, Shouted 'Justice for Floyd,'" *Star Tribune* (Minneapolis), October 23, 2020, https://www.startribune.com.

56  Haley Willis, Muyi Xiao, Christiaan Triebert, Christoph Koettl, Stella Cooper, David Botti, John Ismay, and Ainara Tiefenthäler, "Tracking the Suspect in the Fatal Kenosha Shootings," *New York Times*, August 27, 2020, updated November 3, 2020, https://www.nytimes.com.

57  Ali Watkins, "'Kettling' of Peaceful Protesters Shows Aggressive Shift by N.Y. Police," *New York Times*, June 5, 2020, https://nytimes.com.

58  "N.Y.P.D. Says It Used Restraint During Protests. Here's What the Videos Show," *New York Times*, July 14, 2020, https://www.nytimes.com.

59  Human Rights Watch, *"Kettling" Protesters in the Bronx*.

60  Peter Baker, Maggie Haberman, Katie Rogers, Zolan Kanno-Youngs, and Katie Benner, "How Trump's Idea for a Photo Op Led to Havoc in a Park," *New York Times*, June 2, 2020, https://www.nytimes.com.

61  Thomas Gibbons-Neff, Helene Cooper, Eric Schmitt, and Jennifer Steinhauer, "Former Commanders Fault Trump's Use of Troops Against Protesters," *New York Times*, June 2, 2020, https://www.nytimes.com.

62  Gibbons-Neff et al., "Former Commanders Fault Trump's Use of Troops Against Protesters."

63  Richard Weir, "Reckless Use of U.S. Helicopters to Intimidate Protesters," Human Rights Watch, June 5, 2020, https://www.hrw.org.

64  Physicians for Human Rights, "Now They Seem."

65  Sergio Olmos, Mike Baker, and Zolan Kanno-Youngs, "Federal Officers Deployed in Portland Didn't Have Proper Training, D.H.S. Memo Said," *New York Times*, July 18, 2020, https://www.nytimes.com.

66  Mike Baker, Thomas Fuller, and Sergio Olmos, "Federal Agents Push into Portland Streets, Stretching Limits of Their Authority," *New York Times*, July 25, 2020, https://www.nytimes.com.

67  Olmos, Baker, and Kanno-Youngs, "Federal Officers Deployed in Portland Didn't Have Proper Training, D.H.S. Memo Said;" Ed Pilkington, "'These Are His People': Inside the Elite Border Control Unit Trump Sent to Portland," *The Guardian*, July 27, 2020, https://www.theguardian.com.

68  Olmos, Baker, and Kanno-Youngs, "Federal Officers Deployed in Portland Didn't Have Proper Training, D.H.S. Memo Said."

69  Michael Balsamo, "Barr: Law Enforcement Must 'Dominate' Streets amid Protests," Associated Press, June 1, 2020, https://apnews.com.

70  Baker et al., "How Trump's Idea for a Photo Op Led to Havoc in a Park."

71  Katie Rogers, Jonathan Martin, and Maggie Haberman, "As Trump Calls Protesters 'Terrorists,' Tear Gas Clears a Path for His Walk to a Church,"

*New York Times*, June 1, 2020, https://www.nytimes.com. Trump often referred to protesters as "terrorists": Jordan Muller, "Trump Calls Protesters 'Terrorists,' Pledges 'Retribution' for Tearing Down Statues," *Politico*, June 26, 2020, https://www.politico.com; "'A Beehive of Terrorists': Donald Trump Threatens to Deploy National Guard in Portland," *The Guardian*, July 31, 2020, http://www.theguardian.com; "Trump Visits Kenosha, Calls Protests for Racial Justice 'Domestic Terror,'" *France24*, September 2, 2020, https://www.france24.com.

*Chapter One. Aesthetic Government*

Early versions of parts of chapter 1 were published as "The Governmentality of Consumption," *Interventions* 6, no. 3 (2004) and "Policing Protest in the Post-Fordist City," *Amsterdam Law Forum* 2, no. 1 (2009).

1  Kohn, *Brave New Neighborhoods*, 3.
2  Samantha Hea provided useful background for this example.
3  The Streets at SouthGlenn, "Leasing," accessed July 26, 2019, https://www.shopsouthglenn.com; "The Streets at SouthGlenn FAQs," accessed November 27, 2020, https://www.centennialco.gov/Government/Departments/Economic-Development/The-Streets-at-SouthGlenn/The-Streets-at-SouthGlenn-FAQs.
4  On post-Fordism, see Amin, *Post-Fordism*; on communicative capitalism, see Dean, "Networked Empire," 265–88; Dean, *Democracy and Other Neoliberal Fantasies*; Passavant, "Political Subjectivity"; on semio- and cognitive capitalism, see Berardi, *Soul at Work*; Berardi, *Precarious Rhapsody*; on immaterial labor and capital, see Gorz, *Immaterial*; on the affective and communicative nature of much labor today, see Hardt and Negri, *Empire*; on the communicative mode of production, see Marazzi, *Capital and Affects*.
5  A "social democratic" state recognizes how social inequalities can deny the promise of formally equal legal rights and seeks to ameliorate social or economic inequalities as inconsistent with the democratic principle of equality more broadly. On social rights, see Marshall, "Citizenship and Social Class"; on the relation between social welfare capitalism and democracy, see Habermas, *Legitimation Crisis*. On neoliberalism, see Foucault, *Birth of Biopolitics*; Brown, *Undoing the Demos*; Passavant, "Strong Neo-liberal State."
6  Crouch, *Post-Democracy*.
7  Lochner v. New York, 198 U.S. 45 (1905), Holmes dissenting.
8  United States v. Carolene Products, 304 U.S. 144 (1938), footnote 4.
9  Pritchett, *American Constitution*, 305–8; Marsh v. Alabama, 326 U.S. 501 (1946), 509, footnotes 1 and 7; Jones v. Opelika, 316 U.S. 584 (1942), Stone dissenting; Murdock v. Pennsylvania, 319 U.S. 105 (1943) (vacating Jones v. Opelika).
10  South Carolina v. Katzenbach, 383 U.S. 301 (1966); Gomillion v. Lightfoot, 364 U.S. 339 (1960); Reynolds v. Sims, 377 U.S. 533 (1964).

11 Harper v. Virginia State Board of Elections, 383 U.S. 663 (1966); Oregon v. Mitchell, 400 U.S. 112 (1970).

12 Terry v. Adams, 345 U.S. 461 (1953), is the last in a line of decisions striking down Texas's persistent attempts to exclude African Americans from the Democratic Party's primary elections.

13 Brown v. Board of Education, 347 U.S. 483 (1954).

14 Thompson v. City of Louisville, 362 U.S. 199 (1960).

15 Terminiello v. Chicago, 337 U.S. 1 (1949); Edwards v. South Carolina, 372 U.S. 229 (1963); Cox v. Louisiana, 379 U.S. 536 (1965).

16 Marsh v. Alabama, 505.

17 Marsh v. Alabama, 505–6.

18 Marsh v. Alabama, 506.

19 Marsh v. Alabama, 503, 507–9.

20 Hague v. C.I.O., 307 U.S. 496 (1939), 515; emphasis added.

21 Amalgamated Food Employees Union v. Logan Valley Plaza, 391 U.S. 308 (1968).

22 Amalgamated Food Employees Union v. Logan Valley Plaza, 317.

23 Amalgamated Food Employees Union v. Logan Valley Plaza, 319.

24 Amalgamated Food Employees Union v. Logan Valley Plaza, 324–25.

25 Terry v. Adams, 345 U.S. 461 (1953).

26 Evans v. Newton, 382 U.S. 296 (1966), 301–2.

27 Richard Nixon, "Address Accepting the Presidential Nomination at the Republican National Convention in Miami Beach, Florida," August 8, 1968, American Presidency Project, https://www.presidency.ucsb.edu/documents /address-accepting-the-presidential-nomination-the-republican-national -convention-miami.

28 "Rising Voice of the Right," Time, September 13, 1968, 24; "Republicans: The Politics of Safety," Time, September 13, 1968, 27.

29 Lloyd Corp. v. Tanner, 407 U.S. 551 (1972).

30 Lloyd Corp. v. Tanner, 553–54.

31 Lloyd Corp. v. Tanner, 555–56.

32 Lloyd Corp. v. Tanner, 578–79, Marshall dissenting.

33 Lloyd Corp. v. Tanner, 561–63.

34 Lloyd Corp. v. Tanner, 564–65.

35 Lloyd Corp. v. Tanner, 571.

36 Lloyd Corp. v. Tanner, 580.

37 Lloyd Corp. v. Tanner, 575–80.

38 Lloyd Corp. v. Tanner, 580–86.

39 Hudgens v. National Labor Relations Board, 424 U.S. 507 (1976).

40 Emerson, "First Amendment Doctrine," 440–42.

41 Pruneyard Shopping Center v. Robins, 447 U.S. 74 (1980).

42 SHAD Alliance v. Smith Haven Mall, 66 N.Y. 2d 496 (1985), 505–6.

43 Lloyd Corp. v. Tanner, 561–63. This was also Justice Black's position in *Amalgamated Food Employees Union v. Logan Valley Plaza*, indicating how the political

culture was changing and, along with it, Black's orientation to the First Amendment.

44 Marsh v. Alabama, 506, citation omitted, emphasis added.

45 Shearing and Stenning, "Private Security." The Supreme Court significantly limited the public function doctrine in Jackson v. Metropolitan Edison Co., 419 U.S. 345 (1974); Flagg Bros., Inc. v. Brooks, 436 U.S. 149 (1978).

46 Gruen and Smith, *Shopping Towns, USA*, 23–24.

47 Gruen and Smith, *Shopping Towns, USA*, 110.

48 Gruen and Smith, *Shopping Towns, USA*, 149.

49 Gruen and Smith, *Shopping Towns, USA*, 158, 258 (quoting developer James Rouse).

50 Gruen, "Shopping Centers of Tomorrow," 16. (Issues of *Arts and Architecture* from the mid-twentieth century are now available online: http://www .artsandarchitecture.com.)

51 Gruen, *Heart of Our Cities*, 191, 202. For examples of contemporary mall designs incorporating residences, see Sam Black, "Mall Redevelopment Strategies: Keeping Today's Malls Competitive," *Development Magazine*, winter, 2015–2016, https://www.naiop.org/en/Research-and-Publications/Magazine/2015/Winter -2015-2016/Development-Ownership/Mall-Redevelopment-Strategies.

52 Gruen, *Heart of Our Cities*, 191.

53 State of Hawai'i v. Viglielmo, 105 Haw. 197 (2004), 202.

54 State of Minnesota v. Wicklund, 589 N.W. 2d 793 (1999), 795.

55 United Food and Commercial Workers Union, Local 919 v. Crystal Mall Associates, 270 Conn. 261 (2004), considers and rejects this argument.

56 Shearing and Stenning, "Private Security."

57 Carol Demare, "He Kept His Shirt On—and Got Arrested," *Times Union* (Albany, NY), March 5, 2003, B1; Stephen Downs v. The Town of Guilderland: Town of Guilderland Police Officer Adam Myers; Pyramid Management Group, Inc.; Pyramid Crossgates Co., State of New York Supreme Court, Appellate Division, Third Department, Case No. 507428, "Appellant's Brief" (October 13, 2009); Passavant, "Governmentality of Consumption," 391. I thank Stephen Downs for clarifying the grounds of his arrest and the subsequent withdrawal of the charges against him, and counsel Mark Mishler for making legal documents available to me.

58 Downs v. Guilderland, "Appellant's Brief," 2.

59 Anne Miller, "Mall Drops T-Shirt Charges," *Times Union* (Albany, NY), March 6, 2003, B1; Winnie Hu, "A Message of Peace on 2 Shirts Touches Off Hostilities at a Mall," *New York Times*, March 6, 2003, https://www.nytimes.com.

60 Passavant, "Governmentality of Consumption," 396; Hu, "Message of Peace." Cf. "Malling of Speech," editorial, *Columbus Dispatch* (Ohio), March 10, 2003, 6A; Phil Leavenworth, "Devil Is Alive in America in Form of Capitalism," *Capital Times* (Madison), March 8, 2003, 9A.

61 Hu, "Message of Peace"; Downs v. Guilderland, "Appellant's Brief," 2.

62 In New York, the lower court is known as the "supreme court." His appeal was before an intermediate court of appeals, the Supreme Court of New

York, Appellate Division, Third Department. In New York, the Court of Appeals is its highest court, and it dismissed Downs's appeal of the intermediate appellate court ruling.

63 Adickes v. S. H. Kress, 398 U.S. 144 (1970); Downs v. Guilderland, "Appellant's Brief," 11–12.

64 Downs v. Guilderland, "Appellant's Brief," 16.

65 Stephen Downs v. The Town of Guilderland: Town of Guilderland Police Officer Adam Myers; Pyramid Management Group, Inc.; Pyramid Crossgates Co., State of New York Supreme Court, Appellate Division, Third Department, Case No. 507428, "Appellant's Reply Brief" (December 17, 2009), 8–9.

66 Downs v. Guilderland, "Appellant's Brief," 5.

67 Downs v. Guilderland, "Appellant's Brief," 6; Stephen Downs v. The Town of Guilderland; Town of Guilderland Police Officer Adam Myers; Pyramid Management Group, Inc.; and Pyramid Crossgates Co., State of New York Supreme Court, Appellate Division, Third Department, Case No. 507428, "Brief of Defendants-Respondents" (December 7, 2009), 6.

68 Cantwell v. Connecticut, 310 U.S. 296 (1940); Terminiello v. Chicago, 337 U.S. 1 (1949). If there was any factual disagreement that Stephen or Roger Downs were being disorderly, then the case should not have been decided based on summary judgment. Summary judgment should be granted only when there is no material disagreement on the facts of the case.

69 New York State Executive Law Article 15 Human Rights Law, §296 2(a), 16, accessed March 24, 2020, http://dhr.ny.gov/law#HRL296_2_a.

70 "Creed," Oxford Dictionaries, accessed June 17, 2016, http://www .oxforddictionaries.com/us/definition/english/creed.

71 Downs v. Guilderland, "Appellant's Brief," 21–24; Downs v. Guilderland, "Appellant's Reply Brief," 12–15.

72 People v. Leonard, 62 N.Y. 2d 404 (1984), 408.

73 People v. Leonard, 411. Interestingly, in 1984 the court uses the example of freedom of speech to illustrate its point in a manner that the court must have presumed would have been obvious and compelling to any reader.

74 Downs v. Guilderland, "Brief of Defendants-Respondents," 16.

75 Downs v. Guilderland, "Brief of Defendants-Respondents," 18–19.

76 Downs v. Guilderland, "Brief of Defendants-Respondents," 18, 30.

77 Downs v. Town of Guilderland et al., 897 N.Y.S. 2d 264 (2010), 267.

78 "A Nation Challenged; Excerpts from the President's Remarks on the War on Terrorism," New York Times, October 12, 2001, https://www.nytimes.com.

79 Passavant, "Governmentality of Consumption," 387–89.

80 Passavant, "Governmentality of Consumption," figure 2.

81 Agamben, Means without End, 76; Gorz, Immaterial, 57.

82 "Wave of Patriotism Sweeps Grieving US," BBC News, September 13, 2001, http://news.bbc.co.uk; Marguerite Higgins, "Retailers Build Inventories of September 11 Collectibles to Meet High Demand," Washington Times, September 5, 2002, A1.

83 Higgins, "Retailers Build Inventories."

84 Faisal Islam, "Digital Culture: Masters of War Gaming Meets the Real Thing," *The Guardian–The Observer*, March 2, 2003, 46 (Sec. OTV); "*Conflict: Desert Storm PS2*," Walmart, accessed December 2, 2002, https://www.walmart.com. The Walmart website lists the release date of *Conflict: Desert Storm PS2* as October 3, 2002. According to Wikipedia, it was released in North America September 30, 2002: "Conflict: Desert Storm," Wikipedia, accessed March 5, 2020, https://en.wikipedia.org/wiki/Conflict:_Desert_Storm.

85 "9/11 Trading Cards to Go on Sale for Holidays," CNN.com, November 19, 2002, http://cnn.com; "Iraqi 'Most-Wanted' Deck of Playing Cards," Great USA Flags, accessed January 14, 2004, http://www.greatusaflags.com; "GreatUSAFlags.com Announces Collectors Edition 'Iraqi Most Wanted' Playing Cards in Framed Uncut Sheets," PR Newswire, June 9, 2003, https://www.prnewswire.com.

86 Kay McFadden, "Ads Link Spending with Patriotism," *Seattle Times*, October 1, 2001, http://seattletimes.nwsource.com.

87 Passavant, "Governmentality of Consumption," 390.

88 Linda Feldman, "The Impact of Bush Linking 9/11 with Iraq," *Christian Science Monitor*, March 14, 2003, https://www.csmonitor.com; Gershkoff and Kushner, "Shaping Public Opinion."

89 On branding and associative aesthetic composition, see Passavant, "Political Subjectivity," 38.

90 Hu, "Message of Peace."

91 "Downtown Needs a Lesson from the Suburbs," *Business Week*, October 22, 1955, 64, 68. See also Gruen's comments for the American Planning and Civic Association in "Main Street 1969," 20–22, esp.

92 Gruen, *Heart of Our Cities*, 190.

93 Gruen, *Heart of Our Cities*, 206.

94 McMorrough, "City of Shopping," 194.

95 McMorrough, "City of Shopping," 202.

96 Passavant, "Strong Neo-liberal State"; Passavant, "Mega-Events."

97 Frieden and Sagalyn, *Downtown, Inc.*, 229.

98 New Jersey Coalition against the War v. J.M.B. Realty, 138 N.J. 326 (1994).

99 New Jersey Coalition v. J.M.B. Realty, 333–34.

100 New Jersey Coalition v. J.M.B. Realty, 334.

101 New Jersey Coalition v. J.M.B. Realty, 334–35.

102 New Jersey Coalition v. J.M.B. Realty, 359.

103 New Jersey Coalition v. J.M.B. Realty, 362.

104 New Jersey Coalition v. J.M.B. Realty, 375–76.

105 New Jersey Coalition v. J.M.B. Realty, 393–94.

106 New Jersey Coalition v. J.M.B. Realty, 400.

107 New Jersey Coalition v. J.M.B. Realty, 395.

108 New Jersey Coalition v. J.M.B. Realty, 396.

109 Nixon, "President's State of the Union," 229.

110 Nixon, "President's State of the Union," 228.

111 Passavant, "Governing Sexuality"; Passavant, "Policing Protest." A close reading of these cases involving indecent expression, or secondary effects, demonstrates a substantive concern with racialized poverty, and its association with crime, pervading these texts. See Passavant, *No Escape*, chap. 6.

112 Renton v. Playtime Theatres, 475 U.S. 41 (1986), 53–54.

113 Young v. American Mini Theatres, 427 U.S. 50 (1976); Renton v. Playtime Theatres, 475 U.S. 41 (1986); Barnes v. Glen Theatre, 501 U.S. 560 (1991); Erie v. Pap's A.M., 529 U.S. 277 (2000).

114 Barnes v. Glen Theatre, 501 U.S. 560 (1991), Justice Souter concurring at 586.

115 Young v. American Mini Theatres, 427 U.S. 50, Justice Powell concurring at 80, citations omitted; Renton v. Playtime Theatres, 54, Justice Rehnquist citing "quality of life" concerns in his Opinion of the Court.

116 Dean, "Networked Empire"; Berardi, *Soul at Work*; Marazzi, *Capital and Affects*; Gorz, *Immaterial*; Hardt and Negri, *Empire*.

117 Roost, "Synergy City," 261.

118 Roost, "Synergy City," 270.

119 Adele Buzzetti d/b/a Cozy Cabin and Vanessa Doe v. City of New York, 1997 U.S. Dist. LEXIS 4383 (1997); Adele Buzzetti d/b/a Cozy Cabin and Vanessa Doe v. City of New York, 140 F. 3d 134 (1998) (cert denied 1998 U.S. LEXIS 4846 [1998]).

120 Vitale, *City of Disorder*.

121 On the "creative class," see Florida, *Rise of the Creative Class*.

122 Schneider v. State, 308 U.S. 147 (1939), 163.

123 For a portrayal of social life in Times Square prior to its reconfiguration for Disney, see Delaney, *Times Square Red*.

124 Hotel Employees & Restaurant Employees Union, Local 100 of New York, NY, et al. v. City of New York Department of Parks and Recreation, et al. 311 F. 3d 534 (2002).

125 Hotel Employees & Restaurant Employees Union v. City of New York, 541.

126 Hotel Employees & Restaurant Employees Union v. City of New York, 551–52.

127 Rancière, *Dis-agreement*, 55.

128 Dunn et al., *Arresting Protest*.

129 United for Peace and Justice v. City of New York, 243 F. Supp. 2d 19 (2003). Affirmed: United for Peace and Justice v. City of New York, 323 F. 3d 175 (2003).

130 United For Peace and Justice v. City of New York, 243 F. Supp. 2d 19 (2003).

131 United For Peace and Justice v. City of New York, 243 F. Supp. 2d 19 (2003), at 26.

132 Coalition to Protest the Democratic National Convention v. City of Boston, 327 F. Supp. 2d 61 (2004). Affirmed: Bl(a)ck Tea Society v. City of Boston, 378 F. 3d 8 (2004).

133 Bl(a)ck Tea Society v. City of Boston, 378 F. 3d 8 at 14.

134 Coalition to March on the RNC and Stop the War v. The City of St. Paul, Minnesota, 557 F. Supp. 2d 1014 (2008), at 1031.

135 Felicia Lee, "Thousands Jam Disney's Newest Park to See 'Pocahontas,'" *New York Times*, June 11, 1995, 37 (Section 1).

136 Lee, "Thousands Jam Disney's Newest Park."

137 Michael Cooper, "Look Beyond City's Fiscal Woes, Mayor Tells a Congregation," *New York Times*, November 11, 2002, 5 (Section B); Randal Archibold, "All of New York's a Stage for the G.O.P. Convention," *New York Times*, May 26, 2003, 5 (Section B).

138 National Council of Arab Americans and Act Now to Stop War & End Racism Coalition v. City of New York, et al. 331 F. Supp. 2d. 258 (2004), 262–63; Rosenzweig and Blackmar, *Park and the People*, 519.

139 National Council of Arab Americans v. New York, 263–65.

140 Hague v. C.I.O. (1939).

141 Perry Educators Association v. Perry Local Educators Association (PEA v. PLEA), 460 U.S. 37 (1983); Hudgens v. NLRB (1976); International Society for Krishna Consciousness, Inc. (ISKCON) v. Lee, 505 U.S. 672 (1992); Lee v. ISKCON, 505 U.S. 830 (1992).

142 PEA v. PLEA (1983); Hague v. C.I.O. (1939).

143 Schneider v. State (1939).

144 Meiklejohn, *Free Speech*.

145 Rosenzweig and Blackmar, in *The Park and the People*, observe that in the 1970s, Central Park's decline was attributed to usage by teenagers or Puerto Ricans, when in fact the park's problems were fundamentally economic. During the fiscal crisis, city budgets and workforces were slashed so that, according to one study, by 1982, New York's parks had accumulated almost $3 billion in deferred maintenance needs (501–4).

146 After three and a half more years of litigation, New York City paid damages to the National Council of Arab Americans and ANSWER (and approximately half a million dollars in legal fees) for preventing their protest and agreed to amend the permitting process for Central Park. Evidence developed in the course of the litigation suggested that the city's reasons for denying the permit may have been pretextual, and that the city may not have wanted political demonstrations on Central Park's Great Lawn. National Council of Arab Americans and Act Now to Stop War & End Racism v. City of New York, U.S.D.C. S.D.N.Y. 04 Civ. 6602, "Memorandum and Order" (March 6, 2007), 16–21; National Council of Arab Americans and Act Now to Stop War & End Racism v. City of New York, U.S.D.C. S.D.N.Y. 04 Civ. 6602, "Stipulation and Order of Voluntary Dismissal" (January 10, 2008). See Michael Clancy, "City Settles Great Lawn Protest Lawsuit," *Village Voice*, January 8, 2008, https://www.villagevoice.com; "Central Park Great Lawn Lawsuit Results in Important Victory for Free Speech Rights," Answer Coalition, January 7, 2008, https://www.answercoalition.org/08_01_08_central_park_great_lawn_l. Similarly, Mayor Giuliani and the NYPD governed the steps of City Hall to favor productions of spectacle like New York Yankees World Series celebrations, and to exclude protests by nonprofit groups like

Housing Works, which advocates on behalf of the homeless suffering from HIV/AIDS in New York. See Miller, *Designs on the Public*, chap. 1.

147 Passavant, "Governmentality of Consumption"; Passavant, "Strong Neoliberal State"; Passavant, "Mega-events"; Peck and Tickell, "Neoliberalizing Space."

148 Kohn, "Privatization and Protest."

149 Dean, *Blog Theory*.

*Chapter Two. New York's Mega-Event Security Legacy and the Postlegitimation State*

1 Passavant, "Mega-Events"; Beauregard, *When America Became Suburban*, 84–86; Cohen, *Consumer's Republic*, chaps. 5 and 6. According to Cohen, "between 1959 and 1965 95 percent of new retail jobs in the New York metropolitan area were located in suburbs outside New York City—blacks and Puerto Ricans lost out" (288).

2 Alcaly and Bodian, "New York's Fiscal Crisis," 31; Gerald Ford, "Address to the National Press Club," Gerald R. Ford Presidential Library and Museum, October 29, 1975, 45, https://www.fordlibrarymuseum.gov/library/document /0122/1252562.pdf.

3 Alcaly and Bodian, "New York's Fiscal Crisis," 31–33; Moody, *From Welfare State*, 38–39.

4 Phillips-Fein, *Fear City*, 196–202; Shefter, *Political Crisis/Fiscal Crisis*, 139–48; Moody, *From Welfare State*, 39–47.

5 "Mission Statement," State of New York Financial Control Board, n.d., accessed August 9, 2019, http://www.fcb.state.ny.us/mission_statement.asp; Moody, *From Welfare State*, 286–89; "New York City Government Poverty Measure, 2005–2017," NYC Opportunity, April 2019, accessed August 9, 2019, https://www1.nyc.gov/site/opportunity/poverty-in-nyc/poverty-measure.page.

6 Fuchs, "Permanent Urban Fiscal Crisis," 63.

7 Hackworth, *Neoliberal City*; Sinclair, *New Masters of Capital*.

8 Fainstein, *City Builders*; Eisinger, "Politics of Bread and Circuses"; Judd, "Promoting Tourism in US Cities."

9 Hannigan, *Fantasy City*.

10 Della Porta, Peterson, and Reiter, "Policing Transnational Protest." Gillham, "Securitizing America," however, suggests that the shift away from negotiated management occurred after the attacks of September 11, 2001. See also Gillham, Edwards, and Noakes, "Strategic Incapacitation and the Policing of Occupy Wall Street Protests."

11 Della Porta and Reiter, "Policing of Global Protest"; Noakes and Gillham, "Aspects of the 'New Penology,'" 102; Martin, "Showcasing Security."

12 Noakes and Gillham, "'More Than a March.'"

13 Noakes and Gillham, "Aspects of the 'New Penology.'"

14 Feeley and Simon, "New Penology," 455.

15 Feeley and Simon, "New Penology," 458–59. I use the term "control" to evoke how the new penology is convergent with broader arguments made by Gilles

Deleuze that contemporary society is postdisciplinary due to its neglect of socialization or normalization, and its disposition toward postdisciplinary forms of surveillance, risk management, and selective incapacitation. Today, according to Deleuze, we live in "control societies." See Deleuze, "Postscript on the Societies," 3–7.

16 Feeley and Simon, "New Penology," 456, 466.

17 Vitale, "From Negotiated Management."

18 Shawn Reese, "National Special Security Events: Fact Sheet," Congressional Research Service, CRS Report R43522, January 25, 2017, updated January 11, 2021, https://fas.org/sgp/crs/homesec/R43522.pdf.

19 Wacquant, *Prisons of Poverty*, describes the promotional efforts of New York Mayor Rudolph Giuliani and the Manhattan Institute on behalf of the "Broken Windows" concept of policing. When Giuliani was elected mayor in 1993, he appointed William Bratton to his first tenure as NYPD commissioner, and Bratton institutionalized the "Broken Windows" concept of policing within the NYPD. In between serving as NYPD commissioner under Giuliani and later Mayor Bill de Blasio, he served as the Los Angeles Police Department chief and as a security consultant. John Timoney, who served in the NYPD when it adopted the "Broken Windows" concept of order maintenance policing, helping to pioneer its use of CompStat, later headed the Philadelphia Police Department when it hosted the 2000 RNC, and then headed the Miami Police Department when Miami hosted the Free Trade Agreement of the Americas (FTAA) talks, before becoming a security consultant to Bahrain in the wake of its prodemocracy uprising. Thomas Graham, head of the Disorder Control Unit (DCU) of the NYPD during the 2004 RNC, served as a consultant for security at the 2003 FTAA. For an overview of "Broken Windows" and the NYPD, see Vitale, *City of Disorder*; Bratton with Knobler, *Turnaround*. On Timoney, see Ryan Devereaux, "John Timoney: The Notorious Police Chief Sent to Reform Forces in Bahrain," *The Guardian*, February 16, 2012, https://www.theguardian.com. On the abusive policing of the 2000 RNC in Philadelphia, see Hermes, *Crashing the Party*. Miami's militaristic handling of the FTAA is widely referred to as the Miami Model of policing protest.

20 Bureau of Justice Assistance and CNA, *Managing Large-Scale Events*; Connors, *Planning and Managing Security*; Bickel and Connors, "Planning and Managing Security."

21 Yoder and Tempey, *Developments in the Policing*; Boghosian, *Policing of Political Speech*; Chasan et al., *Out of Control*.

22 Noakes and Gillham, "Aspects of the 'New Penology,'" 97–98.

23 Dinler et al. v. City of New York, 607 F. 3d 923 (2010), 929–30.

24 R. M. McCarthy and Associates in conjunction with Robert Louden, *Preliminary Report for the City of Seattle*, 5–6; *Report to the Seattle City Council*, 3. The City of Seattle posted an archive of reports on the 1999 World Trade Organization meetings at http://www.seattle.gov/archive/wtocommittee/resources .htm, but links to some of these reports are now broken.

25  Chasan et al., *Out of Control*.

26  Chasan et al., *Out of Control*, section 2.

27  Citizens' Panel on WTO Operations, *Report to the Seattle City Council*, 21.

28  Seattle Police Department, *Seattle Police Department After Action Report*, 9.

29  Seattle Police Department, *Seattle Police Department After Action Report*, 8–9, 3.

30  Seattle Police Department, *Seattle Police Department After Action Report*, 17–21.

31  Seattle Police Department, *Seattle Police Department After Action Report*, 49.

32  R. M. McCarthy and Associates in conjunction with Robert Louden, *Preliminary Report for the City of Seattle*, 42.

33  R. M. McCarthy and Associates in conjunction with Robert Louden, *Preliminary Report for the City of Seattle*, 17.

34  R. M. McCarthy and Associates in conjunction with Robert Louden, *Preliminary Report for the City of Seattle*, 13–20.

35  R. M. McCarthy and Associates in conjunction with Robert Louden, *Preliminary Report for the City of Seattle*, 30, 32, 29.

36  R. M. McCarthy and Associates in conjunction with Robert Louden, *Preliminary Report for the City of Seattle*, 23.

37  R. M. McCarthy and Associates in conjunction with Robert Louden, *Preliminary Report for the City of Seattle*, 27.

38  R. M. McCarthy and Associates in conjunction with Robert Louden, *Preliminary Report for the City of Seattle*, 30.

39  Passavant, "Mega-Events," 115–16 (discussing New Orleans).

40  Sarah Ferguson, "Testing Protest in New York," *Mother Jones*, January 24, 2002, http://www.motherjones.com; Al Baker, "Police Vow Zero Tolerance for Violence at Economic Forum," *New York Times*, January 29, 2002, B1.

41  Leslie Eaton, "For City, Good Buzz May Be Best Payoff of Economic Forum," *New York Times*, January 30, 2002, B1.

42  "World Economic Forum Moves from Davos to New York for 2002," CNNMoney.com, December 7, 2001, http://cnnmoney.com.

43  Ferguson, "Testing Protest in New York."

44  Clyde Haberman, "NYC; With Thanks Comes a Call for Restraint," *New York Times*, January 19, 2002, B1.

45  Alice McQuillan, Ralph Ortega, and Bill Hutchinson, "Cop Kudos as Forum Ends Run," *New York Daily News*, February 5, 2002, 8.

46  Raymond Hernandez, "Bloomberg Makes City's Bid for 2004 G.O.P. Convention," *New York Times*, June 18, 2002, http://www.nytimes.com.

47  Randal Archibold, "G.O.P. Makes It Official: New York Is Site of Its 2004 Convention," *New York Times*, February 1, 2003, http://www.nytimes.com.

48  Timothy Hardiman, "Critique of World Economic Forum," Memo from Commanding Officer, Queens South Task Force, to Commanding Officer, Disorder Control Unit, February 5, 2002 (memo on file with author). The memo is erroneously dated February 5, 2001. This and other after-action memos and the "After Action Report" are summarized and contextualized in the

excellent reporting by Jim Dwyer, "Police Memos Say Arrest Tactics Calmed Protest," *New York Times*, March 17, 2006, http://www.nytimes.com.

49 Michael Shortell, "Critique of World Economic Forum Detail," Memo from Commanding Officer, Narcotics Borough Manhattan South, to Commanding Officer, Disorder Control Unit, February 8, 2002 (memo on file with author).

50 Robert Bonifaci, "Critique of World Economic Forum," Memo from Commanding Officer, Queens North Task Force, to Commanding Officer, Disorder Control Unit, February 8, 2002 (memo on file with author).

51 Thomas Graham, "After Action Report on World Economic Forum Meetings and Demonstrations," Memo from Commanding Officer, Disorder Control Unit, to Chief of Department, March 4, 2002 (report on file with author). As noted by Dwyer, "Police Memos Say Arrest Tactics Calmed Protest," Graham's "After Action Report" has "Draft" handwritten on its first page, and it is not signed by Graham.

52 Harcourt, *Counterrevolution*; Ciccariello-Maher, "Counterinsurgency and the Occupy Movement."

53 Dwyer, "Police Memos Say Arrest Tactics Calmed Protest."

54 I understand control technologies, as Deleuze describes them, as becoming integrated within a variety of security apparatuses and thus being situated within a broader framework of security. I understand security here as referring to the way that police forces go beyond law enforcement, strictly speaking. Also encompassed in this understanding of security is the way that the distinction between the purposes and strategies of domestic police forces, and those of armed forces ostensibly dedicated to defense against foreign enemies, is breaking down. Both the logic of control, and that of security as I have described it, are at odds with the logic of public space for a society oriented to the horizon of democracy or the sovereignty of the people.

55 Graham, "After Action Report on World Economic Forum."

56 Personal interview with lawyer who defends protesters, April 27, 2013. (The scope and focus of interviews is discussed in chap. 3, n. 1 of this volume.)

57 Appuzzo and Goldman, *Enemies Within*, 30. The tasks of CIA's New York station chief primarily involve being a CIA liaison with Wall Street firms.

58 When Cohen hired Sanchez, the latter was still actively employed by the CIA. The CIA is prohibited from having any law enforcement or internal security functions. Although CIA agents could be temporarily assigned to other agencies, such agreements were drafted in great detail. None of this occurred when CIA Chief George Tenet sent Sanchez to the NYPD. Sanchez would not even take a leave of absence from the CIA and officially become Cohen's deputy until 2004. See Appuzzo and Goldman, *Enemies Within*, 66–67, 83.

59 Handschu et al. v. Special Services Division, 349 F. Supp. 766 (1972).

60 Handschu v. Special Services, 605 F. Supp. 1384 (1985).

61 The Handschu Guidelines limited the information rightfully obtained for event planning; established procedures for investigations; established a Handschu Authority consisting of the first deputy commissioner of the

Police Department, the deputy commissioner for legal matters, and a civilian member appointed by the mayor in consultation with the police commissioner; limited permissible Intelligence Division investigations to those where there is specific information received by the Police Department that a person or group involved in political activity is involved with, is about to be, or has threatened commission of criminal conduct, and required specific factual predicates be stated as part of the application made to the Handschu Authority for such investigations; established procedures for individuals or groups having reason to believe that they were under investigation to ascertain whether investigations were conducted in compliance with the guidelines by the Handschu Authority; required that the use of undercover personnel be approved by the Handschu Authority; limited the kinds of information lawfully retained by the Intelligence Division; limited the dissemination of such Intelligence Division records; required periodic review of files for compliance with the guidelines to determine, in part, that no files were being retained in violation of the guidelines, and that a report be made to the Handschu Authority every twelve months; and required that a report be made by the Handschu Authority every calendar year on investigations and investigation processes that would be presented to the police commissioner and to the mayor (Handschu v. Special Services, 605 F. Supp. 1384 [1985], Appendix A).

62  Chevigny, "Politics and Law in the Control of Local Surveillance," 735, 766.

63  Apuzzo and Goldman, *Enemies Within*, 50–52; an attorney for Handschu plaintiffs, email message to author, March 28, 2020.

64  Handschu v. Special Services Division, 273 F. Supp. 2d 327 (2003); Arthur Eisenberg, "Police Surveillance of Political Activity—the History and Current State of the Handschu Decree," testimony presented to the New York Advisory Committee to the U.S. Commission on Civil Rights, May 21, 2003, https://www.nyclu.org. For a discussion of John Ashcroft's 2002 FBI guidelines, see Cole and Dempsey, *Terrorism and the Constitution*, 88–96.

65  Handschu v. Special Services Division, 273 F. Supp. 2d 327 (2003).

66  Handschu v. Special Services Division, 288 F. Supp. 2d 411 (2003).

67  Dunn et al., *Arresting Protest*.

68  Dunn et al., *Arresting Protest*, 10, 22.

69  Handschu v. Special Services Division, 288 F. Supp. 2d 411 (2003), 413–14; Dunn et al., *Arresting Protest*, 22.

70  Eavesdropping, video surveillance, and electronic and telephonic monitoring, however, are also governed by federal and state constitutional law, statute, and NYPD regulations.

71  Handschu v. Special Services Division, 288 F. Supp. 2d 411, Appendix A to Second Revised Order and Judgment: Guidelines for Investigations Involving Political Activity (2003).

72  Handschu v. Special Services Division, 475 F. Supp. 2d 331 (2007), 333–34, 336–37.

73 Raza et al. v. City of New York, U.S.D.C. E.D.N.Y., 13 Civ. 3448, "Complaint" (June 18, 2013), https://www.nyclu.org; Handschu v. Police Department of the City of New York, U.S.D.C. S.D.N.Y., 71 Civ. 2203, "Ruling and Order on Proposed Revised Settlement Agreement" (March 13, 2017). The 2017 Revised Handschu Guidelines can be located in Handschu v. Special Services Division, 71 Civ. 2203, "Declaration of Jethro Eisenstein," Tab C (March 6, 2017), https://nyclu.org. Judge Haight was influenced in his modification of the Handschu Guidelines by Peters and Eure, *An Investigation of NYPD's Compliance with Rules Governing Investigations of Political Activity*. This report found significant noncompliance with the rules governing investigations—noncompliance that was predictable in light of the institutional analysis presented here.

74 Handschu v. Special Services Division, 475 F. Supp. 2d 331 (2007), 346–47.

75 Handschu v. Special Services Division, 475 F. Supp. 2d 331 (2007), 346–53.

76 Apuzzo and Goldman, *Enemies Within*, 78, 179, 188, 195–97, 73.

77 Handschu v. Special Services Division, 475 F. Supp. 2d 311 (2007), 350. Critical Mass bicyclists are riders who get together to ride en masse in cities to promote acceptance of bicycle traffic as a more environmentally friendly mode of transportation than car traffic.

78 Chevigny, "Politics and Law in the Control of Local Surveillance," 754–61; Alliance to End Repression v. City of Chicago, 561 F. Supp. 537 (1982).

79 Recall that the Seattle Police Department was faulted by the *Preliminary Report for the City of Seattle* for failing to seek that the Seattle intelligence ordinance be overturned. This *Preliminary Report* was issued in April 2000—again, prior to the attacks of September 11, 2001.

80 Cole and Dempsey, *Terrorism and the Constitution*, 88–94; Alliance to End Repression v. City of Chicago, 742 F. 2d 1007 (1984).

81 Personal interview with lawyer who defends protesters, April 27, 2013; Dunn et al., *Rights and Wrongs*, 14.

82 Michael Schiller v. City of New York, U.S.D.C. S.D.N.Y. 04 Civ. 7922, "Thomas Graham Deposition" (abbreviated hereafter as "Graham Deposition") (April 4, 2006), 112–13 (no-summons policy), 107–110 (fingerprinting for violations); MacNamara v. City of New York, 275 F.R.D. 125 (2011), 135; Dunn et al., *Rights and Wrongs*, 14; Patrick Devlin, Assistant Chief, Commanding Officer, Criminal Justice Bureau, to RNC Coordinator, "Monthly Committee Report for the NYPD Mass Arrest/Prisoner Processing Sub-Committee," May 4, 2004, https://www.nyclu.org/en/policing-protest-nypds-republican-national-convention-documents. (This and other NYPD documents related to NYPD planning for the RNC are hosted online by the NYCLU at this web address. Document on file with the author.)

83 Mandal v. City of New York, U.S.D.C. S.D.N.Y. 02 Civ. 1234, "Memorandum and Order" (October 17, 2006), 3–5.

84 Mandal v. City of New York, 5–6.

85 "Graham Deposition," 211–12.

86 MacNamara v. City of New York, U.S.D.C. S.D.N.Y. 04 Civ. 9216, "Second Amended Class Action Complaint" (hereafter abbreviated as SAC), January 29, 2008, 42.

87 MacNamara v. City of New York, SAC, 36; Dunn et al., *Rights and Wrongs*, 14–15; Raymond Kelly, *Criminal Justice Bureau: Republican National Convention Mass Arrest Plan* (abbreviated hereafter as *RNC Mass Arrest Plan*), August 5, 2004, 19, https://www.nyclu.org/en/policing-protest-nypds-republican-national-convention-documents. (This and other NYPD documents related to NYPD planning for the RNC are hosted online by the NYCLU at this web address. Document on file with the author.)

88 *RNC Mass Arrest Plan*, 6.

89 "Graham Deposition," 65.

90 Personal interview with lawyer who defends protesters, April 27, 2013.

91 *RNC Mass Arrest Plan*, 7, 19; MacNamara v. City of New York, SAC, 27; personal interview with lawyer who defends protesters, April 27, 2013.

92 Personal interview with lawyer who defends protesters, April 27, 2013; Marom v. City of New York, U.S.D.C. S.D.N.Y. 15 Civ. 2017, "First Amended Complaint" (July 21, 2015); Marom v. City of New York, U.S.D.C. S.D.N.Y. 15 Civ. 2017, 2016 U.S. Dist. LEXIS 28466, "Memorandum and Order" (March 7, 2016); Marom v. City of New York, U.S.D.C. S.D.N.Y. 15 Civ. 2017, "Second Amended Complaint" (July 13, 2017).

93 Personal interview with lawyer who defends protesters, April 27, 2013; *RNC Mass Arrest Plan*, 5, 17, 19; MacNamara v. City of New York, SAC, 27 (claiming that the NYPD Legal Bureau attorneys with the knowledge of Criminal Justice Bureau [CJB] supervisors create "perjured sworn statements wherein arresting officers attested that they had personally observed arrestees engaging in conduct that provided a basis for the alleged probable cause to arrest when the officers, in fact, had no personal knowledge of the arrestees' conduct"; Legal Bureau attorneys with the knowledge of CJB supervisors create "arrest paperwork, which contained knowingly false statements . . . for the purpose of insuring that the paperwork was facially sufficient when presented to the Manhattan County District Attorney").

94 Personal interview with lawyer who defends protesters, April 27, 2013.

95 "Intelligence Documents" produced in discovery related to Schiller v. City of New York and Dinler v. City of New York, and released by Judge James Francis's order in Schiller v. City of New York and Dinler v. City of New York, U.S.D.C. S.D.N.Y. 04 Civ. 7921 (May 4, 2007), Bates Stamp Number 000102645. Further references to these Intelligence Division documents will be made as "Intelligence Documents," followed by their Bates stamp number. Cited documents are hosted online at https://www.nyclu.org/en/policing-protest-nypds-republican-national-convention-documents. Some are also hosted online at http://www.nytimes.com/ref/nyregion/RNC_intel_digests.html. All cited "Intelligence Documents" are on file with author.

96 "Intelligence Documents," Bates Stamp 000102762; Lincoln Anderson, "Anarchists Say Smears Were Way Out of Order," *The Villager* 74, no. 20 (September 22–28, 2004), https://www.amny.com/news/anarchists-say-smears-were-way-out-of-order/.

97 Anderson, "Anarchists Say Smears Were Way Out of Order"; Sarah Ferguson, "Coming to a Convention Near You: Scary Anarchist II," *Village Voice*, August 17, 2004, https://www.villagevoice.com; Patrice O'Shaughnessy, "Anarchists Hot for Mayhem, Police on Guard vs. Violent Tactics," *New York Daily News*, August 26, 2004, http://www.nydaily.com. On the ideological effects of police warnings of violence associated with anarchism and the repetition of such warnings in pre-event media coverage, see Fernandez, *Policing Dissent*, chap. 6. On an aesthetics of consent, see Passavant, "Governmentality of Consumption."

98 Jim Dwyer, "City Police Spied Broadly before G.O.P. Convention," *New York Times*, March 25, 2007, http://www.nytimes.com; "Intelligence Documents," Bates Stamp 000102678.

99 Jim Dwyer, "Police Infiltrate Protests, Videotapes Show," *New York Times*, December 22, 2005, http://www.nytimes.com. (A version of this article appeared in print with the title, "New York Police Covertly Join In at Protest Rallies.")

100 "Intelligence Documents," Bates Stamps 000102671, 000102679, 000102749, 000102802, 000103003, 000103046.

101 "Intelligence Documents," Bates Stamp 000102742.

102 Personal interview with lawyer who defends protesters, April 27, 2013.

103 City of New York v. Time's Up, 814 N.Y.S. 2d 890 (February 14, 2006); Bray v. City of New York, 356 F. Supp. 2d 277 (2004), 286; "Intelligence Documents," Bates Stamps 000102716, 000102755.

104 Dwyer, " Police Infiltrate Protests, Videotapes Show."

105 Elizabeth Press, "Critical Mass: Over 260 Arrested in First Major Protest of RNC," *Democracy Now!*, August 30, 2004, https://www.democracynow.org; Oliver, "A Criminal Mess," 38; Dunn et al., *Rights and Wrongs*, 13; City of New York v. Time's Up, 814 N.Y.S. 2d 890 (February 14, 2006).

106 Dunn et al., *Rights and Wrongs*, 28–29.

107 Gorz, *Immaterial*, chap. 2.

108 On communicative capitalism, see Dean, "Networked Empire," 265–88; Dean, *Democracy and Other Neoliberal Fantasies*; Passavant, "Political Subjectivity and Presidential Campaign," 39.

109 "Intelligence Documents," Bates Stamp 00010362.

110 "Intelligence Documents," Bates Stamp 000102719. See Ryan Singel, "NYPD Intelligence Op Targets Dot-Matrix Graffiti Bike," *Wired*, April 10, 2007, https://www.wired.com.

111 "Intelligence Documents," Bates Stamp 000102722; emphasis modified from original.

112 Xeni Jardin, "RNC-NYC: Update on the Arrest of Joshua Kinberg, Bikes against Bush," *Boing-Boing*, August 30, 2004, http://boingboing.net/2004

/08/30/rncnyc-update-on-arr.html; Tim Murphy, "The Disappeared," *New York* magazine, October 24, 2007, http://nymag.com/news/intelligencer /30033/. Kinberg's arrest can be viewed online: "Bicycles against Bush Arrest by Joshua Kinberg and Yury Gitman," Vimeo, n.d., accessed June 12, 2017, https://vimeo.com/21785603.

113 "Intelligence Documents," Bates Stamps 000103025, 000103011.

114 Dunn et al., *Rights and Wrongs*, 32; Dinler v. City of New York, U.S.D.C. S.D.N.Y. 04 Civ. 7921, "Opinion and Order" (September 30, 2012), 17. We should note that the NYCLU documents several instances of the NYPD targeting journalists, legal observers, and street medics for arrest in Dunn et al., *Rights and Wrongs*, 32–34.

115 Dinler v. City of New York, 04 Civ. 7921, "Opinion and Order" (September 30, 2012), 7; War Resisters League, https://www.warresisters.org. Skolnick, *The Politics of Protest*, states, regarding the failure to distinguish absurd from serious threats for the 1968 Democratic National Convention in Chicago, "Surely it is unsatisfactory not to distinguish the absurd from the serious." Such incapacity results in "inadequate protection against real dangers, as well as an increased likelihood of unnecessary suppression and violence" (200).

116 Dinler v. City of New York, "Opinion and Order" (September 30, 2012), 8–9.

117 Dinler v. City of New York, "Opinion and Order" (September 30, 2012), 9; "Victory in Unlawful Mass Arrest during 2004 RNC the Largest Protest Settlement in History" (press release), NYCLU, January 15, 2014, http://www .nyclu.org.

118 Sabrina Tavernise, "Prosecutors Won't Pursue Cases of 227 in Disputed Protest," *New York Times*, October 7, 2004, B1.

119 "Victory in Unlawful Mass Arrest"; John Del Signore, "NYCLU and City Lawyers Square Off over Mass Arrests at Republican National Convention," *Gothamist*, May 31, 2012, http://gothamist.com; Dinler v. City of New York, "Opinion and Order" (September 30, 2012), 12–16.

120 Dunn et al., *Rights and Wrongs*, 34.

121 Erin Durkin and Daniel Beekman, "City Pays $18M to Settle RNC Lawsuits," *New York Daily News*, January 15, 2014, http://www.nydailynews.com.

122 "Intelligence Documents," Bates Stamp 000103061.

123 Jim Dwyer, "City Arrest Tactics, Used on Protesters, Face Test in Court," *New York Times*, September 17, 2004, http://www.nytimes.com.

124 Dwyer, "City Arrest Tactics"; MacNamara v. City of New York, SAC, 44.

125 Dwyer, "City Arrest Tactics"; MacNamara v. City of New York, SAC, 25.

126 Jardin, "RNC-NYC."

127 Press, "Critical Mass."

128 Jardin, "RNC-NYC."

129 Dunn et al., *Rights and Wrongs*, 38.

130 Jardin, "RNC-NYC."

131 Jardin, "RNC-NYC."

132 Earl, "Information Access and Protest Policing," 55–56.

133  Press, "Critical Mass."

134  Dunn et al., *Rights and Wrongs*, 42–44; MacNamara v. City of New York, SAC, 49, 51, 53, 71.

135  Dunn et al., *Rights and Wrongs*, 37–40.

136  Dunn et al., *Rights and Wrongs*, 39–40.

137  MacNamara v. City of New York, SAC, 39.

138  "Victory in Unlawful Mass Arrest."

139  Dunn et al., *Rights and Wrongs*, 7; Rebecca Fishbein, "City Settles All Remaining 2004 RNC Protest Lawsuits with $18 Million Payout," *Gothamist*, January 15, 2014, http://gothamist.com. A conditional dismissal refers to those arrestees who received an ACD or adjournment in contemplation of dismissal. Under New York state law, an ACD means that the charges are dismissed in six months (one year for a marijuana arrest) as long as the individual is not arrested within that period.

140  Tavernise, "Prosecutors Won't Pursue Cases of 227 in Disputed Protest," 1B.

141  Several RNC cases were consolidated in Dinler v. City of New York, 04 Civ. 7921, "Opinion and Order" (September 30, 2012).

142  "Memorandum of Understanding" (Settlement of "RNC cases" including Dinler v. City of New York, 04 Civ. 7921, MacNamara v. City of New York, 04 Civ. 9216, and other plaintiffs), December 9, 2013, accessed November 29, 2020, https://www.nyclu.org/sites/default/files/releases/RNC_settlement_1.15.14.pdf; Fishbein, "City Settles All"; "Victory in Unlawful Mass Arrest"; Packard v. City of New York, U.S.D.C. S.D.N.Y. 15 Civ. 07130, "Complaint" (September 10, 2015), fn. 9.

143  Liu, *City of New York Office of the Comptroller Claims Report Fiscal Year 2011*, 40–42. The growing number of claims against the NYPD is identified as an "area of concern" in this report released prior to the landmark RNC settlement (6).

144  Ron Goldwyn, "Convention Legal Fallout: City, Activists Ready to Square Off in Several Lawsuits Stemming from Republicans' Visit," *Philadelphia Daily News*, February 15, 2001, 5; Gwen Shaffer, "Bully Puppet," *Philadelphia City Paper*, August 15–21, 2002, https://mycitypaper.com/articles/2002-08-15/cover.shtml; Hermes, *Crashing the Party*, 19; Ryan J. Foley, "Taxpayers Off the Hook for GOP Convention Lawsuits," *Common Dreams*, September 4, 2008, https://www.commondreams.org/news/2008/09/04/taxpayers-hook-gop-convention-lawsuits.

145  In addition to Noakes and Gillham, "Aspects of the 'New Penology' in the Police Response to Political Protests"; and Feeley and Simon, "The New Penology"; see Ericson and Haggerty, *Policing the Risk Society*.

146  Brown, *Undoing the Demos*, 63–68. For a critical review of Brown, *Undoing the Demos*, see Dean, "Neoliberalism's Defeat of Democracy."

147  Handschu v. Police Department of the City of New York, U.S.D.C. S.D.N.Y. 71 Civ. 2203, "Ruling and Order on Proposed Revised Settlement Agreement" (March 13, 2017).

148 Schmitt, *Legality and Legitimacy*, 32.

149 Dinler v. City of New York, "Opinion and Order" (September 30, 2012). Consider Skolnick's criticisms of police intelligence, unnecessary suppression, and violence at the Chicago Democratic National Convention of 1968 (see n. 115, above) in relation to my discussion of Judge Sullivan's unquestioning acceptance of NYPD intelligence.

150 Dinler v. City of New York, "Opinion and Order" (September 30, 2012), 24.

151 Dinler v. City of New York, "Opinion and Order" (September 30, 2012), 26–27.

152 Dinler v. City of New York, "Opinion and Order" (September 30, 2012), 26–27. During the middle of the twentieth century, some unrest or disturbance by the exercise of First Amendment rights in a democracy was not unexpected: Terminiello v. Chicago, 337 U.S. 1 (1949); Cox v. Louisiana, 379 U.S. 536 (1965).

153 Dinler v. City of New York, "Opinion and Order" (September 30, 2012), 27.

154 Dinler v. City of New York, "Opinion and Order" (September 30, 2012), 26.

155 John Locke compares "governing without *settled standing laws*" (which he calls absolute arbitrary power) unfavorably with the state of nature, arguing that the "ruling power ought to govern by *declared and received laws* and not by extemporary dictates and undetermined resolutions." Locke, *Second Treatise of Government*, §137.

156 "Graham Deposition," 55–62.

157 Alex Vitale's work highlights the decentralized nature of policing in the United States and frames protest policing as an expression of a city's political culture and political leadership as reflected in its police department. See Vitale, "From Negotiated Management"; Vitale, "Command and Control"; Vitale, "Managing Defiance."

158 For a psychoanalytic approach to enjoyment, see Dean, *Žižek's Politics*, chap. 1.

159 Dunn et al., *Arresting Protest*, 18 (NYPD verbal abuse of antiwar demonstrators on February 15, 2003).

160 Garfinkel, "Conditions of Successful Degradation Ceremonies"; Gusfield, "On Legislating Morals."

161 Foucault, *Discipline and Punish*, part 1.

162 Feeley, *Process Is the Punishment*.

163 Burt, "'Quien Habla es Terrorista,'" explores the debilitating effects on civil society when protest is represented by the state as associated with terrorism.

*Chapter Three. Policing the Uprising*

1 Some events described in interviews are also described in either news media accounts or legal documents, though such sources might not be cited in the note to preserve the anonymity of interviewees. I utilized the snowball method of identifying interviewees, which means that my interviewees suggested others I should interview. Although the sample is fairly representative

in terms of gender and race, experienced, hard-core activists are probably overrepresented. Because activists with greater experience are less likely to self-censor after an encounter with repressive policing, this sample probably understates the chilling effects of the NYPD's protest policing. I did not attempt to interview members of the NYPD for three reasons: I am most interested in the effects of the NYPD's policing on protesters; the lack of success of other protest policing scholars in their efforts to interview members of the NYPD; the long-term reputation of the NYPD as a more insulated and secretive police department. On the insular nature of the NYPD, see Chevigny, *Edge of the Knife*, 63.

2 Wacquant, *Prisons of Poverty*; Bratton with Knobler, *Turnaround*; Ryan Devereaux, "John Timoney: The Notorious Police Chief Sent to Reform Forces in Bahrain," *The Guardian*, February 16, 2012, https://www.theguardian.com.

3 Vitale, *City of Disorder*.

4 Crouch, *Strange Non-Death of Neoliberalism*.

5 Vitale, "From Negotiated Management to Command." For a discussion of protest policing in Montreal, see Fortin, "'Arrest' Is the Punishment."

6 Vitale, "From Negotiated Management to Command."

7 Vitale, "From Negotiated Management to Command," 284.

8 Vitale, "From Negotiated Management to Command," 291-94.

9 Vitale, "Command and Control and Miami," 405-406; Noakes and Gillham, "Aspects of the 'New Penology.'"

10 Vitale, "Command and Control and Miami," 405-6; Noakes and Gillham, "Aspects of the 'New Penology.'" 111-12.

11 Vitale, "Command and Control and Miami," 405-6 (Vitale refers to the new penology as "neoliberal and neoconservative," 405); Feeley and Simon, "New Penology."

12 Feeley and Simon, "New Penology," 456, 466-67.

13 Brown, *Undoing the Demos*, 30-32, 63, 66-67, chap. 5. For a critical review of Brown, *Undoing the Demos*, see Dean, "Neoliberalism's Defeat of Democracy."

14 Brown, *Undoing the Demos*, 140-41.

15 Brown, *Undoing the Demos*, 150 (emphasis in original), 68, 140.

16 Beckett, *Making Crime Pay*, 40-43.

17 Whittaker, "Planned, Mass Violations."

18 David Lawrence, "What's Become of 'Law and Order'?" *U.S. News and World Report*, August 5, 1963, 104.

19 David Lawrence, "The War against Crime," *U.S. News and World Report*, June 29, 1964, 111-12.

20 Richard Nixon, "Address Accepting the Presidential Nomination at the Republican Convention in Miami Beach, Florida," August 8, 1968, American Presidency Project, https://www.presidency.ucsb.edu/documents/address-accepting-the-presidential-nomination-the-republican-national-convention-miami.

21 Nixon, "President's State of the Union."

22 National Advisory Commission on Civil Disorders, *Report of the National Advisory Commission,* 34.

23 Henry Raymont, "Riot Report Book Big Best Seller," *New York Times,* March 14, 1968, 49.

24 Epp, *Making Rights Real.*

25 Schweingruber, "Mob Sociology and Escalated Force," 379–81.

26 Robert Semple Jr., "Nixon Scores Panel for 'Undue' Stress on White Racism," *New York Times,* March 7, 1968, 1.

27 Beckett, *Making Crime Pay,* chap. 4; Hagan, *Who Are the Criminals?*

28 Parenti, *Lockdown America*; Bratton with Knobler, *Turnaround.*

29 George Kelling and James Q. Wilson, "Broken Windows," *The Atlantic,* March 1982, http://www.theatlantic.com.

30 Bernard Harcourt finds the assertion that the appearance of disorder causes crime not to be supported empirically. See Harcourt, *Illusion of Order.* Although the "Broken Windows" concept of policing is often credited with leading to declines in crime, Judith Greene has found the empirical basis for such claims to be lacking because similar declines in crime have been achieved both by cities that have implemented the "Broken Windows" concept of policing and by those that have embraced other approaches to policing. See Greene, "Zero Tolerance."

31 Kelling and Wilson, "Broken Windows."

32 Kelling and Wilson, "Broken Windows."

33 Kelling and Wilson, "Broken Windows."

34 Kelling and Wilson, "Broken Windows."

35 On the psychoanalytic concept of enjoyment, see Dean, *Žižek's Politics.*

36 Slavoj Žižek identifies the discursive frame where one states that others believe in something, while maintaining some distance from those beliefs of others for oneself, as the frame of contemporary ideology. With this insight, we can identify "Broken Windows" as deeply ideological because Kelling and Wilson state that others approve of police kicking ass, while they themselves acknowledge that such approved police brutality could raise questions of due process or fair treatment.

37 Packard v. City of New York, U.S.D.C. S.D.N.Y. 15 Civ. 07130, "Complaint" (September 10, 2015), par. 68; Michael Schiller v. City of New York, U.S.D.C. S.D.N.Y. 04 Civ. 7922, "Thomas Graham, Deposition" (April 4, 2006) (abbreviated hereafter as "Graham Deposition").

38 According to the supremacy clause, U.S. Constitution, Article VI, cl. 2, where there is a conflict between the Constitution, or federal law, and state law, the Constitution, or federal law, takes precedence. In other words, where there is a conflict between the First Amendment and New York's disorderly conduct violation, the First Amendment should take precedence. This was recognized by the "preferred position doctrine," though this doctrine has been neglected since 1968, as discussed in chapter 1.

39  Vitale, "From Negotiated Management to Command," 294.

40  "Timeline: Egypt's Revolution," *Al-Jazeera*, February 14, 2011, https://www
.aljazeera.com.

41  Monica Davey and Steven Greenhouse, "Angry Demonstrations in Wisconsin as Cuts Loom," *New York Times*, February 16, 2011, http://www.nytimes
.com; Mary Spicuzza and Clay Barbour, "Legislators Mum on Walker
Proposal as Union Leaders, Protesters Rage," *Wisconsin State Journal*, February 15, 2011, http://host.madison.com/wsj; Clay Barbour, "Thousands Gather
at Capitol to Protest Walker Budget Bill," *Wisconsin State Journal*, February 16,
2011, http://host.madison.com/wsj.

42  David Chen, "In 'Bloombergville,' Budget Protesters Sleep In," *New York
Times*, June 15, 2011, http://www.nytimes.com; "Welcome to Bloombergville:
New York Activists Fight Budget Cuts by Camping in Front of City Hall,"
*Democracy Now!*, June 24, 2011, http://www.democracynow.org; personal inter-
view with lawyer who defends protesters, February 23, 2013.

43  Reiter, "Pelican Bay Hunger Strike"; Reiter, *23/7*.

44  Schneider, *Thank You, Anarchy*, 10.

45  Andy Kroll, "How Occupy Really Started," *Mother Jones*, October 17, 2011,
https://www.motherjones.com; "August 2—People's Assembly" (video), New
Yorkers against Budget Cuts, accessed August 11, 2017, https://nocutsny
.wordpress.com.

46  Schneider, *Thank You, Anarchy*, 10.

47  Schneider, *Thank You, Anarchy*, chap. 2; Micah White and Kalle Lasn, "The
Call to Occupy Wall Street Resonates around the World," *The Guardian*,
September 19, 2011, https://www.theguardian.com.

48  Kayden, New York City Department of City Planning, and the Municipal
Art Society of New York, *Privately Owned Public Space*, chap. 1; Miller, *Designs
on the Public*, chaps. 4–6.

49  Kayden et al., *Privately Owned Public Space*, 39; Protest and Assembly Project,
*Suppressing Protest*, 7.

50  Joseph Loftus, "Dr. King Suggests 'Camp-In' in Cities," *New York Times*, October 24, 1967, 33. The tactic was ultimately deployed during the Poor People's
Campaign after King's assassination.

51  In this regard, OWS shares much with the autonomy movement in Italy during the 1970s. See Lotringer and Marazzi, *Autonomia*.

52  The Protest and Assembly Project noted, "News coverage of income inequality increased five-fold between September and November" of 2011.
Protest and Assembly Project, *Suppressing Protest*, 14.

53  Cara Buckley and Rachel Donadio, "Buoyed by Wall St. Protests, Rallies
Sweep the Globe," *New York Times*, October 15, 2011, http://www.nytimes.com;
Alan Taylor, "Occupy Wall Street Spreads Worldwide," *The Atlantic*, Octo-
ber 17, 2011, http://www.theatlantic.com.

54  Jodi Dean and Jason Jones, "Occupy Wall Street and the Politics of Representation," *Chto Delat*, n.d., accessed August 18, 2017, https://chtodelat.org

/b8-newspapers/12-38/jodi-dean-and-jason-jones-occupy-wall-street-and-the
-politics-of-representation/.

55 Marina Sitrin, "OWS-NYC: September 21, 2011" (blog post), *Marina Sitrin: Dreaming the Impossible*, accessed March 28, 2020, https://www.marinasitrin .com/entrevistas/; Ryan Devereaux, "Troy Davis Protesters Occupy Wall Street," *Facing South*, originally published by New American Century, September 26, 2011, https://www.facingsouth.org/2011/09/troy-davis-protesters -occupy-wall-street.html.

56 "Over 1,000 Protest Troy Davis Execution in NYC," *Democracy Now!*, September 23, 2011, https://www.democracynow.org; Jen Marlowe and Keeanga-Yamahtta Taylor, "The Execution That Birthed a Movement," *In These Times*, September 17, 2016, http://inthesetimes.com/features/occupy-five-years-troy-davis-black-lives-matter.html; Taylor, *From #BlackLivesMatter to Black Liberation*, 145.

57 Mother Jones News Team, "Map: Occupy Wall Street, a Global Movement," *Mother Jones*, October 4, 2011, https://www.motherjones.com.

58 On OWS, see Schneider, *Thank You, Anarchy*; Schmitt, Taylor, and Creif, *Occupy!* For reporting on a number of different occupations around the United States, see Faraone, *99 Nights with the 99%*. For a timeline of Occupy until its eviction, see Dean, "Introduction." For a theoretical discussion of Occupy's significance, see *Theory and Event* 14, no. 4 (suppl. 2011).

59 Colin Moynihan, "Wall Street Protests Continue, with at Least 6 Arrested," *New York Times*, September 19, 2011, http://www.nytimes.com.

60 Schneider, *Thank You, Anarchy*, 33–34.

61 Schneider, *Thank You, Anarchy*, 39–40.

62 Christina Boyle and John Doyle, "Pepper Spray Videos Spark Furor as NYPD Launches Probe of Wall Street Protest Incidents," *New York Daily News*, September 29, 2011, http://www.nydailynews.com.

63 Associated Press, "New York City Settles with 6 Occupy Wall Street Protesters Pepper-Sprayed by the Police," *New York Times*, July 7, 2015, http://www .nytimes.com; Stephen Rex Brown, "OWS Protester Who Found Love after Pepper-Spraying Wins $55K," *New York Daily News*, July 6, 2015, http://www .nydailynews.com.

64 Al Baker, Colin Moynihan, and Sarah Maslin Nir, "Police Arrest More Than 700 Protesters on Brooklyn Bridge," *New York Times*, October 1, 2011, http:// www.nytimes.com.

65 Schneider, *Thank You, Anarchy*, 78–79; Matt Wells, "Occupy Wall Street Protesters Set for Zuccotti Park Showdown," *The Guardian*, October 13, 2011, https://www.theguardian.com; Josh Harkinson, "Inside Occupy Wall Street's All-Nighter," *Mother Jones*, October 14, 2011, https://www.motherjones.com.

66 Schneider, *Thank You, Anarchy*, 78.

67 Schneider, *Thank You, Anarchy*, 79.

68 Ed Pilkington, "Occupy Wall Street Assault: Lawyer Demands Action on Policeman's Punch," *The Guardian*, October 16, 2011, https://www.theguardian

.com; Christopher Robbins, "HIV Positive Protester Says Cop Who Punched Him Should Get Tested," *Gothamist*, October 14, 2011, http://gothamist.com. The protester sued the city and the case was settled for $55,000. Cardona, though, was granted a disability pension by the NYPD Pension Board for $120,000 a year. The protester's lawyer was "incredulous" upon learning of Cardona's disability pension. On the bright side, he stated, "At least he's off the force." Rocco Parascandola, "Cop Who Punched Occupy Wall Street Protester Gets Tax-Free Disability Pension," *New York Daily News*, June 13, 2014, http://www.nydailynews.com.

69 Al Baker and Joseph Goldstein, "After an Earlier Misstep, a Minutely Planned Raid," *New York Times*, November 15, 2011, http://www.nytimes .com.

70 Baker and Goldstein, "After an Earlier Misstep."

71 "A Surprise Nighttime Raid, Then a Tense Day of Maneuvering in the Streets," *New York Times*, November 15, 2011, http://www.nytimes.com; "Inside Occupy Wall Street Raid: Eyewitnesses Describe Arrests, Beatings as Police Dismantle Camp," *Democracy Now!*, November 15, 2011, http://www.democra-cynow.org.

72 An LRAD, a Long-Range Acoustic Device, emits a loud noise intended to incapacitate an opponent. The LRAD was initially developed through a Department of Defense contract to prevent small ships from approaching U.S. vessels, and has been used by the shipping industry as a defense against pirates. It was also deployed in Iraq. Alec Foege, "Inventor's Killer Sounds Scatter Pirates," *CNN Money*, March 17, 2009, https://money.cnn.com/2009 /03/06/smallbusiness/killer sounds.fsb/.

73 Personal interview with an Occupy activist, June 12, 2014c.

74 Baker and Goldstein, "After an Earlier Misstep"; Dominic Rushe, "Occupy Wall Street: NYPD Attempt Media Blackout at Zuccotti Park," *The Guardian*, November 15, 2011, https://www.theguardian.com; Schneider, *Thank You, Anarchy*, 101.

75 Telephone interview with an Occupy activist, July 23, 2014.

76 "Inside Occupy Wall Street Raid."

77 Adam Martin, "NYPD Raid on Occupy Wall Street Just Cost the City $350,000," *New York Magazine*, April 9, 2013, http://nymag.com.

78 James Barron and Colin Moynihan, "City Reopens Park after Protesters Are Evicted," *New York Times*, November 15, 2011, http://www.nytimes.com.

79 Baker and Goldstein, "After an Earlier Misstep"; telephone interview with an Occupy activist, July 23, 2014.

80 Barron and Moynihan, "City Reopens Park after Protesters Are Evicted"; "A Surprise Nighttime Raid."

81 Barron and Moynihan, "City Reopens Park after Protesters Are Evicted."

82 Personal interview with an Occupy activist, June 12, 2014c; Marom v. City of New York, U.S.D.C. S.D.N.Y. 15 Civ. 2017, "Second Amended Complaint" (abbreviated hereafter as SAC) (July 13, 2017), 19.

83  Jim Dwyer, "In a Wrestling Match over Space, a Sudden Shove," *New York Times*, November 15, 2011, http://www.nytimes.com.

84  Telephone interview with a legal observer, June 12, 2013; Peat et al. v. City of New York, U.S.D.C. S.D.N.Y. 12 Civ. 08230, "First Amended Complaint" (abbreviated hereafter as FAC) (July 30, 2013).

85  Stecklow and Thompson, "Occupy Wall Street: New Year's Day Demonstration, Arrests, and Settlement," YouTube, June 10, 2014, https://www.youtube.com/watch?v=8m2xFteafCQ.

86  Telephone interview with a legal observer, June 12, 2013; Stecklow and Thompson, "New Year's Day Demonstration, Arrests, and Settlement." One reporter who covered the Occupy movement nationally told me, "Cops say horrible things to protesters in New York" (which we also saw in chapter 2). Personal interview with a reporter who covered Occupy, December 29, 2014.

87  Telephone interview with a legal observer, June 12, 2013.

88  Matt Sledge, "Occupy Protesters Reach Major Settlement over 2012 Arrests," *Huffington Post*, June 10, 2014, http://www.huffingtonpost.com; Stecklow and Thompson, "New Year's Day Demonstration, Arrests, and Settlement."

89  Personal interview with an Occupy activist, June 12, 2014a. Names used for interviewees are pseudonyms.

90  Personal interview with an Occupy activist, June 12, 2014c.

91  Personal interview with an Occupy activist, June 12, 2014c.

92  Telephone interview with an Occupy activist, June 25, 2014.

93  Personal interview with an Occupy activist, September 13, 2014.

94  Personal interview with an Occupy activist, June 12, 2014a.

95  Ryan Devereaux, "Occupy Wall Street Demonstrators March to Protest against Police Violence," *The Guardian*, March 24, 2012, https://www.theguardian.com.

96  *Report to the Seattle City Council WTO Accountability Committee*, 21.

97  Telephone interview with an Occupy activist, July 23, 2014; Devereaux, "Occupy Wall Street Demonstrators March to Protest against Police Violence"; Colin Moynihan, "Arrests at Occupy Wall Street Rally," *New York Times*, March 24, 2012, http://www.nytimes.com.

98  Schneider, *Thank You, Anarchy*, 148–50; personal interview with an Occupy activist, June 13, 2014.

99  Adrian Chen, "NYPD Raids Activists' Homes before May Day Protests," *Gawker*, April 30, 2012, http://gawker.com.

100  Schrader v. City of New York, U.S.D.C. S.D.N.Y. 13 Civ. 1995, "Complaint" (March 26, 2013), 10–12.

101  NYPD Shield, "Occupy Wall Street—General Strike," Event Advisory Bulletin, April 29, 2012, http://privacysos.org/sites/all/files/maydayNYPD.pdf. Emphasis in original.

102  Andy Newman and Colin Moynihan, "At May Day Demonstrations, Traffic Jams and Arrests," *New York Times*, May 1, 2012, http://www.nytimes.com.

103  Personal interview with an Occupy activist, June 13, 2014.

104 Personal interview with two Occupy activists, July 27, 2013. Video of a portion of the interaction with Hipster Cop is posted to YouTube: OccupySteph, "Hipster Cop Hates Music," YouTube, May 1, 2012, https://www.youtube.com/watch?v=XxA79rsq1JM. Hipster Cop has since retired: Rebecca Fishbein, "Thanks for the Memories, Hipster Cop," *Gothamist*, February 23, 2017, http://gothamist.com.

105 Personal interview with two Occupy activists, July 27, 2013.

106 We also saw how New York City administers its permit process for political purposes with the denial of Central Park's Great Lawn to the National Council of Arab Americans and Act Now to Stop War and End Racism in chapter 1 (though the city paid significant damages to the affected groups years later). Likewise, Mayor Giuliani's use of permits for gatherings in front of City Hall facilitated the spectacle of major sport team championships and marginalized fair housing advocates' criticisms of his administration (Miller, *Designs on the Public*, chap. 1). These examples show how New York's permitting process is administered to facilitate post-Fordist spectacle while repressing speech and assemblies antagonistic to the neoliberal state formation.

107 Vitale, "From Negotiated Management to Command," 287.

108 Colin Moynihan, "185 Arrested on Occupy Wall St. Anniversary," *New York Times*, September 17, 2012, updated September 18, 2012, http://www.nytimes.com.

109 Gvloanguy, "'Arrest the Bankers!' Sights and Sounds of Occupy Wall Street— September 17, 2012," YouTube, September 17, 2012, https://www.youtube.com/watch?v=jElQ6gUlSsA.

110 Christina Boyle et al., "Financial District in Chaos on 'Occupy Wall Street' Anniversary," *New York Daily News*, September 18, 2012, http://nydailynews.com. According to Moynihan, "185 Arrested on Occupy Wall St. Anniversary," OWS "did not appear to cause much disruption on Wall Street."

111 Moynihan, "185 Arrested on Occupy Wall St. Anniversary." The NYPD crackdown on credentialed journalists covering OWS is also described by Michael Greenberg, "New York: The Police and the Protesters," *New York Review of Books*, October 11, 2012, 58–61, at 59. A journalist covering the one-year anniversary of OWS was standing alone on a sidewalk approximately twenty feet from a protest in a courtyard when a white shirt pointed at him. He was immediately tackled to the ground and his arm violently stretched across his back, causing him injury for which he was forced to seek medical treatment. Despite screaming that he was a reporter, he was taken into custody and processed. His charges were later dismissed, and he sued the city subsequently for false arrest, an illegal search, excessive force, and the violation of his First Amendment rights. Faraone v. City of New York, U.S.D.C. S.D.N.Y. 13 Civ. 9074, "Opinion and Order" (March 21, 2016).

112 Packard v. City of New York, "Complaint" (September 10, 2015), 6, 30; Colin Moynihan, "Suit Says Police Violated Occupy Protesters' Constitutional Rights," *New York Times*, September 14, 2015, A17.

113 Personal interview with four Occupy activists, January 20, 2013.

114 Personal interview with two Occupy activists, July 27, 2013.

115 Personal interview with two Occupy activists, July 27, 2013.

116 Telephone interview with an Occupy activist, July 23, 2014. This activist's personal trajectory complements aspects of Jennifer Earl's research on the effects of arrest at the 2004 RNC upon future willingness to protest. While Earl finds many were deterred or "selectively deterred" from future protest (though she acknowledges these effects were largely due to the extrajudicial aspects of arrest, such as the length and conditions of detention during arrest processing), some were radicalized. For those radicalized, Earl suggests the significance of their prior involvement with activist organizations or movements as preparation for their arrest experience. The OWS activist I interviewed July 23, 2014, began his involvement with OWS fearful of arrest ("the idea of it was terrifying to me"). His work in jail and court support for OWS protesters, however, prepared him to engage in an action involving nonviolent civil disobedience at a later point in the Occupy movement. His arrest did not deter later political activity, though he finds the idea of getting arrested for protesting "still terrifying . . . the police are very scary." For him, police behavior in their interactions with protesters was more of a deterrent to First Amendment activity than the arrest and receiving an Adjournment in Contemplation of Dismissal. In contrast with Earl's focus specifically on the effects of arrest, I am interested in this chapter in the effects of police behavior on protest more broadly (including policing behavior in the streets during their interactions with protesters, or after arrest, while the activist is in custody). See Earl, "Protest Arrests and Future Protest Participation."

117 A lawyer who represented arrested Occupy protesters suggested these lawyers to me for interviews because they had done the most legal observing among those who served as OWS legal observers.

118 Telephone interview with a legal observer, June 12, 2013.

119 Telephone interview with a legal observer, June 12, 2013.

120 Telephone interview with a legal observer, June 12, 2013.

121 Telephone interview with a legal observer, June 20, 2013.

122 Tomlins, "How Autonomous Is Law?"

123 Telephone interview with a legal observer, June 12, 2013.

124 Schmitt, *Legality and Legitimacy*, 32.

125 Telephone interview with a legal observer, June 12, 2013.

126 Telephone interview with a legal observer, June 12, 2013.

127 Personal interview with two Occupy activists, July 27, 2013.

128 Telephone interview with a legal observer, June 12, 2013.

129 Telephone interview with a legal observer, June 12, 2013.

130 Telephone interview with a legal observer, June 20, 2013. Sally also described the NYPD's "excessive show of force" using "four or five police to arrest someone walking in the streets." Telephone interview with a legal observer, June 12, 2013.

131  Telephone interview with a legal observer, June 12, 2013. Policing scholars have pointed to evidence that "surplus stops" and "surplus force" in particular precincts even outside the protest policing context may contribute to civic disengagement: Lerman and Weaver, "Staying Out of Sight?"

132  Some of Earl's interviewees also expressed anger regarding their arrests by the NYPD, and she considers its effect under the subheading of "deterrence." Earl, "Protest Arrests and Future Protest Participation," 160. The anger I am documenting here arises from witnessing the NYPD's treatment of protesters in the streets. In a similar vein, Lerman and Weaver find that civic disengagement is not limited to the person who directly experienced the surplus stop or surplus use of force, but appears to extend to the neighborhood in which the encounter occurred. Lerman and Weaver, "Staying Out of Sight?," 205–6

133  Telephone interview with a legal observer, June 12, 2013.

134  Personal interview with four Occupy activists, January 20, 2013.

135  Telephone interview with a legal observer, June 20, 2013.

136  Personal interview with an Occupy activist, June 13, 2014.

137  Floyd v. City of New York, U.S.D.C. S.D.N.Y. 08 Civ. 1034, "Opinion and Order" (August 12, 2013), 7, 34.

138  Floyd v. City of New York, 74.

139  Floyd v. City of New York, 6–7, 33–34.

140  Floyd v. City of New York, 72–73, 76.

141  Michael Greenberg, "The Problem of the New York Police," *New York Review of Books*, October 25, 2012, http://www.nybooks.com.

142  Colin Moynihan, "Wall Street Protesters Complain of Police Surveillance," *New York Times*, March 11, 2012, http://www.nytimes.com.

143  "Occupy's Undercover Cop: 'Shady,' Ubiquitous, and Willing to Get Arrested," *Gothamist*, October 10, 2013, http://gothamist.com.

144  Adrian Chen, "NYPD Raids Activists' Homes before May Day Protests," *Gawker*, April 30, 2012, http://gawker.com.

145  Schrader v. City of New York, "Complaint," 10–15.

146  Personal interview with an Occupy activist, June 13, 2014.

147  Telephone interview with an Occupy activist, June 25, 2014.

148  Personal interview with an Occupy activist, June 13, 2014.

149  Moynihan, "Wall Street Protesters Complain of Police Surveillance."

150  Moynihan, "Wall Street Protesters Complain of Police Surveillance."

151  John Del Signore, "3 Occupy Wall Street Protesters Win $50K Settlement over 'Thought Crime' Arrest," *Gothamist*, November 9, 2012, http://gothamist.com.

152  Del Signore, "3 Occupy Wall Street Protesters Win $50K Settlement."

153  Telephone interview with an Occupy activist, June 25, 2014; personal interview with an Occupy activist, September 13, 2014; personal interview with an Occupy activist, June 13, 2014.

154  Faraone v. City of New York, U.S.D.C. S.D.N.Y. 13 Civ. 9074, "Complaint" (December 23, 2013), 5; Faraone v. City of New York, 13 Civ. 9074, "Opinion and Order" (March 21, 2016), 5.

155  Faraone v. City of New York, "Opinion and Order," 5.

156  Personal interview with an Occupy activist, September 13, 2014.

157  Personal interview with an Occupy activist, September 13, 2014.

158  Marom v. City of New York, U.S.D.C. S.D.N.Y. 15 Civ. 2017, "Complaint" (March 17, 2015); Marom v. City of New York, U.S.D.C. S.D.N.Y. 15 Civ. 2017, "First Amended Complaint" (abbreviated hereafter as "FAC") (July 21, 2015); Marom v. City of New York, U.S.D.C. S.D.N.Y. 15 Civ. 2017, 2016 U.S. Dist. LEXIS 28466, "Memorandum and Order" (March 7, 2016); Marom v. City of New York, 15 Civ. 2017, "Memorandum and Order on Reconsideration" (July 29, 2016).

159  Marom v. City of New York, 2016 U.S. Dist. LEXIS 28466, "Memorandum and Order," *18–21.

160  Taibbi, *I Can't Breathe*, 104–5.

161  Marom v. City of New York, FAC, 29–31.

162  Marom v. City of New York, "Memorandum and Order," *21–22.

163  Marom v. City of New York, "Memorandum and Order," *22–23.

164  Marom v. City of New York, FAC, 31–32; Marom v. City of New York, "Memorandum and Order," *22.

165  Personal interview with a lawyer who defends protesters, February 23, 2013; personal interview with a lawyer who defends protesters, April 27, 2013.

166  Marom v. City of New York, FAC, 6, 10; Mandel v. City of New York, 02 Civ. 1234, "Memorandum and Order" (October 17, 2006), 2–6.

167  Raymond Kelly, *Criminal Justice Bureau: Republican National Convention Mass Arrest Plan* (abbreviated hereafter as RNC Mass Arrest Plan), August 5, 2004, https://www.nyclu.org/en/policing-protest-nypds-republican-national -convention-documents (document on file with author); Patrick Devlin, Memo from Commanding Officer, Criminal Justice Bureau, to RNC Coordinator, "Monthly Committee Report for the NYPD Mass Arrest/Prisoner Processing Sub-committee," May 4, 2004, 1 (stating a no-summons policy for the RNC), https://www.nyclu.org/en/policing-protest-nypds-republican-national -convention-documents (memo on file with the author); personal interview with a lawyer who defends protesters, February 23, 2013; personal interview with a lawyer who defends protesters, April 27, 2013.

168  Personal interview with a lawyer who defends protesters, February 23, 2013; personal interview with a lawyer who defends protesters, April 27, 2013.

169  Personal interview with a lawyer who defends protesters, April 27, 2013. See also Marom v. City of New York, FAC, 16–17, 23–25.

170  Caravalho v. City of New York, U.S.D.C. S.D.N.Y. 13 Civ. 4174, "Complaint" (June 17, 2013) (recaptioned Guest v. City of New York); Caravalho v. City of New York, U.S.D.C. S.D.N.Y. 13 Civ. 4174, 2016 U.S. Dist. LEXIS 44280, "Memorandum and Order" (March 31, 2016).

171  Caravalho v. City of New York, "Memorandum and Order," *14–24.

172  Caravalho v. City of New York, "Complaint."

173  Caravalho v. City of New York, "Complaint," 9.

174 Caravalho v. City of New York, "Complaint," 8–12.

175 Caravalho v. City of New York, "Complaint."

176 Caravalho v. City of New York, "Memorandum and Order," *29–37. Only one plaintiff, whom NYPD officers carried onto an MTA bus by knocking his head against each step and seat they carried him up or past, had his excessive force claim sustained at summary judgment because one of the officers "escorting" him through the bus could be identified (at *37–41).

177 Marom v. City of New York, FAC.

178 Marom v. City of New York, "Memorandum and Order"; Marom v. City of New York, "Memorandum and Order on Reconsideration."

179 Marom v. City of New York, "Memorandum and Order," *23–26; Marom v. City of New York, "Memorandum and Order on Reconsideration," 8–10.

180 Marom v. City of New York, "Memorandum and Order," *69–79.

181 Dinler v. City of New York, U.S.D.C. S.D.N.Y. 04 Civ. 7921, "Opinion and Order" (September 30, 2012), 24.

182 Dinler v. City of New York, 26–27.

183 Dinler v. City of New York, 26.

184 Balbus, *Dialectics of Legal Repression.* As a point of comparison, when Philadelphia hosted the 2000 RNC, it used excessive bail to keep activists off the streets during the RNC. See Hermes, *Crashing the Party.* The NYPD's innovation for the 2004 RNC was to extend the length of time spent processing the arrest by utilizing a MAPC, deciding to fingerprint all RNC arrestees, and choosing a MAPC location that lacked fingerprinting capacity.

185 Personal interview with a lawyer who defends protesters, April 27, 2013.

186 Depew v. New York, U.S.D.C. S.D.N.Y. 15 Civ. 3821, "Complaint" (May 18, 2015), par. 93–104. See also Packard v. City of New York, 15 Civ. 7130, "Complaint" (September 10, 2015); and Marom v. City of New York, FAC, SAC.

187 Depew v. City of New York, U.S.D.C. S.D.N.Y. 15 Civ. 3821, "Order" (December 13, 2016), 15.

188 Schmitt, *Concept of the Political,* discusses how the state must decide upon the "domestic enemy" for "internal peace" (46) and castigates liberalism's failures (from his conservative or fascistic perspective) in this regard (23, 61, 70–71).

189 This incident chimes with the case of an OWS livestreamer who was "brutalized" by a then–NYPD deputy inspector (later promoted to full chief) with subordinate officers cheering, "Kick his ass, Tom!" Boss v. City of New York, U.S.D.C. S.D.N.Y. 12 Civ. 8728, cited in Depew v. City of New York, "Complaint," 11.

190 Brown, *Undoing the Demos,* 150, emphasis in original.

191 Habermas, *Legitimation Crisis.*

192 Offe, *Contradictions of the Welfare State.*

193 On democratic demands overloading the state, see Huntington, " United States."

194 Streek, *Delayed Crisis of Democratic Capitalism.*

195 On the changed organizational landscape of the state, see Hacker and Pierson, *Winner-Take-All Politics.*

Chapter Four. Violent Appearances and Neoliberalism's Disintegrated Political Subjects

An early version of part of chapter 4 was published as "Neoliberalism and Violent Appearances," in *Capital at the Brink: Overcoming the Destructive Legacies of Neoliberalism*, edited by Jeffrey Di Leo and Uppinder Mehan (Open Humanities Press, 2014).

1 Brown, *Undoing the Demos*, 63, 66, 68, 150, emphasis in original.
2 Epp, *Making Rights Real*, 25.
3 Epp, *Making Rights Real*, 50, 72–76.
4 Epp, *Making Rights Real*, 14.
5 Epp, *Making Rights Real*, 17, 70, 84.
6 Epp, *Making Rights Real*, 60–68.
7 Epp, *Making Rights Real*, 77–80.
8 Epp, *Making Rights Real*, 86–87.
9 Epp, *Making Rights Real*, 226, citations omitted.
10 Epp, *Making Rights Real*, 227, citation omitted.
11 Epp, *Making Rights Real*, 132.
12 Epp, *Making Rights Real*, 132.
13 Epp, *Making Rights Real*, 97–98.
14 Epp, *Making Rights Real*, 97–98.
15 Epp, *Making Rights Real*, 117–28.
16 For instance, attention to departmental reputation as a factor leading to processes to reduce the likelihood of legal liability could be driven more by a concern for maintaining an urban brand and its assessment by bond-rating agencies rather than the value of norms like due process or human dignity.
17 Foucault, *Discipline and Punish*.
18 Foucault, *Discipline and Punish*, 205 (the panoptic prison is premised on a diagram of power).
19 I am adjusting George Herbert Mead slightly here. Mead, *Mind, Self, and Society*. See also Elias, *Civilizing Process*. On the spread of disciplinary logics beyond enclosed institutions, see Foucault, *Discipline and Punish*, 211–12.
20 Foucault, *Discipline and Punish*, 16.
21 Foucault, *Discipline and Punish*, 16.
22 Foucault, *Discipline and Punish*, 233.
23 Foucault, *Discipline and Punish*, 135–37.
24 Foucault, *Discipline and Punish*, 170.
25 Foucault, *Discipline and Punish*, 161–62, 166, 174, 181.
26 Foucault, *Discipline and Punish*, 179–80, quotation removed.
27 Foucault, *Discipline and Punish*, 190–91.
28 Foucault, *Discipline and Punish*, 183.
29 Foucault, *Discipline and Punish*, 242, 183–84, 193, 254, 277.
30 Foucault, *Discipline and Punish*, 146.
31 Foucault, *Discipline and Punish*, 222.
32 Foucault, *Discipline and Punish*, 252–53.
33 Foucault, *Discipline and Punish*, 146, 169, 222.

34 Foucault, *Discipline and Punish*, 162.

35 Foucault, *Discipline and Punish*, 90, 184.

36 Foucault, "On the Genealogy of Ethics," 272.

37 Foucault, "On the Genealogy of Ethics," 272–73.

38 Foucault, "Ethics of the Concern," 288.

39 Foucault, "On the Genealogy of Ethics," 254.

40 Dean and Villadsen, *State Phobia and Civil Society*; Zamora and Behrent, *Foucault and Neoliberalism*.

41 Foucault, *Discipline and Punish*, 227.

42 Virno, *Multitude*, 107– 109.

43 Epp, *Making Rights Real*, 46–47, 50–51.

44 McPhail, Schweingruber, and McCarthy, "Policing Protest," 54–57.

45 Joseph Loftus, "Riot Panel to Ignore Costs in Making Proposals," *New York Times*, December 19, 1967, 37.

46 John Herbers, "Riot Study Is Said to Express Alarm," *New York Times*, February 18, 1968, 63.

47 National Advisory Commission on Civil Disorders, *Report of the National Commission*, 411.

48 National Advisory Commission on Civil Disorders, *Report of the National Commission*, 413.

49 Skolnick, *Politics of Protest*, 261–62.

50 Morris, *Origins of the Civil Rights*, 270–71; King, "Behind the Selma March," 127. Passavant, "Neoliberalism and Violent Appearances," 42–46, provides a more extended discussion.

51 Balibar, *Philosophy of Marx*, 84; Rose, "Death of the Social?," 325–56.

52 Hardt and Negri, *Labor of Dionysus*, 261; Hardt and Negri, *Empire*, 328. For a discussion, see Passavant, "Multitude," 1473–81.

53 Foucault, *Discipline and Punish*, 179 (prison as correctional), 205 (the panoptic prison is premised on a diagram of power).

54 National Advisory Commission on Civil Disorders, *Report of the National Advisory Commission*, appendix C. A portion of President Johnson's speech also serves as the report's epigraph.

55 Garland, *Culture of Control*, chap. 3. Garland also refers to this model as "penal-welfarism" (chap. 2).

56 Hardt and Negri, *Empire*, 329; Deleuze, "Postscript on the Societies."

57 Deleuze, "Postscript on the Societies," 5, 7.

58 Hardt and Negri, *Empire*, sections 3.2–3.4.

59 Bauman, *Globalization*, 112. See also Amin, *Post-Fordism*.

60 Deleuze, "Postscript on the Societies," 6, highlights the significance of marketing for societies of control.

61 Garland, *Culture of Control*, 72–73.

62 The Kerner Commission's report was expectantly awaited, received serious coverage in the press and on television, and became a best seller, and its famous sentence about the United States becoming two societies, black, white,

"separate and unequal," was the *New York Times* quote of the day on March 1, 1968, 39. Henry Raymont, "Riot Report Book Big Best Seller," *New York Times*, March 14, 1968, 49. Criticism that the Johnson administration was not moving fast enough to implement the report's recommendations was bipartisan: Richard Madden, "3 in Senate Charge Johnson with Inaction on Riots," *New York Times*, March 14, 1968, 37. The *New York Times* buried criticisms of the report by Georgia's segregationist governor, Lester Maddox: "Maddox Scores Riot Report as Incitement to Disorder," *New York Times*, March 3, 1968, 71. Nixon's response, however, was covered on the front page: Robert Semple Jr., "Nixon Scores Panel for 'Undue' Stress on White Racism," *New York Times*, March 7, 1968, 1. Perlstein, *Nixonland*, 240–41, discusses Nixon's response.

63  Semple, "Nixon Scores Panel," 1.

64  The profound shift in political culture that occurred, between President Johnson's legislative victories in 1964–65 and the 1968 election, is also described in Perlstein, *Nixonland*. Exemplifying the conflation of protests, riots, and crime, see Richard Nixon, "Address Accepting the Presidential Nomination at the Republican National Convention in Miami Beach, Florida," August 8, 1968, American Presidency Project, https://www.presidency.ucsb.edu/ws/?pid=25968. The 1968 presidential election's corrosive effects on political culture were observed even prior to Election Day: see "Rising Voice of the Right," *Time*, September 13, 1968, 24; "Republicans: The Politics of Safety," *Time*, September 13, 1968, 27.

65  Garland, *Culture of Control*, 61, 63, 69. Although Garland does not point to the particular expressions of crisis that I do, his representation of the collapse of support for penal modernism resonates with the sense of trauma produced when crises cause settled values, and the ways of life built around such values, to collapse. Garland discusses changes in the ecology of everyday life that undermined the social solidarity penal modernism presupposes. The politicization of these changes, according to Garland, produced a dramatic change in the U.S. incarceration rate and in policing. Though his discussion is rich and fascinating, why these dramatic changes occurred precisely when they did remains an open question, and my discussion of the crises of the late 1960s and 1970s may help flesh out a better answer to this question.

66  Garland, *Culture of Control*, appendix, fig. 3. The rise in incarceration rates is noticeable in the 1970s and becomes exponential in the 1980s and 1990s.

67  Beckett, *Making Crime Pay*, 89; Reiter, *23/7*, 39–40.

68  Scheingold, "Constructing the New Political Criminology"; Feeley and Simon, "New Penology."

69  Deleuze, "Postscript on the Societies," 7; Simon, *Poor Discipline*.

70  Reiter, *23/7*.

71  Reiter, *23/7*, chap. 2.

72  Reiter, *23/7*, 41–53.

73  Reiter, *23/7*, 52, 54.

74  Reiter, 23/7, 102, 91, 52.

75  Reiter, 23/7, 138.

76  Reiter, 23/7, 57.

77  Reiter, 23/7, 21–22. On gladiator fights in the California prison system, see also Parenti, *Lockdown America*, 205.

78  Reiter, 23/7, 131.

79  Reiter, 23/7, 158.

80  Reiter, 23/7, 181.

81  Reiter, 23/7, 163–65.

82  Reiter and Coutin, "Crossing Borders and Criminalizing Identity."

83  Reiter, 23/7, chap. 7.

84  Reiter, 23/7, 25–26.

85  Fisher, *Capitalist Realism*; Berardi, *Soul at Work*.

86  George Kelling and James Q. Wilson, "Broken Windows," *The Atlantic*, March 1982, http://www.theatlantic.com.

87  Kelling and Wilson, "Broken Windows."

88  Kelling and Coles, *Fixing Broken Windows*.

89  Kelling and Coles, *Fixing Broken Windows*, chap. 2.

90  Kelling and Coles, *Fixing Broken Windows*. See also Wilson, *Thinking about Crime*, xv esp.

91  Shearing and Stenning, "Private Security," 494–97.

92  Shearing and Stenning, "Private Security," 501.

93  Bayley and Shearing, "Future of Policing."

94  Bayley and Shearing, "Future of Policing," 593.

95  See also Bayley and Shearing, "New Structure of Policing."

96  Floyd v. City of New York, U.S.D.C. S.D.N.Y. 08 Civ. 01034, "Opinion and Order" (August 12, 2013), 6–11.

97  Floyd v. City of New York, 66, emphasis in original.

98  Floyd v. City of New York, 64.

99  Floyd v. City of New York, 91, emphasis in original.

100 Beckett and Herbert, *Banished*, 79.

101 Beckett and Herbert, *Banished*, 73, 67.

102 Beckett and Herbert, *Banished*, chap. 2.

103 Beckett and Herbert, *Banished*, 96.

104 Beckett and Herbert, *Banished*, 98.

105 Beckett and Herbert, *Banished*, 67.

106 Beckett and Herbert, *Banished*, chap. 5.

107 Beckett and Herbert, *Banished*, chap. 5.

108 Passavant, "Strong Neo-liberal State."

109 Passavant, "Strong Neo-liberal State"; Deleuze, "Postscript on Societies," discusses how the proliferation of control technologies renders subjects as "dividuals" (5) and as "man in debt" (6). Brayne, "Big Data Surveillance," provides a good update of the developments traced in Passavant, "Strong Neo-liberal State." She discusses the Los Angeles Police Department's use of the

data aggregation platform Palantir at length. Palantir's founder, Peter Thiel, is cofounder of PayPal and a prominent supporter of Donald Trump. See Ellen Mitchell, "How Silicon Valley's Palantir Wired Washington," *Politico*, August 14, 2016, https://www.politico.com.

110 Passavant, "Strong Neo-liberal State."
111 Brayne, "Big Data Surveillance," 991.
112 Passavant, "Strong Neo-liberal State."
113 Brayne, "Big Data Surveillance," 1003.
114 Passavant, "Strong Neo-liberal State."
115 Joseph Goulden, "The Cops Hit the Jackpot," *The Nation* 211 (November 23, 1970), 528–59.
116 Noakes and Gillham, "Aspects of the 'New Penology,'" 101.
117 Noakes and Gillham, "Aspects of the 'New Penology.'" See also McCarthy and McPhail, "Institutionalization of Protest," 102–3.
118 George Joseph, "How Police Are Watching You on Social Media," *CityLab*, December 14, 2016, https://www.citylab.com. See also Jonah Engel Bromwich, Daniel Victor, and Mike Isaac, "Police Use Surveillance Tool to Scan Social Media, A.C.L.U. Says," *New York Times*, October 11, 2016, https://www.nytimes.com.
119 Joseph, "How Police Are Watching You on Social Media."
120 Michael Cabanatuan, "BART Admits Halting Cell Service to Stop Protests," *San Francisco Gate*, August 12, 2011, https://www.sfgate.com. For a discussion, see Community Oriented Policing Services and Police Executive Research Forum, *Social Media and Tactical Considerations for Law Enforcement*. Chicago #BlackLivesMatter protesters experienced disruptions to their cell phone service, which appears to be due to Chicago Police Department surveillance efforts. See George Joseph, "Cellphone Spy Tools Have Flooded Local Police Departments," *CityLab*, February 7, 2017, https://www.citylab.com.
121 George Joseph, "Inauguration Protesters Targeted for Facebook Searches," *CityLab*, February 3, 2017, https://www.citylab.com.
122 Bl(a)ck Tea Society v. City of Boston, 378 F. 3d 8 (July 30, 2004), 14.
123 Dean, *Democracy and Other Neoliberal Fantasies*, chap. 1.
124 The framework provided here helps contextualize Epp's later work in relation to *Making Rights Real*. See Epp, Maynard-Moody, and Haider-Markel, *Pulled Over*.
125 Jodi Dean has discussed communicative capitalism at length in several important works: Dean, "Networked Empire"; Dean, *Democracy and Other Neoliberal Fantasies*; Dean, *Blog Theory*. See also Passavant, "Yoo's Law, Sovereignty and Whatever"; Passavant, "Neoliberalism and Violent Appearances," 36–42.
126 Marazzi, *Capital and Affects*, 31.
127 Pariser, *Filter Bubble*, 70–71.
128 Dean, *Aliens in America*, is an initial exploration of this problem.
129 "Shepard Smith Tours the Fox News Deck," Fox News Channel, October 7, 2013, http://video.foxnews.com/v/2727500025001/?#sp=show-clips. Smith

left Fox in the fall of 2019: Michael Grynbaum, "Shepard Smith, Fox New Anchor, Abruptly Departs from Network," *New York Times*, October 11, 2019, https://nytimes.com.

130 Hardt, "Withering of Civil Society," 32.

131 Hardt, "Withering of Civil Society," citation removed.

132 Agamben, *Coming Community*, 1–2.

133 Agamben, *Coming Community*, 83.

134 Agamben, *Means without End*, 58–59.

135 Agamben, *Coming Community*, 82–83, 87.

136 See "Internet Meme," Wikipedia, accessed August 8, 2017, https://en .wikipedia.org/wiki/Internet_meme.

137 "Kim Kardashian's Awkward Photoshoot Is Now a Viral Meme; These Will Leave You ROFL-ing," Trends Desk, *Indian Express*, August 8, 2018, https:// indianexpress.com.

138 "Casually Pepper Spray Everything Cop," Know Your Meme, accessed August 8, 2018, https://knowyourmeme.com/memes/casually-pepper-spray -everything-cop.

139 Crouch, *Post-Democracy*, 26, 37–38.

140 Dean, *Blog Theory*, chap. 3.

141 Žižek, *Plague of Fantasies*, 26, 63, 107, 120.

142 Žižek, "From Desire to Drive."

143 Dean, *Democracy and Other Neoliberal Fantasies*, 63–66; Dean, *Blog Theory*, 5.

144 "Rep. Wilson Yells 'You Lie,' to Obama during Speech," CNN Politics, September 10, 2009, http://www.cnn.com/2009/POLITICS/09/09/joe.wilson/; Byron Wolf, "Read This: How Trump Defended Criticism of Judge for Being 'Mexican,'" CNN, April 20, 2017, https://www.cnn.com/2017/04/20/politics /donald-trump-gonzalo-curiel-jake-tapper-transcript/index.html. Symptomatically, in the opening paragraph prior to the transcript of Jake Tapper's interview with Trump, the article has a typo, referring to the judge being "partial," rather than being "impartial."

145 Dean, *Blog Theory*, 76–77.

146 Perlstein, *Nixonland*, 240–41.

147 Semple, "Nixon Scores Panel," 1.

148 Perlstein, *Nixonland*, 68.

149 Nixon, "Address Accepting the Presidential Nomination."

150 Campbell, Sahid, and Stang, *Law and Order Reconsidered*, chap. 4.

151 Žižek, *Tarrying with the Negative*, 201–7.

152 This sheds light upon how Fox Network's Tucker Carlson continues to complain about a "liberal elite" as a "ruling class." See Amanda Marcotte, "Tucker Carlson Claims There Is No Such Thing as White Nationalism. His Show's Obsessive Racism Suggests Otherwise," *Salon*, August 15, 2018, https://www.salon.com. I do not mean to imply that only conservatives or Republicans have affective political attachments, but to show how particular affective tendencies have been incited, captured, and given political

direction. Emerging scholarship suggests that affective attachment and motivation is an increasingly significant attribute of contemporary electoral politics in the United States. Moreover, some of these particular affective characteristics in the task force's discussion of the Forgotten Man are quite prominent among liberals or the left in contemporary American politics, such as being distrustful of authorities and being disinclined to believe or trust. This further supports the argument pointing to a decline in the symbolic order and symbolic efficiency. On affect in politics, see Thomas Edsall, "Which Side Are You On?," editorial, *New York Times*, May 10, 2018, https://www.nytimes.com. Edsall's essay is informed by recent scholarly work, including Pierce, Rogers, and Snyder, "Losing Hurts" (happiness impact on those who identify as Republicans of the Republican loss of the 2012 presidential election was greater than the happiness impact of the Newtown killings of schoolchildren on parents or the Boston Marathon bombing on Boston residents); Huddy, Mason, and Aarøe, "Expressive Partisanship" (discussing the role of expressive political partisanship as driving political involvement).

153 Žižek, "From Desire to Drive."

154 Salecl, "Satisfaction of Drives."

155 Salecl, "Satisfaction of Drives."

156 Salecl, "Satisfaction of Drives," 106; Žižek, "Desire: Drive = Truth."

157 Dean, "Real Internet," 14.

158 Perlstein, *Nixonland*, chap. 5, includes illustrative instances.

159 Dean, "Real Internet," 15.

160 Dean, "Real Internet," 14.

161 Žižek, "Desire: Drive = Truth," 149.

162 Marcus, *Hating Breitbart*.

163 On contributions, see Dean, *Democracy and Other Neoliberal Fantasies*, 26–28.

164 Hermes, *Crashing the Party*, 222. These numbers understate the settlements because they do not include other elements that may be included in a settlement, such as First Amendment training or conditions placed on policing and detentions. Also, because of the length of time civil litigation requires, other settlements may have occurred since the publication of Hermes's book (or settlements other than the most prominent civil rights case may not be included in the financial figures: for instance, the 2004 RNC sum does not include the settlement regarding New York City's illegitimate denial of access to Central Park for a major planned demonstration).

165 "Know Your Meme: Pepper Spray Cop," Know Your Meme, accessed September 17, 2018, https://knowyourmeme.com/memes/casually-pepper-spray -everything-cop.

166 USLAWdotcom, "NYPD Police Pepper Spray Occupy Wall Street Protesters (Anthony Balogna) [sic]," YouTube, September 24, 2011, https://www.youtube .com/watch?v=TZ05rWxIpig.

167 #OccupyWallStreet, "Peaceful Female Protesters Penned in the Street and Maced!-," YouTube, September 24, 2011, https://www.youtube.com/watch?v=moD2JnGTToA.

168 USLAWdotcom, "NYPD Police Pepper Spray Occupy Wall Street Protesters." All further references to comments from this thread are from this source. Quotes are not corrected, and I have refrained from numerous insertions of *sic* where spelling or grammar is in error.

169 Agamben, *Means without End*, 57–60.

170 "Occupy Portland: How Photojournalist Randy L. Rasmussen Captured That Image," *The Oregonian*, November 18, 2011, http://www.oregonlive.com/multimedia/index.ssf/2011/11/occupy_portland_how_photojourn.html. The original article—but only the first page of comments—is archived. See https://web.archive.org/web/20111123005911/oregonlive.com/multimedia/index.ssf/2011/11/occupy_portland_how_photojourn.html.

171 Other comments on the video of Bologna pepper spraying the Occupy women exhibit communicative cross-fertilization that recalls the Fox News Deck. For example, several echo then–Fox News personality Megyn Kelly who, appearing on Bill O'Reilly's show to discuss the Pike pepper spraying incident, downplayed its significance by calling pepper spray "a food product, essentially." The comment went viral as a meme (the Megyn Kelly "Essentially" meme). Other comments reiterate rhetoric from the *New York Post*'s consistently disparaging coverage of Occupy. Cf. "Time to Throw the Bums Out," editorial, *New York Post*, November 3, 2011, http://www.nypost.com.

172 Jim Dwyer, "Videos Challenge Accounts of Convention Unrest," *New York Times*, April 12, 2005, https://www.nytimes.com; Nick Pinto, "Jury Finds Occupy Wall Street Protester Innocent after Video Contradicts Police Testimony [Updated: Video]," *Village Voice*, March 1, 2013, https://www.villagevoice.com/2013/03/01/jury-finds-occupy-wall-street-protester-innocent-after-video-contradicts-police-testimony-updated-video/.

173 Mosi Secret, "Police, Too, Release Videos of Arrests on Bridge," *New York Times*, October 2, 2011, http://www.nytimes.com.

174 Thomas Graham, "After Action Report on World Economic Forum Meetings and Demonstrations," Memo from Commanding Officer, Disorder Control Unit, to Chief of Department, March 4, 2002 (report on file with author).

175 Dunn et al., *Arresting Protest*, 18; MacNamara v. City of New York, U.S.D.C. S.D.N.Y. 04 Civ. 9216, "Second Amended Complaint" (January 29, 2008), 49, 51, 53, 71; Dunn et al., *Rights and Wrongs at the RNC*, 36–43.

176 Caravalho v. City of New York, U.S.D.C. S.D.N.Y. 13 Civ. 4174, "Complaint" (June 17, 2013) (recaptioned Guest v. City of New York), 9.

177 Caravalho v. City of New York, 8–12.

178 Personal interview with an Occupy activist, September 13, 2014.

179 Bl(a)ck Tea Society v. City of Boston, 378 F. 3d 8 (July 30, 2004), 14.

180 Habermas, *Legitimation Crisis*; Offe, *Contradictions of the Welfare State*.

*Chapter Five. Political Antagonism*

An early version of part of chapter 5 was published as "I Can't Breathe: Heeding the Call of Justice," *Law Culture, and Humanities* 11, no. 3 (2015): 330–39.

1   Elahe Izadi, "'I Can't Breathe,'" *Washington Post*, December 9, 2014, https://www.washingtonpost.com. For key critical discussions of neoliberalism and black politics, see Spence, *Knocking the Hustle*; Taylor, *From #BlackLivesMatter to Black Liberation*.

2   National Advisory Commission on Civil Disorders, *Report of the National Advisory Commission*, 299. The significance of this assessment is underscored by its quotation by the Task Force on Law and Law Enforcement to the National Commission on the Causes and Prevention of Violence. Campbell, Sahid, and Stang, *Law and Order Reconsidered*, 315–16.

3   National Advisory Commission on Civil Disorders, *Report of the National Advisory Commission*, 305.

4   National Advisory Commission on Civil Disorders, *Report of the National Advisory Commission*, chap. 17.

5   Habermas, *Legitimation Crisis*; Offe, *Contradictions of the Welfare State*.

6   Phillips-Fein, *Fear City*, 183; Moody, *From Welfare State*, 47; Shefter, *Political Crisis/Fiscal Crisis*, chap. 6.

7   Fuchs, "Permanent Urban Fiscal Crisis," 63; Judd, "Promoting Tourism in US Cities"; Fainstein, *City Builders*; Eisinger, "Politics of Bread and Circuses."

8   Passavant, "Mega-Events"; Hackworth, *Neoliberal City*.

9   Huntington, "United States," 113–14; Habermas, *Legitimation Crisis*.

10  Huntington, "United States," 113–14.

11  George Kelling and James Q. Wilson, "Broken Windows," *The Atlantic*, March 1982, http://www.theatlantic.com.

12  Derrida, *Specters of Marx*.

13  On negotiated management, see McCarthy and McPhail, "Institutionalization of Protest."

14  Derrida, *Specters of Marx*, 37, 54, 61; Derrida, *Politics of Friendship*, 84.

15  Other scholars are also perceiving the hybridity of policing in the United States: Martinot, "Militarisation of the Police," 215.

16  Deleuze, "Postscript on the Societies of Control," 5.

17  National Advisory Commission on Civil Disorders, *Report of the National Advisory Commission*, 299–301.

18  National Advisory Commission on Civil Disorders, *Report of the National Advisory Commission*, 410–12.

19  National Advisory Commission on Civil Disorders, *Report of the National Advisory Commission*, chap. 17.

20  Habermas, *Legitimation Crisis*.

21  Perlstein, *Nixonland*.

22  Beckett, *Making Crime Pay*, 30–32, 40–43.

23  David Lawrence, "What's Become of 'Law and Order'?" *U.S. News and World Report*, August 5, 1963, 104.

24 Richard Nixon, "Address Accepting the Presidential Nomination at the Republican National Convention in Miami Beach, Florida," August 8, 1968, American Presidency Project, https://www.presidency.ucsb.edu/documents /address-accepting-the-presidential-nomination-the-republican-national -convention-miami.

25 Cowie, *Stayin' Alive*, 3, 11 (citation removed).

26 Blumenson and Nilsen, "Policing for Profit."

27 American Civil Liberties Union, *War Comes Home*, 24–25; Spencer Ackerman, "US Police Given Billions from Homeland Security for 'Tactical' Equipment," *The Guardian*, August 20, 2014, https://www.theguardian.com.

28 Kraska and Kappeler, "Militarizing American Police"; Chambliss, "Policing the Ghetto Underclass."

29 Beckett, *Making Crime Pay*.

30 Feeley and Simon, "New Penology"; Scheingold, "Constructing the New Political Criminology."

31 Deleuze, "Postscript on the Societies of Control."

32 Hagan, *Who Are the Criminals?*

33 Kelling and Wilson, "Broken Windows."

34 Kelling and Wilson, "Broken Windows."

35 Loïc Wacquant observes that by the end of the 1990s, California's spending on its prisons had exceeded its spending on the state's university system. Likewise, in Washington, DC, the number of students attending University of the District of Columbia had declined so significantly, and the number of inmates in its prison had increased so significantly, that their respective totals roughly reversed positions between 1980 and 1997 (in 1980, UDC had 15,340 students enrolled and there were 2,873 inmates in DC, but by 1997, the number of students enrolled at UDC had fallen to 4,729 while the number of inmates in DC had risen to 12,745). Wacquant, *Punishing the Poor*, 154, 163. Orfield and Lee, *Historic Reversals, Accelerating Resegregation*.

36 Wacquant, *Punishing the Poor*, 84–85; Wacquant, *Urban Outcasts*, 80–81.

37 Wacquant, *Punishing the Poor*, 160.

38 Floyd v. City of New York, U.S.D.C. S.D.N.Y. 08 Civ. 1034, "Opinion and Order" (August 12, 2013) (slip op.), 7.

39 Center for Constitutional Rights, "2011 NYPD Stop and Frisk Statistics," accessed January 16, 2019, https://ccrjustice.org/sites/default/files/assets/files /CCR-Stop-and-Frisk-Fact-Sheet-2011.pdf. See also *Floyd v. City of New York*, "Opinion and Order," 32–33.

40 Floyd v. City of New York, "Opinion and Order," 32.

41 Adam Serwer and Jaeah Lee, "Charts: Are NYPD's Stop-and-Frisks Violating the Constitution?," *Mother Jones*, April 29, 2013, https://www.motherjones.com.

42 Serwer and Lee, "Charts."

43 Floyd v. City of New York, "Opinion and Order," 9.

44 Floyd v. City of New York, "Opinion and Order," 9.

45 Floyd v. City of New York, "Opinion and Order," 72–81.

46 John Marzulli, Rocco Parascandola, and Thomas Tracy, "NYPD No. 3's Order to Crack Down on Selling Loose Cigarettes Led to Chokehold Death of Eric Garner," *New York Daily News*, August 7, 2014, http://www.nydailynews.com.

47 Ali Winston, "Eric Garner Death Was 'Not a Big Deal,' Police Commander Said," *New York Times*, May 16, 2019, https://www.nytimes.com.

48 U.S. Department of Justice, *Investigation of the Ferguson Police Department*, 4–5.

49 U.S. Department of Justice, *Investigation of the Ferguson Police Department*, 28.

50 U.S. Department of Justice, *Investigation of the Ferguson Police Department*, 46–48, 55–56.

51 U.S. Department of Justice, *Investigation of the Ferguson Police Department*, 56.

52 U.S. Department of Justice, *Investigation of the Ferguson Police Department*, 56.

53 Julia Lurie and Katie Rose Quandt, "How Many Ways Can the City of Ferguson Slap You with Court Fees? We Counted," *Mother Jones*, September 12, 2014, https://www.motherjones.com; Arch City Defenders, "Arch City Defenders: Municipal Court White Paper" (St. Louis: Arch City Defenders, n.d.), 25–30, accessed April 14, 2020, https://www.archcitydefenders.org/wp-content/uploads/2019/03/ArchCity-Defenders-Municipal-Courts-Whitepaper.pdf.

54 U.S. Department of Justice, *Investigation of the Ferguson Police*, 9–15.

55 U.S. Department of Justice, *Investigation of the Ferguson Police*, 71–73, 79–80.

56 On the de-democratization of the relation between the state and capital, see Streeck, *Delayed Crisis of Democratic Capitalism*, chap. 2 (especially); Kirkpatrick, "New Urban Fiscal Crisis." The use of fines to fund municipal government is strongly correlated with the percentage of a city's population that is black. See Sances and You, "Who Pays for Government?" See also Wong, *Carceral Capitalism*.

57 Nancy Fraser distinguishes expropriation from exploitation as distinct means of accumulation. See Fraser, "Expropriation and Exploitation." See also Harvey, "'New' Imperialism."

58 Amnesty International, *On the Streets of America*; Institute for Intergovernmental Research and COPS Office Critical Response Initiative, *After-Action Assessment of the Police Response*, 56 (hereafter abbreviated as IIR and COPS, *After-Action Assessment*). St. Louis County and Ferguson had received military surplus through the Pentagon's 1033 program: David Mastio and Kelsey Rupp, "Pentagon Weaponry in St. Louis County: Updated Column," *USA Today*, August 13, 2014 (updated May 20, 2015), https://www.usatoday.com.

59 Barbara Starr and Wesley Bruer, "Missouri National Guard's Term for Ferguson Protesters: 'Enemy Forces,'" CNN, April 17, 2015, https://www.cnn.com.

60 Rancière, *Dis-agreement*.

61 Robert Lewis, "NYPD Officers on the Ground in Ferguson," *WNYC News*, November 25, 2014, http://www.wnyc.org.

62 Ashley Southall, "Protesters Fill Streets across U.S. over Decision in Garner Case," *New York Times*, December 4, 2014, https://www.nytimes.com; "Marchers Stop Traffic in New York to Protest Death at Hands of Police," *Newsweek*, December 5, 2014, https://www.newsweek.com.

63 James Logue v. New York City Police Department, Index No. 153965/16, "Opinion and Order," February 6, 2017 (slip op.), 1; Nick Pinto, "Lawyers for Black Lives Matter Protestor Seek to Hold NYPD in Contempt for Stonewalling Release of Surveillance Video," *Village Voice*, July 17, 2017, https://www .villagevoice.com.

64 Logue v. NYPD, "Opinion and Order," 1–2; James Logue to Lieutenant Richard Matellino, August 9, 2018, https://docs.wixstatic.com/ugd/02d7a5_b20cc 66fbd104a05a150ab537ffaf6e2.pdf. (A link to NYPD documents and communications with the NYPD is available at M. J. Williams Law, https://www.mjw -law.com.)

65 Claire Lampen, "NYPD Ordered to Turn Over Photos, Intel from Surveillance of Black Lives Matter Protesters," *Gothamist*, January 17, 2019, http:// gothamist.com.

66 George Joseph, "Years after Protests, NYPD Retains Photos of Black Lives Matter Activists," *The Appeal*, January 17, 2019, https://theappeal.org/years -after-protests-nypd-retains-photos-of-black-lives-matter-activists/.

67 In the Matter of Millions March NYC v. New York City Police Department, Index No. 100690/17, "Petition" (May 23, 2017), 1–2.

68 Millions March NYC v. NYPD, "Petition," 4–6; Ali Winston, "Did Police Spy on Black Lives Matter Protesters? The Answer May Soon Come Out," *New York Times*, January 14, 2019, https://www.nytimes.com.

69 Millions March NYC v. NYPD, "Petition," 5.

70 Millions March NYC v. NYPD, "Petition," 4–8; Winston, "Did Police Spy?"

71 In the Matter of Abdur-Rashid v. New York City Police Department, N.Y. 3d 217, No. 19 (March 29, 2018).

72 George Joseph, "Undercover Police Have Regularly Spied on Black Lives Matter Activists in New York," *The Intercept*, August 18, 2015, https:// theintercept.com; Shawn Cohen and Kevin Fasick, "NYPD to Launch a Beefed-Up Counterterrorism Squad," *New York Post*, January 30, 2015, https:// www.nypost.com; "Commissioner Bratton Unveils Plans for New High-Tech Anti-terror Police Unit," *CBS New York*, January 29, 2015, https://newyork .cbslocal.com.

73 Joseph, "Undercover Police Have Regularly Spied on Black Lives Matter Activists"; George Joseph, "NYPD Sent Undercover Officers to Black Lives Matter Protest, Records Reveal," *The Guardian*, September 29, 2016, https:// www.theguardian.com.

74 Joseph, "Undercover Police Have Regularly Spied on Black Lives Matter Activists"; Jake Offenhartz, "Video Shows NYPD Officers Violently Arresting Black Lives Matter Activist," *Gothamist*, June 15, 2018, http://gothamist.com.

75 George Joseph, "NYPD Sent Video Teams to Record Occupy and BLM Protests over 400 times, Documents Reveal," *The Verge*, March 22, 2017, https:// www.theverge.com; Adam Johnson and Keegan Stephan, "From Abu Ghraib to Black Lives Matter: Meet the NYPD'S Most Notorious Anti-activist Cop," *Gothamist*, September 23, 2015, http://gothamist.com. Joseph, "NYPD

Sent Video Teams," describes how BLM surveillance documents show that Lombardo requested copies of NYPD videos of BLM mass arrests from the December 4, 2014, protests on May 19, 2016—an unusual request because he is with the SRG and not the Legal Bureau.

76  George Joseph, "NYPD Officers Accessed Black Lives Matter Activists' Texts, Documents Show," *The Guardian*, April 4, 2017, https://www.theguardian.com. Giacalone added, "as long as you have reasonable cause to do so," a qualification that, given its context, is unclear (if not contradictory), as he was describing how the NYPD engages in pretextual arrests of political activists to disorganize political movements.

77  Stephen Rex Brown, "NYPD Must Disclose Surveillance of Black Lives Matter Protesters," *New York Daily News*, February 8, 2017, http://www.nydailynews.com; Stephen Rex Brown, "NYPD Must Provide Videos of Black Lives Matter Activists within 30 Days after Contempt of Court Ruling," *New York Daily News*, November 29, 2017, https://www.nydailynews.com.

78  Millions March NYC v. New York City Policy [*sic*] Department, Supreme Court of the State of New York, New York County, Index No. 100690/2017, "Decision and Order" (January 11, 2019, received January 14, 2019); Winston, "Did the Police Spy?"

79  Joseph, "NYPD Officers Accessed Black Lives Matter Activists' Texts."

80  New York Police Department Freedom of Information Law Production, November 13, 2018, emails 6, 330, 18, 18, and 330 (hereafter abbreviated NYPD FOIL Production, November 13, 2018), https://www.mjw-law.com/foil-release-nypd-nov-2018.

81  New York Police Department Freedom of Information Law Production to James Logue, July 2, 2018, email 767 (hereafter abbreviated NYPD FOIL Production, July 2, 2018), https://www.mjw-law.com/foil-release-nypd-july-2018.

82  Joseph, "Years after Protests, NYPD Retains Photos of Black Lives Matter Activists."

83  NYPD FOIL Production, November 13, 2018, email 16.

84  NYPD FOIL Production, November 13, 2018, emails 242, 297, 467, 610.

85  NYPD FOIL Production, November 13, 2018, emails 306, 443.

86  NYPD FOIL Production, November 13, 2018, emails 68, 125.

87  NYPD FOIL Production, November 13, 2018, emails 68, 396.

88  NYPD FOIL Production, November 13, 2018, emails 125, 407, 413, 494, 696.

89  NYPD FOIL Production, November 13, 2018, emails 81, 140, 252, 266, 328, 348, 704, 742, 756.

90  NYPD FOIL Production, November 13, 2018, email 23.

91  NYPD FOIL Production, November 13, 2018, email 618.

92  NYPD FOIL Production, November 13, 2018, email 635.

93  NYPD FOIL Production, November 13, 2018, email 637. Similarly, on December 18, 2014, at 8:17 p.m., "Team 1" reports that Zuccotti Park is "clear" (email 707), but at 9:27 p.m., they report that fifteen to twenty people are "circling

the park" (email 716), and approximately ten minutes later report back that the "protesters [are] still inside [the] park" (email 717).

94 NYPD FOIL Production November 13, 2018, emails 57, 125, 312, 336, 358, 455, 461, 476, 487, 496, 507, 524, 722, 731 (Times Square); 453, 457 (indicates "higher ups" are "very concerned" about this site), 474, 480, 484, 494, 495, 501, 504, 505, 506, 694, 696 (Barclays Arena).

95 NYPD FOIL Production November 13, 2018, email 350.

96 Handschu v. Police Department of the City of New York, U.S.D.C. S.D.N.Y. 71 Civ. 2203, "Ruling and Order on Proposed Revised Settlement Agreement" (March 13, 2017); Handschu v. Special Services Division, U.S.D.C. S.D.N.Y. 71 Civ. 2203, "Declaration of Jethro M. Eisenstein" (March 6, 2017), Tab C, "Guidelines for Investigations Involving Political Activity," V. D. ("Terrorism Enterprise Investigation"), VII. ("Investigative Techniques"). Section V. D. 4e. of the Revised Handschu Guidelines defines the presumptive duration of a Terrorism Enterprise Investigation as "5 years." Under the New York Law of Criminal Procedure, Article 700, "Designated Offenses" for which eavesdropping and video surveillance warrants are justified include "Riot," "Criminal Anarchy," and making a threat, providing support for, or engaging in the "Crime of Terrorism" (see also New York Penal Law §240.05–§240.15 [riot, unlawful assembly, and criminal anarchy], and New York Penal Law §490.05–§490.25 [terrorism]).

97 Derrida, *Politics of Friendship*. Derrida explores the ambiguous status of the enemy in Carl Schmitt's work as a spectral idea, on the one hand, and as existential, on the other.

98 Mandal v. City of New York, U.S.D.C. S.D.N.Y. 02 Civ. 1234, "Memorandum and Order" (October 17, 2006), 1–5.

99 Colin Moynihan, "Concerns Raised over Shrill Device New York Police Used during Garner Protests," *New York Times*, December 12, 2014, https://www.nytimes.com. For a discussion of "military urbanism," see Graham, *Cities under Siege*.

100 Edrei v. Bratton, United States Court of Appeals Second Circuit, Docket No. 17-2065, "Opinion" (June 13, 2018) (slip op.), 4–5; Edrei v. City of New York, U.S.D.C. S.D.N.Y. 16 Civ. 1652, "First Amended Complaint" (FAC), (August 3, 2016), 2–4; Gideon Oliver to William Bratton, December 12, 2014, Edrei v. City of New York, U.S.D.C. S.D.N.Y. 16 Civ. 1652, "Document 21-2" (August 3, 2016), 1 (hereafter abbreviated Oliver to Bratton, December 12, 2014).

101 Oliver to Bratton, December 12, 2014, 2–3 (quoting Tom Hays, "Authorities to Turn Up the Volume for GOP Convention: A 150-Decibel Megaphone," Associated Press, August 19, 2004, in part).

102 Oliver to Bratton, December 12, 2014, 3; Moynihan, "Concerns Raised over Shrill Device"; Edrei v. City of New York, FAC, 14; Edrei v. City of New York, U.S.D.C. S.D.N.Y. 16 Civ. 1652, "Opinion" (May 31, 2017) (slip op.), 4.

103 Edrei v. City of New York, "Opinion" (May 31, 2017), 4–5.

104 Edrei v. Bratton, "Opinion" (June 13, 2018), 7.

105 Edrei v. City of New York, "Opinion" (May 31, 2017), 6.

106 Edrei v. Bratton, "Opinion" (June 13, 2018), 7–8.

107 Edrei v. Bratton, "Opinion" (June 13, 2018), 8.

108 Edrei v. City of New York, "Opinion" (May 31, 2017), 8.

109 Edrei v. Bratton, "Opinion" (June 13, 2018), 8; Edrei v. City of New York, FAC, 26.

110 Edrei v. City of New York, FAC, 6–7.

111 Edrei v. Bratton, FAC, 15; New York Police Department, Disorder Control Unit, "Briefing on the LRAD (Long Range Acoustical Device)," January, 2010, Edrei v. City of New York, U.S.D.C. S.D.N.Y. 16 Civ. 1652, "Document 21-1" (August 3, 2016), 5.

112 Edrei v. City of New York, FAC, 5–6.

113 Edrei v. Bratton, "Opinion" (June 13, 2018), 8–9.

114 Edrei v. City of New York, FAC, 14–15.

115 Wilderson, *Red, White and Black*, 4–5. In what follows, I adhere to Wilderson's capitalization of Black, White, and Human where appropriate to designate when these are being used as ontological terms.

116 Wilderson, *Red, White and Black*, 11.

117 Wilderson, *Red, White and Black*, 11.

118 Wilderson, *Red, White and Black*, 12, 18.

119 Wilderson, *Red, White and Black*, 11.

120 Wilderson, *Red, White and Black*, 19.

121 For a critique of "black exceptionalism," see Johnson, "Panthers Can't Save Us Now"; Cedric Johnson, "Black Political Life and the Blue Lives Matter Presidency," *Jacobin*, February 19, 2019, https://jacobinmag.com. For critical engagements with Afro-pessimism, see Gordon et al., "Afro Pessimism."

122 Wilderson, *Red, White and Black*, 5–6, 30–31.

123 Wilderson, *Red, White and Black*, 11, 73.

124 Wilderson, *Red, White and Black*, 58.

125 Wilderson, *Red, White and Black*, 70, 72.

126 Wilderson, "Social Death and Narrative Aporia," 135, 139.

127 Wilderson, *Red, White, and Black*, 91, 283 (emphasis in original).

128 Wilderson, *Red, White and Black*, 74.

129 Wilderson, *Red, White and Black*, 66–67.

130 Hartman and Wilderson, "Position of the Unthought," 191, 195.

131 Walsh, "Afro-pessimism and Friendship," 78–79.

132 Walsh, "Afro-pessimism and Friendship," 79. Wilderson is referring to videos of police murdering black people posted online.

133 Schmitt, *Concept of the Political*, 29, emphasis added.

134 Schmitt, *Concept of the Political*, 27, 30, emphasis added.

135 Wilderson, *Red, White and Black*, 52–53, 181–82.

136 Wilderson, *Red, White and Black*, 283.

137 Derrida, *Politics of Friendship*.

138 Rancière, *Disagreement*. For a critique of Rancière highlighting the importance of the decline of symbolic efficiency in contemporary society, see
Dean, "Politics without Politics."

139 Rancière, *Disagreement*, 16.

140 Rancière, *Disagreement*, 33.

141 Rancière, *Disagreement*, 33.

142 Rancière, *Disagreement*, 16.

143 Rancière, *Disagreement*, 10–15, 19.

144 Rancière, *Disagreement*, 13, 24–26, 29–30, 49.

145 Rancière, *Disagreement*, 30.

146 Rancière, *Disagreement*, 32.

147 Rancière, *Disagreement*, 36–39.

148 Rancière, "Comments and Responses."

149 Skolnick, *Politics of Protest*.

150 Skolnick, *Politics of Protest*, 183, quoting Baldwin, *Nobody Knows My Name*,
65–67.

151 Skolnick, *Politics of Protest*, 183–84. In a similar vein, the Kerner Commission
quotes a passage from a *Michigan Law Review* article, written by the former
commissioner of the Detroit Police Department and a federal appeals court
judge, describing how local police, when on patrol in predominantly black
areas of the city, tend to perceive "each person on the streets as a potential criminal or enemy, and all too often that attitude is reciprocated." See
National Advisory Commission on Civil Disorders, *Report of the National
Advisory Commission*, 85.

152 National Advisory Commission on Civil Disorders, *Report of the National
Advisory Commission*, 303, 299.

153 National Advisory Commission on Civil Disorders, *Report of the National
Advisory Commission*, 304–5.

154 Epp, *Making Rights Real*.

155 Floyd v. City of New York, "Opinion and Order," 145–49.

156 The Department of Justice's Report on the Baltimore Police Department,
finding the latter's zero tolerance policing practices to be racially disproportionate, documents instances where arrests are retaliation for the communication of disrespect of police—the arrests are a product of the communication of mutual enmity. See U.S. Department of Justice, *Investigation of the
Baltimore City Police*, 116–21.

157 U.S. Department of Justice, *Investigation of the Ferguson Police*, 79–81.

158 Epp, Maynard-Moody, and Haider-Markel, *Pulled Over*.

159 Garfinkel, "Conditions of Successful Degradation Ceremonies."

160 Amnesty International, *On the Streets of America*, 15.

161 Abdullah v. St. Louis, 52 F. Supp. 3d 936 (2014).

162 Amnesty International, *On the Streets of America*, 7.

163 Amnesty International, *On the Streets of America*, 10.

164 Amnesty International, *On the Streets of America*, 16.

165  Starr and Bruer, "Missouri National Guard's Term for Ferguson Protesters."

166  Benjamin Mueller and Al Baker, "2 N.Y.P.D. Officers Killed in Brooklyn Ambush; Suspect Commits Suicide," *New York Times*, December 20, 2014, https://www.nytimes.com.

167  Mueller and Baker, "2 N.Y.P.D. Officers Killed in Brooklyn Ambush"; Shawn Cohen, Kristan Conley, and Amber Jamieson, "Police Turn Their Back on de Blasio," *New York Post*, December 20, 2014, https//nypost.com.

168  Cohen, Conley, and Jamieson, "Police Turn Their Back on de Blasio."

169  Jeremy Diamond, "Blame Piles on NYC Mayor for Cop Shooting," CNN, December 21, 2014, http://edition.cnn.com.

170  Diamond, "Blame Piles on NYC Mayor for Cop Shooting."

171  Amanda Holpuch, "Police Turn Backs on de Blasio at Funeral of NYPD Officer Rafael Ramos," *The Guardian*, December 27, 2014, https://www .theguardian.com.

172  Alex Altman, "Why New York Cops Turned Their Backs on Mayor de Blasio," *Time*, December 22, 2014, http://time.com.

173  Blue Lives Matter joined Twitter using the Twitter handle @bluelivesmtr in December, 2014, https://twitter.com/bluelivesmtr?lang=en. Its Twitter homepage includes a link to its webpage, https://bluelivesmatter.blue. Blue Lives Matter also maintains a Facebook page.

174  Blue Lives Matter, "History," n.d., accessed April 27, 2019, http://archive. bluelivesmatter.blue/organization/. An edited version of this narrative can be found more easily at Christopher Berg, "Home of the Official Blue Lives Matter Organization. America's Largest Law Enforcement Support Community," June 6, 2018, accessed December 1, 2020, https://policetribune.com /about-blue-lives-matter/. On melodramatic political discourse, see Anker, *Orgies of Feeling*.

175  Blue Lives Matter, "History." One can only speculate what Blue Lives Matter is referring to with the phrase "big law enforcement media companies." Perhaps this refers to the major policing professional associations, such as the International Association of Chiefs of Police and PERF. If so, the us-versus-them relationship Blue Lives Matter constructs in opposition to the major policing professional associations may exemplify the split in policing between those committed to policing in terms of legalized accountability and order maintenance, and how the latter are a reaction against policing as law enforcement, as discussed in chapter 4.

176  Justin Wm. Moyer, "Louisiana Bill Would Make Offenses Committed against Police Hate Crimes," *Washington Post*, April 22, 2016, https://www .washingtonpost.com.

177  Ed Pilkington, "Louisiana Passes 'Blue Lives Matter' Statute for Hate Crimes against Police," *The Guardian*, May 27, 2016, https://www.theguardian.com; Natasha Lennard, "Call Congress's 'Blue Lives Matter' Bills What They Are: Another Attack on Black Lives," *The Intercept*, May 19, 2018, https:// theintercept.com. On the ambiguous significance of the enemy as specter or

as existential, see Derrida, *Politics of Friendship*. This conflation of person and public office that the Blue Lives Matter law presupposes is reminiscent of feudalism. Or it is illustrative of a weakening of the symbolic order.

178 Reinforcing this imaginary of war is the semiotic migration from policing to militarization that occurs when the Blue Lives Matter website visitor clicks the link to "Store," which is hosted by "Warrior XII" (Warrior 12). Warrior 12 is an organization claiming to be founded by those with both police and military backgrounds. It believes not only in offering "quality apparel" but also in "embracing the warrior mindset and the essence of what it means to stand on the thin blue line, serve in our military, or simply be a patriotic American." According to Warrior 12's website, all its apparel is printed in St. Louis, Missouri. Warrior XII, "About Us," accessed April 29, 2019, https://warrior12 .com/pages/about-us.

179 Kraska and Kappeler, "Militarizing American Police."

180 Kraska and Kappeler, "Militarizing American Police"; Kraska, "Militarization and Policing"; Lawson, "Trends"; Amnesty International, *On the Streets of America*, 11; Ackerman, "US Police Given Billions from Homeland Security."

181 Kraska and Kappeler, "Militarizing American Police," 6–11; Chambliss, "Policing the Ghetto Underclass."

182 Martin, "Showcasing Security" (discussing the phenomenon in Australia); Brian Bowling, "Pittsburgh to Pay Researcher Who Suffered Hearing Loss during G-20 Summit," *TribLive*, November 14, 2012, https://archive.triblive .com/news/pittsburgh-to-pay-researcher-who-suffered-hearing-loss-during-g -20-summit/.

183 Shawn Reese, "National Special Security Events" (Congressional Research Service, November 6, 2007, Order Code RS22754) (on file with author). Shawn Reese, "National Special Security Events" (Congressional Research Service, March 24, 2009, RS22754), https://fas.org/sgp/crs/natsec/RS22754 .pdf, covers much of the same ground as the 2007 report, but lacks the list of past events designated as NSSEs. The 2009 report, however, remains archived online.

184 Wilderson, *Red, White and Black*, 30, 142.

185 Passavant, "Contradictory State of Giorgio Agamben"; Passavant, "Democracy's Ruins, Democracy's Archive."

186 Derrida, *Specters of Marx*, 161.

187 Derrida, *Specters of Marx*, xvii–xx.

188 Fisher, *Ghosts of My Life*; Fisher, "What Is Hauntology?"; Dean, *Communist Horizon*.

189 Derrida, *Specters of Marx*, 37, 48, 61; Derrida, *Politics of Friendship*, 84.

190 Deleuze, "Postscript on the Societies"; Graham, *Cities under Siege*, 63–64; Iveson and Maalsen, "Social Control in the Networked" (it is unclear, however, if the "discipline" discussed in this article is disciplinary in the sense that Michel Foucault elaborated the concept).

191 Dean, "Networked Empire."

192  Jeremy Scahill and Glenn Greenwald, "The NSA's Secret Role in the U.S. Assassination Program," *The Intercept*, February 10, 2014, https://theintercept .com/2014/02/10/the-nsas-secret-role/; Jeremy Scahill and Margot Williams, "Stingrays: A Secret Catalogue of Government Gear for Spying on Your Cell Phone," *The Intercept*, December 17, 2015, https://theintercept.com/2015/12/17 /a-secret-catalogue-of-government-gear-for-spying-on-your-cellphone/.

193  G. Lage Dyndal, T. Arne Berntsen, and S. Redse-Johansen, "Autonomous Military Drones: No Longer Science Fiction," *NATO Review Magazine*, July 28, 2017, https://www.nato.int/docu/review/2017/Also-in-2017/autonomous -military-drones-no-longer-science-fiction/EN/index.htm. See generally, Graham, *Cities under Siege*, chap. 5.

194  Terminiello v. Illinois, 337 U.S. 1 (1949), 4.

195  Edwards v. South Carolina, 372 U.S. 229 (1963); Cox v. Louisiana, 379 U.S. 536 (1965).

196  Blanchard et al. v. City of Memphis, U.S.D.C. W.D.T.N. 17 Civ. 02120, "Complaint for Enforcement of Order, Judgment and Decree" (February 22, 2017).

197  Chevigny, "Politics and Law in the Control of Local Surveillance," 747–67.

198  Chevigny, "Politics and Law in the Control of Local Surveillance," 751–54; Kendrick v. Chandler, U.S.D.C. W.D.T.N. No. C 76–499, "Order, Judgment and Decree" (September 18, 1978).

199  Blanchard and ACLU of Tennessee v. City of Memphis, U.S.D.C. W.D.T.N. 17 Civ. 2120, "Opinion and Order" (October 26, 2018), 22.

200  Blanchard and ACLU of Tennessee v. City of Memphis, "Opinion and Order," 22.

201  Blanchard and ACLU of Tennessee v. City of Memphis, "Opinion and Order," 3.

202  Blanchard and ACLU of Tennessee v. City of Memphis, "Opinion and Order," 3.

203  Blanchard and ACLU of Tennessee v. City of Memphis, U.S.D.C. W.D.T.N. 17 Civ. 02120, "Plaintiff's Undisputed Statement of Material Facts" (July 24, 2018), "Deposition of Major Stephen Chandler" (April 25, 2018), 3428. References to evidence use "Page ID" numbering unless otherwise noted. ("Plaintiff's Undisputed Statement of Material Facts" includes hundreds of pages of exhibits and excerpts of depositions that permit independent inspection of the evidence on which the "Statement" is based.)

204  Blanchard and ACLU of Tennessee v. City of Memphis, "Plaintiff's Undisputed Statement of Material Facts," "Deposition of Major Stephen Chandler," 3427; "Family: Officer Killed 19-Year-Old after Mistaking Him for Someone Else," WMC5, July 18, 2015, https://www.wmcactionnews5.com/story /29578116/man-dead-after-struggle-with-mpd-officer/.

205  Blanchard and ACLU of Tennessee v. City of Memphis, "Plaintiff's Undisputed Statement of Material Facts" (July 24, 2018), 3.

206  Blanchard and ACLU of Tennessee v. City of Memphis, "Plaintiff's Undisputed Statement of Material Facts," 3.

207 Blanchard and ACLU of Tennessee v. City of Memphis, "Deposition of Major Stephen Chandler," 3430.

208 Blanchard and ACLU of Tennessee v. City of Memphis, "Plaintiff's Undisputed Statement of Material Facts," 3–4.

209 Blanchard and ACLU of Tennessee v. City of Memphis, "Plaintiff's Undisputed Statement of Material Facts," 5.

210 Blanchard and ACLU of Tennessee v. City of Memphis, "Plaintiff's Undisputed Statement of Material Facts," 7; Blanchard and ACLU of Tennessee v. City of Memphis, "Plaintiff's Undisputed Statement of Material Facts," "Deposition of Timothy Reynolds" (April 24, 2018), 3508ff.

211 Blanchard and ACLU of Tennessee v. City of Memphis, "Plaintiff's Undisputed Statement of Material Facts," 8; Exhibit LL, 3358.

212 Blanchard and ACLU of Tennessee v. City of Memphis, "Deposition of Major Stephen Chandler," 3432; Blanchard and ACLU of Tennessee v. City of Memphis, "Plaintiff's Undisputed Statement of Material Facts," "Deposition of Bradley Wilburn" (April 26, 2018), 3540.

213 Blanchard and ACLU of Tennessee v. City of Memphis, "Plaintiff's Undisputed Statement of Material Facts," 6; Blanchard and ACLU of Tennessee v. City of Memphis, "Plaintiff's Undisputed Statement of Material Facts," "Deposition of Eddie Bass" (April 26, 2018), 3410.

214 Blanchard and ACLU of Tennessee v. City of Memphis, "Plaintiff's Undisputed Statement of Material Facts," 7.

215 Blanchard and ACLU of Tennessee v. City of Memphis, "Plaintiff's Undisputed Statement of Material Facts," 9; Exhibit PP, 3364.

216 "Accurint LE Plus," Accurint for Law Enforcement, accessed July 10, 2019, http://www.accurint.us/lePlus.html"; "Accurint for Law Enforcement," Lexis Nexis Risk Solutions, accessed July 10, 2019, https://risk.lexisnexis.com/products/accurint-for-law-enforcement.

217 "IBM Security i2 Analyst's Notebook," IBM, accessed July 10, 2019, https://www.ibm.com/us-en/marketplace/analysts-notebook.

218 Blanchard and ACLU of Tennessee v. City of Memphis, "Plaintiff's Undisputed Statement of Material Facts," Exhibit PP, 3364–65.

219 Blanchard and ACLU of Tennessee v. City of Memphis, "Plaintiff's Memorandum in Support of Its Motion for Summary Judgment," 2–3; Blanchard and ACLU of Tennessee v. City of Memphis, "Plaintiff's Undisputed Statement of Material Facts," 1–2; Blanchard and ACLU of Tennessee v. City of Memphis, "Deposition of Timothy Reynolds" (April 24, 2018), 3522–28.

220 Blanchard and ACLU of Tennessee v. City of Memphis, "Plaintiff's Undisputed Statement of Material Facts," Exhibit U, 3248.

221 Blanchard and ACLU of Tennessee v. City of Memphis, "Plaintiff's Undisputed Statement of Material Facts," "Deposition of Bradley Wilburn," 3547–48.

222 Blanchard and ACLU of Tennessee v. City of Memphis, "Plaintiff's Undisputed Statement of Material Facts," Exhibit V, 3249.

223 Blanchard and ACLU of Tennessee v. City of Memphis, "Plaintiff's Undisputed Statement of Material Facts," Exhibit HH, 3330.

224 Blanchard and ACLU of Tennessee v. City of Memphis, "Plaintiff's Undisputed Statement of Material Facts," Exhibit KK, 3339–57.

225 Blanchard and ACLU of Tennessee v. City of Memphis, "Plaintiff's Undisputed Statement of Material Facts," 4.

226 Adrian Sainz, "Graceland Black Lives Matter Protest Leads to Lawsuit," Associated Press, January 20, 2017, https://www.apnews.com.

227 "Elvis Week Wraps Up with Vigil, Black Lives Matter Protests," *Clarion Ledger*, August 16, 2016, https://www.clarionledger.com.

228 Jody Callahan and John Beifuss, "Legislators Ask Why Protesters Blocked from Graceland during Elvis Vigil," *USA Today*, August 16, 2016, https:// www .usatoday.com.

229 Sainz, "Graceland Black Lives Matter Protest Leads to Lawsuit."

230 Adrian Sainz, "Trial in Lawsuit over Police Surveillance of Protesters Ends," Associated Press, August 23, 2018, https://apnews.com; Bill Dries, "Police Documents Show Protest Spreadsheet and Fear of 'Radicals,'" *Memphis Daily News*, July 31, 2018, https://www.memphisdailynews.com.

231 Blanchard and ACLU of Tennessee v. City of Memphis, "Plaintiff's Undisputed Statement of Material Facts," Exhibit Q, 3207–8.

232 Blanchard and ACLU of Tennessee v. City of Memphis, "Plaintiff's Undisputed Statement of Material Facts," Exhibit Q, 3207–31.

233 Blanchard and ACLU of Tennessee v. City of Memphis, "Plaintiff's Undisputed Statement of Material Facts," "Deposition of Director Michael Rallings," 3480–82; "Civil Disturbance Law and Legal Definition," US Legal, accessed July 11, 2019, https://definitions.uslegal.com/c/civil-disturbance/.

234 Harcourt, *Counterrevolution*, also represents contemporary governance in the United States in terms of counterinsurgency. Harcourt describes the inception of these practices as coalescing in anticolonial and Cold War struggles and as receiving more recent stimulation by the attacks of September 11, 2001 (1–35). He also describes current governmental policies as "counterinsurgency without insurgency" (12). In contrast, I have tried to be more historically nuanced here by discussing protest policing as a result of institutional and cultural reactions to the protests and riots of the 1960s. One cannot draw a straight line from the Cold War and anticolonial era to the present, albeit with a tick up after September 11, 2001, because that fails to account for important gains made by the mobilizations of the 1960s and 1970s, one of which is the *Kendrick* Consent Decree itself. In an additional contrast with Harcourt, I have highlighted important mobilizations of the present, like OWS and BLM, that the state seeks to contain, if not defeat, through security practices very much akin to COIN.

235 Blanchard and ACLU of Tennessee v. City of Memphis, "Plaintiff's Undisputed Statement of Material Facts," Exhibit Q, 3222, 3227, 3231.

236 U.S. Department of the Army, *Counterinsurgency*, 1–8 (references are to page numbers, not subsections, unless otherwise noted).

237 U.S. Department of the Army, *Counterinsurgency*, 1–23.

238 U.S. Department of the Army, *Counterinsurgency*, 1–24.

239 Offe, *Contradictions of the Welfare State*.

240 Hackworth, *Neoliberal City*; Sinclair, *New Masters of Capital*.

241 Blanchard and ACLU of Tennessee v. City of Memphis, "Deposition of Timothy Reynolds" (April 24, 2018), 3518–20.

242 Blanchard and ACLU of Tennessee v. City of Memphis, "Deposition of Timothy Reynolds," 3518–19.

243 Blanchard and ACLU of Tennessee v. City of Memphis, "Plaintiff's Undisputed Statement of Material Facts," Exhibit Q, 3210; Blanchard and ACLU of Tennessee v. City of Memphis, "Deposition of Timothy Reynolds," 3520; Jody Callahan, "Marchers Shut Down I-40 Bridge at Memphis during Black Lives Matter Rally," *Commercial Appeal*, July 10, 2016, http://archive.commercialappeal.com/news/tennessee-black-caucus-calls-for-calm-amid-racial-unrest—3714d93e-1078-6a7d-e053-0100007f134e-386214081.html/.

244 Blanchard and ACLU of Tennessee v. City of Memphis, "Plaintiff's Undisputed Statement of Material Facts," Exhibit F, 3154.

245 Blanchard and ACLU of Tennessee v. City of Memphis, "Deposition of Timothy Reynolds," 3521.

246 Blanchard and ACLU of Tennessee v. City of Memphis, "Plaintiff's Undisputed Statement of Material Facts," Exhibit R, 3238–40; Blanchard and ACLU of Tennessee v. City of Memphis, "Deposition of Timothy Reynolds," 3522; Memphis Coalition of Concerned Citizens, Facebook, accessed July 12, 2019, https://www.facebook.com/pg/CoalitionOfMemphis/about/.

247 Kelsey Ott and Michael Quander, "12 Arrested at Anti-pipeline Protest at Valero Memphis Refinery," WREG Memphis, January 16, 2017, https://wreg.com/news/group-at-valero-memphis-refinery-to-protest-pipeline/; Blanchard and ACLU of Tennessee v. City of Memphis, 17 Civ. 02120, "Defendant's Memorandum in Support of Motion for Summary Judgment on Civil Contempt" (June 18, 2018), 10.

248 Blanchard and ACLU of Tennessee v. City of Memphis, "Plaintiff's Undisputed Statement of Material Facts," Exhibit R, 3238–40; Blanchard and ACLU of Tennessee v. City of Memphis, "Deposition of Timothy Reynolds," 3523; "Elvis' Birthday Celebration," Graceland, accessed July 16, 2019, https://www.graceland.com/elvis-birthday.

249 Michael Quander, "Memphis Mayor Woke Up to People Playing Dead in His Front Yard," WREG Memphis, December 19, 2016, https://wreg.com/news/memphis-mayor-woke-up-to-people-playing-dead-in-his-front-yard/.

250 Hacker and Pierson, *Winner-Take-All Politics*, 110–12; Page, Bartels, and Seawright, "Democracy and the Policy Preferences."

251 U.S. Department of Justice, *Investigation of the Ferguson Police*, 42–62; Western and Pettit, "Incarceration and Social Inequality"; Natapoff, *Punishment without Crime*.

252 Blanchard and ACLU of Tennessee v. City of Memphis, U.S.D.C. W.D.T.N. 17 Civ. 02120, "Defendant's Memorandum in Support of Motion for Summary Judgment," 5.

253 Blanchard and ACLU of Tennessee v. City of Memphis, "Defendant's Memorandum in Support of Motion for Summary Judgment," 6.

254 Statement from Memphis Police Director Michael W. Rallings, "City Unseals Documents in Ongoing Lawsuit," July 24, 2018, https://memphis.hosted. civiclive.com/news/what_s_new/city_unseals_documents_in_ongoing_lawsuit.

255 Blanchard and ACLU of Tennessee v. City of Memphis, U.S.D.C. W.D.T.N. 17 Civ. 02120, "Motion for Relief from Judgment or Order" (August 15, 2018), 3–4.

256 Blanchard and ACLU of Tennessee v. City of Memphis, U.S.D.C. W.D.T.N. 17 Civ. 02120, "Joint Motion to Stay City's Motion to Modify and/or Vacate Judgment and Incorporated Memorandum of Law" (December 20, 2018); Blanchard and ACLU of Tennessee v. City of Memphis, U.S.D.C. W.D.T.N. 17 Civ. 2120, "Order Granting Joint Motion, Modifying Discovery Schedule, and Maintaining Sanctions Compliance Schedule" (December 31, 2018). Ultimately, the Kendrick decree was modified to accommodate the emergence of social media and to protect First Amendment activities from First Amendment–related intelligence gathering given the emergence of social media: ACLU of Tennessee v. City of Memphis, U.S.D.C. W.D.T.N. 17 Civ. 02120, "Opinion and Order" (September 21, 2020); ACLU of Tennessee v. City of Memphis, U.S.D.C. W.D.T.N. 76 Civ. 00449, "Amended Judgment and Decree 'Modified *Kendrick* Decree'" (September 21, 2020). Importantly, the modified Kendrick decree and the "Order and Opinion" prohibit Memphis from using third parties to evade the decree.

257 IIR and COPS, *After-Action Assessment*, 59–60.

258 IIR and COPS, *After-Action Assessment*, 60. The *AAA* is either contradictory or hypocritical on whether the LRAD should be considered a military weapon. On the one hand, the LRAD is considered in the chapters "Use of Force" and "Militarization," which acknowledge it is a weapon. On the other hand, in the "Militarization" chapter, the *AAA* states that it considers the LRAD "a technique and not a weapon" (55).

259 IIR and COPS, *After-Action Assessment*, 83.

260 IIR and COPS, *After-Action Assessment*, 83.

261 Lewis, "NYPD Officers on the Ground in Ferguson."

262 IIR and COPS, *After-Action Assessment*, 84.

263 IIR and COPS, *After-Action Assessment*, 85.

264 IIR and COPS, *After-Action Assessment*, 82–83.

265 IIR and COPS, *After-Action Assessment*, 131.

266 Police Executive Research Forum, *Managing Major Events*, 37. According to Rachel Levinson-Waldman, more than 150 police departments use software to monitor social media, but "only eighteen ha[ve] publicly available policies detailing how social media is used for investigative or intelligence purposes." See Levinson-Waldman, "Government Access," 560–61.

267 Community Oriented Policing Services and Police Executive Research Forum, *Social Media and Tactical Considerations*, 14–15. See also Police Executive Research Forum, *Lessons Learned from the 2015 Civil Unrest in Baltimore*, 26–27 (recommending that the Baltimore Police Department review its "current intelligence software," determine whether other software might be "more effective," and designate that its Analytical Intelligence Section "serve under the Operations Section," rather than the Planning Section, during conditions of "civil unrest").

268 IIR and COPS, *After-Action Assessment*, 126.

269 Bl(a)ck Tea Society v. City of Boston, 378 F. 3d 8 (2004), at 14; American Civil Liberties Union v. City and County of Denver, 569 F. Supp. 2d 1142 (August 6, 2008); Citizens for Peace in Space v. City of Colorado Springs, 477 F. 3d 1212 (2007).

270 Zusha Elinson and Shoshana Walter, "Latest BART Shooting Prompts New Discussion of Reforms," *New York Times*, July 16, 2011, https://www.nytimes.com; Zusha Elinson, "After Cellphone Action, BART Faces Escalating Protests," *New York Times*, August 20, 2011, https://www.nytimes.com; Michael Cabanatuan, "BART Admits Halting Cell Service to Stop Protests," *San Francisco Gate*, August 12, 2011, https://www.sfgate.com. The case of BART shutting down internet access to prevent a protest is discussed extensively in Community Oriented Policing Services and Police Executive Research Forum, *Social Media and Tactical Considerations*, 33–38.

271 Elinson, "After Cellphone Action, BART Faces Escalating Protests"; Matt Richtell, "Egypt Cuts Off Most Internet and Cell Service," *New York Times*, January 28, 2011, http://www.nytimes.com.

272 Matt Ehling, "Examining the Costs of Hosting the Super Bowl," editorial, *Minnesota Post*, June 9, 2014, https://www.minnpost.com; Mara Gottfried, "Police Cast an Electronic Eye," *Politico*, August 13, 2008, https://www.politico.com; Jessica Vander Velde, "Tampa Mayor Bob Buckhorn to Keep RNC Security Cameras Focused Downtown," *Tampa Bay Times*, September 12, 2012, https://www.tampabay.com.

273 Stanley, *Dawn of Robot Surveillance*, 3–5.

274 Stanley, *Dawn of Robot Surveillance*, 6–8.

275 Stanley, *Dawn of Robot Surveillance*, 9–10.

276 Police Executive Research Forum, *Managing Major Events*, 38.

277 Monte Reel, "Secret Cameras Record Baltimore's Every Move from Above," *Bloomberg Business Week*, August 23, 2016, https://www.bloomberg.com. The FBI also monitored BLM protests in Baltimore from the air, though its surveillance was focused on specific targets in contrast with the aerial surveillance

offered by Persistent Surveillance Systems. See also Police Foundation, *A Review of the Baltimore Police Department's Use of Persistent Surveillance* (providing a policing perspective on persistent aerial surveillance); Pavletic, "Fourth Amendment" (raising Fourth Amendment questions about persistent aerial surveillance).

278 We can situate "community" in the context of communicative capitalism and control, in contrast to "society," which we can situate within disciplinary power. See Rose, *Powers of Freedom*, chap. 5; Hardt, "Withering of Civil Society."

279 For example, St. Louis Metropolitan Police and St. Louis County police enjoy beating up BLM protesters: Tim Elfrink, "'It's Still a Blast Beating People': St. Louis Police Indicted in Assault of Undercover Officer Posing as Protester," *Washington Post*, November 30, 2018, https://www.washingtonpost.com.

## Conclusion

An early version of my research on the Wisconsin uprising appeared as "Uneven Developments and the End to the History of Modernity's Social Democratic Orientation: Madison's Pro-Union Demonstrations," in *The Ends of History: Questioning the Stakes of Historical Reason*, edited by Amy Swiffen and Joshua Nichols (Routledge, 2013).

1 Deleuze, "Postscript on the Societies."

2 I use "social reproduction" to refer broadly to that which is needed to reproduce society and a society oriented to doing justice to the needs of all. Social reproduction refers to what we need to produce and reproduce the conditions of possibility for lives better than mere life, that is, lives with value. Like Silvia Federici, I am concerned with the "profound crisis of social reproduction" we are experiencing today around the world. See Federici, "Social Reproduction Theory"; Silvia Federici and Marina Sitrin, "Social Reproduction: Between the Wage and the Commons," *ROAR Magazine*, no. 2 (n.d.), accessed September 14, 2019, https://roarmag.org/magazine/social-reproduction-between-the-wage-and-the-commons/.

3 David Lawrence, "What's Become of 'Law and Order'?," *U.S. News and World Report*, August 5, 1963, 104; David Lawrence, "The War against Crime," *U.S. News and World Report*, June 29, 1964, 111–12.

4 Richard Nixon, "Address Accepting the Presidential Nomination at the Republican Convention in Miami Beach, Florida," August 8, 1968, American Presidency Project, https://www.presidency.ucsb.edu/documents/address-accepting-the-presidential-nomination-the-republican-national-convention-miami; Beckett, *Making Crime Pay*, 30–32, 41–43.

5 Garland, *Culture of Control*.

6 Beckett, *Making Crime Pay*, 33–36; Soss, Fording, and Schram, *Disciplining the Poor*. A forum on the thirtieth anniversary of the Kerner Commis-

sion's report, hosted by the Heritage Foundation, exemplifies the mutually reinforcing relations between the crises. Indicative of how it was haunted by the figure of black insurrection, the forum framed the urban fiscal crisis as resulting from the Kerner Commission's advocacy for ameliorating inequalities. For forum participants, the potential for black political mobilization resulted in black people on welfare, which, in turn, produced the urban fiscal crisis. Thernstrom, Siegel, and Woodson, "Kerner Commission Report."

7  United States v. Carolene Products, 304 U.S. 144 (1938), n. 4.

8  Natapoff, *Punishment without Crime*; Camp and Heatherton, *Policing the Planet*.

9  Sernatinger, "Capitalist Crisis"; Clay Barbour and Mary Spicuzza, "Education, Local Government Bear Brunt of $1 Billion in Cuts in Walker's First Budget," *Wisconsin State Journal*, March 1, 2011, https://madison.com; Abby Sewell, "Wisconsin Governor Proposes Austerity Measures to Balance Budget," *Los Angeles Times*, March 1, 2011, https://www.latimes.com.

10  John Nichols, "Upwards of 125,000 March in Madison, as Activists Rally Nationwide to Back Wisconsin Workers," *The Nation*, February 26, 2011, http://www.thenation.com; John Nichols, "Undaunted! More Than 100,000 Wisconsinites Rally to 'Take Our State Back!,'" *The Nation*, March 12, 2011, http://www.thenation.com.

11  Jessica Vanegeren, "'Chaos in the Streets' of Madison? Hardly," *Capital Times*, February 19, 2011, https://madison.com.

12  Mary Spicuzza, "Chief of Peace: During Protests at Capitol, Charles Tubbs Emerged as Force for Calm," *Wisconsin State Journal*, March 29, 2011, https://madison.com.

13  Bill Novak, "Protests Build on Square, in Capitol Again; Streets Shut Down," *Capital Times*, February 17, 2011, https://madison.com.

14  "Respect for Constitution Trumps Walker's Assault on Free Speech," editorial, *Capital Times*, February 28, 2011, https://madison.com.

15  Personal interview with Charles Tubbs, June 23, 2011.

16  Passavant, "Uneven Developments," 38–39.

17  Personal interview with Noble Wray, June 22, 2011.

18  Personal interview with Dave Mahoney, June 24, 2011.

19  Dee Hall, "Madison Police Chief, Mayor Ask Governor to Explain 'Troubling' Statements," *Wisconsin State Journal*, February 25, 2011, https://madison.com; "Chief Wray Responds . . . to Reporters' Questions," City of Madison News Release, February 24, 2011, https://www.cityofmadison.com/news/chief-wray-responds (copy on file with author).

20  Bill Lueders, "Dane County DA Ismael Ozanne, Sheriff Dave Mahoney Weigh In on Capitol Access," *Isthmus*, March 1, 2011, http://www.thedailypage.com.

21  Personal interview with Dave Mahoney, June 24, 2011.

22  Jessica Vanegeren and Shawn Doherty, "South of the Border: Dem Senators Talk of Life on the Lam," *Capital Times*, March 2, 2011, https://madison.com; Ruth Conniff, "Citizens Jam Capitol after WI Republicans' Sudden Vote

to Pass Union-Busting Measure," *The Progressive*, March 9, 2011, http://www
.progressive.org; Sernatinger, "Capitalist Crisis," 56.

23 Mary Spicuzza and Clay Barbour, "Budget Bill Passes Senate, Thursday Vote Set in House," *Wisconsin State Journal*, March 10, 2011, https://
madison.com; State of Wisconsin ex rel. Ismael Ozanne v. Jeff Fitzgerald
et al., Circuit Court, Dane County, 11 Civ. 1244, "Complaint" (March 16, 2011),
"Attachment 2."

24 Dee Hall, "Multiple Complaints Are Filed Charging Legislature Violated
Law," *Wisconsin State Journal*, March 11, 2011, https://madison.com; Judith Dav-
idoff and Kristin Czubkowski, "Tears and Resolve after Capitol Vote," *Capital
Times*, March 11, 2011, https://madison.com; Ed Treleven, "DA: Vote Broke
State Open Meetings Law," *Wisconsin State Journal*, March 17, 2011, A1.

25 "Hasty Action Violates Public Trust," *Wisconsin State Journal*, March 11, 2011,
http://madison.com.

26 Steven Verburg, "Calls, Preparations for General Strike Grow," *Wisconsin
State Journal*, March 10, 2011, https://madison.com; Jessica Vanegeren, "Next
Step for Protesters: Recall Republicans," *Capital Times*, March 13, 2011, https://
madison.com.

27 John Nichols, "'Dictator Governor Checked, Balanced by Pesky Third
Branch of Government," *The Nation*, March 19, 2011, http://www.thenation
.com.

28 Patrick Marley and Jason Stein, "Collective Bargaining Law Published
Despite Restraining Order," *Milwaukee Journal Sentinel*, March 25, 2011, http://
archive.jsonline.com/news/statepolitics/118677754.html/.

29 Dan Simmons and Sandy Cullen, "Battle for Capitol Access Heads to the
Court Room," *Wisconsin State Journal*, March 1, 2011, https://madison.com.

30 Sandy Cullen, "Judge Orders Capitol Restrictions Lifted but Bars Overnight
Stays," *Wisconsin State Journal*, March 4, 2011, https://madison.com.

31 John Nichols, "Kloppenburg Wins More Than an Election," *Capital Times*,
April 7, 2011, https://madison.com.

32 Dee Hall, "Waukeshaw County Clerk Has Drawn Criticisms in the Past,"
*Wisconsin State Journal*, April 9, 2011, https://madison.com.

33 Molly Beck, "State Supreme Court Justice David Prosser to Retire," *Wisconsin
State Journal*, April 27, 2016, https://madison.com; Patrick Marley, "Ethics
Violations Filed against Prosser," *Milwaukee Journal Sentinel*, March 16, 2012,
https://archive.jsonline.com/news/statepolitics/ethics-violations-filed-
against-prosser-4c4k50c-142975425.html/.

34 Patrick Marley, "Supreme Court Tensions Boil Over," *Milwaukee Journal
Sentinel*, March 19, 2011, http://archive.jsonline.com/news/statepolitics/118310479
.html/.

35 "David Prosser Is Stepping Down under a Cloud of Shame," editorial, *Capital
Times*, May 18, 2016, https://madison.com; "Bradley Says Prosser Choked
Her," *Milwaukee Journal Sentinel*, June 25, 2011, http://archive.jsonline.com/
news/wisconsin/124551874.html/.

36 State of Wisconsin ex rel. Ismael Ozanne v. Jeff Fitzgerald et al., 2011 AP 613-LV, 2011 AP 765-W, "Order and Opinion" (June 14, 2011), 7–8 (slip op.).

37 State of Wisconsin ex rel. Ismael Ozanne v. Jeff Fitzgerald, Shirley Abrahamson dissenting at 2, 9; Patrick Crooks dissenting at 12–15 and n. 24.

38 State of Wisconsin ex rel. Ismael Ozanne v. Jeff Fitzgerald, Crooks dissenting at 8–11.

39 State of Wisconsin ex rel. Ismael Ozanne v. Jeff Fitzgerald, Crooks dissenting at 3–8; Abrahamson dissenting at 4.

40 State of Wisconsin ex rel. Ismael Ozanne v. Jeff Fitzgerald, Abrahamson dissenting at 2–3, 19; Crooks dissenting at 1.

41 Dan Simmons, "Anatomy of a Protest: From a Simple March to a National Fight," *Wisconsin State Journal*, February 27, 2011, https://madison.com.

42 Cowie, *Stayin' Alive*, 363.

43 Leslie Bennetts, "An Uneasy Time for Strikers," *New York Times*, August 13, 1981, A1, D22; Cowie, *Stayin' Alive*, 362.

44 This is a key event for Michael Hardt and Antonio Negri as well. Hardt and Negri, *Labor of Dionysus*, 241.

45 Hacker and Pierson, *Winner-Take-All Politics*, 59.

46 Barbour and Spicuzza, "Education, Local Government Bear Brunt"; Igor Volsky, "Scott Walker Cuts State Health Services, Then Rejects Health Reform's Public Health Grants," ThinkProgress, August 5, 2011, http://thinkprogress.org; Patrick Marley and Jason Stein, "Walker Signs Budget Bill, Vetoes Just 50 Items," *Milwaukee Journal Sentinel*, June 26, 2011, http://archive.jsonline.com/news/statepolitics/124563073.html/; "Scott Walker Budget," SourceWatch, n.d., accessed December 8, 2020, https://www.sourcewatch.org/index.php/Scott_Walker_Budget/.

47 Barry Adams, "Walker Wants to Increase Tourism Marketing Budget," *Wisconsin State Journal*, March 7, 2011, https://madison.com.

48 Danielle Kaeding, "Income Inequality in Wisconsin at Highest Level since Great Depression," Wisconsin Public Radio, August 30, 2017, https://www.wpr.org.

49 Cooper, *As Wisconsin's and Minnesota's Lawmakers Took Divergent Paths, So Did Their Economies*.

50 Shawn Johnson and Laurel White, "As Voting Begins, a Look Back at the Fight over Wisconsin's Voter ID Law," Wisconsin Public Radio, September 26, 2016, https://www.wpr.org.

51 Michael Wines, "Wisconsin Strict ID Law Discouraged Voters, Study Finds," *New York Times*, September 25, 2017, https://www.nytimes.com. For a discussion of the significance of race in Wisconsin politics, see Ani Mukherji, "Racism and the Wisconsin Idea," *Boston Review*, October 29, 2018, http://bostonreview.com. For a discussion of how Scott Walker sought to position himself to run a Nixonian law-and-order campaign for president in 2016, see Eli Hager, "Scott Walker on Crime and Punishment: Back to the '90s," Marshall Project, June 26, 2015, https://www.themarshallproject.org.

52  Craig Gilbert, "New Election Data Highlights the Ongoing Impact of 2011 GOP Redistricting in Wisconsin," *Milwaukee Journal Sentinel*, December 6, 2018, https://www.jsonline.com/story/news/blogs/wisconsin-voter/2018/12/06/wisconsin-gerrymandering-data-shows-stark-impact-redistricting/2219092002/.

53  Rucho v. Common Cause, 588 U.S. __ (2019).

*Abdullah v. St. Louis*, 52 F. Supp. 3d 936 (2014).

*ACLU of Tennessee v. City of Memphis*, U.S.D.C. W.D.T.N. 17 Civ. 02120, "Opinion and Order" (September 21, 2020).

*ACLU of Tennessee v. City of Memphis*, U.S.D.C. W.D.T.N. 76 Civ. 00449, "Amended Judgment and Decree 'Modified *Kendrick* Decree'" (September 21, 2020).

*Adele Buzzetti d/b/a Cozy Cabin and Vanessa Doe v. City of New York*, 140 F. 3d 134 (1998).

*Adickes v. S. H. Kress*, 398 U.S. 144 (1970).

Agamben, Giorgio. *The Coming Community*. Translated by Michael Hardt. Minneapolis: University of Minnesota Press, 1993.

Agamben, Giorgio. *Means without End*. Translated by Vincenzo Binetti and Cesare Casarino. Minneapolis: University of Minnesota Press, 2000.

Agamben, Giorgio. *State of Exception*. Translated by Kevin Attell. Chicago: University of Chicago Press, 2005.

Alcaly, Roger, and Helen Bodian. "New York's Fiscal Crisis and the Economy." In *The Fiscal Crisis of American Cities*, edited by Roger Alcaly and David Mermelstein, 30–58. New York: Vintage, 1977.

*Alliance to End Repression v. City of Chicago*, 561 F. Supp. 537 (1982).

*Amalgamated Food Employees Union v. Logan Valley Plaza*, 391 U.S. 308 (1968).

*American Civil Liberties Union v. City and County of Denver*, 569 F. Supp. 2d 1142 (August 6, 2008).

American Civil Liberties Union. *The War Comes Home: The Excessive Militarization of American Policing*. New York: ACLU Foundation, 2014. https://www.aclu.org.

Amin, Ash, ed. *Post-Fordism: A Reader*. Malden, MA: Blackwell, 1994.

Amnesty International. *On the Streets of America: Human Rights Abuses in Ferguson*. New York: Amnesty International Publications, 2014.

Anker, Elisabeth. *Orgies of Feeling: Melodrama and the Politics of Freedom*. Durham, NC: Duke University Press, 2014.

Appuzzo, Matt, and Adam Goldman. *Enemies Within: Inside the NYPD's Secret Spying Unit and Bin Laden's Final Plot against America*. New York: Touchstone, 2013.

Balbus, Isaac. *The Dialectics of Legal Repression: Black Rebels before the American Criminal Courts*. New York: Russell Sage, 1973.

Baldwin, James. *Nobody Knows My Name*. New York: Dell, 1962.

Balibar, Etienne. *The Philosophy of Marx*. Translated by Chris Turner. New York: Verso, 1995.

*Barnes v. Glen Theatre*, 501 U.S. 560 (1991).

Bauman, Zygmunt. *Globalization: The Human Consequences*. New York: Columbia University Press, 1998.

Bayley, David, and Clifford Shearing. "The Future of Policing." *Law and Society Review* 30, no. 3 (1996): 585–606.

Bayley, David, and Clifford Shearing. *The New Structure of Policing: Description, Conceptualization, and Research Agenda*. Washington, DC: U.S. Department of Justice, Office of Justice Programs, National Institute of Justice, July 2001.

Beauregard, Robert. *When America Became Suburban*. Minneapolis: University of Minnesota Press, 2006.

Beckett, Katherine. *Making Crime Pay: Law and Order in Contemporary American Politics*. New York: Oxford University Press, 1997.

Beckett, Katherine, and Steve Herbert. *Banished: The New Social Control in Urban America*. New York: Oxford University Press, 2009.

Berardi, Franco. *Precarious Rhapsody: Semiocapitalism and the Pathologies of the Post-Alpha Generation*. London: Minor Compositions, 2009.

Berardi, Franco. *The Soul at Work: From Alienation to Autonomy*. Los Angeles: Semiotext(e), 2009.

Bickel, Karl, and Ed Connors. "Planning and Managing Security for Major Special Events: Best Practices for Law Enforcement Administrators." *Police Chief* 74, no. 12 (December 2007).

*Bl(a)ck Tea Society v. City of Boston*, 378 F. 3d 8 (July 30, 2004).

*Blanchard and ACLU of Tennessee v. City of Memphis*, U.S.D.C. W.D.T.N. 17 Civ. 2120, "Opinion and Order" (October 26, 2018).

*Blanchard and ACLU of Tennessee v. City of Memphis*, U.S.D.C. W.D.T.N. 17 Civ. 02120, "Plaintiff's Undisputed Statement of Material Facts" (July 24, 2018).

*Blanchard, et al. v. City of Memphis*, U.S.D.C. W.D.T.N. 17 Civ. 02120, "Complaint for Enforcement of Order, Judgment and Decree" (February 22, 2017).

Blumenson, Eric, and Eva Nilsen. "Policing for Profit: The Drug War's Hidden Economic Agenda." *University of Chicago Law Review* 65 (Winter 1998): 35–114.

Boghosian, Heidi. *The Policing of Political Speech: Constraints on Mass Dissent in the U.S., A National Lawyers Guild Report*. New York: National Lawyers Guild, 2010.

Bourdieu, Pierre. *Acts of Resistance: Against the Tyranny of the Market*. New York: New Press, 1998.

Bratton, William, with Peter Knobler. *Turnaround: How America's Top Cop Reversed the Crime Epidemic*. New York: Random House, 1998.

*Bray v. City of New York*, 356 F. Supp. 2d 277 (2004).

Brayne, Sarah. "Big Data Surveillance: The Case of Policing." *American Sociological Review* 82, no. 5 (2017): 977–1008.

*Brown v. Board of Education*, 347 U.S. 483 (1954).

Brown, Wendy. *Undoing the Demos: Neoliberalism's Stealth Revolution*. Brooklyn: Zone, 2015.

Bureau of Justice Assistance and CNA. *Managing Large-Scale Security Events: A Planning Primer for Local Law Enforcement Agencies*. Arlington, VA: CNA, May 2013. https://bja.ojp.gov/sites/g/files/xyckuh186/files/Publications/LSSE-planning-Primer.pdf.

Burt, Jo-Marie. "'Quien Habla es Terrorista': The Political Use of Fear in Fujimori's Peru." *Latin American Research Review* 41, no. 3 (October 2006): 32–62.

Butler, Judith. *Precarious Life: The Powers of Mourning and Violence*. New York: Verso, 2004.

Camp, Jordan, and Christina Heatherton, eds. *Policing the Planet: Why the Policing Crisis Led to Black Lives Matter*. New York: Verso, 2016.

Campbell, James, Joseph Sahid, and David Stang. *Law and Order Reconsidered: Report of the Task Force on Law and Law Enforcement to the National Commission on the Causes and Prevention of Violence*. New York: Praeger, 1970.

*Cantwell v. Connecticut*, 310 U.S. 296 (1940).

*Caravalho v. City of New York*, U.S.D.C. S.D.N.Y. 13 Civ. 4174, "Complaint" (June 17, 2013) (recaptioned *Guest v. City of New York*).

*Caravalho v. City of New York*, U.S.D.C. S.D.N.Y. 13 Civ. 4174, 2016 U.S. Dist. LEXIS 44280, "Memorandum and Order" (March 31, 2016).

Chambliss, William. "Policing the Ghetto Underclass: The Politics of Law and Law Enforcement." *Social Problems* 41, no. 2 (May 1994): 177–94.

Chasan, Daniel Jack, and Christianne Walker, with Doug Honig and Kathleen Taylor. *Out of Control: Seattle's Flawed Response to Protests against the World Trade Organization*. Seattle: American Civil Liberties Union of Washington, July 2000.

Chevigny, Paul. *Edge of the Knife: Police Violence in the Americas*. New York: New Press, 1995.

Chevigny, Paul. "Politics and Law in the Control of Local Surveillance." *Cornell Law Review* 69 (April 1984): 735–84.

Ciccariello-Maher, George. "Counterinsurgency and the Occupy Movement." In *Life during Wartime: Resisting Counterinsurgency*, edited by Kristin Williams, Will Munger, and Lara Messersmith-Glavin, 219–41. Oakland: AK Press, 2013.

*Citizens for Peace in Space v. City of Colorado Springs*, 477 F. 3d 1212 (2007).

Citizens' Panel on WTO Operations. *Report to the Seattle City Council WTO Accountability Committee by the Citizens' Panel on WTO Operations*. September 7, 2000.

Report on file with the author. http://www.seattle.gov/archive/wtocommit-tee/panel3_report.htm.

*City of New York v. Time's Up*, 814 N.Y.S. 2d 890 (February 14, 2006).

*Coalition to March on the RNC and Stop the War v. The City of St. Paul, Minnesota*, 557 F. Supp. 2d 1014 (2008).

*Coalition to Protest the Democratic National Convention v. City of Boston*, 327 F. Supp. 2d 61 (2004).

Cohen, Lizabeth. *A Consumer's Republic: The Politics of Mass Consumption in Postwar America*. New York: Alfred Knopf, 2003.

Cole, David, and James Dempsey. *Terrorism and the Constitution: Sacrificing Civil Liberties in the Name of National Security*, rev. and updated ed. New York: New Press, 2006.

Community Oriented Policing Services and Police Executive Research Forum. *Social Media and Tactical Considerations for Law Enforcement*. Washington, DC: U.S. Department of Justice, Office of Community Oriented Policing Services and Police Executive Research Forum, May 2013.

Connors, Edward. *Planning and Managing Security for Major Special Events: Guidelines for Law Enforcement*. Alexandria, VA: Institute for Law and Justice, March 2007.

Cooper, David. *As Wisconsin's and Minnesota's Lawmakers Took Divergent Paths, So Did Their Economies*. Washington, DC: Economic Policy Institute, May 8, 2018. https://www.epi.org/files/pdf/145177.pdf.

Cowie, Jefferson. *Stayin' Alive: The 1970s and the Last Days of the Working Class*. New York: New Press, 2010.

*Cox v. Louisiana*, 379 U.S. 536 (1965).

Crouch, Colin. *Post-Democracy*. Malden, MA: Polity, 2004.

Crouch, Colin. *The Strange Non-Death of Neoliberalism*. Malden, MA: Polity, 2011.

Dean, Jodi. *Aliens in America: Conspiracy Cultures from Outer Space to Cyberspace*. Ithaca, NY: Cornell University Press, 1998.

Dean, Jodi. *Blog Theory: Feedback and Capture in the Circuits of Drive*. Malden, MA: Polity, 2010.

Dean, Jodi. *Communist Horizon*. New York: Verso, 2012.

Dean, Jodi. *Democracy and Other Neoliberal Fantasies*. Durham, NC: Duke University Press, 2009.

Dean, Jodi. "Introduction." *Theory and Event* 14, no. 4 (suppl., 2011).

Dean, Jodi. "Neoliberalism's Defeat of Democracy." *Critical Inquiry* 42, no. 4 (Summer 2016): 979–82.

Dean, Jodi. "The Networked Empire: Communicative Capitalism and the Hope for Politics." In *Empire's New Clothes: Reading Hardt and Negri*, edited by Paul A. Passavant and Jodi Dean, 265–88. New York: Routledge, 2004.

Dean, Jodi. "Politics without Politics." *Parallax* 15, no. 3 (2009): 20–36.

Dean, Jodi. "The Real Internet." *International Journal of Žižek Studies* 4, no. 1 (2010): 1–22. https://zizekstudies.org/index.php/IJZS/article/view/280.

Dean, Jodi. *Žižek's Politics*. New York: Routledge, 2006.

Dean, Mitchell, and Kaspar Villadsen. *State Phobia and Civil Society: The Political Legacy of Michel Foucault*. Stanford, CA: Stanford University Press, 2016.

Delaney, Samuel. *Times Square Red, Times Square Blue*. New York: New York University Press, 1999.

Deleuze, Gilles. "Postscript on the Societies of Control." *October* 59 (Winter 1992): 3–7.

della Porta, Donatella, Abby Peterson, and Herbert Reiter. "Policing Transnational Protest: An Introduction." In *The Policing of Transnational Protest*, edited by Donatella della Porta, Abby Peterson, and Herbert Reiter, 1–12. Burlington, VT: Ashgate, 2006.

della Porta, Donatella, and Herbert Reiter. "Policing of Global Protest: The G8 at Genoa and Its Aftermath." In *The Policing of Transnational Protest*, edited by Donatella della Porta, Abby Peterson, and Herbert Reiter, 13–41. Burlington, VT: Ashgate, 2006.

*Depew v. City of New York*, U.S.D.C. S.D.N.Y. 15 Civ. 3821, "Order" (December 13, 2016).

*Depew v. New York*, U.S.D.C. S.D.N.Y. 15 Civ. 3821, "Complaint" (May 18, 2015).

Derrida, Jacques. *Politics of Friendship*. Translated by George Collins. New York: Verso, 1997.

Derrida, Jacques. *Specters of Marx: The State of the Debt, the Work of Mourning, and the New International*. Translated by Peggy Kamuf. New York: Routledge, 1994.

*Dinler et al. v. City of New York*, 607 F. 3d 923 (2010).

*Dinler v. City of New York*, U.S.D.C S.D.N.Y. 04 Civ. 7921, "Opinion and Order" (September 30, 2012).

*Downs v. Town of Guilderland, et al.*, State of New York Supreme Court, Appellate Division, Third Department, Case No. 507428, 897 N.Y.S. 2d 264 (2010).

Dunn, Christopher, Arthur Eisenberg, Donna Lieberman, Alan Silver, and Alex Vitale. *Arresting Protest: A Special Report of the New York Civil Liberties Union on New York City's Protest Policies at the February 15, 2003 Antiwar Demonstration in New York City*. New York: New York Civil Liberties Union, April 2003.

Dunn, Christopher, Donna Lieberman, Palyn Hung, Alex Vitale, Zac Zimmer, Irum Taqi, Steve Theberge, and Udi Ofer. *Rights and Wrongs at the RNC: A Special Report about Police and Protest at the Republican National Convention*. New York: New York Civil Liberties Union, 2005.

Earl, Jennifer. "Information Access and Protest Policing Post-9/11: Studying the Policing of the 2004 Republican National Convention." *American Behavioral Scientist* 53, no. 1 (September 2009): 44–60.

Earl, Jennifer. "Protest Arrests and Future Protest Participation: The 2004 Republican National Convention Arrestees and the Effects of Repression." *Studies in Law, Politics, and Society* 54 (2011): 141–73.

*Edrei v. Bratton*, U.S. Court of Appeals Second Circuit, Docket No. 17-2065, "Opinion" (June 13, 2018).

*Edrei v. City of New York*, U.S.D.C. S.D.N.Y. 16 Civ. 1652, "First Amended Complaint" (August 3, 2016).

*Edrei v. City of New York*, U.S.D.C. S.D.N.Y. 16 Civ. 1652, "Opinion" (May 31, 2017).

*Edwards v. South Carolina*, 372 U.S. 229 (1963).

Eisinger, Peter. "The Politics of Bread and Circuses: Building the City for the Visitor Class." *Urban Affairs Review* 35, no. 3 (January 2000): 316–33.

Elias, Norbert. *The Civilizing Process*. Translated by Edmund Jephcott. 1939. Reprint, Cambridge: Blackwell, 1994.

Emerson, Thomas. "First Amendment Doctrine and the Burger Court." *California Law Review* 68 (1980): 422–81.

Epp, Charles. *Making Rights Real: Activists, Bureaucrats, and the Creation of the Legalistic State*. Chicago: University of Chicago Press, 2009.

Epp, Charles, Steven Maynard-Moody, and Donald Haider-Markel. *Pulled Over: How Police Stops Define Race and Citizenship*. Chicago: University of Chicago Press, 2014.

Ericson, Richard, and Kevin Haggerty. *Policing the Risk Society*. Toronto: University of Toronto Press, 1997.

*Erie v. Pap's A.M.*, 529 U.S. 277 (2000).

*Evans v. Newton*, 382 U.S. 296 (1966).

Fainstein, Susan. *The City Builders: Property Development in New York and London, 1980–2000*, 2nd ed., rev. Lawrence: University of Kansas Press, 2001.

Faraone, Chris. *99 Nights with the 99%: Dispatches from the First Three Months of the Occupy Revolution*. Boston: Write to Power, 2012.

*Faraone v. City of New York*, U.S.D.C. S.D.N.Y. 13 Civ. 9074, "Opinion and Order" (March 21, 2016).

Federici, Silvia. "Social Reproduction Theory: History, Issues and Present Challenges." *Radical Philosophy* 2, no. 4 (Spring 2019). https://www.radicalphilosophy.com/article/social-reproduction-theory-.

Feeley, Malcolm. *The Process Is the Punishment*. New York: Russell Sage, 1992.

Feeley, Malcolm, and Jonathan Simon. "The New Penology: Notes on the Emerging Strategy of Corrections and Its Implications." *Criminology* 30, no. 4 (1992): 449–74.

Fernandez, Luis. *Policing Dissent: Social Control and the Anti-globalization Movement*. New Brunswick, NJ: Rutgers University Press, 2009.

Fisher, Mark. *Capitalist Realism: Is There No Alternative?* Washington, DC: Zero, 2009.

Fisher, Mark. *Ghosts of My Life: Writings on Depression, Hauntology and Lost Futures*. Washington, DC: Zero, 2014.

Fisher, Mark. "What Is Hauntology?" *Film Quarterly* 66, no. 1 (Fall 2012): 16–24.

*Flagg Bros., Inc. v. Brooks*, 436 U.S. 149 (1978).

Florida, Richard. *The Rise of the Creative Class Revisited*. New York: Basic Books, 2012.

*Floyd v. City of New York*, U.S.D.C. S.D.N.Y. 08 Civ. 1034, "Opinion and Order" (August 12, 2013).

Fortin, Véronique. "The 'Arrest' Is the Punishment: How Montreal Deals with 'Disturbances of the Peace' in Public Space." Paper presented at the annual meeting of the Law and Society Association, Seattle, Washington, May 28–31, 2015.

Foucault, Michel. *The Birth of Biopolitics: Lectures at the Collège de France 1978–1979.* Translated by Graham Burchell. Edited by Michel Senellart. New York: Palgrave Macmillan, 2008.

Foucault, Michel. *Discipline and Punish: The Birth of the Prison.* Translated by Alan Sheridan. 1977. Reprint, New York: Random House, 1995.

Foucault, Michel. "The Ethics of the Concern of the Self as a Practice of Freedom." In *Essential Works of Foucault, 1954–1984. Vol. 1: Ethics,* edited by Paul Rabinow, 281–301. New York: New Press, 1997.

Foucault, Michel. "On the Genealogy of Ethics: An Overview of a Work in Progress." In *Essential Works of Foucault, 1954–1984. Vol. 1: Ethics,* edited by Paul Rabinow, 253–80. New York: New Press, 1997.

Fraser, Nancy. "Expropriation and Exploitation in Racialized Capitalism: A Reply to Michael Dawson." *Critical Historical Studies* 3, no. 1 (Spring 2016): 163–78.

Frieden, Bernard, and Lynne Sagalyn. *Downtown, Inc.: How America Rebuilds Cities.* Cambridge, MA: MIT Press, 1989.

Fuchs, Ester. "The Permanent Urban Fiscal Crisis." In *Breaking Away: The Future of Cities,* edited by Julia Vitullo-Martin, 49–73. New York: Twentieth Century Fund Press, 1996.

Garfinkel, Harold. "Conditions of Successful Degradation Ceremonies." *American Journal of Sociology* 61, no. 5 (March 1956): 420–24.

Garland, David. *The Culture of Control: Crime and Social Order in Contemporary Society.* Chicago: University of Chicago Press, 2001.

Gershkoff, Amy, and Shana Kushner. "Shaping Public Opinion: The 9/11-Iraq Connection in the Bush Administration's Rhetoric." *Perspectives on Politics* 3, no. 3 (September 2005): 525–37.

Gillham, Patrick. "Securitizing America: Strategic Incapacitation and the Policing of Protest since the 11 September 2001 Terrorist Attacks." *Sociology Compass* 5, no. 7 (2011): 636–52.

Gillham, Patrick, Bob Edwards, and John Noakes. "Strategic Incapacitation and the Policing of Occupy Wall Street Protests in New York City, 2011." *Policing and Society* 23, no. 1 (2013): 81–102.

*Gomillion v. Lightfoot,* 364 U.S. 339 (1960).

Gordon, Lewis, Annie Menzel, George Shulman, and Jasmine Syedullah. "Afro Pessimism." *Contemporary Political Theory* 17, no. 1 (February 2018): 105–37.

Gorz, André. *The Immaterial: Knowledge, Value, Capital.* Translated by Chris Turner. New York: Seagull, 2010.

Graham, Stephen. *Cities under Siege: The New Military Urbanism.* New York: Verso, 2010.

Greenberg, Miriam. *Branding New York: How a City in Crisis Was Sold to the World.* New York: Routledge, 2008.

Greene, Judith. "Zero Tolerance: A Case Study of Police Policies and Practices in New York City." *Crime and Delinquency* 45, no. 2 (April 1999): 171–87.

Gruen, Victor. *The Heart of Our Cities: The Urban Crisis: Diagnosis and Cure.* New York: Simon and Schuster, 1964.

Gruen, Victor. "Main Street 1969—The Concepts of New Shopping Center Design and How They Can Be Applied to Existing Main Streets." In *American Planning and Civic Annual*, 13–30. Washington, DC: American Planning and Civic Association, 1957.

Gruen, Victor. "Shopping Centers of Tomorrow." *Arts and Architecture*, January 1954, 12–17.

Gruen, Victor, and Larry Smith. *Shopping Towns, USA: The Planning of Shopping Centers.* New York: Reinhold, 1960.

Gusfield, Joseph. "On Legislating Morals: The Symbolic Process of Designating Deviance." *California Law Review* 56, no. 1 (January 1968): 54–73.

Habermas, Jürgen. *Legitimation Crisis.* Translated by Thomas McCarthy. Boston: Beacon, 1975.

Hacker, Jacob, and Paul Pierson. *Winner-Take-All Politics: How Washington Made the Rich Richer—and Turned Its Back on the Middle Class.* New York: Simon and Schuster, 2010.

Hackworth, Jason. *The Neoliberal City: Governance, Ideology, and Development in American Urbanism.* Ithaca, NY: Cornell University Press, 2007.

Hagan, John. *Who Are the Criminals? The Politics of Crime Policy from the Age of Roosevelt to the Age of Reagan.* Princeton, NJ: Princeton University Press, 2010.

*Hague v. C.I.O.*, 307 U.S. 496 (1939).

*Handschu et al. v. Special Services Division*, 349 F. Supp. 766 (1972).

*Handschu v. Police Department of the City of New York*, U.S.D.C. S.D.N.Y., 71 Civ. 2203, "Ruling and Order on Proposed Revised Settlement Agreement" (March 13, 2017).

*Handschu v. Special Services*, 605 F. Supp. 1384 (1985).

*Handschu v. Special Services Division*, 288 F. Supp. 2d 411 (2003).

Hannigan, John. *Fantasy City: Pleasure and Profit in the Postmodern Metropolis.* New York: Routledge, 1998.

Harcourt, Bernard. *The Counterrevolution: How Our Government Went to War against Its Own Citizens.* New York: Basic Books, 2018.

Harcourt, Bernard. *Illusion of Order: The False Promise of Broken Windows Policing.* Cambridge, MA: Harvard University Press, 2001.

Hardt, Michael. "The Withering of Civil Society." In *Deleuze and Guattari: New Mappings in Politics, Philosophy, and Culture*, edited by Eleanor Kaufman and Kevin Jon Heller, 23–39. Minneapolis: University of Minnesota Press, 1998.

Hardt, Michael, and Antonio Negri. *Empire.* Cambridge, MA: Harvard University Press, 2000.

Hardt, Michael, and Antonio Negri. *Labor of Dionysus: A Critique of the State Form.* Minneapolis: University of Minnesota Press, 1994.

*Harper v. Virginia State Board of Elections*, 383 U.S. 663 (1966).

Hartman, Saidiya, and Frank Wilderson III. "The Position of the Unthought." *Qui Parle* 13, no. 2 (Spring/Summer 2003): 183–201.

Harvey, David. "The 'New' Imperialism: Accumulation by Dispossession." *Socialist Register* 40 (2004): 63–87.

Hermes, Kris. *Crashing the Party: Legacies and Lessons from the RNC 2000*. Oakland: PM Press, 2015.

Honig, Bonnie. *Emergency Politics: Paradox, Law, Democracy*. Princeton, NJ: Princeton University Press, 2009.

*Hotel Employees & Restaurant Employees Union, Local 100 of New York, NY, et al. v. City of New York Department of Parks and Recreation, et al.* 311 F. 3d 534 (2002).

Huddy, Leonnie, Lilliana Mason, and Lene Aarøe. "Expressive Partisanship: Campaign Involvement, Political Emotion, and Partisan Identity." *American Political Science Review* 109, no. 1 (February 2015): 1–17.

*Hudgens v. National Labor Relations Board*, 424 U.S. 507 (1976).

Human Rights Watch. *"Kettling" Protesters in the Bronx: Systematic Police Brutality and Its Costs in the United States*. New York: Human Rights Watch, September 2020.

Huntington, Samuel. "The United States." In *The Crisis of Democracy*, edited by Michel Crozier, Samuel Huntington, and Joji Watanuki, 59–118. New York: New York University Press, 1975.

Institute for Intergovernmental Research and COPS Office Critical Response Initiative. *After-Action Assessment of the Police Response to the August 2014 Demonstrations in Ferguson, Missouri*. Washington, DC: Office of Community Oriented Policing Services, 2015.

*International Society for Krishna Consciousness, Inc. (ISKCON) v. Lee*, 505 U.S. 672 (1992).

*In the Matter of Abdur-Rashid v. New York City Police Department*, N.Y. 3d 217, No. 19 (March 29, 2018).

*In the Matter of Millions March NYC v. New York City Police Department*, Index No. 100690/17, "Petition" (May 23, 2017).

Iveson, Kurt, and Sophia Maalsen. "Social Control in the Networked City: Datafied Dividuals, Disciplined Individuals, and Powers of Assembly." *Environment and Planning D: Society and Space* 37, no. 2 (2019): 331–49.

*Jackson v. Metropolitan Edison Co.*, 419 U.S. 345 (1974).

*James Logue v. New York City Police Department*, Index No. 153965/16, "Opinion and Order" (February 6, 2017).

Johnson, Cedric. "The Panthers Can't Save Us Now." *Catalyst* 1, no. 1 (Spring 2017). https://catalyst-journal.com.

*Jones v. Opelika*, 316 U.S. 584 (1942).

Judd, Dennis. "Promoting Tourism in US Cities." *Tourism Management* 16, no. 3 (1995): 175–87.

Kayden, Jerold, New York City Department of City Planning, and the Municipal Art Society of New York. *Privately Owned Public Space: The New York City Experience*. New York: John Wiley, 2000.

Kelling, George, and Catherine Coles. *Fixing Broken Windows: Restoring Order and Reducing Crime in Our Communities*. New York: Touchstone, 1996.

Kendrick v. Chandler, U.S.D.C. W.D.T.N., No. C 76-499, "Order, Judgment and Decree" (September 18, 1978).

King, Martin Luther, Jr. "Behind the Selma March." In *A Testament of Hope: The Essential Writings of Martin Luther King, Jr.,* edited by James Melvin, 126-31. New York: Harper and Row, 1986.

Kirkpatrick, L. Owen. "The New Urban Fiscal Crisis: Finance, Democracy, and Municipal Debt." *Politics and Society* 44, no. 1 (2016): 45-80.

Kishi, Roudabeh, and Sam Jones. "Demonstrations and Political Violence in America: New Data for Summer 2020." Princeton, NJ: U.S. Crisis Monitor and Armed Conflict Location and Event Data, September 2020.

Kohn, Margaret. *Brave New Neighborhoods: The Privatization of Public Space.* New York: Routledge, 2004.

Kohn, Margaret. "Privatization and Protest: Occupy Wall Street, Occupy Toronto, and the Occupation of Public Space in a Democracy." *Perspectives on Politics* 11, no. 1 (March 2013): 99-110.

Kotsko, Adam. *Neoliberalism's Demons: On the Political Theology of Late Capital.* Stanford, CA: Stanford University Press, 2018.

Kraska, Peter. "Militarization and Policing—Its Relevance to 21st Century Police." *Policing* 1, no. 4 (2007): 1-13.

Kraska, Peter, and Victor Kappeler. "Militarizing American Police: The Rise and Normalization of Paramilitary Units." *Social Problems* 44, no. 1 (February 1997): 1-18.

Lawson, Edward, Jr. "Trends: Police Militarization and the Use of Lethal Force." *Political Research Quarterly* 72, no. 1 (March 2019): 177-89.

*Lee v. International Society for Krishna Consciousness, Inc. (ISKCON),* 505 U.S. 830 (1992).

Lerman, Amy, and Vesla Weaver. "Staying Out of Sight? Concentrated Policing and Local Political Action." *Annals of the American Academy of Political and Social Science* 651 (January 2014): 202-19.

Levinson-Waldman, Rachel. "Government Access to and Manipulation of Social Media: Legal and Policy Challenges." *Howard Law Journal* 61, no. 3 (2018): 523-62.

Liu, John. *City of New York Office of the Comptroller Claims Report Fiscal Year 2011.* New York: Office of the Comptroller, December 27, 2012. https://comptroller.nyc.gov/wp-content/uploads/documents/2012_Claims_Report.pdf.

*Lloyd Corp. v. Tanner,* 407 U.S. 551 (1972).

*Lochner v. New York,* 198 U.S. 45 (1905).

Locke, John. *Second Treatise of Government.* 1690. Edited by C. B. Macpherson. Indianapolis: Hackett, 1980.

Lotringer, Sylvère, and Christian Marazzi, eds. *Autonomia: Post-political Politics* Cambridge, MA: Semiotext(e), 2007.

*MacNamara v. City of New York,* U.S.D.C. S.D.N.Y. 04 Civ. 9216, "Second Amended Complaint" (January 29, 2008).

*MacNamara v. City of New York,* U.S.D.C. S.D.N.Y. 04 Civ. 9216, 275 F.R.D. 125 (May 19, 2011).

*Mandal v. City of New York*, U.S.D.C. S.D.N.Y. 02 Civ. 1234, "Memorandum and Order" (October 17, 2006).

Marazzi, Christian. *Capital and Affects: The Politics of the Language Economy*. Translated by Giuseppina Mecchia. Los Angeles: Semiotext(e), 2011.

Marcus, Andrew, dir. *Hating Breitbart*. Freestyle Digital Media, 2012.

*Marom v. City of New York*, U.S.D.C. S.D.N.Y. 15 Civ. 2017, 2016 U.S. Dist. LEXIS 28466, "Memorandum and Order" (March 7, 2016).

*Marom v. City of New York*, U.S.D.C. S.D.N.Y. 15 Civ. 2017, "Memorandum and Order on Reconsideration" (July 29, 2016).

*Marom v. City of New York*, U.S.D.C. S.D.N.Y. 15 Civ. 2017, "Second Amended Complaint" (July 13, 2017).

*Marsh v. Alabama*, 326 U.S. 501 (1946).

Marshall, T. H. "Citizenship and Social Class." In *Class, Citizenship, and Social Development*, 65–122. Westport, CT: Greenwood, 1973.

Martin, Greg. "Showcasing Security: The Politics of Policing Space at the 2007 Sydney APEC Meeting." *Policing and Society* 21, no. 1 (March 2011): 27–48.

Martinot, Steve. "The Militarisation of the Police." *Social Identities* 9, no. 2 (2003): 205–24.

Martinot, Steve, and Jared Sexton. "The Avant-Garde of White Supremacy." *Social Identities* 9, no. 2 (2003): 169–81.

McCarthy, John, and Clark McPhail. "The Institutionalization of Protest in the United States." In *The Social Movement Society: Contentious Politics for a New Century*, edited by David Meyer and Sidney Tarrow, 83–110. Lanham, MD: Rowman and Littlefield, 1998.

McMorrough, John. "City of Shopping." In *Harvard Design School Guide to Shopping: Project on the City*, edited by Chuihua Judy Chung, Jeffrey Inaba, Rem Koolhaas, and Sze Tsung Leong, 193–202. New York: Taschen, 2001.

McPhail, Clark, David Schweingruber, and John McCarthy. "Policing Protest in the United States: 1960–1995." In *Policing Protest: The Control of Mass Demonstrations in Western Democracies*, edited by Donatella della Porta and Herbert Reiter, 49–69. Minneapolis: University of Minnesota Press, 1998.

Mead, George Herbert. *Mind, Self, and Society*. Edited by Charles Morris. Chicago: University of Chicago Press, 1962.

Meiklejohn, Alexander. *Free Speech and Its Relation to Self Government*. New York: Harper, 1948.

*Michael Schiller v. City of New York*, U.S.D.C. S.D.N.Y. 04 Civ. 7922 (April 4, 2006).

Miller, Kristine. *Designs on the Public: The Private Lives of New York's Public Spaces*. Minneapolis: University of Minnesota Press, 2007.

*Millions March NYC v. New York City Policy [sic] Department*, Supreme Court of the State of New York, New York County, Index No. 100690/2017, "Decision and Order" (January 11, 2019, received January 14, 2019).

Moody, Kim. *From Welfare State to Real Estate: Regime Change in New York City, 1974 to the Present*. New York: New Press, 2007.

Morris, Aldon. *The Origins of the Civil Rights Movement: Black Communities Organizing for Change*. New York: Free Press, 1984.

*Murdock v. Pennsylvania*, 319 U.S. 105 (1943).

Natapoff, Alexandra. *Punishment without Crime: How Our Massive Misdemeanor System Traps the Innocent and Makes America More Unequal*. New York: Basic Books, 2018.

National Advisory Commission on Civil Disorders. *Report of the National Advisory Commission on Civil Disorders*. New York: Bantam, 1968.

*National Council of Arab Americans and Act Now to Stop War & End Racism Coalition v. City of New York, et al.*, 331 F. Supp. 2d. 258 (2004).

*National Council of Arab Americans and Act Now to Stop War & End Racism v. City of New York*, U.S.D.C. S.D.N.Y. 04 Civ. 6602, "Memorandum and Order" (March 6, 2007).

*New Jersey Coalition against the War v. J.M.B. Realty*, 138 N.J. 326 (1994).

Nixon, Richard. "President's State of the Union Message." *Vital Speeches of the Day* 36, no. 8 (February 1, 1970): 226–29.

Noakes, John, and Patrick Gillham. "Aspects of the 'New Penology' in the Police Response to Major Political Protests in the United States, 1999–2000." In *The Policing of Transnational Protest*, edited by Donatella della Porta, Abby Peterson, and Herbert Reiter, 97–115. Burlington, VT: Ashgate, 2006.

Noakes, John, and Patrick Gillham. "'More Than a March in a Circle': Transgressive Protests and the Limits of Negotiated Management." *Mobilization* 12, no. 4 (December 2007): 341–57.

Offe, Claus. *Contradictions of the Welfare State*. Edited by John Keane. Cambridge, MA: MIT Press, 1984.

Oliver, Gideon. "A Criminal Mess: New York City's Response to Critical Mass Bike Rides, 2004–2010." *National Lawyers Guild Review* 67, no. 1 (Spring 2010): 37–51.

*Oregon v. Mitchell*, 400 U.S. 112 (1970).

Orfield, Gary, and Chungmei Lee. *Historic Reversals, Accelerating Resegregation, and the Need for New Integration Strategies*. Los Angeles: Civil Rights Project/Proyecto Derechos Civiles, UCLA, August 2007. http://civilrightsproject.ucla.edu/research/k-12-education/integration-and-diversity/historic-reversals-accelerating-resegregation-and-the-need-for-new-integration-strategies-1/orfield-historic-reversals-accelerating.pdf.

*Packard v. City of New York*, U.S.D.C. S.D.N.Y. 15 Civ. 07130, "Complaint" (September 10, 2015).

Page, Benjamin, Larry Bartels, and Jason Seawright. "Democracy and the Policy Preferences of Wealthy Americans." *Perspectives on Politics* 11, no. 1 (March 2013): 51–73.

Parenti, Christian. *Lockdown America: Police and Prisons in the Age of Crisis*. New York: Verso, 1999.

Pariser, Eli. *Filter Bubble: How the New Personalized Web Is Changing What We Read and How We Think*. New York: Penguin, 2011.

Passavant, Paul A. "The Contradictory State of Giorgio Agamben." *Political Theory* 35, no. 2 (April 2007): 147–74.

Passavant, Paul A. "Democracy's Ruins, Democracy's Archive." In *Reading Modern Law: Critical Methodologies and Sovereign Formations*, edited by Ruth Buchanan, Stewart Motha, and Sundhya Pahuja, 49–73. New York: Routledge, 2012.

Passavant, Paul A. "Governing Sexuality: The Supreme Court's Shift to Containment." In *Between Law and Culture: Relocating Legal Studies*, edited by David Theo Goldberg, Michael Musheno, and Lisa Bower, 306–323. Minneapolis: University of Minnesota Press, 2001.

Passavant, Paul A. "The Governmentality of Consumption." *Interventions* 6, no. 3 (2004): 381–400.

Passavant, Paul A. "Mega-Events, the Superdome, and the Return of the Repressed in New Orleans." In *The Neoliberal Deluge: Hurricane Katrina, Late Capitalism, and the Remaking of New Orleans*, edited by Cedric Johnson, 87–129. Minneapolis: University of Minnesota Press, 2011.

Passavant, Paul A. "Multitude." In *The Wiley-Blackwell Encyclopedia of Globalization*, vol. 3, edited by George Ritzer, 1473–81. Malden, MA: Blackwell, 2012.

Passavant, Paul A. "Neoliberalism and Violent Appearances." In *Capital at the Brink: Overcoming the Destructive Legacies of Neoliberalism*, edited by Jeffrey Di Leo and Uppinder Mehan, 30–71. Ann Arbor: University of Michigan Press and Open Humanities Press, 2014.

Passavant, Paul A. *No Escape: Freedom of Speech and the Paradox of Rights*. New York: New York University Press, 2002.

Passavant, Paul A. "Policing Protest in the Post-Fordist City." *Amsterdam Law Forum* 2, no. 1 (2009): 93–115.

Passavant, Paul A. "Political Subjectivity and Presidential Campaign Ads." *PS: Political Science and Politics* 49, no. 1 (January 2016): 36–42.

Passavant, Paul A. "The Strong Neo-liberal State: Crime, Consumption, Governance." *Theory and Event* 8, no. 3 (2005).

Passavant, Paul A. "Uneven Developments and the End to the History of Modernity's Social Democratic Orientation: Madison's Pro-Union Demonstrations." In *The Ends of History: Questioning the Stakes of Historical Reason*, edited by Amy Swiffen and Joshua Nichols, 23–43. New York: Routledge, 2013.

Passavant, Paul A. "Yoo's Law, Sovereignty and Whatever." *Constellations* 17, no. 4 (2010): 549–71.

Pavletic, John. "The Fourth Amendment in the Age of Persistent Aerial Surveillance." *Journal of Criminal Law and Criminology* 108, no. 1 (2018): 171–96.

*Peat et al. v. City of New York*, U.S.D.C. S.D.N.Y. 12 Civ. 08230, "First Amended Complaint" (July 30, 2013).

Peck, Jamie, and Adam Tickell. "Neoliberalizing Space." In *Spaces of Neoliberalism: Urban Restructuring in North America and Western Europe*, edited by Neil Brenner and Nik Theodore, 33–57. Malden, MA: Blackwell, 2002.

*People v. Leonard*, 62 N.Y. 2d 404 (1984).

Perlstein, Rick. *Nixonland*. New York: Simon and Schuster, 2008.

*Perry Educators Association v. Perry Local Educators Association (PEA V. PLEA)*, 460 U.S. 37 (1983).

Peters, Mark, and Philip Eure. *An Investigation of NYPD's Compliance with Rules Governing Investigations of Political Activity*. New York: New York City Department of Investigation, Office of the Inspector General for the NYPD [OIG-NYPD], August 23, 2016. https://www1.nyc.gov/assets/oignypd/downloads/pdf/oig_intel_report_823_final_for_release.pdf.

Phillips-Fein, Kim. *Fear City: New York's Fiscal Crisis and the Rise of Austerity Politics*. New York: Metropolitan, 2017.

Physicians for Human Rights. *Now They Seem to Just Want to Hurt Us: Dangerous Use of Crowd-Control Weapons against Protesters and Medics in Portland, Oregon*. New York: Physicians for Human Rights, October 2020.

Pierce, Lamar, Todd Rogers, and Jason Snyder. "Losing Hurts: The Happiness Impact of Partisan Electoral Loss." *Journal of Experimental Political Science* 3, no. 1 (Spring 2016): 1–16.

Police Executive Research Forum. *Lessons Learned from the 2015 Civil Unrest in Baltimore*. Washington, DC: Police Executive Research Forum, September 2015.

Police Executive Research Forum. *Managing Major Events: Best Practices from the Field*. Washington, DC: Police Executive Research Forum, June 2011.

Police Foundation. *A Review of the Baltimore Police Department's Use of Persistent Surveillance*. Washington, DC: Police Foundation, January 30, 2017.

Preparations and Planning Panel. *Report to the Seattle City Council WTO Accountability Review Committee*. August 24, 2000. Report on file with the author. http://www.seattle.gov/archive/wtocommittee/panel2_report.htm.

Pritchett, C. Herman. *The American Constitution*. New York: McGraw-Hill, 1977.

Protest and Assembly Project. *Suppressing Protest: Human Rights Violations in the U.S. Response to Occupy Wall Street*. New York: Global Justice Clinic and Walter Leitner International Human Rights Clinic, 2012.

*Pruneyard Shopping Center v. Robins*, 447 U.S. 74 (1980).

Rafail, Patrick, Sarah Soule, and John McCarthy. "Describing and Accounting for the Trends in US Protest Policing, 1960–1995." *Journal of Conflict Resolution* 56, no. 4 (August 2012): 736–65.

Rancière, Jacques. "Comments and Responses." *Theory and Event* 6, no. 4 (2003).

Rancière, Jacques. *Dis-agreement*. Translated by Julie Rose. Minneapolis: University of Minnesota Press, 1999.

*Raza et al. v. City of New York*, U.S.D.C. E.D.N.Y. 13 Civ. 3448, "Complaint" (June 18, 2013).

Reiter, Keramet. "The Pelican Bay Hunger Strike: Resistance within Structural Constraints of a US Supermax Prison." *South Atlantic Quarterly* 113, no. 3 (Summer 2014): 579–611.

Reiter, Keramet. *23/7: Pelican Bay Prison and the Rise of Long-Term Solitary Confinement*. New Haven, CT: Yale University Press, 2016.

Reiter, Keramet, and Susan Bibler Coutin. "Crossing Borders and Criminalizing Identity: The Disintegrated Subjects of Administrative Sanctions." *Law and Society Review* 51, no. 3 (September 2017): 567–601.

*Renton v. Playtime Theatres*, 475 U.S. 41 (1986).

*Reynolds v. Sims*, 377 U.S. 533 (1964).

R. M. McCarthy and Associates in conjunction with Robert Louden. *Preliminary Report for the City of Seattle Focusing on Planning and Preparation: An Independent Review of the 1999 World Trade Organization Conference Disruptions in Seattle, Washington*. San Clemente, CA: R. M. McCarthy and Associates in conjunction with Robert Louden, April 2000. Report on file with the author. http://www.seattle.gov/archive/wtocommittee/resources.htm.

Roost, Frank. "Synergy City: How Times Square and Celebration Are Integrated into Disney's Marketing Cycle." In *Rethinking Disney: Private Control, Public Dimensions*, edited by Mike Budd and Max Kirsch, 261–98. Middletown, CT: Wesleyan University Press, 2005.

Rose, Nikolas. "The Death of the Social? Refiguring the Territory of Government." *Economy and Society* 25 (August 1996): 325–56.

Rose, Nikolas. *Powers of Freedom: Reframing Political Thought*. Cambridge: Cambridge University Press, 1999.

Rosenzweig, Roy, and Elizabeth Blackmar. *The Park and the People: A History of Central Park*. Ithaca, NY: Cornell University Press, 1992.

*Rucho v. Common Cause*, 588 U.S. __ (2019).

Salecl, Renata. "The Satisfaction of Drives." *UMBR(a): On the Drive* 1 (1997): 105–109.

Sances, Michael, and Hye Young You. "Who Pays for Government? Descriptive Representation and Exploitative Revenue Sources." *Journal of Politics* 79, no. 3 (July 2017): 1090–94.

Scheingold, Stuart. "Constructing the New Political Criminology: Power, Authority, and the Post-liberal State." *Law and Social Inquiry* 23, no. 4 (autumn 1998): 857–95.

*Schiller v. City of New York and Dinler v. City of New York*, U.S.D.C. S.D.N.Y. 04 Civ. 7922, 04 Civ. 7921, "Memorandum and Order" (May 4, 2007).

Schmitt, Carl. *The Concept of the Political*. Translated by George Schwab. 1932. Reprint, Chicago: University of Chicago Press, 1996.

Schmitt, Carl. *Legality and Legitimacy*. Translated by Jeffrey Seitzer. Durham, NC: Duke University Press, 2004.

Schmitt, Eli, Astra Taylor, and Mark Creif. *Occupy! Scenes from an Occupation*. New York: Verso, 2011.

*Schneider v. State*, 308 U.S. 147 (1939).

Schneider, Nathan. *Thank You, Anarchy: Notes from the Occupy Apocalypse*. Berkeley: University of California Press, 2013.

*Schrader v. City of New York*, U.S.D.C. S.D.N.Y. 13 Civ. 1995, "Complaint" (March 26, 2013).

Schweingruber, David. "Mob Sociology and Escalated Force: Sociology's Contribution to Repressive Police Tactics." *Sociological Quarterly* 41, no. 3 (2000): 371–89.

Seattle Police Department. *The Seattle Police Department after Action Report: World Trade Organization Ministerial Conference Seattle, Washington November 29–December 3, 1999*. Seattle: Seattle Police Department, April 4, 2000.

Sernatinger, Andrew. "Capitalist Crisis and the Wisconsin Uprising." In *Wisconsin Uprising: Labor Fights Back*, edited by Michael Yates, 45–58. New York: Monthly Review Press, 2010.

*SHAD Alliance v. Smith Haven Mall*, 66 N.Y. 2d 496 (1985).

Shearing, Clifford, and Philip Stenning. "Private Security: Implications for Social Control." *Social Problems* 30, no. 5 (June 1983): 493–506.

Shefter, Martin. *Political Crisis/Fiscal Crisis: The Collapse and Revival of New York City*. New York: Basic Books, 1985.

Simon, Jonathan. *Governing through Crime: How the War on Crime Transformed American Democracy and Created a Culture of Fear*. New York: Oxford University Press, 2007.

Simon, Jonathan. *Poor Discipline*. Chicago: University of Chicago Press, 1993.

Sinclair, Timothy. *The New Masters of Capital: American Bond Rating Agencies and the Politics of Creditworthiness*. Ithaca, NY: Cornell University Press, 2005.

Skolnick, Jerome. *The Politics of Protest: Violent Aspects of Protest and Confrontation*. Washington, DC: Government Printing Office, 1969.

Sorkin, Michael, ed. *Variations on a Theme Park: The New American City and the End of Public Space*. New York: Hill and Wang, 1992.

Soss, Joe, Richard Fording, and Sanford Schram. *Disciplining the Poor: Neoliberal Paternalism and the Persistent Power of Race*. Chicago: University of Chicago Press, 2011.

Soule, Sarah, and Christian Davenport. "Velvet Glove, Iron Fist, or Even Hand? Protest Policing in the United States, 1960–1990." *Mobilization* 14, no. 1 (March 2009): 1–22.

*South Carolina v. Katzenbach*, 383 U.S. 301 (1966).

Spence, Lester. *Knocking the Hustle: Against the Neoliberal Turn in Black Politics*. Brooklyn, NY: Punctum, 2015.

Stanley, Jay. *The Dawn of Robot Surveillance: AI, Video Analytics, and Privacy*. Washington, DC: American Civil Liberties Union, June 2019.

*State of Hawaiʻi v. Viglielmo*, 105 Haw. 197 (2004).

*State of Minnesota v. Wicklund*, 589 N.W. 2d 793 (1999).

*State of Wisconsin ex rel. Ismael Ozanne v. Jeff Fitzgerald, et al.*, Dane County Circuit Court, 11 Civ. 1244, "Complaint" (March 16, 2011).

*State of Wisconsin ex rel. Ismael Ozanne v. Jeff Fitzgerald, et al.*, 2011 AP 613-LV, 2011 AP 765-W, "Order and Opinion" (June 14, 2011).

Streek, Wolfgang. *The Delayed Crisis of Democratic Capitalism*, 2nd ed. Translated by Patrick Camiller and David Fernbach. New York: Verso, 2017.

Taibbi, Matt. *I Can't Breathe: A Killing on Bay Street*. New York: Spiegel and Grau, 2017.

Taylor, Keeanga-Yamahtta. *From #BlackLivesMatter to Black Liberation*. Chicago: Haymarket, 2016.

*Terminiello v. Chicago*, 337 U.S. 1 (1949).

*Terry v. Adams*, 345 U.S. 461 (1953).

Thernstrom, Stephen, Fred Siegel, and Robert Woodson. "The Kerner Commission Report." Lecture 619 on Poverty and Inequality. Heritage Foundation, June 24, 1998. https://www.heritage.org/poverty-and-inequality/report/the-kerner-commission-report.

*Thompson v. City of Louisville*, 362 U.S. 199 (1960).

Tomlins, Christopher. "How Autonomous Is Law?" *Annual Review of Law and Social Science* 3 (2007): 45–68.

*United Food and Commercial Workers Union, Local 919 v. Crystal Mall Associates*, 270 Conn. 261 (2004).

*United for Peace and Justice v. City of New York*, 243 F. Supp. 2d 19 (2003).

*United States v. Carolene Products*, 304 U.S. 144 (1938).

U.S. Department of the Army. *Counterinsurgency: Field Manual No. 3-24*. Washington, DC: Headquarters, Department of the Army, December 2006.

U.S. Department of Justice, Civil Rights Division. *Investigation of the Baltimore City Police Department*, August 10, 2016. https://www.justice.gov/opa/file/883366/download.

U.S. Department of Justice, Civil Rights Division. *Investigation of the Ferguson Police Department*. March 4, 2015. https://www.justice.gov/sites/default/files/opa/press-releases/attachments/2015/03/04/ferguson_police_department_report.pdf.

Virno, Paolo. *Multitude: Between Innovation and Negation*. Translated by Isabella Bertoletti, James Cascaito, and Andrea Casson. Los Angeles: Semiotext(e), 2008.

Vitale, Alex. *City of Disorder: How the Quality of Life Campaign Transformed New York Politics*. New York: New York University Press, 2008.

Vitale, Alex. "The Command and Control and Miami Models at the 2004 Republican National Convention: New Forms of Policing Protests." *Mobilization* 12, no. 4 (2007): 403–15.

Vitale, Alex. "From Negotiated Management to Command and Control: How the New York Police Department Polices Protest." *Policing and Society* 15, no. 3 (September 2005): 283–304.

Vitale, Alex. "Managing Defiance: The Policing of the Occupy Wall Street Movement." Paper presented at the annual meeting for the Law and Society Association, Boston, MA, May 30–June 2, 2013.

Wacquant, Loïc. *Prisons of Poverty*. Expanded ed. Minneapolis: University of Minnesota Press, 2009.

Wacquant, Loïc. *Punishing the Poor: The Neoliberal Government of Social Insecurity*. Durham, NC: Duke University Press, 2009.

Wacquant, Loïc. *Urban Outcasts: A Comparative Sociology of Advanced Marginality*. Malden, MA: Polity, 2008.

Walsh, Shannon. "Afro-pessimism and Friendship in South Africa: An Interview with Frank B. Wilderson III." In *Ties That Bind: Race and the Politics of Friendship in South Africa*, edited by Shannon Walsh and Jon Soske, 69–98. Johannesburg: Wits University Press, 2016.

Western, Bruce, and Becky Pettit. "Incarceration and Social Inequality." *Daedalus* 139, no. 3 (Summer 2010): 8–19.

Whittaker, Charles. "Planned, Mass Violations of Our Laws: The Causes, and the Effects upon Public Order." *Vital Speeches of the Day* 33, no. 11 (March 15, 1967): 322–28.

Wilderson, Frank, III. *Red, White, and Black: Cinema and the Structure of U.S. Antagonisms*. Durham, NC: Duke University Press, 2010.

Wilderson, Frank, III. "Social Death and Narrative Aporia in *12 Years a Slave*." *Black Camera* 7, no. 1 (Fall 2015): 134–49.

Wilson, James Q. *Thinking about Crime*. New York: Basic Books, 1975.

Wong, Jackie. *Carceral Capitalism*. South Pasadena, CA: Semiotext(e), 2018.

Wood, Lesley. *Crisis and Control: The Militarization of Protest Policing*. London: Pluto, 2014.

Yoder, Traci, and Nathan Tempey. *Developments in the Policing of National Special Security Events: An Analysis of the 2012 RNC and DNC*. New York: National Lawyers Guild, 2013.

*Young v. American Mini Theatres*, 427 U.S. 50 (1976).

Zamora, Daniel, and Michael Behrent, eds. *Foucault and Neoliberalism*. Malden, MA: Polity, 2016.

Žižek, Slavoj. "Desire: Drive = Truth: Knowledge." *UMBR(a): On the Drive* 1 (1997): 147–51.

Žižek, Slavoj. "From Desire to Drive: Why Lacan Is Not Lacaniano." *Atlántica de las Artes* 14 (autumn 1996). https://zizek.livejournal.com.

Žižek, Slavoj. *The Plague of Fantasies*. New York: Verso, 1997.

Žižek, Slavoj. *Tarrying with the Negative*. Durham, NC: Duke University Press, 1993.

# Index

Page numbers in italics refer to figures.

"camp-ins," 107–8

capitalism: and automation, 151; as communicatively productive, 13–15; social reproduction capitalized, 23. *See also* communicative capitalism

capitalist democracies, 139

*Caravalho v. City of New York*, 133, 181–82, 285n176

Cardona, Johnny (police officer), 110, 279n69

Castel, Kevin P. (judge), 131–35

"catfishing," 225

cell phones, interruption of service to, 162, 199, 290n120

Central Booking (Manhattan), 79–80

Central Intelligence Agency (CIA), 73–74, 199

Chauvin, Derek, 20

Chicago Police Department, 78, 105, 180

Chickasaw, Alabama, 29–30, 33c, 34

Ciorra, Paul, 201

cities: bond markets, dependence on, 63, 229, 247, 286n16; malls as models for urban design, 44–48; market logics forced on, 9–10, 56, 60, 63, 65, 139, 173, 186, 228–29, 240–41; neoliberal, post-Fordist, 49–59, 54–55, 58–60, 86, 112; "quality of life" agenda, 48–50; visitor economy, 9, 27, 38, 51, 56, 58, 63–64, 67; zoning, 49–50. *See also* Baltimore Police Department; branding; Madison, Wisconsin; mega-events; Memphis Police Department (MPD); New York City; Portland, Oregon; Seattle, Washington; security legacy; urban fiscal crisis; urban political economy; Wisconsin

citizens, 14, 25, 29–30, 34–35; police as fellow, 5, 35, 68; "theft of enjoyment" and, 171

Citizens' Panel on WTO Operations, 67, 116

*Citizens United v. Federal Election Commission*, 108

City Hall Escort List ("blacklist") (Memphis), 224, 226

City Parks Department, 52

civil-criminal hybrid order, 158–59, 219

civil disobedience, 5, 67, 84, 102, 116, 123, 189, 203, 282

civil liberties, restriction of, 56

Civil Rights Act of 1871, 143

Civil Rights Act of 1964, 29

Civil Rights movement, 57, 141, 149, 178; crime associated with by conservatives, 8, 11, 15, 102, 189, 227, 241; and *Terminiello* decision, 222–23

civil society, decline of, 137, 149–52

Clinton, Bill, 11, 189

Coalition for the Homeless, 77

Cohen, David, 74, 264n1

Cohen, Steve (member of Congress), 226

collective outrage, decline of, 4, 78, 179, 182–83

college and university campuses, 4, 84, 166–67

color of law, 40

*Coming Community* (Agamben), 165–66

command and control protest policing, 100–101, 106, 119. *See also* order maintenance policing

commerce, priority of, 32–36, 52, 93–94

commodity images, 45–46, 83, 88, 152

communication, 5, 83; of communicativity, 164–66, 179; cynicism, 176–77, 183, 184, 233; disempowerment of people of ordinary means, 35, 49, 60; disintegrated mediality of, 164–66; of enmity, 212–15; and memes, 14–15, 166–67, 167, 175, 177–79, 182–83; multiplicity of interpretations, 14, 168, 175–79, 182–83, 184–85

communicative capitalism, 55; associative reason, logic of, 166–67, 172, 176, 225–26; "canals," drive as, 172–73; communicative production sustains, 60, 86–87, 97, 163–64, 167; and control technologies, 17–18, 167; and doppelganger, 14, 169, 172–75, 179; Nixon's comments underscore social democratic collapse, 169–70; oligopolistic

Crooks, Patrick (justice), 248
cynicism, 176–77, 183, 184, 233

Dakota Access Pipeline, 3
data aggregation, 160–61, 167, 180–81;
Accurint, 225; Geofeedia, 162, 166, 223,
225; Stingray technology, 199, 222
Davis, Troy, 108
Dean, Jodi, 142, 168, 169, 172–73
de Blasio, Bill, 215–16, 265n19
defeat of protesters, as police goal, 19,
179, 239, 306n235; and BLM protests,
16, 188, 204, 221, 236–37, 242; and OWS
protests, 12–13, 131, 137–38
defunding police, calls for, 22
degradation rituals, 16, 90, 195,
213–14
dehumanization of police, 121
Deleuze, Gilles, 17, 150, 264–65n15,
267n54
democracy: capitalist, 139; constitutional, 28, 78, 223, 235, 240, 242;
demise of, 32–36; and discipline,
144–49; "excess" of, 139, 186, 240; free
speech as practice of, 222–23; priority
of, 28–32; privatization of public space
undermines, 9, 25–26; undermined by
protest policing, 6, 72, 122–23
democracy, crisis of, 7–9, 61, 103, 150,
152–53, 222–36, 240–42; and control
technologies, 222–23, 227; and Memphis Police Department's policing,
223–28; as reaction against Black political mobilization, 15–16, 185–86, 242;
and Supreme Court shift, 27
Democratic National Convention
(DNC) (1968), 4, 142, 272n115
Democratic National Convention
(DNC) (1996), 5
Democratic National Convention
(DNC) (2004), 54–55
demonstration zone (DZ), 54–55
Department of Defense, 78
Department of Health Services, 250
Department of Homeland Security, 66,
190

Department of Justice, 66; Community
Oriented Policing Services (COPS),
232, 233; *Investigation of the Ferguson
Police Department*, 193–94, 213, 237
Derrida, Jacques, 221
desire, 168–69
desk appearance ticket (DAT), 79, 81
despotism, primary, 209
detention, 65–66, 129–30, 285n184; in
areas remote from arrest site, 129, 201;
excessive and degrading, 2, 6, 13, 83,
88–90, 94–95; federal vs. New York
standards, 65, 80, 89, 134; fingerprinting used to lengthen, 80–81, 83,
88–89, 96, 285n184; non-prison-based,
153; preventative, 66, 79, 89. *See also*
arrests
Diallo, Amadou, 80, 132
die-ins, 87, 197, *198*, 202, 225–26, 230
Dinler, Hacer, 90, 97
Direct Action, 115
direct confrontation as necessary, 137,
149–50
dirt, symbolic association of protesters
with, 111–12
disciplinary institutions, 145, 149–50,
163–64, 181; decline of, 152–53; prisons,
153–56
disciplinary power, 145–49, 222; consequences of weakened, 152–63; decline
of, 149–52, 181; prison as site of, 155–56;
and prison control, 152–56; progressive
orientation of, 148
disciplinary punishment, 64, 147
disciplinary society, 145, 149–52, 170; as
socially integrative, 150
*Discipline and Punish* (Foucault), 64, 147
discourse ethics, 165
disintegration: of mediality, 164–66; of
subjectivity, 14, 18, 149–52, 155, 158, 160,
163, 167, 182–83
Disney, 50, 55–56
Disney brand, 50
disorder: disagreement with ideology
as, 41–42; disruption of aesthetic
regime as, 33, 49–51, 60, 71; "feeling

reassured" through aggressive policing, 105, 190–91; indiscriminate arrests, 88; legal legitimacy sacrificed to suppress, 135–36; as legally arbitrary determination, 19; police production of, 21, 23, 87–88, 94–95, 117, 126–27, 185; shutting people out as cause of, 246; unmet social needs as, 104–106; and visibility, 37, 117, 191. *See also* minor disorder, policing of

disorderly conduct, 42, 76, 106, 109, 119, 132–33, 138, 199, 227, 276n38

diversity, criminalization of democratic strength vs., 53–55

"dividuals," 17–18, 160, 188, 222, 289n109

doppelganger, 14, 169, 172–75, 179

Douglas, William O., 222

Downs, Roger, 39–44, 45, 47–48, 260n68

Downs, Stephen, 39–44, 45, 47–48, 260n68

drive, 172–73

Duarte Square, 112–13, *113*, 119

Ducati, Steffano, 178

due process and equal protection, policing delinked from, 105, 149, 156, 160, 180, 191, 276n36, 286n16

Dwyer, Jim, 83

Earl, Jennifer, 282n116

economic precarity, 106–7, 168, 171–72, 243

education and training, as disciplinary techniques, 145–48

efficiency, 10–11, 65, 80, 97, 100, 101, 120, 138; scientific, 165; symbolic, 142, 152, 168–69, 172–74, 179, 181, 292

Egypt, 106–7

Eisner, Michael, 50

Elvis Presley Enterprises, 227, 230

Elvis Week (Graceland), 226–27, 230

Emergency Financial Control Board (New York City), 63

enemies, political, 17; BLM treated as, 204, 209–15; Blue Lives Matter as response to, 215–19, *216*; communicating enmity, 212–15; Ferguson protesters treated as, 195–96, *196*; illiberal

logic of guilt by association, 226; OWS treated as, 128–37; protesters as, 67–68, 78, 106, 189–90; residents in areas of racialized poverty as, 127, 212, 301n151. *See also* political antagonism

enjoyment: "Broken Windows" policing legitimizes, 106, 138; bullying and taunts by police officers, 90, 114, 118, 120, 130, 181, 213, 280n86; *jouissance*, 172; of "kicking ass," 12, 106, 120, 138, 162, 179, 182, 191, 193, 276n36; ontological, of violence against Blacks, 209; of others' suffering, by "forgotten Americans," 171–72; "theft of," 171; of violence against protesters, 177–79, 182–83. *See also* appearance; neoliberal authoritarianism

Enlightenment project, 147

Epp, Charles, 142–48, 156, 163, 173, 180

escalated force, 3–4, 23, 96, 145, 193–94, 213, 223, 227, 232, 252

Esper, Mark, 22

Esposito, Joseph, 158

expertise, diminishment of, 164, 169

expressivity of protest policing, 13–14, 21, 65, 72, 120; similar to sovereign power cruelties, 95–96. *See also* affective attachments; enjoyment

expropriation of resources, 17, 194–95, 204, 208, 214, 215, 243, 296n57; asset forfeiture, 11, 190; fines, 194, 296n56; lack of accountability in, 190, 194–95

extrajudicial punishment, 2, 67, 79, 90, 94–97, 99; fines as, 194; LRADs as, 2, 16, 19; of OWS activists, 116, 120, 130–32

extralegal practices, 12–13, 65, 70–73, 96, 106, 120, 127; authoritarianism, 248

eye contact, as reason for police abuse, 213

"Failure to Comply" charges, 193–96

"failure to disperse" orders, 3, 21, 85, 114, 206, 214

*Fanciful Images of Prisons* (Piranesi), 55

Fanon, Frantz, 209

Federal Bureau of Investigation (FBI), 73–75, 78

Matthew Shepard Emergency Demonstration (1998), 6
Maurer, Ann, 88, 97
Mauro, Paul, 201
May Day, May 1, 2012, 116–17, 119–20, 129
McCalla, Jon (judge), 224, 231
McClain, Elijah, 20
McCord, Mary, 22
McMorrough, John, 46
mediality, disintegrated, 164–66
medical care, lack of access to, 90
medics, targeting of, 22
mega-events, 9, 13, 15, 64, 173; actuarial calculations for risk management, 10, 73; and communicative production, 55–56; as demonstration of city recovery, 56, 64, 69–70; security legacy of, 10, 16, 65–69, 97, 99, 163, 206, 220, 242; and symbolic production, 55–59. *See also* National Special Security Events (NSSEs); specific events
memes, 14–15, 177–79, 182–83, 293n171; "Casually Pepper Spray Everything Cop," 166–67, *167*, 175
Memphis Coalition of Concerned Citizens (CCC), 229–30
Memphis Police Department (MPD), 16, 18, 78, 223–28, 243; "Blue Suede Shoes" PowerPoint, 227–28; Joint Intelligence Briefings (JIBs), 224; Office of Homeland Security (OHS), 224–25; Organized Crime Unit, 225
mentally ill, treatment of, 22–23, 106, 155
Metropolitan Transit Authority (MTA), 199–200
Miami Police Department, 100, 265n19
Microsoft, 235
Middle Passage, 207
militarized policing, 16–17, 67, 72, 187–88, 191, 220–21, 242; military-grade weapons at protests, 2–3, 11, 67, 195, 214–15. *See also* security model of policing protest
militias, right-wing, 20
Millions March NYC, 199
Million Youth March (1998), 6

Minneapolis police, 20
Minnesota, 250–51
minor disorder, policing of, 5, 11–12, 77, 86, 158–59, 174, 192, 194; by NYPD, 12, 68, 87, 92–93, 97, 101, 106, 120, 125–26, 134–35, 203, 243. *See also* disorder
Missouri National Guard, 195, 204, 215, 219
Moeser, Daniel, 248
Monahan, Terrence, 87–88
*Monnell v. New York Department of Social Services*, 143
*Monroe v. Pape*, 143
Moran, Christopher (police officer), 213
MSNBC, 86–87, 90
Mubarak, Hosni, 107
Municipal Assistance Corporation (New York City), 63
Murphy, Patrick, 143
Muslims, groundless surveillance of, 77

"naked title," 31
National Advisory Commission on Civil Disorders (Kerner Commission), 4, 147–48, 301n151; backlash against recommendations, 185, 191–92, 212–13, 310–11n6; crime prevention through addressing social ills, 150, 170, 185, 188–89, 240; implementation not fast enough, 188–89, 287–88n62; Nixon's rejection of report, 7–8, 103–4, 148, 153, 169–70
National Association for the Advancement of Colored People (NAACP), 143
National Commission on the Causes and Prevention of Violence, 148, 170
*National Council of Arab Americans and Act Now to Stop War & End Racism Coalition v. City of New York*, 56–59, 263n146, 281n106
National Crime Information Center, 161
National Guard, 4, 21–22; Missouri, 195, 204, 215, 219
nationalism, 44–45
National Labor Relations Act, 30, 250
National Lawyers Guild, 143, 201

New York Police Department (*cont.,*) Community Affairs Unit, 125; consent decrees, 74–75; Counterterrorism Division, 200; Disorder Control Unit (DCU), 70, 206; "event advisory bulletin," 117; extralegal practices, 12–13, 70–73; Ferguson, travel to, 196–97, 232–33; First Amendment ignored by, 106; "Handschu Guidelines," 74–78; high-ranking officers, aggression by, 21; institutional development and expressive policing at 2004 RNC convention, 83–90; kettling of protesters, 53; Legal Bureau, 81; marking shift in protest policing, 85; Mass Arrest Processing Centers (MAPCs), 132–37; Mass Arrest Processing Plan (MAPP), 128, 132–35, 205; mass arrests, processing of, 79–83, 94–95; minor infractions, aggressive response to, 12, 68, 87, 92–93, 97, 101, 106, 120, 125–26, 134–35, 203, 243; mosques, monitoring of, 77; Organized Crime Control Bureau (OCCB), 202; Patrol Guidelines, 74, 77; permits denied by, 53–54; post-legal-legitimation institutional orientation, 72–73, 94, 126–27; Strategic Response Group (SRG), 200, 201; vengeful actions by, 85, 110, 134, 154, 301n156; "white shirts," 21, 87, 109, 118, 281n111. *See also* Intelligence Division (Intel) (NYPD); Occupy Wall Street (OWS); Republican National Convention (RNC), 2004

*New York Post* (newspaper), 178

New York State Commission on Judicial Conduct, 39

New York state discrimination provisions, 42–43

*New York Times, The* (newspaper), 20, 21, 83, 103, 109, 111, 148

*Nightline* (television program), 84

Nixon, Richard, 11, 239–40; "forgotten Americans" rhetoric of, 7, 14, 32, 102, 170–71, 241; Kerner Commission results, rejection of, 7–8, 103–4, 148,

153, 169–70, 241; "Law and Order" campaign, 189; Southern strategy, 11, 102–3, 171, 241; State of the Union Address, 1970, 48, 102

Noakes, John, 101

*Nobody Knows My Name* (Baldwin), 212

non-criminal law violations, 76, 80

no-protest zones, 68

norms, 146, 147–49; constitutional, 65; eroded by control technologies, 168–69; legal, 64, 123; legitimation, 10, 140; weakening of, 149, 157

Northland Center, Michigan, 37

no-summons policy for arrests: constitutionality of sustained, 92–93, 134; and OWS activists, 132–35; and RNC 2004, 80, 81, 83, 88–90, 92–93, 96, 205

NYC and Company, 69

Obama, Barack, 216

obedience, 211

Occupy Wall Street (OWS), 12–13, 65, 97, 98–140, *110*; Bloombergville, 107; Brooklyn Bridge march, 109, 130; Day of Outrage (September 21, 2011), 108–9; disappearance of arrested protesters, 200–201; as enemy of police, 131; extrajudicial punishment against, 116, 120, 128, 130–37; general assemblies, 107, 108; Hurricane Sandy relief efforts, 109, 128; intelligence gathering against, 10, 13; interviews with activists, 99, 274–75n1; intimidation of activists by police, 117–18; March 17 protest, and police aggression, 2, 98, 114–16, 119, 120, 130–33; Mass Arrest Processing Centers (MAPCs) used against, 132–37; May Day 2012, 116–17, 119–20, 129; New Year's Eve arrests, 113–14, 119–20, 130; Occupy Homes, 109; Occupy Town Squares, 109; October 15 day of action, 108; one-year anniversary, 118–19; pepper spraying of protesters, 1–2, 109, 120, 176; political concerns supplanted by police behavior, 123–24,

political economy: and legal development, 51–52; post-Fordist urban, 7–9,
26, 49–59, 95, 159, 162, 174, 220, 229,
241; urban, 7–10, 15, 23, 53, 60, 64,
94–95
political equality, as crime, 11, 211–14
political favoritism by police, 93, 135
politically based targeting, 5, 42, 54, 57,
92–93, 201, 252
political parties, 23
political relation, 17, 211
political speech, 47–48, 113; First Amendment protections needed for, 54,
58–59. See also free speech
political subjects, 14, 18, 141–83; appearance of agency disorganized by police,
72, 83, 87–88, 95, 97, 117, 184, 188, 223,
298n76; of communicative capitalism,
165–73. See also subjectivity
Popular Science (magazine), 86
Portland, Oregon, 22, 32–36
Portland Oregonian (newspaper), 178
Post Arrest Staging Site (PASS), Pier 57,
2, 80–83, 88–90, 95
post-Fordism, 33, 83, 240; commodity
images, 45–46; and control technologies, 151–52; "partition of the perceptible," 53; state policies and reduction of
First Amendment rights, 54; subjective experience under, 151–52; of urban
political economy, 7–9, 26, 49–59, 95,
159, 162, 174, 220, 229, 241
postlegitimation, post-democratic state
formation, 1, 16, 18–23, 27, 36–37, 59,
126; exceptions suggest emergence
of, 136; extrajudicial policing as, 120;
malls as models for urban design,
44–48; and NYPD's policing, 72–73;
political favoritism by police, 93,
135; post-democratic, 22, 27, 36–37,
47–48; postlegitimation and post-
democratic, 18–19; and Seattle policing, 68; and selective enforcement, 65,
83, 86–87, 94, 97, 119, 121–25; and Supreme Court jurisprudence, 8, 27–28,
32, 35–36, 44, 108, 240; unevenness in,

252. See also neoliberal authoritarianism; state
poverty, 23, 63, 103, 106, 157, 170, 190,
220, 243
Powell, Lewis, 32–34
"preferred position" doctrine, 28, 30,
34–35, 60, 240, 276n38
presidential commissions, 4, 212. See also
National Advisory Commission on
Civil Disorders (Kerner Commission)
preventative/proactive arrests, 5, 68,
71–72; abuse by police during, 129;
detentions, 66, 79, 89; Intelligence
Division surveillance used, 83, 129;
Kinberg targeted, 86; of OWS activists, 129
prisons, 153–56; correctional officers
(COs), 154–55; and discipline, 145;
hunger strikes, 107, 155; permanent
lockdown, 154; secure housing units
(SHUs), 153, 155; solitary confinement,
107, 153, 154–55; supermaxes, 107,
154–55; torturous treatment of inmates, 154, 156; "waste management"
function, 153, 190
private property, 157, 159; imaginary association of public accommodations
with, 8, 30, 43–44
private security forces, 3, 13, 157
privatization: and aesthetic production,
26–27, 32–33; of public spaces, 8–9,
25–27, 61; state role in, 59–61
processing of arrests, 79–83, 89, 94–95.
See also Mass Arrest Processing Centers (MAPCs); Mass Arrest Processing
Plan (MAPP)
"professional agitators," as label for
protesters, 197, 233
Professional Air Traffic Controllers
Organization (PATCO), 250
professional networks for police, 143–44
progress, diminished idea of, 148
property of protesters, destruction of, 112
Proposition 2½ (Massachusetts), 63
Proposition 13 (California), 63
Prosser, David, 248

Torres, Analisa (judge), 136
torturous conditions, 95, 121, 128, 137, 148, 155; denial of medical care as, 90; lengthy detention as, 4, 83, 89–90
transnational protesters, 64, 69
trapping, 85
trespass admonishments, 158–59
Trinity Church (New York City), 112, *113*, 119
Trump, Donald, 21–22, 119, 162, 169
trust, 170, 292n152
truth, 164–65
Tubbs, Charles (chief of Madison Capitol Police), 244
Tunisian Revolution, 106–7

unarmed people, killing of, 80, 219
undercover operations, 70–71, 72, 76, 84, 202
"undesirable people," 105, 156, 159
union activities, 3, 30–31; Lincoln Center, 51–53
Union Square (New York City), 113
United for Peace and Justice (UFPJ), 53, 84, 89
United Nations Security Council, 53–54, 74
*United States v. Carolene Products*, 28
uprising of 2020, 20–23; Cadman Plaza, Brooklyn, 20–21; Lafayette Square incident, June 1, 21–22; Portland, Oregon, 22
urban design, malls as models for, 44–48
urban fiscal crisis, 7, 9–11, 15, 94, 104, 152–53; and Ferguson, 204; manufacturing relocated, 8–9, 62–63, 190, 192. *See also* cities; New York City
urban political economy, 7–10, 15, 23, 53, 60, 64, 94–95; neoliberal urbanism, BLM resistance to, 228–31; post-Fordist, 7–9, 26, 49–59, 95, 159, 162, 174, 220, 229, 241. *See also* cities
"urban riots," 4, 7, 102, 105, 135, 138–39, 148, 150, 153, 254n18; Black insurrection evoked by, 156–57; and legalized accountability, 163

USA PATRIOT Act (November 2001), 78
*U.S. News and World Report* (magazine), 102, 189, 227
USS *Cole*, attack on, 205

Valero Memphis Refinery, 230
verbal abuse by police, 2, 5, 95, 114, 120, 130, 194
victim narrative, of police, 218–19
video recording by police, 77
Viglielmo, Frances, 37–38
Villepin, Dominique de, 53
violence: appearance of, 173–79; escalation of by police, 3–4, 23, 96, 145, 193–94, 213, 223, 227, 232, 252; "excessive" eschewed, 19, 91–92, 101, 138, 141; gratuitous, 207–9; as ontological condition for Blacks, 208–9
Violent Crime Control and Law Enforcement Act (1994), 189
Viscardi, William, 201
visibility. *See* appearance
visitor economy, 9, 27, 38, 51, 56, 58, 63–64, 67
visual barriers to protest, 54 55
visual culture, 59
Vitale, Alex, 100–101, 106, 119, 120, 137–38, 187, 274n157
voter suppression, 251
voting rights, 29, 31
Voting Rights Act of 1965, 29

Wacquant, Loïc, 295n35
Walker, Samuel, 1
Walker, Scott, 107, 244–51
Wallace, George, 14, 170–71
Wallace, Walter, Jr., 20
Wall Street Financial District, 118–19
"War on Crime, The" (Lawrence), 102
"war on drugs," 103
"war on terrorism," 44–45
warrants, pretextual, 129
Warren, Lovely, 23
War Resisters League, 87–88
weak state, as misperception, 59, 61